On Becoming a Social Scientist

On Becoming a Social Scientist

*From Survey Research
and Participant Observation
to Experiential Analysis*

Shulamit Reinharz

With a New Introduction by the Author

Transaction Publishers
New Brunswick (U.S.A.) and Oxford (U.K.)

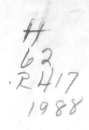

Second Printing, 1988.
New material this edition copyright © 1984 by Transaction Publishers,
New Brunswick, New Jersey 08903. Originally published in 1979 by
Jossey-Bass, Inc.

Library of Congress Catalog Number: 84-2484
ISBN: 0-87855-968-x (paper)
Printed in the United States of America

Library of Congress Cataloging in Publication Data

Reinharz, Shulamit.
On becoming a social scientist.

Reprint. Originally published San Francisco:
Jossey-Bass, 1979. (Jossey-Bass social and behavioral
science series)
Bibliography: p.
Includes index.
1. Social sciences—Methodology. 2. Social sciences—
Research—Case studies. 3. Sociology—Research.
4. Social scientists—Biography. 5. Reinharz, Shulamit.
6. Socialization. I. Title.
[H62.R417   1984]   300'.72   84-2484
ISBN 0-87855-968-X (pbk.)

Introduction to the Transaction edition

Shulamit Reinharz

The original version of this book was published in the spring of 1979. Although a relatively short period has elapsed since then, it certainly has been enough time for me to have new thoughts about my past efforts. The reader will not see in this paperback version of *On Becoming a Social Scientist* any evidence of these new insights or experiences, however. Rather, the text has remained completely unaltered, and the results of new thinking are confined entirely to this preface.

In the past five years two developments led me to place this book in new frameworks. First is the overlap between the ideas expressed here and feminist concerns with method in the social sciences; second is the similarity between my efforts to defend an experiential method and the efforts of others in disparate fields to do the same. After discussing these two ideas briefly, I will add some reflections on the reviews and other forms of feedback I have received about the book. All of this reconsideration of my original work has been enhanced, of course, by several years of teaching, additional research experiences, supervising doctoral dissertations, and serving, with Peter Conrad, as editor of *Qualitative Sociology*.

Shortly after *On Becoming a Social Scientist* appeared, a feminist graduate student at the University of Michigan, where I was then a member of the community psychology area in the Department of Psychology, informed me that feminist scholars had found my book useful because it articulated a critique of social science methodology that was essentially a feminist critique even though it did not use feminist theory or terminology. She had recently attended the annual meeting of the National Women's Studies Association in which several sessions concerning method had used my book as a model. Soon thereafter I began receiving letters from feminist scholars telling me how the book had helped them conceptualize and conduct their research. There followed invitations to contribute to a book on this theme,[1] to run workshops, to give lectures, to write a column for a newsletter, to help form a feminist research methodology study group,[2] to publish a bibliography of materials on feminist methodology,[3] and to write a review essay on the topic.

Although the ideology of the women's movement had always appealed to me, when I wrote *On Becoming a Social Scientist* I had been active in the women's movement in only limited ways. My life was not really shaped by feminist consciousness, even if some of my work did deal with women's experiences. Now that I was being reached out to by feminists, however, I took another look at the connection between my work and theirs, and found it to be pervasive. Simultaneously, but without being aware of one another, we had recognized the same problems and had reached similar conclusions.

For example, sociologist Dorothy E. Smith had written about the disjunction between women's experiences and the concepts available to think about them.[4] Smith had reached this conclusion about the ideological socialization of sociologists: "As graduate students learning to become sociologists . . . we learn to discard our experienced world as a source of reliable information about the world" (p. 8). Smith helped me understand something I wish I had known while writing my book, namely that a large part of my socialization in academia was influenced by my being a woman.

Having gone to Barnard, an all-women's college, one might have expected me to avoid developing an identity as "marginal woman." Yet, even in an all-female environment that has positive role models for its students, women can develop a marginalized identity if the profession or academic discipline into which they are being trained is dominated by concepts that women have had very little part in forming.[5] This marginal position, created in part by the misogyny of respected "fathers of sociology," leads some women sociologists to develop a critical view of the whole field, sharpened by the vantage point of being an outsider. These insider-outsiders may feel compelled to create an alternative definition of the field and to seek an alternative community within the field. Not only are they likely to seek new subject matter to study but also new methods to address the subject matter, as they attempt to break out from what feels like a monolithic definition of proper procedures. As Smith explained, "Women sociologists stand at the centre of a contradiction in the relation of our discipline to our experience of the world. . . . An alternative approach must somehow transcend this contradiction . . . [this involves a reorganization which makes the female sociologist's] direct experience of the everyday world the primary ground of her knowledge" (p. 11). Without having been aware of Smith's analysis or the link between my interest in the examination of experience and my role as a woman, I reached Smith's conclusion in chapter eight of this book.

The experience of being affirmed in this way led me to examine feminist writing on methodological issues in the social sciences. It turned out, as many readers are undoubtedly aware, that this literature is vast and very diverse. Although there is no consensus among feminists interested in this topic, one major subgroup argues that the methods of modern social science have distorted matters because in the quest for objectivity the researcher has distanced him/herself from the person(s) studied.[6] With this distancing, the researcher is denied access to understanding the researched person's experiences, and therefore the findings or interpretation based on these "data" are inaccurate. What is called for, some feminist critics have argued, is the creation of new methods that utilize a new paradigm of research.[7] In addition, the feminist critique of the dominant methods in the social sciences includes new ethical standards such as the elimination of deception, striving to use research to empower subjects (in a way analogous to Paolo Friere's conscientization), the limiting of claims of expertise to researchers who have close personal acquaintance with the phenomenon studied, disclosure of the political context surrounding the research endeavor, and revamping research team organization to be nonhierarchical.

One outcome of these feminist methods is the reaffirmation of the experience of women, an experience that has been largely ignored, trivialized, or misunderstood (until studied by feminists) because of the system of values underlying supposedly value-free traditional social science. Unfortunately, even though there is increasing attention paid to the general need for more experiential approaches to the creation of knowledge, feminist approaches are still largely overlooked even by other critics within the social sciences who claim to be harbingers of new paradigms. There is thus a need for better communication between feminist critics and others attempting to alter the basic paradigm in the social sciences. For instance, it would be useful to explore the relation of the radical critique of the "verification paradigm" in sociology as contained in Glaser's and Strauss's *Discovery of Grounded Theory* (1967) with feminist criticism. Would feminists necessarily see the Glaser and Strauss book as part of the male-dominated tradition; could we consider it feminist even if it does not discuss feminism at all? As one colleague commented after I had given a talk on this question: Is one alternative paradigm striving for dominance and imperialistically crowding out other alternatives?

It has become clear to me that in order for communication to occur among those interested in alternative paradigms, there must be more teaching about this topic in academic departments. Similarly, there should be interaction among the various groups attempting to develop alternatives and those more committed to the mainstream. One way to achieve this is to encourage journals to have the policy of inviting many types of scholars to respond in print to significant articles. There is also much work to be done to determine the relation between the various critiques (e.g., Marxist, phenomenological, humanist, feminist, to name a few) that have developed out of the conventional "value-free" positivist paradigm in the social sciences.

Finally, it has become apparent to me through the consideration of feminist theory that white middle-class academics such as myself must question how their research would be affected by membership in other "invisible groups," such as racial or ethnic minorities. One typical product of developing feminist consciousness is the interest in forming bonds with women of various backgrounds in order to compare and contrast perspectives on our work. Thus, the feminist research groups with which I have been involved since the publication of this book have attempted to be broad-based with regard to age, race, status, sexual orientation, and more. In this regard, I have become involved in a manuscript draft exchange with women different from myself, so that we can critique each other's work for omissions, blindspots, and prejudice.

The second issue relevant to a reconsideration of this book is my effort to teach the perspective contained in its pages. Not only did I try to build experiential methods into my methods courses and other teaching, but shortly after publication of *On Becoming a Social Scientist,* I received a request to write material about the implications of my ideas for teaching.[8] Graduate students at other universities who were "stuck," unable to formulate, start, or complete their dissertations, began to write that this book helped them, regardless of the specific methods they used. Surprisingly, I received such letters from students in nursing, education, and management, as well as sociology and psychology. In one case a woman wrote from Colorado that upon reading the book, she gained the confidence and resources she needed to convince her dissertation committee to allow her to do a qualitative study. In another case, the book somehow assisted a graduate student to recognize what topic she wanted to study. Teachers of methods courses wrote about urging students to read the book at the outset of their careers since it "articulates the feelings they will have." Several people expressed thoughts such as this:

> The purpose of this letter is to share with you some of my personal reactions to your book, *On Becoming a Social Scientist*. It is a book which is very dear to me. I have found much solace within its pages; it has helped validate that the kind of identity confusion, which I have experienced since coming to [this university], is, indeed, growthful, and part of the process of socialization into the field of psychology.

Even senior faculty wrote how the book revived memories of their socialization and helped clarify how they had become social scientists.

The comments people wrote about how and why the book "validated their experience" was to me of great interest. Clearly, in many places, students experience conventional methodological training as tyranny (to use Mary Daly's phrase) but feel constrained to keep their doubts about their training to themselves until after they get their degree or tenure. Apparently, this effect is not limited to students. In one case an eminent senior scholar wrote: "In my 28 years as an academic I have never before been moved to write a letter like this (an academic love letter?) to any other author, even those that I might have known well. So for me this is a special experience." He then went on to tell me a bit about his biography as a researcher and his "conversion experience" to a qualitative methodological orientation. To have their concerns about social science in print gave many students a sense of confirmation and thus normalized what they feared was their personal deviance. The letters in which people shared the autobiographical accounts of socialization reinforced my desire to continue to write in a personalized way. The interaction between some of these letter-writers and the book is reminiscent of the dynamics of consciousness-raising.

Equally important to me was my work with graduate students who wanted to use these methodological ideas to guide a study from beginning to end. I have found that each person who wanted to do an experiential study ended up combining these ideas with others drawn from various sources. In part this was the result of pressure from other dissertation committee members. Nevertheless, this was completely appropriate since it was never my intention to exclude other methods. On the contrary, as some reviewers of my book acknowledged, my point is not to cast off "normal science completely . . . but rather to enrich it," by openly acknowledging what actually goes on in social research, by utilizing serendipity and intuition, by examining processes as well as structures, by focusing on understanding and explanations of specific instances, by having the research "subject" teach, and by generating concepts in vivo.[9]

In some cases the blending of methodological perspectives by students led to the creation of new techniques such as "dialogic retrospection," which earned one student an American Psychological Association prize for his dissertation.[10] There were some who successfully blended "experiential analysis" with phenomenology[11] or with participant observation.[12] Even more frequent was the use of "experiential analysis" by students to clarify what they wanted to study. Interestingly, when they worked through the procedures that reduced the split between their private and public selves as social scientists, they produced, in my view, informative, pathbreaking studies.[13] I hope that some of the procedural ideas discussed in the first chapters, such as the importance of seeing a research project as a challenge on three fronts—to understand the substantive problem studied, to allow personal change to occur at least in the researcher, and to create methodological innovation because of the unique features of each project—will continue to assist students in formulating new or blended methods.

I hope that people will consider both the book as a whole and also the specific arguments of each part, such as the discussion of survey research, which John Van Maanen characterized as the only material in print that is close to "coming clean" about the conditions under which data are gathered.[14] In other words, I am as interested in people exploring the potential of "experiential analysis" as I am in their considering my critique of survey research, my elaboration on participant observation field research,[15] and my suggestion of "temporary affiliation" as a form of action research.[16] It is gratifying to see the recent increased interest in methods of qualitative research as indicated by many new books on the subject as well as a more balanced presentation in research methods textbooks. In addition, it has become obvious to me that there will be even more interest in qualitative methods in the future when, through computer-assistance, its time-consuming aspects will be handled in a more efficient manner.[17]

Finally, I want to turn to a brief discussion of the criticism this book has received. The content of the positive reviews echoed the private letters of faculty and students mentioned above. They pointed to the importance of looking at professional training as a socialization experience in which the internalization of research methodology plays a critical function, the necessity of considering alternative paradigms to counterbalance that of "normal science," the value of developing a method that is grounded in the experiences both of the researcher and those studied, and the need to examine the research process itself as an influence on the research findings.

On the other hand, some reviewers admonished me for being overly critical and wordy. I accept the latter criticism and would have liked the opportunity to shorten this new edition. Others criticized me for being "overly anxious." The personal letters I continue to receive attesting to the problems I have described lead me to conclude that the socialization process for social scientists has varied effects on different types of people. I believe it would be worthwhile to investigate these differences. I have been criticized for developing an ethic of research that is limited to "consistency with one's values," an ethic that is essentially "therapeutic" rather than moral. My response to this is simply that when "consistency with one's values" and "therapeutic" elements are lacking, the problem of personal alienation is more likely to develop, as are incomplete understanding, callousness, and even exploitation. Finally, I have been criticized for some of my choices of examples of good research, such as Agee's *Let Us Now Praise Famous Men*. Instead of engaging in a discussion of the merits of Agee's work, I would like to mention additional studies that in my view were conducted in the experiential paradigm. They include, in anthropology, Barbara Meyerhoff's *Number Our Days*, Liz Stanley's and Sue Wise's articles in feminist sociology, and Graham Rowles's work in humanistic geography,[18] to mention a few. In each case, the author(s) illuminated a subject matter, engaged in reciprocally meaningful relations with others or underwent significant personal change, and made methodological contributions.

I ended the original version of this book with the statement, "I recognize now that I need the rest of my life to finish my socialization." As this preface indicates, my previous prediction that my attitudes toward the social sciences and my self-definition as a social scientist would continue to change, was borne out. It is also evident that it has been as rewarding yet demanding to receive responses as it has been to write the book. My hope is that students and social scientists, whether they agree with the ideas in these pages or not, will use them as a springboard to a deepened understanding of their own work, values, and identity.

Notes

1. Shulamit Reinharz, "Experiential analysis: A contribution to feminist research," in *Theories of Women's Studies,* ed. Gloria Bowles and Renate Duelli-Klein (Boston: Routledge and Kegan Paul, 1983), pp. 162-91.
2. Shulamit Reinharz, "Feminist research methodology groups: Origins, forms, and functions," in *Feminist Visions and Re-Visions,* ed. Louise Tilly and Vicki Petraka (University of Michigan, Women's Studies, 1983), pp. 197-228.
3. Shulamit Reinharz, Marti Bombyk, and Janet Wright, "Methodological issues in feminist research: A bibliography of literature in women's studies, sociology and psychology," *Women's Studies International Forum* 6 (1983): 437-54.
4. Dorothy E. Smith, "Women's perspective as a radical critique of sociology," *Sociological Inquiry* 44 (1974): 7-13.
5. Mary Jo Deegan, "Early women sociologists and the American Sociological Society: The patterns of exclusion and participation," *American Sociologist* 16 (1981): 14-24.
6. Ann Oakley, "Interviewing women: A contradiction in terms," in *Doing Feminist Research,* ed. Helen Roberts (Boston: Routledge and Kegan Paul, 1981), pp. 30-61.
7. See, for example, The Nebraska Feminist Collective: "A feminist ethic for social science research," *Women's Studies International Forum* 6 (1983): 535-43.
8. Shulamit Reinharz, "Implementing new paradigm research: A model for training and practice," in *Human Inquiry : A Sourcebook of New*

Paradigm Research, ed. Peter Reason and John Rowan (New York: John Wiley, 1981), pp. 415-36.

9. Gerald Zaltman, "Review," in *Journal of Marketing Research* 18 (1981): 124-31.

10. Charles Kieffer, "The emergence of empowerment: The development of participatory competence among individuals in citizen organizations," University of Michigan, Ph.D. diss., 1981.

11. Ann Wood, "Growing up with divorced parents: A phenomenological study of preschool children's experiences," University of Michigan, Ph.D. diss., 1981.

12. Janet Wright, "Open communication and conflict in alternative organizations: A case study of a higher education program," University of Michigan, Ph.D. diss., 1982.

13. For example, Marcia J. Bombyk, "Social parenting: An exploratory study of informal relationships between adults, unrelated children, and the children's parents," University of Michigan, Ph.D., diss., 1983.

14. "Introduction," in *Varieties of Qualitative Research,* ed. John Van Maanen, James M. Dabbs, Jr., and Robert Faulkner (Beverly Hills, Calif.: Sage, 1982).

15. See Robert M. Emerson's use of "experiential analysis" in *Contemporary Field Research* (Boston: Little, Brown, 1983).

16. See Nevitt Sanford, "Social psychology: Its place in personology," *American Psychologist* 37 (1982): 896-903.

17. See, for example, Peter Conrad and Shulamit Reinharz, "Computers and Qualitative Data," in a special double issue of *Qualitative Sociology: Computers and Qualitative Data* 7 (1984).

18. Liz Stanley and Sue Wise, "Feminist research, feminist consciousness and experiences of sexism," *Women's Studies International Quarterly* 2 (1979): 259-79; Graham Rowles, "Reflections on experiential fieldwork," in *Humanistic Geography: Prospects and Problems,* ed. David Ley and Marwyn Samuels (Chicago: Maaroufa Press, 1978), pp. 173-93.

Preface

The social sciences have the potential to reduce human anxiety and uncertainty by clarifying the social world in which we live. They hold out a great promise and thus attract many students. The transformation of wide-eyed, eager students into competent, productive social scientists is encompassed in the term *socialization*. At some point in the socialization process, many students find themselves confronting unexpected discomfort with what they are learning to think and do. Some become quite alienated and confused and are thus led to drop out; others bury their questions and set them aside as epistemological problems to be tackled someday "when they have time." This book is about students who are setting out, in the midst of, or finishing their socialization—who are attempting to forge identities as social scientists and trying to cope with the problems strewn along the way, particularly problems related to research methodology.

Although the socialization of social scientists is fueled with the combined influence of special mentors, assorted faculty, and a cohort of peers, it is particularly among peers that questions concerning the emergence of identity are raised. In private introspection and informal discussion among students, the large questions—how knowledge should be acquired and how identities are being shaped—can be discussed without concern of evaluation. This book is intended to continue those discussions in a systematic way. Sometimes problems of identity formation are discussed in the scholarly literature when accomplished social scientists reflect on their experiences during a particular research project or during an entire career. This book provides another case to this "studies of studies" literature— referred to as the sociology of sociology—in which social scientists share the backstage of their work.

What began as a series of introspective essays to myself concerning my struggle and disillusionment with certain research approaches and the hegemony of "science" has become in this book an extended discussion of the strengths and weaknesses of several methods (survey research, participant observation, and experiential analysis) as they are experienced—not as they are ideally described. I report a series of experiences reconstructed by a framework that emerged at the end of those experiences, rather than report the results of a study designed in advance. My argument is couched in the model of discovery rather than the model of testing because I believe that the experiences of socialization and of research must first be adequately described before they can be tested.

My suggestions for an appropriate, alternate research method and for a model for understanding the dynamics of socialization, as discussed in Chapter Eight, are grounded in the research projects described in Chapters Two, Three, Four, Six, and Seven. In fact, one of the major hypotheses with which the book concludes is that socialization can be fruitfully understood precisely as the creation of a sense of identity hinged on the resolution of conflicts concerning method. In other words, as one is involved in being socialized, one encounters conflicts, and as they are resolved, one develops an internalized sense of identity. Socialization is thus the production of individuals who have adopted an identity linked to their competence in carrying out action, which in the case of social science is the action of social research. But, since the actual activity of research is frequently blurred in deference to the ideal image of research, the process of identity formation is muddled and problematic. If we wish to produce social scientists who are at peace with themselves and who do not alienate others in society by their actions as researchers, it would seem useful to examine the way they are trained and how they feel about themselves during that training.

My perspective on social science can be classified as part of the branch that uses case studies, qualitative data analysis, and an inductive understanding of grounded experience and that adopts a reflexive stance on the research endeavor. With this book I add my voice to those who wish to reduce the monopoly of quantitative methods on the production of social science knowledge. My work synthesizes some of the key approaches of two seminal works in the contemporary sociological scene—Glaser and Strauss (1967) and Gouldner (1970). These studies helped shape my resistance to and protest against sociological conventions and guided my search for alternatives. I hope that I have opened the way for others to share their experiences without embarrassing those whom I discuss in these pages. My description and analysis of actual experiences for public scrutiny make it necessary for me to forgo the detachment enjoyed by most social scientists. Although I delight in reasserting the experience of the individual, my training within the guidelines of communicating about ideas rather than about ourselves leaves me with some unresolved concerns. The dilemma is that the closer I come to accurately describing my reality the greater is the potential of illuminating the situation; yet, at the same time, the greater is the risk of discomforting someone else who is involved. Thus, I have sometimes changed the names of locales and personalities in the case histories I report.

In the course of conducting a survey, a participant observation field study, and an experiential team study, I experienced both the emergence and fusion of my method and identity. My concern in this book is less with the details of each study than with illustrating the intertwined development of method and identity. It is my hope that this description of the cycle of search and rejection will facilitate the socialization of other students by articulating their conflicts and encourage both students and faculty to return to their own experiences. By grounding ourselves in our own experiences, perhaps we will be able to rehumanize social research and allow experience to become the foundation of useful knowledge.

One last prefatory comment: Although I have been trained as a sociologist, I frequently speak of social science in general terms. My reasons for doing so are because the boundaries between the content areas and the perspectives of the various social science disciplines are, in my opinion, almost meaningless. The only real distinction can be found in the professional identification of the various constituencies. Similarly, the conflicts and problems I uncovered during my socialization process as a sociologist were referred to frequently in the literature of other disciplines, particularly anthropology and psychology. The issues seem to be the same, although the actors are different. For this reason, I believe the book will be of use to members of many disciplines within social science.

Since this work is an exercise in reflexive sociology, I mention in each chapter significant individuals who shaped my socialization. Professors Mirra Komarovsky and Renee Fox, then of Barnard College, introduced me to sociology's potential and served as much-admired models. The staff at the Bureau of Applied Social Research, Columbia University, opened the world of survey research and permitted me to experience its inner workings. I am grateful for the individual and collective influence of the faculty of Brandeis University's Department of Sociology. Professors Philip Slater, Kurt Wolff, Everett Hughes, Lewis Coser, Maurice Stein, and many others (who were all at Brandeis at the time) pushed, prodded, stimulated, and provoked me in pursuing my interests. I am most indebted to Professors Morris Schwartz, Gordon Fellman, Rosabeth Kanter, and Irving Zola of Brandeis University and Severyn Bruyn of Boston College who read my rough drafts with care and offered me valuable criticism. Their thoughtful comments sharpened my ideas; their support buoyed my determination. But it is Morris Schwartz to whom I owe my greatest debt for creating opportunities that I could use to pursue this project. He has been the ideal guide, encouraging me on every step of the way, eager to learn with me. And his wife, Charlotte Green Schwartz, shared with me many of her discoveries and scholarly concerns. This couple's brilliant contributions to sociology will continuously influence my thinking and development.

The director and members of the activity therapies staff of the mental hospital I studied aided my efforts at becoming a participant observer. The patients tolerated my curiosity as a researcher and showed me how to remain human in the context of a mental hospital. My Israeli mentor, colleague, and collaborator, Ruth Gruschka, guided me through team research, consultation, and data analysis. A consummate social practitioner and theoretician, her work has consistently filled me with admiration. To the families of the Israeli border town and the public health nurses who served them, I am grateful for their open doors, minds, and hearts.

I thank the members of the Department of Psychology, University of Michigan, Ann Arbor, for granting me a leave from my academic duties to write the first draft of this book. For financial assistance, I thank the Danforth Foundation and the Horace H. Rackham School of Graduate Studies, University of Michigan. For cheerful, prompt, and high-quality technical assistance, I acknowledge Esther Rentschler and Barbara Toler.

My two-year-old daughter Yael does not yet know the extent to which she inspired me to complete this book. Finally, my husband Jehuda gave me marvelous practical advice, concrete help, and encouragement when I needed it most. Without his continuous support this book would still be "in progress."

Shulamit Reinharz

March 1979

Contents

The Author

Shulamit Reinharz is assistant professor of psychology at the University of Michigan, where she specializes in community psychology and is director of Project Outreach, an undergraduate experiential education program that places nearly 1,000 students a semester in community settings.

Reinharz was born in Amsterdam, Holland, in 1946 and was raised in the United States. She was awarded the B.A. degree with honors in sociology from Barnard College (1967) and the M.A. and Ph.D. degrees in sociology from Brandeis University (1969, 1977). Among the awards she received during her graduate education were the Kent Fellowship, Woodrow Wilson Fellowship, and a National Institute of Mental Health fellowship. In addition to her academic training as a sociologist, she has had clinical experience in family and group therapy. After teaching at the schools of social work of Simmons College and the University of Michigan, she joined the faculty of the Department of Psychology at the University of Michigan, Ann Arbor, in 1972.

Among her publications are several articles on experiential education and on the development of community mental health practice and philosophy, particularly in Israel, with special emphasis on ethnically heterogeneous communities, holocaust survivors' children, and conflicting cultural ideologies. Her recent research activities include developing formative evaluation models for experiential education and creating consultation networks for alternative human services organizations. On leave from the University of Michigan in 1979-80, she is conducting an experiential study of the kibbutz elderly. She is also working on a historical study that attempts to locate the "place of experience" in the discipline of psychology.

Reinharz lives with her husband, Jehuda, a professor of history at the University of Michigan, and their two-year-old daughter, Yael.

For my husband, Jehuda

CHAPTER 1

Encountering the World of Sociology

Becoming a Sociologist

Two themes—the socialization of a sociologist as a researcher, and the search for and discovery of an alternative method for sociological research—are interwoven in this book through a detailed examination of three of my own research experiences. These three cases are linked both chronologically and with regard to a personal developmental process. My purpose is to demonstrate the struggle that is involved in socialization—the accommodations, doubts, compromises, and insights that culminate in a position one can finally call one's own. This kind of personal struggle is important not only to the individual but also to the entire profession, for sociology is revitalized through critical examination by its newcomers. The resolution of a stu-

1

dent's socialization crisis is a potential contribution to the field's development. My resolution and proposed contribution is "experiential analysis," the product of difficulties I encountered as a student trying to adopt a satisfactory method for doing research.

The three research project descriptions are presented as if I was aware of my analytic framework at the time. The analysis emerged, however, only in retrospect and as a product of those research experiences. I anticipate my conclusion, for example, by writing this book in the first person singular—from the perspective of the researcher's self.

My discussion is concerned with issues about sociology rather than problems within sociology because it assumes that sociology itself is problematic. To work on a circumscribed substantive problem within sociology is to imply that the discipline is nonproblematic, an assumption I cannot make.

> The usual instruction to a prospective sociologist is to identify a problem and, solving it, bring into the discipline new knowledge. That this is a betrayal in its inception and a fraud in its completion should be understood.
>
> To deal with problems is to ignore issues; to solve problems requires consensus methods, while to resolve issues requires conflict methods. The idea of "stating problems" is an idea which derives from the interest of academia to serve the power structure. A problem is something which can be solved within existing rules; issues require political action in the course of settling the rules. The focus on problem-oriented topics requires information available by following the existing rules of sociological method. The focus on issues would require one to obtain relevant information closed off from the researcher by existing rules about how to gain quality data [Young, 1974, p. 137].

For me, the problem with much of sociology is the shallowness of its methods, representing a simplistic attitude toward the question of how we can know that something is the case, and its techniques for accomplishing its mission. It is precisely the adoption of these methods that is the task of those who are being socialized and transformed into members of the profession.

The first of the three case histories employs the quantitative method of survey research. The second uses the qualitative method of participant observation. Both proved personally disappointing: the first because of its relation to "subjects" and the nature of the data this method produced, and the second because of its constraints, assumptions, and focus. The third case, which I retrospectively labeled *experiential analysis*, represents a collection of discoveries resulting from a search for a replacement for survey research and an extension of participant observation. I have applied this phenomenological approach to the search for method itself and have thus created a critique of sociological traditions from an experiential viewpoint. This search for a valid, meaningful, fruitful method for doing sociological research was also my search for a personally satisfying role in sociology. I was trying to find a way to become a humanistic sociologist.

The term *sociology* implies an activity (to study) and a target of that activity (society). Both components have taken on countless meanings over time. The debates concerning exactly what is meant by *study* and by *society* provide sociology with vitality. The diversity of opinions is stimulating for the profession, but for newcomers or students whose identities are being shaped by the nature of their work, the lack of consensus becomes personally problematic. In a commissioned examination of graduate education in sociology, Sibley (1963, p. 103) concluded:

> An essential function of graduate education, in addition to imparting a certain body of knowledge and skills, is the development of a sense of identification with a profession. In the case of sociology this process of professional socialization, of internalizing professional norms, is often slow and difficult for several reasons [partially because there are] only vague and distorted notions of what a professional sociologist does.

While students learn "to do" sociology and "to become" sociologists, they acquire an implicit, personally defined understanding of what sociology is. In this process there are occasions in which students experience intellectual satisfaction stemming from both the substance and process of their studies. But there are also profoundly dissatisfying occasions. Studies do not seem fruitful, the methods seem to miss the essence, the endeavors disappoint. Sibley (1963), in fact, characterized initiates into the culture of sociology as suffering fron anomie, disillusionment, and frustration.

Assuming that both positive and negative experiences are expected during the sociologist's socialization, we can examine case histories to determine if particular issues predominate, if these issues emerge in sequence, and which resolutions are made. This book presents the case history of one individual. It examines a process of several years during which I was attracted to the field of sociology, entered the field, engaged in a few studies, drew some tentative conclusions, and formulated some recommendations for change.

A student's career is a combination of self-selected, prescribed, and fortuitous activities. These are affected by the student's desire to meet the degree requirements, the faculty's consensus concerning offerings, and the availability of research activities. A student's intellectual growth is a product of directed and undirected readings, planned and unplanned research experiences, and numerous personal contingencies. As their work proceeds, students' explicit and implicit understanding of what sociology is forms the assumptions underpinning their work.

Students quickly learn that contemporary sociology contains numerous research methods or ways of approaching reality for the purpose of gaining knowledge. These methods include models that quantify information derived from surveys, interviews and questionnaires specifically constructed for the research project, and records and data banks that have accumulated. When archival records are used in this way, we have historical social science. By contrast, some methods involve the creation of experimental situations in which researchers manipulate one of the limited number of variables that they believe are in effect. There are techniques, such as participant observation, which depend on the researcher's involvement in a natural setting. Closer to psychology and infrequently adopted is the case study approach, based on intensive examination of individuals by interviews and other means to produce an analysis profound enough to permit generalization.

The profusion of these methods and models reflects sociology's borrowing from other sciences, such as mathematics, which have already achieved methodological rigor. Even where it has not borrowed, sociology has been conscious of its relation to other disciplines, especially the natural sciences, and has established its own mission in the context of these others. Sociology's partnership with other disciplines in interdisciplinary research, such as medical sociology, social psychiatry, urban planning, and criminology, has led to methodological exposure and exchange.

Social scientists approach problems, therefore, with many strategies at their disposal. Their first responsibility, after reviewing the literature on a given topic, is to select methods that best fit the problem at hand. If researchers work on a variety of problems, they might be expected to employ a wide range of methods. This, however, is not the case. Instead, the discipline is characterized by methodological specialization for several reasons: Sociologists are interested in particular methods; they need extensive experience to use one well; they are reinforced by success; and they typically have received exclusive training. In addition, researchers are convinced that some approaches are superior not only for a given research project but for *all* research projects. Methods are selected not by asking "Which particular method is useful for this problem?" but by asking "Which methods are legitimate at all?"

Proponents of different methods justify their choice by referring to different epistemological positions. These methods differ first as to *what is a fact* or datum and second as to *what to do with a fact* to produce knowledge. Much of Durkheim's delineation of the new science of sociology was precisely his novel definition of facts and the discovery of social facts. His definition of facts can be paraphrased as "rates of quantifiable behavior." The mathematical manipulations using this definition are limitless. But just as mathematics rests on assumptions about quantities and their relation, so too the definition of facts rests on value-laden assumptions, such as that instances of a linguistically defined behavior can be equivalent. To argue against Durkheimian assumptions is to reject the notion that human behavior consists of discrete units that can be labeled, compared, and quantified. One could say instead that social behavior is continuous, that social life is greater than the sum of its parts, and that social phenomena are ambiguous rather than clearly definable and unique rather than replicable. From these definitional disagreements stem myriad others within the research enterprise, such as the nature of evidence and validity. These debates are unresolved.

Advocates of an alternative image of social behavior espouse qualitative methodologies. Their definition of facts—descriptions of naturally occurring phenomena—is shaped by the pursuit of meaning rather than rate. Some social scientists, such as Lewis (1953, p. 454) and Reiss (1968, pp. 351-367), argue for different methods utilized at different stages in the research process. This compromise ignores epistemological problems in the belief that the weakness of one method is cancelled by the strength of another. I claim, however, that the weakness of any renders the whole enterprise unsound.

Just as each historical period preferred certain methods, so too students of sociology prefer different methods at different stages of their socialization. Methods are in a state of flux, both historically and individually. When there is conflict within the discipline, there is conflict within the individual.

As a student, I experienced both the historic conflict between models and the individual journey in search of a method. This journey has not been an amusing excursion of playful experimentation with different models, but rather a wrenching process in which each temporary model claimed to be *true*. It was particularly difficult to free myself of the overwhelming power of the scientific model to search for other paradigms.

In addition, each epistemological and methodological

preference shapes a particular research career and life-style. Different sociological methods lead to different sociological identities. Horowitz (1968) categorizes these as mainliners and marginals. Mainliners view sociology as a profession or occupation, and marginals are antisociologists and unsociologists. Merton (1957, pp. 439-528) differentiates between the American empiricists and the European grand theorists. Deutscher (1968, p. 326) suggests that English-speaking social scientists have a limited conception of ways of knowing because the English language employs only one verb, *to know*, whereas French, German, and Spanish utilize at least two. Other choices reflect different research life-styles and values. The kind of sociology that is possible, valuable, and personally desirable becomes integrated for each student in the socialization process. As Horowitz (1968, p. 218) states, "In this competition between sociological styles . . . the struggles over the kind of theories and methods sociology should have is directly proportional to the institutional questions—what kind of agency should the sociologist have, and what kind of man should the sociologist be?"

In addition, there appears to be a connection between gender and style of knowing. The "machismo" style of discovery (Bernard, 1973; Millman and Kanter, 1975) reflected in science is characterized as hard, rational, and controlled. The feminine style is characterized as soft, deep, humanistic, and concerned with the inner world. Erikson (1964, p. 38), for example, portrays Freud as having been able to combine "feminine intuition, childlike curiosity, and artistic freedom of style with the masculine 'inner tyrant' " of science. The female social scientist chooses among following the feminine style of discovery, adopting the masculine one, or disguising the masculine one as "feminist." In my view, the feminine discovery modalities should be introduced and not discounted. Such a perspective, however, is professionally jeopardizing, because as Bird (1972, p. 296) has written, "to be professional is to be objective, detached, impersonal, authoritative, competitive, stoic, tribal and tough. To be professional, in short, is 'to be a man.' I believe that suggestions for making professional practice more responsive, more concerned with social welfare, more people-oriented are resisted as soft, effeminate threats to professional 'manhood.' " This culturally defined association between gender and discovery style hinders both sexes from free exploration. This book represents an effort to overcome this sexist barrier by presenting *experiential analysis* as a contribution to sociological method in an unapologetically female modality.*

Merton's "American" and Horowitz's "mainline professional" sociologists comprise an *ideal type* whose work claims to be value-free and bias-free and uses quantified data, statistical theory, precise problems, careful research design, controls, and prescribed data-gathering techniques such as questionnaires and interviews. Students who accept this model prepare for a career within a research institute or academic department with its accompanying career life-style. As an undergraduate at Barnard College, I was exposed to the problems and benefits of this model. My analysis of this experience, the first of the three case histories, is contained in Chapter Two.

Dissatisfaction with this model prompted me to explore other possibilities. In the graduate department of sociology at Brandeis University, I encountered the world of Horowitz's marginal sociologists. Sociologists with philosophical, historical, psychological, and anthropological interests became role models. Among them were even some unsociologists who had recently rejected sociology as meaningless and were about to abandon academia. This eclectic group was too diverse to be a school, yet it did favor certain methods—participant observation, applied sociology, clinical work, ethnomethodology, historical analysis, theory construction, and phenomenology. They worked alone rather than in bureaucratic research institutes, and they chose research problems from among their personal concerns. In Chapter Three I describe my research experience while following this model.

My search for a way to become a sociologist did not end

---

*Despite this intention, the language in the book is at times sexist, using *he* as the general pronoun, since the traditional pronoun has not yet been superseded by a convenient, generally accepted pronoun that means either *he* or *she*.

in graduate school. Rather, I discovered that becoming a sociologist represented an ongoing search for method and identity. At times both role and method would crystallize; at other times both would be in flux.

Developing Values

As a result of these experiences, I came to believe that methodological debates are essentially polemic, since there is no consensus as to how agreement should be reached. Since method debates advocate one view over another, they are not capable of determining the "correct" way of doing sociology. The sociology I would do, therefore, would stem from my personal values as much as from my understanding of methods. The task before me, in that case, was to clarify my values and adopt or develop a fitting method. Values underlie definitions, and definitions of concepts and procedures are the first step of any research method. To select certain issues to study rather than others reflects researchers' choices in the context of their socially structured opportunities and values. These values are the assumptions of the research project and are particularly problematic in stratified research sites, as Becker and Horowitz (1972, p. 48) point out: "Prison research has for the most part been oriented to problems of jailers rather than those of prisoners; industrial research, to the problems of managers rather than those of workers; military research, to problems of generals rather than those of privates. . . . Wherever someone is oppressed, an 'establishment' sociologist seems to lurk in the background, providing the facts which make oppression more efficient and the theory which makes it legitimate to a larger constituency."

Methodological preferences stem from several sources: formal training, experience-based or personal values, and the institutional constraints of the setting in which the research is conducted. Values of individual researchers are clarified as they confront each component of the research process, from obtaining sponsorship, to defining a problem for study, to determining what will constitute evidence, to selecting a manner of presenting research results and developing a relation with the user or reader of the results. With continued practice, more and more elements of the research process become differentiated as issues around which value positions form.

As I progressed through my socialization and had to make decisions concerning research issues, I became aware that I held the following values:

1. Research should be *unalienated labor.* Since research activities require commitment, we should attempt to minimize conflict within ourselves by selecting research activities that coincide with personal concerns (Coser, 1969). We can further reduce conflict by obtaining sponsorship from funders or institutions that accept the values expressed in the research (Vidich and Bensman, 1971). The most effective means for reducing alienation is to create a sense of community among sponsors, researchers and subjects, a value that is operationalized in collaborative research.

2. My basic image of the world stems from a preference for seeing process and change rather than order and continuity. I imagine an elusively organized social system rather than one which is governed by inexorable laws. Therefore, it is not disconcerting to confront contradiction or conflict. As researchers, we are not in control of the forces shaping our environment but are instead controlled by them in ways we do not yet understand.

3. The researcher's most productive stance is curiosity and dissatisfaction with current paradigms for understanding social life. The researcher should be oriented to discovering fresh insights beyond conventional understanding, not just building incremental bits of knowledge by using conventional techniques.

4. The problems we study should be important according to a standard the researcher is able to specify. The significance of findings should be demonstrable in terms of larger social relevance.

5. Since research is a personal activity, research reports should contain a vivid description of the experience of researching.

In these reports the value positions of the researcher should be faced squarely and addressed fully. Results of the research activities should be presented not only in terms of findings but also of questions that provoke the reader. To accomplish this, researchers should acquire writing skills that will enable them to reach the reader.

If my research is unalienated, then it must coincide with my values. To proceed with my socialization, therefore, I had to clarify what my values were as related to research. I set out on my search for method by reading, thinking, and sitting before my typewriter, spilling onto the pages thousands of words about how I felt about research, its methods, purposes, and process. After recording all of this very personal material over a period of several months, I then sifted and sorted the pages looking for themes. This reductive process produced a set of major themes which I posed in this form: "I am concerned with _____ rather than _____" or "I believe in _____ rather than _____." These preference statements summarized my methodological stance. I then pulled out the contrasts contained in each preference statement and listed the contrasting claims of the major sociological research models. The following list represents the major themes I discovered in my search for method, with the right-hand column indicating my preferences. The right-hand column embodies the rehumanization of sociology to reflect the fact that its researchers are human beings dealing with human problems in humane ways.

Contrasting Claims of Sociological Research Models

Mainstream sociology claims to be:	*An alternative method would acknowledge that it is:*
Exclusively rational in the conduct of research and the analysis of data	A mix of rational, serendipitous and intuitive phenomena in research and analysis
Scientific	Accurate but artistic
Oriented to carefully defined structures	Oriented to processes

Mainstream sociology claims to be:	*An alternative method would acknowledge that it is:*
Completely impersonal	Personal
Oriented to the prediction and control of events and things	Oriented to understanding phenomena
Interested in the validity of research findings for scholars	Interested in the meaningfulness of research findings to the scholarly and user communities
Objective	A mix of objective and subjective orientations
Capable of producing generalized principles	Capable of producing specific explanations
Interested in replicable events and procedures	Interested in unique although frequently occurring phenomena
Capable of producing completed analyses of a research problem	Limited to producing partial discoveries of ongoing events
Interested in addressing problems with predefined concepts	Interested in generating concepts *in vivo*, in the field itself

The preceding clarification of my values and orientations is the fruit of my effort to resolve the "chronic conflicts" (Hughes, 1958, p. 160) or the "professional tensions" (Berg, 1978, pp. 1-20) that abound in the social sciences. In the conduct of research, the action preferences rooted in these values are expressed. As each research project is begun, the chronic conflicts reemerge, asking to be resolved. With the passage of time and the accumulation of experience, researchers discover the significance of the choices they have made. During the socialization process students confront the conflicts but are unsure of the extent to which they can explore them since strong pressures to specialize compel students to choose a substantive camp early and develop a firm commitment expressed in competence. In addition, the student does not know to what extent the values inherent in the discipline can be challenged. Are there certain questions that may not be asked at all without violating the definition of the profession itself?

As I reflected on my own work, I differentiated between two sets of attitudes toward the conduct of social research. Although some have argued that these sets represent a false dichotomy (Berg, 1978), members of the sociology profession act as if these perspectives compete for legitimacy. The left-hand column in the preceding list represents the mainstream perspective commonly used as the sole set of characteristics defining sociology. The set on the right represents contrasting methodological preferences, which I discovered I espoused.

After separating the contrasting claims of sociological research models, my next task was to identify the critical dimensions of research models in general so that the contrasts could be presented in a manner that depicted all the elements of a research model. I could thus recognize if I had overlooked a contrast and could sharpen the contrasts I had defined. I undertook this disciplined search for method clarification only after I had completed the three research projects described in this book; therefore, this analysis represents a reconstruction of my socialization with regard to method.

The right-hand column of Table 1 represents the self attempting to contest the mystification of science's claim to be the only way of acquiring truth or knowledge. Graduate training as currently organized in the social sciences trains people to act primarily in terms of the research claims represented in the left-hand column. To act in terms of the alternative model requires courage to withstand the charge of holding these views because one is improperly or inadequately socialized. It also requires special forms of training, including the following:

1. Undergoing some form of *self-analysis*, such as psychoanalysis (see Nader, 1970; Powdermaker, 1966), group process experiences, or other self-awareness methods, such as yoga or zen. Through this training students can learn to recognize their way of shaping reality; they can discover the problems

Table 1. Research Models in Contemporary Sociology

Units of study	predefined, operationalized concepts stated as hypotheses	natural events encased in their ongoing contexts
Sharpness of focus	limited, specialized, specific, exclusive	broad, inclusive
Data type	reports of attitudes and actions as in questionnaires, interviews and archives	feelings, behavior, thoughts, insights, actions as witnessed or experienced
Topic of study	manageable issue derived from scholarly literature, selected for potential scholarly contribution, sometimes socially significant	socially significant problem sometimes related to issues discussed in scholarly literature
Role of researcher		
In relation to environment	control of environment is desired, attempt to manage research conditions	openness to environment, immersion, being subject to and shaped by it
In relation to subjects	detached	involved, sense of commitment, participation, sharing of fate
As a person	irrelevant	relevant, expected to change during process
Impact on researcher	irrelevant	anticipated, recorded, reported, valued
Implementation of method	as per design, decided a priori	method determined by unique characteristics of field setting
Validity criteria	proof, evidence, statistical significance; study must be replicable and yield same results to have valid findings	completeness, plausibility, illustrativeness, understanding, responsiveness to readers' or subjects' experience; study cannot however be replicated
The role of theory	crucial as determinant of research design arranged in advance relying on deductive logic, done when all data are "in"	emerges from research implementation done during the study, relying on inductive logic
Data analysis	utilization of statistical analyses	creation of gestalts and meaningful patterns
Manipulation of data		
Research objectives	testing hypotheses	development of understanding through grounded concepts and descriptions

Presentation format	research report form; report of conclusions with regard to hypotheses stated in advance, or presentation of data obtained from instruments	story, description with emergent concepts; including documentation of process of discovery
Failure	statistically insignificant variance	pitfalls of process illustrate the subject
Values	researchers' attitudes not revealed, recognized or analyzed, attempts to be value-free, objective	researchers' attitudes described and discussed, values acknowledged, revealed, labelled
Role of reader	scholarly community addressed, evaluation of research design, management, and findings	scholarly and user community addressed and engaged; evaluate usefulness and responsiveness to perceived needs

they need to study; and they can ascertain how others perceive them. In addition, as they develop an increasing sense
of autonomy, they can develop the courage needed to self-
disclose and pursue the "truth."

2. Undergoing many different kinds of *experiences* in order to
   formulate grounded questions and feel comfortable immersing oneself in a variety of research settings.

3. Developing *literary skills* so that the actual writing is clear
   and forceful, recognizing that writing descriptions of events
   as data and analyses of data as products are the essence of
   the alternative method.

In addition, as in all socialization processes, it is useful
for the person in training to surround himself with living and
written examples of the model which represents an ideal. In this
case, the implementation of a project based on the alternative
research model would benefit from reading discussions of methodological debates and reports of completed projects and working with proponents of the desirable model.

Learning Methodology

My socialization into the sociology profession was difficult, since I seriously examined the conflicts among the various
methods and tried to account for my choices. Choosing a sociology, like choosing "between cultivating theory or experiment, is
one of those existential dilemmas with which the scientist simply has to live" (A. Kaplan, 1964, p. 214). To become a fully
socialized member of a society, one has to internalize its values.
Problematic socialization occurs, however, when the values
within that society are conflict ridden and correspond to inconsistent behavior. Students must unlearn behavior associated
with other roles (see G. Jacobs, 1970), while at the same time
learning sociological behavior that is rather incoherent. In Sussman's (1964, p. 216) words, "Ambivalence, confusion and conflict exist regarding what [the sociologist's] proper role behavior should be." According to Butts (1975, p. 185), "[There is]
unprecedented doubt and confusion about the character of the

sociological enterprise" (see also Gamberg, 1969). The multiple ways of learning the activities of sociology, the paucity of opportunities for the newcomer to directly observe or witness the full-fledged member's activity, and the discrepancy between the real and the ideal reports of practice render socialization problematic. How then does the student sociologist learn the appropriate role behavior of the profession? What kinds of material are available to learn about method?

Figure 1 presents the variety of means by which students learn methodology. Becker (1970) lists four categories of methodological writing: proselytization, technical, analytic, and sociological; I list three: experiential, didactic, and descriptive.

Figure 1. Ways of Learning Sociological Research Methods.

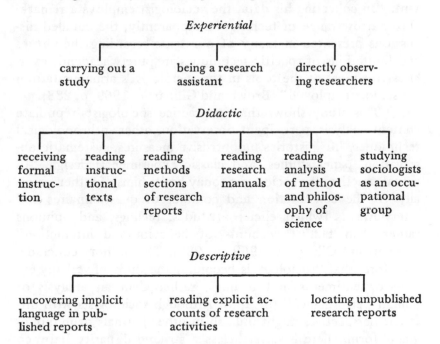

Experiential

| carrying out a study | being a research assistant | directly observing researchers |

Didactic

| receiving formal instruction | reading instructional texts | reading methods sections of research reports | reading research manuals | reading analysis of method and philosophy of science | studying sociologists as an occupational group |

Descriptive

| uncovering implicit language in published reports | reading explicit accounts of research activities | locating unpublished research reports |

The experiential form emphasizes the responsibility of students to carry out, relatively unassisted, an investigation for the purpose of analyzing the nature of the research experience. This experiential method is closely linked with direct observation of sociologists doing their research. Students who observe seasoned researchers are given an opportunity to formulate accounts of their activities (see Diesing, 1971, for an example). Falling between assuming the responsibility for investigation and observing research with detachment is an apprenticeship frequently in the form of research assistantship.

In the descriptive modality for learning sociological methods, much can be learned from published accounts. Brown and Gilmartin (1969) analyzed 402 articles published in the *American Sociological Review* and the *American Journal of Sociology* in 1940-1941 and 1965-1966 to determine how published sociology is actually practiced. They concluded that sociological research is time- and culture-bound, provincial, and unlikely to concern topics that sociologists themselves claim to be important. "In collecting his data, the sociologist employs a remarkably narrow range of techniques. Apparently, the detailed discussions presented in many of our texts regarding the virtues and limitations of specific techniques are purely academic exercises, for most of the tools in the sociologist's armamentarium are seldom employed" (Brown and Gilmartin, 1969, p. 288).

This study shows that in practice sociologists repudiate content analysis, participant observation, other anthropological techniques, life histories, unobtrusive measures, systematic observation, panel studies, and classic experimental design. "In actual practice, the sociologist today limits himself rather generally to the construction and conduct of questionnaires and interviews ... [which elicit] attitudes, feelings, and opinions rather than factual accounts of behavior and interaction" (Brown and Gilmartin, 1969, p. 288). The authors conclude, therefore, that "sociology is becoming the study of verbally expressed sentiments and feelings, rather than an analysis of human performance" (p. 288). Although sociologists with different perspectives might publish in other journals or in monograph form, there is nevertheless a striking disparity between the scope of published research and sociology's claims. In a similar content analysis (of the journal *Social Problems* from the beginning of its publication through December 1964), McCartney (1970, p. 34) proposes the following basis for the "premature obsolescence of case-study and qualitative analysis":

The potential sponsors of sociological research have exerted pressure on sociologists (and other social scientists) to become scientific in their research and use statistics because they assume that only scientific research will be useful in solving problems. The pragmatic concern of the sponsor interacts with the professional concern of the sociologist, who seeks recognition by making his discoveries known to his colleagues (i.e., publication of his research). The sociologist who decides to use statistics in his research is more likely to have it published eventually. He will avoid research strategies that sponsors and his colleagues define as "pre-scientific" or "unscientific." One does not find explicit encouragement (or discouragement) for use of the case-study method from the major public and private sponsors of sociological research, but their enthusiasm for statistics is undisguised.

McCartney's conclusion puts methodology training into a form that a student being socialized can understand:

> A sociologist who adopts a rigorous scientific stance, complete with the use of statistics, will have more success in obtaining funds to do research and a greater probability of having the results published in the major professional journals. Conducting case-study or qualitative research, which important peers (and nonpeers) view as unscientific or unsystematic, involves some risk for one's professional career [p. 37].

The discrepancy between the broad array of methods presented formally in texts and the narrow range that is actually practiced and published is disconcerting. Students typically respond by using methods that the profession actually accepts.

Another socializing device is the subtly disparaging and condescending tone used to describe nonquantitative methods, which damns with faint praise. The following is an example:

> Prior to 1940, most sociologists—conducting their studies alone and with limited resources—relied on informal methods. Many of the major empirical studies were based on "participant observation," in which the investi-

gator immersed himself in a social setting to study it intensively. . . . Sociologists still use informal research methods when they study situations about which little is known or situations in which everyday behavior is so familiar that it is likely to be taken for granted. . . . Studies of this sort are often extraordinarily rich in original insights that would have been difficult to obtain through formal methods, such as survey research or experimentation. Their results suffer, however, from lack of generalizability, since they are based on small samples of carefully selected respondents. Many sociologists argue that such studies are essential for developing hypotheses, but inadequate for testing them [Smelser and Davis, 1969, pp. 38-39].

Dewey's (1954, p. 49) "collateral learning" refers to attitudes that students learn to adopt toward the subject matter as distinct from the learning of the material itself. Lofland's (1974) analysis of unpublished *qualitative* research reports is a similar socialization tool, affording an insight into the actual practice of qualitative research, which was unsuccessful from the criterion of publishability.

The methodological norms of the profession are also revealed in academic hiring practices, methods utilized in accepted dissertations, research styles of officers of professional organizations, and features of work that has been awarded academic prizes. Examining both the approved and disapproved instances of each of these categories leads students to understand the real methodological practices in contrast with the idealized ones. Each process chosen for obtaining information about method, whether by questionnaire, observation of researchers at work, interview, examination of publications, manuscript review practices, grant proposal analysis, or personal experience, leads to particular conclusions.

Finally, there are explicit accounts of research activities that give students access to other researchers' experiences. By revealing the events of a particular research project, they instruct newcomers as to how sociology is actually done. Ironically, this valuable material is scarce, since sociologists under-report their own activities and separate the private behavior of the research experience from the public, published document. Sociologists guard their privacy as academicians, as well as the details of their methods as researchers. When Daniels (1974) published descriptions of professional, unprofessional, and controversial behavior of sociologists identified by name, her report was criticized as indiscreet. Thousands of social researchers have performed research; libraries are full of "findings"; yet the number of reports about the actual research process is small in absolute terms and miniscule relative to other products. There are frequent calls for publishing more of these reports, yet few are forthcoming.* Glaser and Strauss (1967, p. 8) state that their "principal aim is to stimulate other theorists to codify and publish their own methods for generating theory." Such exposure involves risk (Hart, 1957). In addition, researchers are problem oriented rather than process oriented. They consider the research process an irrelevant or insignificant variable and believe there is no more process in a research project than its formal method.

Despite this disclaimer about the limited quantity of published research accounts and analyses, there are several anthologies that do contribute to a researchers-at-work literature. These accounts ground sociology in the reality of everyday life and contribute to understanding sociology as an occupation. Through these accounts the human and social dimensions of being a researcher emerge. Horowitz's *Sociological Self-Images* contains contributions by sociologists willing to "risk the disapproval of colleagues who prefer to think that personal reflections are better kept out of print, or at least out of the scientific

---

*A similar situation seems to exist in the discipline of anthropology. "Teachers of anthropology have previously been handicapped by the lack of clear, authoritative statements of how anthropologists collect and analyze relevant data. The results of fieldwork are available . . . (but) they rarely tell students much about how the facts have been gathered and interpreted. Without this information [we are] left uninformed about the processes of our science" (Langness, 1965, p. v). Powdermaker (1966, p. 11) writes, "Among all field workers—sociologists, anthropologists, and others—there is an increasing awareness of the need for personal chronicles of their research."

purview of the young" and by an interest in the "subjective processes by which science gets done" (1969, p. 9).

Hammond's *Sociologists at Work* is developed around the theme of the "role of the circumstantial, the irrational and non-rational, as well as the logical and systematic, nature of social research" (1964, p. 2). These authors demystify science by telling the sociological research story as it really is. The impetus of Hammond's work is this deficit in social science reporting: "For very few social scientific reports, it appears, with all their discussion of methods, contain accounts of the 'method' by which they came about. There are almost no chronicles of social research. And yet this missing component is an important one, as seen in the frequency with which existing chronicles are cited as well as by the number of times eminent and experienced researchers have called for more such accounts" (Hammond, 1964, p. 2).

Vidich, Bensman, and Stein's *Reflections on Community Studies* (1964), Adams and Preiss's *Human Organization Research* (1960), and Sjoberg's *Ethics, Politics and Social Research* (1967) contain research accounts that focus primarily on the process rather than the product. These reports contribute to the sociologists' shared experiential culture to which students can have access. These social scientists risk their privacy in order to share this culture. However, by violating the standards of impersonal research, they make a reflexive sociology possible. Through self-revelation they diminish the gap between the real and the ideal in social science. For as Merton (1962, p. 19) wrote, the method literature is concerned with "how social scientists OUGHT to think, feel, and act and fails to give the necessary detail on what they ACTUALLY DO, think and feel." These reports uncover significant but unexamined aspects of the research process. They reduce "the detachment of the sociologist from the milieu in which his professional role unfolds. Such detachment brings with it special problems in the sociologist's understanding of his own behavior within the context of the research process, e.g., strategies in the research process may at times be less a function of intellectual canons of procedure and more a function of pressures emanating elsewhere; pressures to publish and pressures to maintain one's position with colleagues may influence the strategic decisions made in research" (Lantz, 1969, p. v).

Reflexive research accounts serve students as a corrective to the idealization inherent in methodological instruction.* They speed the transition from naive novice to mature member. With these reports students learn "what everybody knows," to see past the scientific \"front" into the backstage of sociological performances. As the socialization process unfolds, students gain more and more access to the backstage. They overhear and then participate in private discussions concerning the ways in which actual professional work is done. They come to see that "few practicing social scientists today believe their research resembles the orderly intellectual presentations in textbooks on method: selection of problem, formulation and testing of hypotheses, and analysis and interpretation of data" (Powdermaker, 1966, p. 10). Whyte (1971, p. 3) complained of being

> severely handicapped by the paucity of reading matter that I can assign to students. There are many good published studies of communities or organizations, but generally the published reports give little attention to the actual process whereby the research was carried out. . . . They fail to note that the researcher, like his informants, is a social animal. . . . A real explanation of how the research was done necessarily involves a rather personal account of how the researcher lived during the period of study.

That these publications involve risk can be detected by several characteristics. Typically, many short pieces are collected in such a volume; pseudonyms are used for the author (Bowen, 1964; Field, 1936; West, 1945); the material is difficult to publish (Watson, 1968; Agee and Evans, 1972) or is published posthumously (Malinowski, 1967); and the material is located in peripheral places of a manuscript, such as footnotes,

---

*For parallel discussions concerning anthropology, see Langness (1965) and Jongmans and Gutkind (1967).

prefaces, acknowledgments, appendices, and dedications (Gans, 1962; Whyte, 1961; Liebow, 1967), or where rules can be broken; much time elapses between the occurrence of the events and the appearance of the analysis (Wax, 1957; Bogart, 1961).

The severe limitations on exposing the researcher's experience or the actual dynamics of the research process reinforce the scientific ideal. A truly reflexive, descriptive report of the experience of seeking knowledge compels a revelation of self, with frailties, shortcomings, passions, and biases. In writing about attempts to understand social reality, the sociologist typically defends himself against his humanity and reveals "little of [his] feelings . . . as he continuously participates, observes and interviews, of his discouragements and pleasure, and of the possible relationship of these to the type of work he does" (Powdermaker, 1966, p. 9).

When sociologists omit the actual processes involved in their work, they emulate the natural sciences and presume an "unembodied" method. In so doing, they implicitly deny the "boundedness" of their research activities. Boundedness refers to all concepts that sociologists have created to account for other people's behavior. Sociologists claim that behavior is class bound, gender related, historically rooted, and situationally determined by expectations of others. To be consistent with this belief, sociologists' perceptions and behavior in their research activities must be considered bound to their social position. Their responsibility as sociologists, then, is to understand how their work is shaped by these factors. However, rarely if ever do investigators take into account their roles in the social system under investigation or their impact on the thing studied (see Webb and others, 1966). Moreover, the isolation of the so-called Hawthorne effect demonstrates that subjects attempt to please their investigators. Sudman and Bradburn (1974) similarly show how subjects relate to their questioners. Their dissection of the influence of interview components on respondents' behavior should dispel dusty notions of obtaining objective data from respondents as if they transcended time, situation, or interest.

Since knowledge is situated in particular contexts, researchers must discover their own role imbeddedness. Their definition of what is going on is but one of several definitions grounded in different perspectives and useful for different purposes. An illuminating instance is Manocchio and Dunn (1970), who offer two views of a prison—through the eyes of a habitual criminal and a prison counselor. Methodological instruction that lifts sociologists out of reality implies that social science can be perspective-free. But the postulate of an unembodied researcher refutes sociology's very foundations.

Failing and Falsifying

Because reflexive research accounts are scarce in comparison with idealized reports, research almost always appears to succeed. Yet Denzin (1970, p. 7) claims that "an investigation seldom runs to successful completion." The demands of clients or subjects, problems in the research organization, political pressure, vagueness or untestability of theory, inappropriateness of research methods, problems of the investigators themselves, demands and pressures of academia and the community, and the influence of the research auspices affect the process (Andrew, 1967). The American adoration of "success" for any undertaking and its inevitability if one works hard enough influence reporting. The idealized reporting of research projects the image of an ability to control the environment (the variables), the power of reason to predict the outcome of events, and the clearcut distinction of success and failure. But failures occur in social research, as the few published accounts attest, and they reflect problems encountered during all research programs. Sometimes obstacles are avoided; other times they become termination points. Failure can occur at the beginning, middle, or end—before the project begins, while it should be sustained, or when results should be forthcoming. The following are some examples of these three types of failure:

Failure To Get Started

- failure to develop appropriate research team and methods (Riesman and Watson, 1964; Cherniss, 1977)
- failure to obtain funding

- failure to conduct research without undue influence of sponsor
- failure to locate appropriate research site or subject population (New and Priest, 1968; Deutscher, 1956)
- failure to obtain entry into a setting
- failure to enter a setting to which one has obtained access (Madan, 1967)

Failure To Sustain

- failure to develop desired role relations with subjects (Daniels, 1967)
- failure to win subject compliance with research purposes (Powdermaker, 1966; Bain, 1950; Horowitz, 1965a)
- failure to carry out research techniques (Josephson, 1970; Miller, 1965; Vaughan, 1967; Voss, 1966)
- failure to remain independent of special group interests (Wax, 1971)

Failure To Complete

- failure to produce desired outcomes in applied research (Cumming and Cumming, 1957; Klein, 1971)
- failure to produce results at all (den Hollander, 1967)
- failure to obtain publisher (Lofland, 1974)
- failure to submit results for publication (Madan, 1967)
- failure to avoid censorship of manuscript (Record, 1967)
- failure to achieve client utilization of results (Gouldner, 1965b)
- failure to achieve client approval of findings or interpretations (Lewis, 1961; Horowitz, 1967; Beals, 1969; Barnes, 1963; Vidich and Bensman, 1960)

Projects can also fail on ethical grounds, produce insignificant findings, or in some way dissatisfy the researcher. Given all these opportunities for failure, every project partially succeeds and partially fails, but they are reported less ambiguously and create misleading role models for students.

Practically and theoretically, the disinclination to discuss failures is unfortunate, because it would be useful to know how and why a particular community or group rejected a particular researcher. It would also be useful to know under what conditions a researcher was not able to accomplish his proposed aims and objectives, how he found himself blocked; whether he gave up completely, or whether he found some way to circumvent his difficulties. And finally, it might strengthen the morale of inexperienced fieldworkers to know that many attempts at research turn out badly and some turn into total flops. Perhaps the true professional is characterized not by his own grand success but by his ability to transcend a resounding failure and keep on with his work [Wax, 1971, p. 279].

Jean Briggs's *Never in Anger* (1970) is a case in point. She came to study Eskimo shamans, but when to her dismay she discovered they were "either in hell or in hiding," she turned instead to study the Eskimos' patterning of emotional expression. Similarly, the three research projects of this book are presented in terms of the structured sources of success and failure characteristic of the particular method used.

Since revelations about the experience of researching are scarce, researchers modify their activities to fit the impressions created by most published studies. Others model their work in line with this reinforced image, which is challenged only when deviant accounts are published. Students construct an image of social research unilluminated by discussions of "failures."

The reporting of negative results is not rewarded. Unless a sociologist can show positive relationships between his variables, his research typically remains unpublished. Yet the obvious value of reporting studies that failed—another way of stating that negative cases should be examined—is clear. Sociologists could certainly benefit by learning what causal propositions, what designs, and what strategies failed for others; at the very least the mistakes of the past might not be repeated [Denzin, 1970, p. 33].

The notion of failure is redefined whenever the research process is reconceptualized from a closed to an open process of discovering, in which the process itself is significant. The open process yields new knowledge on three levels: the researcher as a human being, the problem under investigation, and the process of research—in other words, *person, problem, and method.*

The underreporting of sociologists' actual activities and research failures follows from the idealized social science model. Fuller documentation of the realities of researching would demystify the research process and rehumanize the researcher. Factors useful in developing the public's trust and in gaining access to sources of power would be clarified. Publication of research-as-process would also assist the profession in developing guidelines of ethical conduct since procedures would be open to scrutiny.

Kaplan discusses the problem of the mystification of research as the difference between "logic-in-use" and "reconstructed logic." Logic-in-use is the "more or less logical cognitive style used by scientists," whereas reconstructed logic "idealizes the logic of science only in showing us what it would be if it were extracted and refined to utmost purity" (A. Kaplan, 1964, p. 11). Since this distinction is easily forgotten, reconstructed logic becomes the standard for logic-in-use, with the adverse effect of eliminating the special discovery features of logic-in-use. Logic-in-use is dynamic and unsure of the future; it is becoming and creating knowledge. Reconstructions account for past behavior and order the past to inexorably yield the present. Logic-in-use attends to extralogical factors, such as inspiration, intuition, and coincidence.

In a less benign manner, Barber and Fox (1958) differentiate between actual and reported research. Their term "retrospective falsification" refers to the standardizing of research reporting in accordance with norms, guidelines, and formats rather than actual experience (see also Casagrande, 1960). In their opinion, research reports are distorted. Mack (1970) considers the simplification used by social scientists to be misleading as a description of their work. If revelations of logic-in-use are scarce, if analysts claim the standard research report is a falsification, and if those reporters claim they are scientific—then how should students learn method and attempt research?

The cases of this book document this problematic socialization process.

My struggle to resolve the perplexing contradictions within sociological research could have been short-circuited by the availability of documents of research-as-process rather than the customary research-as-product. Reports of research as a social psychological activity would have eliminated retrospective falsification. Reports intended as contributions to the literature of research-as-practice as well as to a substantive area require researchers to communicate their individuality rather than presume an unembodiedness. In expressing this individuality, the researcher reinforces the humanistic potential of sociology. A demystified sociology seeks to recreate rather than justify the research process. A full account includes the subjects', colleagues', friends', and families' perceptions of the research activities. This multidimensional view would reflect sociology's conceptualization of the multidimensionality of "definitions of situations" and would contribute a rich account of logic-in-use or research-as-process.

In this review of the processes involved in becoming a sociologist, I discuss conflicts with regard to sociology's definition, purpose, and methods. Focusing on the research component of the socialization process, I claim that methods reflect personal values. The adoption of a critical position involves a risk because the sociology students are taught is the only sociology for which they will be rewarded. Finally, the idealized scientific version seems rather unsociological since it contains the implicit assumptions of an unembodied investigator.

The experiential, didactic, and descriptive means of learning method present different images of the norms governing sociological research. Since descriptions of real, in contrast with ideal, research are not highly valued, the student is left with partial accounts constructed retroactively to justify findings that conform with the scientific ideal. Those writings that claim to be sociology "as it really is" frequently debunk "establishment sociology." How can one form a reasonably well-integrated professional identity from all of these strains?

Overcoming Alienation

When students encounter discrepancies between ideal and real methods, they have several options: denial of the problem, withdrawal from the discipline, unquestioning conformity, or attempt at innovation. "The general way in which sociologists I knew coped with [the sense of their profession's meaninglessness] was in disputatiousness and, growing in part out of it, the formation of 'schools' and sects that recruited, rewarded, and penalized, scanned for evidence of the true faith and demanded loyalty and forensic fire" (Seeley, 1971, p. 176). Since I wavered between withdrawal and innovation, my tactic was to try and redefine sociology. Where would that sociology begin? What knowledge did I trust? What were my standards?

The sociologist in training encounters conflicts not only between the ideal and real ways in which sociology is practiced but also in the contradictory sets of models for the discipline. The limited accounts of sociologists performing their work and the infrequent discussion of failure produce images of sociological research not always verified in practice. The total effect of this problematic socialization is alienation or dehumanization. Dehumanization is not confined to any particular research method but occurs when sociologists attempt to transform themselves into something other than that which they are—whenever they repress their values, attitudes, and goals for the sake of professionalization. Sociologists are expected to adopt a professional attitude and then transform themselves into more fully human beings when they are "out of role." Cicourel (1964, p. 101), for example, advises that "canons of research demand that the interviewer operate somewhat like a computer with all the appearances of a fellow human being." If the professional role constitutes a major portion of the identity, however, then there is an invitation not only to a dehumanized researching self but to a dehumanized general self. This splitting of the experienced self from the presented self could be labeled schizophrenic.

The sociologists' model of the dehumanized sociologist at work reflects their concept of men and women as fragmented selves. Their methods assume that attitudes are always formed and readily expressible (for attitude polling). They assume that sociologists are not value-laden citizens and that ethical and human considerations are properly suspended at work. Weber is frequently cited for his passionate advocacy of detachment lest professional prestige lead to moral persuasion. As a student in the turbulent 1960s and early 1970s, however, I condemned acts of omission or value neutrality, not only those of commission.

Merton has suggested a compromise between affective neutrality and passionate advocacy with his notion of "detached concern," which is perhaps the forerunner of Moynihan's "benign neglect." Like most compromises, however, it placates rather than resolves the conflict. By contrast, Berger (1963, p. 5) acknowledges the struggle necessary to transform the self:

> The sociologist will normally have many values as a citizen, a private person, a member of a religious group or as an adherent of some other association of people. But within the limits of his activities as a sociologist there is one fundamental value only—that of scientific integrity. Even there, of course, the sociologist, being human, will have to reckon with his convictions, emotions and prejudices. But it is part of his intellectual training that he tries to understand and control these as bias that ought to be eliminated, as far as possible, from his work. It goes without saying that this is not always easy to do, but it is not impossible.

Aside from the suspension of all values other than "scientific integrity," another characteristic of sociologists is the nature of the variables they utilize for explanations. Phillips (1971, p. 57) notices that "sociologists have long gone out of their way to avoid having to utilize such concepts as needs, motives, and drives in their explanations of social behavior, despite the fact that many sociologists frequently employ such concepts in their more casual interpretations and explanations of their own and other people's everyday behavior." The definition of a sufficient explanation or an exploratory variable hinges on whether sociologists are "in role." Their image of people as composites of parts reflects their own self-image. Matson (1966) says we have created an image of mechanical people from the mechanical means we use to study them. When social scientists learn to acquire their special "social scientist self" for doing research, they simultaneously learn to suppress aspects of their humanness that conflict with the scientific value system (Maslow, 1966). Schlesinger (1962, p. 768) confirms that "inside every sociologist there is a humanist struggling to get out." The struggle develops when the student sociologist is confronted with "the empirical mystique that it is the only way to knowledge, and that its only true expression is mathematical" (Schlesinger, 1962, p. 768). This constraint on method and explanation can inspire a liberation attempt when sociologists begin to deal with problems outside the realm of these quantitative methods.

Sociologists behave differently as sociologists than they do as human beings in three respects—with regard to their values, their definition of what they consider to be an adequate explanation, and their conception of people. Zinn (1967, p. 172) sees a split within those who are "embarrassed by their own humanity" and those who try to keep separate "human drives and professional mores." To keep these separate, it is necessary to "avoid direct confrontation with contemporary problems," apologize "for any sign of departure from 'objectivity,'" and spurn any "liaison with social action." Zinn (1967, p. 176) has introduced a fourth difference between the sociologist as professional and as person—the definition of relevant problems. He suggests that we "remove the shame from subjectivity" and overcome the "fear of engagement." Only when the work of sociologists is both therapeutic and academic can practical action test the efficacy of their understanding. This therapeutic purpose begins with sociologists' influence on the people they study. In the suggestion that we develop a sociology of evil, Wolff contributes a final notion to the rehumanization of the sociologist. He believes sociology should be morally directed, oriented to praxis, concerned with the study of "universal human preoccupations," and therapeutic for those who do the research as well as all those who "in any way come in contact with it" (Wolff, 1969, p. 120). The humanization of the subject matter and of the researcher are intimately related.

Sociologists do not have to remain alienated but require courage to defy current norms and reclaim subjectivity and experience, as I advocate. This book is an attempt to realize this alternative definition of a sociological product: a human document depicting the sociologist as a human being working towards a rehumanized sociology. It attempts to be the model for what it is trying to create. Because the model conceives of the world as becoming rather than being, the model is unfinished and expanding. Some features disappear as they prove unworkable or unuseful. Others are confirmed by repeated or additional experience. Features of the model include rejection of past methodological traditions in order to foster creativity, focus on process as the content of research, abandonment of the scientific ideal, and utilization of the self. These features portray sociologists at work in an active, unfragmented way. Such sociological studies begin only when sociologists are aware of themselves in the act of experiencing and then making sense out of reality. Reflection on the experiencing self becomes the indicator, in contrast with questionnaires, experiments, and tests. A human method is used for a human subject matter.

This definition of sociological method allows me to be myself, to use my own mind, and to not rely on disguises, deceptions, or indirections. In this way, sociology becomes not a collection of facts nor even a series of integrated concepts, but rather a fundamental way of studying. The sociology I am interested in using as a source of my identity would have to be adequate for understanding the world beyond the confines of sociological research. It must not split my consciousness but permit me to be whole.

A humanizing sociologist overcomes the self-rejecting, selfless scientific stance and produces not merely an increment in sociological theory but self-knowledge that emerges from catharsis, reflection, and reintegration. Personal knowledge requires emotional involvement, not merely logical and rational analysis. Through self-examination, problems are defined and the motivation to study them is clarified. Self-knowledge discards pseudoproblems and highlights significant issues. In my case, these problems were concerned with the nature of sociology since I was in the process of being socialized into the profession, and I experienced this socialization as problematic. My concerns during this period were many: What is the process of discovery? What kinds of relationships do sociologists have with representatives of the real world, their own families, research subjects, and fellow sociologists? How does one go about sociologizing? Is there a way of getting closer to experience than participant observation? Should science be the model for sociology? What could an alternative model be? What things are worth predicting, controlling, and replicating? How can the sociology of knowledge be used to understand more about sociology itself? In what ways do our very research processes create our image of society? Should sociology be value-free, valueless, or value laden? What could a radical sociology, a humanistic sociology, a liberated sociology, be?

My desire to resolve these questions became my source of energy. To confront such broad questions is to invite a liberating dialectical process of considering major alternatives. When illuminated with one's own experience, the range of explanatory variables is opened to include those with little sociological respectability. Sociologists thereby reintegrate themselves in their work and ground both their work and their selves in the everyday world. Through reflection, the experiencing self discovers integrating resolutions that reduce alienation. Since person and profession mesh in the process of identity formation, the process of liberating the self produces an impact on sociology. "The process of the person becoming a sociologist is intimately linked to the sociologist becoming a person" (Horowitz, 1968, p. 12). My struggle with sociology was part of my struggle to form an identity. My search for both was grounded in a search for data that could not be questioned as meaning anything other than what they claimed. The search for something that could not be doubted led me to my own experiences, the self in its social psychological environment. Those data eventually became the experiencing self, reflecting the social psychological environment. When self-reflective sociologists understand and communicate experiences, they rehumanize readers who can then develop insights into their own experiences. Similarly, Dewey (1954) considered the essential characteristic of experience to be its generation of other experience. In dealing with alienation, the assistance rendered by colleagues is situational and cannot do the work of making the self whole. To deal with alienation, one must recognize the experiencing self and explore personal relevance. The battle with alienation is a protracted struggle characteristic of being human in contemporary society.

Humanizing Society

To overcome alienation, the discipline of sociology must be changed. Such innovations are frequently defined as a new branch of sociology, but sometimes the branch influences the tree itself. In the case of sociology, change is impeded because of the disproportionate funding of empirical research. The debate over what sociology is to become is influenced by factors beyond its own membership. If the transitions made within sociology are primarily responses to scarce resources, then we can expect no change other than intensified retrenchment (Dynes, 1974). The humanities will not provide an alternative home for sociology. Ferris (1965, p. 18) reports on the Commission on the Humanities in which an American Sociological Association group participated and "concluded that there was very little 'working affinity' between sociology and the humanities despite the 'humanistic character' of the research interests of a number of prominent sociologists. . . . [Instead,] the majority of sociologists in the U.S. today show no evidence in their works of either interest in or affinity with the humanities." The prejudice against this link is expressed in such dire warnings as "Humanistic regression would be deplorable" (Gamberg, 1969, p. 115). Science, as perceived by social scientists, contains an antihumanistic folklore: "Only that is scientific that proceeds from an unambiguous and precisely delimited problem, drawn from statistically aseptic data, to a carefully tailored hypothesis.

All else is, by definition, art or philosophy" (Nisbet, 1963, p. 154). This view has diverted sociology from focusing on problems with "intrinsic intellectual importance" to problems in which "quantitative methodologies can work frictionlessly" (Nisbet, 1963, p. 154). Few believe, as does Bierstedt (1960), that sociology shares its impulses and functions with both the humanities and science and can therefore serve as a bridge between the two. The lack of mutual stimulation between the humanities and sociology reflects their different conceptions of humanity. The humanities by and large view people holistically, whereas the social sciences are interested in fragments of behavior or opinions. Sociology has not yet developed a model based on the unique humanness of individuals or groups. Wrong's (1961, p. 190) criticism is still timely:

> Modern sociology, after all, originated as a protest against the partial view of man contained in such doctrines as utilitarianism, çlassical economics, social Darwinism, and vulgar Marxism. All of the great 19th and early 20th century sociologists saw it as one of their major tasks to expose the unreality of such abstractions as economic man, the gain-seeker of the classical economists; political man, the power-seeker of the Machiavellian tradition in political sciences; self-preserving man, the security seeker of Hobbes and Darwin; sexual or libidinal man, the pleasure-seeker of doctrinaire Freudianism; and even religious man, the God-seeker of the theologians. It would be ironic if it should turn out that they have merely contributed to the creation of yet another reified abstraction in socialized man, the status-seeker of our contemporary sociologists.

Sociology's disinterest in conceptualizing human beings as sentient, experiencing, passionate creatures (or "simply human" in H. S. Sullivan's terms) stems in part from methodological rigidity. When concepts are not quantifiable, they are irrelevant. The concepts used to study people eventually replace them through a process of reification. Wrong (1961) urges us to let people back into sociology, but first sociology must be changed to incorporate them. One starting point is the re-humanization of the sociologist. From that starting point, a rehumanized sociology can emerge.

This altered sociology could develop in several directions. The most traditional would be to define new topics for study: "the humanistically inclined sociologist might ask what are the social correlates of trust, interdependency, autonomy, and other individual characteristics in terms of groups, associations, and other social structures from the family to the giant corporation" (Glass, 1970, p. 14). Which values guide people's behavior, and what functions does the sociologist have beyond clarifying those values? Another humanistic stance begins with the study of the researcher's humanness, a concern included in the sociology of sociology (Friedrichs, 1970; Reynolds and Reynolds, 1970). This revision of the sociological focus corrects the tradition of non-self-reflectiveness. Gouldner (1970, pp. 25, 26, 30) believes that the rehumanization of sociology will follow precisely from sociologists' self-examination:

> For if, as the sociologist says, it is his special job to see man-in-society, then shouldn't he also see and talk about *himself* in society? Unfortunately, no more than other men do sociologists tell us what they are really doing in the world, as distinct from what they think they should be doing. . . . The sociologists' task today is not only to see people as they see themselves, nor to see *themselves* as they see other people. What is needed is a new and heightened self-awareness among sociologists, which would lead them to ask the same kinds of questions about themselves as they do about taxicab drivers or doctors, and to answer them in the same ways. . . . We have failed to become aware of ourselves and to take our experience seriously.

This perspective leads to the rehumanization of the sociological enterprise or at least the demythologizing of the ideal sociologist. To achieve either goal requires an understanding at least of the "social structure of sociology, the culture of sociology, the stratification of sociology, and the socialization of sociologists" (Oromaner, 1972, p. 11). The redirection of sociology rather than the creation of just another subspecialty therefore begins with the examination of our socialization. The case study method offers the missing link between the social sciences and the humanities. This intentional linking underlies my use of the case history format in this book. Some will predict unfortunate outcomes arising from the process of reducing alienation. Self-study reduces the grip of previously held assumptions and meaning structures. Anomie may emerge, as Berger (1971) argues, leaving the grim choice between two unattractive options—alienation or anomie.

The humanization of sociology involves a relation with the humanities, a concept of humanity, the study of peculiarly human subject matter, a concern with the values of the groups that are studied, and the centrality of the human researcher. Together these elements support active engagement in social issues relevant to the quality of life. But active engagement is grounded in values other than the value of scholarly integrity. "To have values or not to have values; the question is always with us. When sociologists undertake to study problems that have relevance to the world we live in, they find themselves caught in a crossfire. [But] the question is not whether we should take sides, since we inevitably will, but rather whose side we are on" (Becker, 1967, p. 239). Our humanness is not an obstacle but the foundation of our ability to study and understand others. Our responsibility is to be aware of our own perspective and to share it explicitly.

As a critique of mainstream sociology, humanistic sociology's initial position was formulated by C. Wright Mills' *The Sociological Imagination* (1959). Contemporary critics, following Mills, prefer the label *new sociology* to humanistic sociology (Horowitz, 1965b; Anderson, 1971; Means, 1969). "As sociology moves into the 1970s, the image of the sociologist appears to be undergoing a revolutionary revision. An activist-oriented sociology appears, in this time of general academic discontent, to be gathering support among both sociologists and students. The current movement is commonly labeled 'new sociology' " (Medley and Conyers, 1972, p. 6).

Humanistic sociologists are "those sociologists who feel the need and the responsibility to be actively involved in guiding the processes of history. They wish to relinquish the secluded haven of academic life with its esoteric interests, its professional jargon, its limited (in scope) and limitless (in numbers) research projects, its value-free search for what they consider a valueless truth, and to become involved in the real problems facing the world today. They wish to be free to analyze and question, to criticize and condemn, to construct and propose; free to feel the pulse-beat of their society and to sense its inner mechanism; free to follow the imaginations of their minds and the emotions of their hearts—free to bare themselves before both their academic peers and the mass of ordinary men and unashamedly declare, "This I believe." Forsaking to a certain extent the refined methodological tools that have served American sociologists for over two generations, they look to personal insight to carry them into new climes of intellectual thought beyond the reach of less perceptive men. Abandoning the ever-growing alignment between the natural and social sciences, they have turned back to the days when sociology drew intellectual inspiration from the humanities [Shaskolsky, 1967, p. 26].

The activist sociologist replaces value neutrality with value responsibility because "objectivism seeks to relieve us from all responsibility for the holding of our beliefs" (Polanyi, 1958, p. 323). Humanistic sociologists thereby challenge the norms of society and sociology. This definition of humanistic sociology, in other words, permits and encourages disruption for a larger social good. Such a stance, however, makes the work of future sociologists contingent on the record of their predecessors, particularly the reaction of subjects of sociological research and to the disruption of the researchers. Sociologists are faced with the choice of "protecting" a setting for future research or living up to their definition of sociology. Their decision rests on the differential claim of their values.

The two major thrusts of humanistic sociology are increased action in the real world and increased attention inward.

As it reduces the mystique of the natural science model, humanistic sociology engages in political activism, political analysis, and espousal of "causes," asking "to what useful purposes can social research be put?" The other direction is the push inward. The world cannot be rebuilt until the house (of sociology) has been straightened. I suggest we begin by analyzing what we actually do, who we pretend to be and why, and what the effects of our work on others and on ourselves are. One example is Derek Phillips (1971, p. xi), who writes of his "dissatisfaction with the state of sociology as it is practiced on the contemporary American scene" and offers an alternative. The foundation for a humanistic sociology is built on self-reflection and activism. Only in their combination is there a "basis wherein both the outer and the inner worlds of man, with their conceptual systems and special vocabularies, can be viewed from a human standpoint" (Bruyn, 1966, p. 84).

Beginning with My Own Case

The case history can serve as a bridge between the humanities and sociology, since it provides an alternative to commonsense generalization on the one hand and isolated, distorted empiricism on the other. Langness' (1965) review of the use of life histories in the humanities, history, literature, psychology, and medicine demonstrates its usefulness in understanding the experience of individuals and groups. In sociology the case history was used to understand the development of a sociological type through an "account of experiences, written as an autobiography, as a diary, or presented in the course of a series of interviews. The unique feature of such documents is that they are recorded in the first person, and not translated into the language of the person investigating the case. . . . [The investigator provides] supplementary case material which might serve as a check on the authenticity of the story and afford a basis for a more reliable interpretation of the experiences and situations described in the documents" (Shaw, 1966, p. 2). The subjects join the sociologists in producing, interpreting, and evaluating material. Sutherland's *The Professional Thief* (1956) and Rainwater's *Behind Ghetto Walls* (1970) use case studies to inform the reader without much investigator interference. They "are intended not merely as illustrations or citations of data to support generalizations . . . but . . . allow the reader an opportunity to become acquainted with the complexity and multi-faceted quality of the information from which we draw conclusions, and to confront more directly the continuous nature of an individual experience in the [Pruitt-Igoe] community" (Rainwater, 1970, p. 16).

The informant's case history must still be understood as a production within the context of a sociological investigation. Particular case histories are inevitably grounded in particular contexts. Another term applied to this approach is *oral sociology*, which creates records of people whose lives otherwise do not typically enter archives. Studs Terkel's *Working* (1972) is a model accomplishment within this perspective. Sociology thus "serves the people" by giving them a mouthpiece and by altering the one-sided view of experience afforded by outsiders. For Becker (1966, pp. vi-vii), the case history instrumentalizes George Herbert Mead's social psychology: "To understand why someone behaves as he does you must understand how it looked to him, what he thought he had to contend with, what alternatives he saw open to him; you can only understand the effects of opportunity structures, delinquent subcultures, social norms, and other commonly invoked explanations of behavior by seeing them from the actor's point of view." The life history method seeks interpretations that people impose on their own experiences.

Burgess (1939) referred to this method as "socioanalysis" to emphasize its similarity with psychoanalysis, a view supported by Dollard's (1936, pp. 24-25) description of the method:

> The informant was invited to talk about his life in his own way, beginning where he chose and saying what he chose. It was stressed that the researcher would use the material in no way to the detriment of the informant and that communication of more than ordinary freedom

would be appropriate. I explained that I would not ask questions because I could not know in advance what questions would bring out the important information about the informant; surely that was something which only he could know, and I might spoil his chance to give an account of himself if I intruded with inappropriate questions.

A further modification of the technical analytical method was that I made as few comments as possible and did not press for material from the unconscious level, although unintentionally I sometimes got it. It seemed unethical for me to raise problems that could not be settled in the time at my disposal, which was far short of that required for a thorough analysis. Informants were specifically told that they were not undergoing analysis, although they might incidentally learn some things which psychoanalytic research has made available to us.

The resulting life history yields not only a description of a human life, but a key to the socioemotional culture of the community.

Interest continued for about a decade and then the case history fell into disuse because of the "romantic sentimentality" danger (Langness, 1965, p. 19) and the time-consuming and difficult nature of gathering the data. In addition, there were difficulties differentiating case history analysis from social casework, developing methods of comparative case analysis, and combining case histories with statistics to permit a higher level of generalization (Znaniecki, 1934).

The repudiation of the life history as a method fits the general repudiation of experience in the social sciences (Toby, 1955). The case history, conversely, compels the researcher to utilize and analyze experience. There are several ways in which this can be done: transform the sociologist from *investigator* to a *collector* of personal materials, create in-depth interview situations and compose a case history, join people in their activities and write the history of the experience, and join others in order to examine the impact on the self, thereby utilizing the researcher's experience as the basis of the study (for example, Reynolds and Farberow, 1976). In the three case studies of this book, I attempt to do the latter, that is, analyze my personal experience of three research projects.

The case history possesses a dynamic dimension since it spans across time periods. Processes unfold and are explained or at least described. Readers reach conclusions with the researcher as they accompany each other through the processes. This book is such a case history with the unifying theme of the socialization of a sociology student, particularly with regard to identifying with the profession and adopting a research method. The presentation of this case illustrates the conclusions of my search for method, which include the centrality of the researcher in the research enterprise, the necessity of developing sociology on the foundation of experience, and the suitability of experiential analysis for revealing the impact of institutions and social structures on individuals. This comparative analysis of my research experiences covers my major socialization phases. The report combines the perspectives of an insider and outsider because the actor is the analyst; the sociologist analyzes her own experiences. Of course, it is merely one of many possible accounts for any series of events and is designed for a specific purpose. This particular account only reflects not the actual educational process but is influenced greatly by you, the reader, and my anticipation of your response.

This case history serves as a vehicle for understanding my self, my experiences with method, and my conclusions about appropriate methodology. In addition, it is a historical document that reveals how some people currently study sociology and become sociologists. In addition to Wax (1971) and Powdermaker (1966), two other accounts attempted to achieve these goals. The first example is Beatrice Webb's discovery of a method that resolved her intellectual and identity problems.

It was in the summer of 1883 that I took the first step as a social investigator. . . . What had been borne into me during my book studies was my utter ignorance of the manual-working class, that is, of four-fifths of my fellow-countrymen. During the preceding London season I had joined the Charity Organization Committee and acted as one of its visitors in the slums of Soho; but it was clear to me that these cases of extreme destitution, often distorted by drink and vice, could (not be) regarded as a fair sample of the wage-earning class. . . . How was I to get an opportunity of watching, day by day, in their homes and in their workshops, a sufficient number of normal manual-working families to enable me to visualize the class as a whole; to understand what was meant by chronic poverty and insecurity of livelihood; to ascertain whether such conditions actually existed in any but a small fraction of the great body of the people? [Webb, 1938, pp. 175-176].

Beatrice Webb concluded that she must go and see for herself. She became a rent collector and settled in a poor section of London. She called herself a social scientist because she intended to learn by first-hand experience and to avoid received notions.

Closer to my time is Derek Phillips (1971), who introduces his investigation of contemporary sociological methods with an autobiographical statement explaining his traumatic abandonment of the dominant paradigm. Bruyn, too, claims his contribution to sociological methodology did "not build from a preconceived plan, but builds instead from the ruins of expectations I shared with others to study the human community solely from the traditional standards of science" (1966, p. xi). Phillips began to doubt sociology's significance, but his fellow sociologists considered this very question insignificant. He questioned the morality of deferring sociology graduate students' military service by virtue of their national value. He rejected radical sociologists' accusation that sociology is harmful, contending instead that sociology is impotent. He discovered that few sociologists actually observed behavior in their area of expertise and that their data did not correspond to actual behavior. After uncovering technical errors in his own work, he realized that sociologists are concerned more with refining data analysis than with improving data collection. In his view, the key to a meaningful sociology lies in recognizing data collection itself as a social act in which the situation is being defined continuously by all the participants. Phillips (1971, p. xv) discovered a method: "By understanding what happens when the sociologist collects his data, we can better accomplish our goal of learning about everyday human behavior."

From Phillips's brief case history, the following stages of socialization and identity formation are evident:

1. mastering sociology as it is presented; learning its values, beliefs, and heroes
2. internalizing and utilizing prescribed procedures; acting on these beliefs
3. becoming disillusioned; feeling alienated with regard to meaningfulness and sense of community; increased isolation leading to increased alienation
4. developing antipathy to sociological identity; attributing immorality and bankruptcy to the discipline
5. feeling curious about this perspective; wanting to understand and create meaning and satisfaction
6. communicating with colleagues; attempting to revise sociology in accordance with revision of self

These stages coincide with those of my own socialization except that I was compelled to repeat stages 3 through 5 before reaching 6. My journey consisted of learning, using, becoming dissatisfied, rejecting, and then creating a method of my own. Each of the following chapters is a link in this chain of learning, rejecting, and creating. I was able to break the cycle of expectation, alienation, and rejection by examining the process itself and using, rather than denying, my own experiences.

Through this process, I learned that rejection is an instrumental component of development and creativity. The child rejects the parents to differentiate an identity. Rejection is not nihilism: The past need not be destroyed, nor does the self have to be repudiated. Proceeding on one's own, rather than on the shoulders of giants (or midgets), requires courage. The very act of rejecting that which others take for granted or hold sacred releases creativity at the social cost of assuming the status of deviant. To reject social conventions creates the possibility of social invention. So, too, with ways of knowing: with the courage to reject comes the potential for developing new forms. A remarkable feature of the accounts of Phillips and several others was their willingness to question and abandon their past. No matter how deep one's alienation, it requires courage to let go of the structure and security of past arrangements. Nevertheless, unquestionable creativity has arisen out of this process of "letting go," such as the therapeutic advances of Freud, who first realized that his patients improved whether he touched them or not and whether he hypnotized them or not (Jones, 1963). His genius was partially the result of his willingness to let go of cherished ideas. Letting go is liberating; it implies demystification of former received notions, such as the necessity of sociology's modeling itself on science. Letting go liberates the student to be imaginative and individualistic. By contrast, discovering can be enslaving. Like a conversion experience, once you find it, it grabs hold of you and will not let go. Your way of perceiving the world is shaped, and you experience an inner response that binds you to this perspective.

Because of previous disillusionment, I am reluctant to claim longevity for the method I propose in this book. I would rather advocate the process than the end point. The certainty I sought eludes me; I am left with a close approximation. My present conclusions are relative to my own methodological concerns and not necessarily those of the reader. Readers must examine their own experiences as researchers and students and compare those with the case histories in this book. The conclusion of a private journey creates a reluctance to generalize too broadly, as Descartes (1960, pp. 38, 47) noted:

> Thus, my present design is not to teach the method which each one is bound to employ for the proper conduct of his reason, but only to show how I have conducted mine. . . . I offer what I have written simply as a record, or, if you prefer the term, a tale in which, with a few examples that may be followed, there will be many,

perhaps, that it will be right to avoid. I hope that it will be useful to some, without being harmful to any, and that all will be grateful to me for my frankness. I should be glad, however, in this discourse, to describe for the benefit of others the paths I have followed, to paint a picture as it were, of my life, of which each one may judge as he pleases; and I should be happy to learn what public opinion has to say of me, and so discover a fresh mode of instruction for myself, which I shall add to those I am already accustomed to employ. If, since what I have done has pleased me well enough, I display it as a model, that does not mean that I advise anyone to follow it.

Each reader's experience will differ based on unique personal characteristics. From these varying perspectives emerge distinctive styles that modify the norm of scientific uniformity.

The model of my presentation is neither verification nor validation, but process analysis. I describe the background prehistory of my formulations and their contexts. I can no longer attribute meaning to sociological reports unless they contain such self-critical discussions of the knowledge acquisition process. This book reports on this process of searching for a sociological method and identity. If the process itself is instructive, then it is suitable to express its open-endedness by posing questions and being reluctant with answers. The questions, dilemmas, and continuing paradoxes provide the energy for further movement in the journey of identity and method refinement. Dilemmas are the potential source of self-liberation among perplexed students. Too many definitions and answers are, in Sartre's (1967, p. xxxiii) view, distasteful and a hindrance to the student's growth: "It is the nature of an intellectual quest to be undefined. To name it and to define it is to wrap it up and tie the knot. What is left? A finished, already outdated mode of culture, something like a brand of soap—in other words, an idea." So, too, does the Socratic method of education rely on questions, paradoxes, and student self-development.

I have applied my discovery of the "experiential method," which developed at the end of my search, to the very journey that produced it in order to account for both the method and its discovery. This, then, is an experiential analysis of three different research experiences—survey empiricism, participant observation, and experiential analysis. In those research programs described, I used particular methods but also observed my experiences using those methods. I searched for their essential features to account for my experience and identity formation. Experiential analysis released me from the compelling immediacy of these concerns and helped me resolve retroactively the personal conflicts I experienced in these projects. Whyte (1969b, pp. 35-37) describes a similar process:

> Since 1955, I have no longer been in a position to spend substantial time myself in field work, but I have sought to maintain the excitement of personal involvement by regarding myself as a participant observer in administrative activities. . . . My participant-observer-as-research-administrator role grew out of an attempt to resolve the problems of role conflict in research administration: personal involvement in research versus project administration. . . . To the extent that I could treat myself as a participant-observer in the process of developing a new form of (social research) organization, I would be gathering data for analysis and report-writing in the process of administration. . . . I am finding this experience not only productive in data but in the stimulus it provides toward building new and better theories of organizational behavior and inter-organizational relations.

To resolve my questions of sociology's meaning, I had to examine my experiences themselves. What was I actually doing; what were its satisfying and dissatisfying features? After examining experience itself, I could connect private and social realities.

Experiential analysis of the search for method and of the socialization process of the sociologist required a redefinition of myself as a field site in which discovery would emerge without intervening instruments. Removing the crutches of scientific methods, I relied on my own powers of observation, understanding, imagination, creativity, and organization. My data are my experiencing self; my comparative analysis stems from my experiencing self in different situations.

The personal discovery of what appeared to be the bankruptcy of sociological survey research was disillusioning, confusing, and enraging. What is rejected, however, must be replaced. The need for substitutes brought me to a new method to be learned, accepted, and perhaps rejected. In retrospect, the process seems logical and inevitable (from survey empiricism to participant observation to experiential analysis), but at the time no resolution was evident. In my personal search for method, I experienced the pendular swing between polarities in the history of methodology. These apparently parallel processes in the history of method and in my socialization experience are explored in the three research project case histories that follow.

CHAPTER 2

The Ritual of
Survey Empiricism

Initiation

I was an undergraduate woman at Barnard College just before
the student revolt of 1968 across the street at Columbia. I lived
in a delicate balance between wanting to explore and needing to
succeed. This tension was expressed in the conflict between
studying a wide range of academic disciplines and selecting only
those courses in which I expected to excel. On a deeper level
the tension represented the competing pulls of dependency and
autonomy, of security and competence—an issue that women
characteristically resolve later than men. Continuous evaluation
created an atmosphere of vulnerability, which Jules Henry
(1966) identifies as a major characteristic of our educational
system. For me education was compelling and inviting but also
fraught with the danger of failure. Exceptionally self-confident
students transcended this atmosphere. They released themselves
from the grip of grades and chose to follow their intellectual

curiosity. Some found ways to manipulate the educational system while reaping its benefits. I fell in the latter category and survived the college years by pitting my strengths against the system's design or matching my wits with the college's demands. A useful asset was my ability to become interested in nearly anything; the college's weak point was its definition of success as superior graded performance in a major area. To become less vulnerable, I had merely to select one area and perform well. Of course, the price paid was premature specialization, which could develop into incompetence in all but one field.

These conservative forces in favor of specialization were compounded by pressure from administration, faculty, and fellow students to form an academic identity or major as soon as possible in order to begin professionalization. The division of students by major enabled the college to function bureaucratically in terms of categories rather than individuals. Once a category had been applied to originally unformed, undifferentiated students, the various academic departments made claims on them and fashioned them in their own image.

Choosing a major field of study is a significant decision made by young people in our society today. The domino theory of future career decisions applies. Each year brings increasing inbeddedness and investment in the choice; a career change in later years is traumatic, if attempted at all. As with most important life decisions, this choice of a major is made with little knowledge of the consequences.

One well-taught course in sociology in which I succeeded according to the established criteria and which interested me during the crucial period of career path selection became the foundation of a new identity as sociologist. As is true with women students, however, a real commitment to the discipline was to develop only gradually (Tidball, 1976). As soon as the fateful choice was made, I began to examine my role models— Mirra Komarovsky, Renee Fox, Philip Zimbardo, Alan Blum, Roberta Simmons, Gladys Meyer, and Amitai Etzioni among others. These were the people who represented the "future me." They were bright and enthusiastic, and they conveyed an attractive image of the social scientist. Their enthusiasm communicated a basic belief that sociology and social psychology are viable fields of study into which I could pour my life energies. The student peer culture strongly steered me away from models considered unattractive, thus these individuals rarely had the chance to prove their reputations wrong. Students used the same identification category—the major—as did the administration, but peers asked for a justification of my identity and a defense of my selection of courses and plans.

All of my sociology courses "sold" sociology to us students because the teachers desired a confirmation of their identity choices, and the department won favors from the administration in relation to the number of students it attracted. Once a student completed the introductory course and agreed to continue in the discipline, it was assumed that he or she had no ulterior motives.

The next task for the department was to convince students that sociology was a social *science* resting on scientific credentials for its value, prestige, and validity. That basic foundation firmly in place, the rest of my college education in sociology was devoted to theories about numerous aspects of our society. In these relatively abstract courses, we read the masters of classic and contemporary sociological thought. As a newcomer, I was unable to know what was being omitted; my sociology universe was encompassed by my selected courses. Each element of this incremental education redefined the boundaries of the field for me, just as each new experience of children redefines their world. I was taught to grasp and criticize the works of other sociologists without being shown how to be a sociologist myself.

The introductory courses rigorously presented scientific method so we could evaluate published research. These criteria were presented as basic or ultimate, the only ones to be applied. Although the scientific model itself was never criticized, we were taught that sociologists have a variety of methods at their disposal. In the methodology course, the particular assignments defined the scope of my methodological awareness and helped to form my basic methodological positions and concerns. Particularly significant was the required analysis of Elinore Smith Bowen's *Return to Laughter* (1964), a fictionalized account of Laura Bohanan's struggles with fieldwork, especially her conflict between emotional involvement and scientific detachment. My indoctrination in the value of scientific detachment and my utter lack of experience as a researcher in a field setting led me to criticize this anthropologist harshly. I condemned Bohanan for not thinking through her methodological problems, not defining her status carefully, and succumbing to errors and agony. Mirroring my educational environment, I was more concerned with evaluating what Bohanan had done than I was in understanding her experience. I attributed her imperfect performance to the personal failure of inadequate preparation.

Because I had already adopted the notion that social scientists could achieve nearly perfect control of their activities with participant observation or other methods, I was unaware of the differences between experiential and abstract learning. The only impediment to the pure application of method was, I believed, personal inadequacies or unpredictable and overwhelming external constraints. My understanding of methodology was coated from the start with a veneer of moralism. When a social scientist such as Bohanan explained the shortcomings and actual processes of her research, I assumed it was a confession of wrongdoing, of wandering from the path of methodological righteousness.

A course paper makes it clear that my indoctrination in the virtue of the scientific model shaped my passionate critique of Bohanan: "She betrayed her status as an anthropologist; she was not an impartial observer but reacted with personal likes and dislikes to the people with whom she dealt. This inhibited her fact-finding. Forgetting her job as an anthropologist and befriending the community by befriending individuals within it biased her data because it forced her to take sides in community affairs. Rather than merely recording their behavior, she judged it" (Rothschild [maiden name], 1965a, p. 7). With an indignant tone, I expressed my disdain for Bohanan's slovenliness. Her "betrayal of her status as an anthropologist" was heresy; "befriending," her sin; "bias," the price she paid; and "fact-finding," her salvation. This undergraduate paper culminated in the following sentence, which won the professor's praise: "The researcher represents science, not himself as an individual" (Rothschild, 1965a, p. 8). The force behind this condemnation stemmed from bewilderment with my teachers, who had inculcated in me a set of beliefs and then presented me with a perplexing deviant model. Because I was new to these methodological debates, I did not yet pose the questions that would have been most helpful: What is the place of the scientific model in the study of behavior? What possible alternative models can be employed to gain knowledge?

In my first attempt to elucidate these methodological concerns, I was reinforced for statements such as "Impartiality is essential for professional equanimity, but indifference is inhuman and immoral. Although Bohanan wrote that 'one learns by seeing with the eyes, not hearing with the ears,' I submit that one learns by seeing with the mind, not with the heart or immature personality" (Rothschild, 1965a, p. 10). The mastery of proper methodological techniques and their strict procedural performance had personal meaning as a way of controlling immaturity, sensitivity, and impulses. The mind was safe and guaranteed results, whereas the emotions were dangerous and could abort my work. My criticism of Bohanan was as much a reflection of my disappointment in her as it was an indication of my psychosocial needs. Her "failure" reinforced my adherence to the scientific model, which formed the basis of my critique.

Anthropological participant observation as evidenced by Bohanan was certainly not the social science method of choice, but it raised the question of whether research could ever be free of "contamination" by social processes. To find the answer, I longed to know what scientists actually do, and I wrote a paper expressing my longing for a substitution for the Bohanan model. I complained as follows:

> The norm of humility in the scientific community forbids the glorification of one's own work. Unfortunately this norm has become generalized to such a degree that a scientist hesitates to discuss his personal experiences in

research. Very little has been written therefore about the psycho- and socio-dynamics of research. Findings are reported in scientific journals and follow a highly structured form with an emphasis on logic as opposed to the leisurely autobiographical style of the last century. Contemporary reports are presented with this outline: hypotheses, methods, findings, interpretation, implications, and discussion. Is this a false model—has retrospective falsification taken place (Barber and Fox, 1958)? According to Barber and Fox this neat, systematic unfolding simply does not occur. These reports are dysfunctional in creating an incorrect stereotype of the research process. We are left with almost no notion as to how the scientist worked, what his thought patterns were, and which ideas he discarded. By selecting only those components of the actual research process that serve their primary purpose, scientific papers leave out a great deal.

Barber and Fox called on their colleagues to explicate the process of scientific discovery. As my teacher, Fox explicated the irrational, idiosyncratic, and environmental factors that invade the scientific project. Under her guidance, I began to soften my views, as evidenced in a term paper: "The social scientist who recognizes that personal factors affect his choice of a topic will be better able to control their covert entry into his methods than will one who is unwilling to acknowledge this fact" (Rothschild, 1965b, p. 4).

From these deliberations on social scientists' approximation of scientific method in their actual work, my image of "the researcher," my future identity, gradually developed. The budding image was of a curious, practical, and orderly individual always attuned to the potential conflict of scientific procedures and everyday social interaction but loyal to science when put to the test. Researchers chose to study particular problems because of intense personal dedication, I believed, or because their reading of the literature in their field of specialization led them to formulate hypotheses for the cumulative production of knowledge. They immersed themselves in the subject by studying existing literature, referring casually to commonsense notions and personal experiences, and exploring the problem with other colleagues and experts through interviews, observation, and discussion. Research was propelled by difficulties researchers had to resolve. They foresaw the future problems to be investigated and selected methods in accordance with the research demands. Frequently they had to devise ingenious new methods to deal with the particular research problem and to provide data that could substantiate or invalidate the hypotheses. Researchers were familiar with the whole range of available methodological tools.

They were flexible and willing to change their methods and the very formulation of their problems on the basis of data pouring in from the pilot studies. Pilot studies were so essential that it could be taken for granted that they would be utilized. Similarly, my model researchers developed cooperative, constructive relationships with colleagues and sponsors based on open communication. Researchers, I believed, had time to contemplate their work and develop their creativity. After patiently observing their subject matter, an insight or conceptual scheme emerged that organized the whole into manageable parts. Although detached from their subjects, researchers were always intimate with their work. This intimacy and involvement provided opportunities for chance occurrences to develop into fresh insights. The intense interest, clear definition of the problem, and massive associated knowledge coalesced in marvelous creativity.

In retrospect, two problems were paramount for me. First, I had no experience as a researcher or observer of research, so my notions were limited to a few published project descriptions or my idealization of the research process. Second, I was confused about the difference between what research was and what research ought to be. The only limit on my idealized image was the social context of research. I understood that sponsored research led to conflicts between being an employee and being an impartial researcher. I expected researchers to defend sponsors out of gratitude or fear, or to criticize the sponsor to demonstrate impartiality. This relationship between the sponsor and the investigator was a test of the researcher's integrity. Since social research was a socially imbedded, rather than a context-free, activity, then moral and ethical considerations applied as they did everywhere. When conflict arose, however, researchers had to choose to be loyal to truth rather than to friends, economic gain, or political pressure. Strict adherence to scientific method protected researchers against a sponsoring agency's wrath resulting from unflattering findings. The basic tenets of research morality—confidentiality and honesty—assured that data were not divulged, distorted, or plagiarized.

In the more advanced seminars, invited guests discussed their actual research experiences and students were encouraged to join an ongoing research project. Such participation would teach us the necessary skills and help us identify with and make a professional commitment to social research. Following through on this suggestion, I successfully applied for a position as research assistant to a former instructor who had recently accepted responsibility for one component of a larger study granted to the Bureau of Applied Social Research and Columbia University Teachers College. Fortunately, the project's time span from beginning to completion was exactly as long as I would be able to work, September 1966 through June 1967. The small size of the staff—two codirectors, myself, and additional personnel for special assignments—would allow me to perform a wide range of activities. I was proud to be associated with the prestigious research organization, and my expectations were high for a rewarding, positive experience. The sociological theory I had studied extensively and my professors' encouragement gave me the confidence needed to undertake this work. The pay was adequate, the location perfect, the hours satisfactory. Everything was set for a fine meshing of my needs with this opportunity. Grateful for this chance to enter the inner sanctum of sociological research, I approached the project with trust and high hopes.

If this experience is generalizable, then research assistants become involved with projects that happen to be available. These low-level researchers mold their interests to fit the project they join. As I continued in the project, I discovered that what is true for the research assistant can hold as well for the project

directors. Their involvement, too, blended training, chance, and
flexibility. But I began with the belief that I alone was acci-
dentally connected to the project. I had not yet grasped the
notion of a method so universal and a researcher so replaceable
that the identity of the investigator in a particular project was
insignificant. Within this framework, however, research institutes can "farm out" projects that will then be subjected to a
predictable series of operations, regardless of the project personnel.

    From the day I joined the project, I experienced the dis-
crepancies between the ideal and real versions of research. The
case study that comprises this chapter is an account of my disillusionment and my attempt to convert this personal experience into a generalizable methodological critique. This disillusionment was abetted by the retrospectively falsified reports
referred to previously: "All these accounts of investigations that
have been put neatly into shape afterwards tend to give research
students unreasonable expectations so that they quite unneces-
sarily develop a bad conscience and cease to believe in themselves when they are forced to adopt doubtful maneuvers which
their esteemed predecessors—though they kept it to themselves
—made before them" (Gouldner, 1969, p. 15). At first the discrepancy disheartened me and left me cynical and suspicious of
all activity labeled "social research." Gradually I began to
understand social research as an ideal type, in a Weberian sense,
with inevitable imperfections. "However successful may be a
particular scientific achievement, it always and inevitably falls
short of the scientist's highest standards of perfection, and it is
essential to know those standards as the goal toward which he is
striving" (Znaniecki, 1934, p. vii). The certainty of partial failure cloaks research with a tragic dimension (Gouldner, 1969).
Despair follows from the inadequacy of observation, description, explanation, and understanding. Since reality is elusive,
inexhaustible, and forever changing, its understanding is condemned to a sorry approximation. The difference in the phenomenological status of experience and language renders reality
ultimately indescribable. Our claims are blatant dishonesties and
failed generalizations. Our products are merely impressions of

knowledge. There are several possible responses to this despair: abandonment of the activity altogether, attempts to join the real with the ideal, or setting a new standard that reflects the real. The response reflects the student's existential and methodological positions.

My work on the project began in an informationless, meaningless vacuum. I learned only that the U.S. Congress had granted Teachers College $250,000 to assess the quality of Washington, D.C.'s public education and to recommend school policy changes. Congressional sponsorship and the request of policy recommendations gave me an impression that our research would be used. Spending taxpayers' money imbued me with a sense of added responsibility. In addition, I assumed naively that the decision to fund the project stemmed from congressional concern for the quality of public education in Congress' immediate environs. The Bureau of Applied Social Research's piece was a survey of the teachers, while other Columbia University research facilities were to study other components. Apparently, the bureau's administrators offered this project to one of its staff researchers who was unoccupied at the time. Thus began the process of accommodation to the predefined social conditions rather than adherence to maximally effective research conditions for this project.

This introduction to the project produced two principles for my subsequent work. First was the importance of familiarization with an activity's history in order to create a dynamic framework. Our little project was part of a chain of events, none of whose links I understood. I learned the significance of an event's background and the drawback of a time-free perspective. Second, research assistants perceive research projects as inadequately planned if they have not participated in the planning. When assistants are unaware of the project's rationale, then its tasks appear disjointed and disorganized. Without full knowledge of the project's origins, research assistants are unimpressed by the project's coherence or design.

As I began work on the project, I was struck by its enormous cost and by the lack of fit between the project director and the research problem. (I did not recognize the similar lack

of fit between the research assistant and the research problem.)
I was overwhelmed that Congress was willing to spend so much
money on this study. Never before had I been involved in an
activity with such a large budget. The largesse contrasted vividly
with my shoestring student budget. Since I had not known that
research is so expensive, this discrepancy made me suspicious
and angry. Why was this large a sum being spent on the project?
Would Congress, the taxpayer, or the Washington, D.C., school
system users get their money's worth? Who was actually bene-
fiting from this grant? Why was research so expensive? Was this
exorbitance common or was someone milking the government?
Would it have been more beneficial to give the money to the
school system than to buy the research? As a mere research
assistant, however, I did not feel it was my place to question a
project director about these things, so I mulled over these
doubts privately.

     By torturing myself through these questions, I began to
glimpse the fiscal and political implications of social research
and to recognize the relationship between the government, researchers, and the underclasses (the help recipients). Sociologists and other middle-class professionals and academicians
benefit from other groups' problems or poverty while professing
liberal views. They enjoy the spoils of a society rich in both social problems and resources. Their wages are linked to another
group's failure, which makes sociologists doubly parasitic: They
live off the rich and the poor, the government and the dispos-
sessed. I did not apply this harsh criticism to myself, however,
since I was earning a mere minimum wage. I identified more
with the teachers and pupils who I imagined wrongly to be poor
than with the parasitic professionals.

     My critique should be tempered now with qualifications,
since at the time my perspective was rather limited on the particular project that I assisted, let alone on the full project. But
in my naivete I assumed the best: that the director of the overall study cared about his work and was performing in a meticulous, brilliant fashion; that other team members like myself
were task oriented; and that interpersonal relations were divorced from the research activities. Now I recognize, however,

that we affected our research: Our assumptions were expressed in our questions; our personalities were at play in our decisions; our prejudices, ignorance, and expectations were everywhere.

Who composed the team? The principal codirector, a female, and the associate codirector, a male, were distinctive personalities. The former was a glamorous woman, preoccupied with an extensive social life in New York and characterized by a work style consisting of fluctuating productive and dry periods. Her counterpart was more anxious about his productivity and achievements, was heavily involved in other research problems, and had a sense of humor and a quieter life-style.

Who was I at that time? A twenty-year-old woman at work on her first research project, curious about what researchers really do, eager to learn, reluctant to criticize, and concerned with numerous personal issues that seemed far more significant than the research job (such as deciding whether to marry my future husband, learning how to separate from my family, and coping with the demands of college). My attitude was not suspicious but helpful. I was inquisitive, cooperative, polite, and modest. I was not a spy looking for contradictions and inadequacies, rather the contradictions jumped out at me and provoked me to inquire further. I did not scrutinize the project directors' activities. There was no subculture of stories, complaints, and gossip about "boss" behavior, because there was only one research assistant and two bosses. Rather my observations were based on our working together, side by side, day by day, sharing, overhearing, participating in discussions, attending occasional meetings, and talking about joint work. As time passed, however, the processes of the project rather than my tasks alone began to preoccupy me. Observation became my means of coping with alienation. I focused my attention on the research project itself since we were not observing subjects in the field. I was a student rudely awakened from a dream of the ideal to the reality of professional banality. For the record, the following acknowledgment appeared in the manuscript: "Shulamit Rothschild's enthusiasm and efficiency were those of a model Research Assistant."

The role for which I was hired was ambiguous. My basic

qualifications were a background in sociology, good typing skills, and a satisfactory but somewhat remote relationship with one of the codirectors. I expected that as a research assistant I would be guided, taught, and placed in the role of apprentice. I strove to be accepted as a colleague or fellow sociologist. The small size of the research team increased my expectations of intimacy, partnership, and personal investment. Although I assumed my functions would be similar to those of a student or a researcher, they actually approximated those of a clerk. The directors perceived me as a jane-of-all-trades, including secretary, coder, errand girl, confidante, and fellow researcher. Whereas I thought there should be a precise role definition for research assistant, the directors defined the position generally, loosely, and ambiguously. The variety of tasks that I performed were a product of our implicit role negotiation. I accommodated the request for secretarial tasks such as arranging flight reservations and other personal matters; they accommodated my wish to write bits and pieces of the final research report. Within these extremes fell the bulk of my work.

Shortly after we began I asked for background information to determine precisely what we were trying to discover or describe. I met with a surprised response—Why should a research assistant be interested in the background of a research project? Whereas in my classes I was being taught that sound research is carefully planned and guided by clearly formulated hypotheses, in the actual project these principles were suspended to accommodate practical considerations. This discrepancy did not necessarily reflect on the personal shortcomings of the project directors but could be explained by the unrealistic time schedule (Andrew, 1967).

Others have noted that failure to read the literature is common. Andrew lists fourteen different kinds of problems that characterized four research projects analogous to this case, among which are the "limited use of available knowledge from appropriate areas; the tendency, under pressure of beginning project, to fail to read the literature, leading to needless errors; the development of new rather than tried instruments; and no conceptual clarification of project" (1967, p. 86). The clash between the standards presented in class and those operationalized at work in the research institute was vivid as I moved back and forth between them.

Ritualism

"Why did we select our particular method?" I asked the director. It appeared that since the technology of abstracted empiricism was available, it could be applied to any and all problems, from the trivia of advertising research to the most crucial issues facing humanity. Our method was taken for granted rather than selected for its appropriateness: a large-scale survey of self-administered questionnaires whose responses would be converted into variables that could be correlated and adapted to multivariate analyses. Because the method was assumed, we appeared to be enacting a ritual that began with a knock on the doors of the bureau and the deposit of a "problem" on the altar. A team was then formed to pick up the "problem" and "do research on it," performing mysterious operations, juggling tests of significance, and eventually converting the "problem" into a little book that "deals with it," scientifically, objectively, certainly. The method was sacred; the particular "problem" incidental, peripheral. Frequently I wondered if the particular problem at hand—the attitudes of Washington, D.C., public schoolteachers—imposed any constraints on our work, or if instead the method was completely unaffected by the problem. We avoided the freedom of studying and learning about our subject matter by becoming willing slaves to the rigorous method of survey research.

The survey has been the standard tool of sociologists for decades. In fact, it has become so standard that many sociologists have little idea of how to study behavior other than by accumulating paper and pencils and heading for a representative sample of the target population they wish to investigate. They are rewarded for their efforts by hours and hours of computer storage and statistical manipulation of their pencil marks. . . . Questionnaires ask a person to report on himself, to respond to

unreal hypothetical situations, and the results are taken
as indicative of some future set of behaviors [Tarter,
1973, p. 157].

If in fact the choice of research method was discussed by our
project directors, I never observed such a discussion.

Nor did we delay the development of the research design
until the study problem was clarified. We presupposed the suitability of the large-scale survey ritual for the project. Such fitting of the problem to the method rather than the reverse has
begun to disturb some sociologists.

All I am urging is that the sociologist use a method
that is appropriate to his particular area of investigation. I
am questioning the value of highly complex measuring
devices that become ends in themselves rather than inter-
mediary tools used to increase the amount of sociological
understanding. It is inexcusable to force the research
problem in an a priori scheme of technical paraphernalia
rather than *observing it in the context of the empirical
world being investigated* [Filstead, 1970, p. vii; emphasis
added].

Whereas I believed that research should develop out of a clearly
defined problem even if only for the purpose of exploration, we
began not with a problem but with a contract and a deadline.
As contrasted with my ideal image of isolated, compulsive
scholars consumed by the quest for knowledge and working
arduously to solve gnawing problems, I was faced with real researchers more concerned with meeting deadlines and producing
a respectable document than with discovering anything. Our
purpose was to finish rather than to discover. I began to realize
that the success of the project rested not on discoveries but
rather on prompt completion. The behavior of the codirectors
abetted my growing suspicion that professional sociologists considered research something that was *done to* an issue or a target
population, rather than an investigative undertaking into which
one threw oneself existentially.

For me the project became an opportunity to learn about

research, researchers, and substantive issues; for the directors the project was a piece of routinized work. Their routine activity was my initiation into a new world; their run-of-the-mill research project was my formative experience. I was frankly dismayed at the project directors' lack of personal involvement in the study problem. This detachment not only from subjects but also from the research itself affected me like a career trauma. This major disillusionment of unfulfilled expectations was the anticlimax of education. The conflict between the ideology of research and the practices in which we engaged became a conflict within myself. Should I challenge the directors; should I "report" them (and to whom); should I shed my overly sensitive research morality and moralizing; should I just live out the conflict and observe the process?

I decided on the path of alienation. Although I would continue to act as if I believed in what we were doing, I would treat the project as a game rather than as science. My observational stance would provide me with the needed distance but not allow anyone to recognize my detachment. My coping mechanism of inner detachment was ironically similar to the initial problem, that is, the detachment of the project directors. Did their detachment reflect a response to conflicts they were experiencing? Were these conflicts induced by the social organization of applied social research? I also quickly lowered my standards and unconsciously began to express my disillusionment and detachment by performing less than optimal work. Although my performance was adequate, my energy was not invested in this work. Despite my intentions, I modeled myself after the directors and became the alienated research assistant. Alienated labor begets alienated labor.

Another source of disillusionment was the process by which the partnership of the two project directors was formed. The match was arbitrary and stemmed from availability rather than suitability. Although the two individuals were interpersonally compatible, there was no effort to match skills or to balance perspectives. As the project proceeded, however, the expectable breakdown of our triad into ever-changing dyadic alliances did occur. Since one of the codirectors was simultaneously engaged in another project, his limited time resulted in abbreviated relationships between him and the remaining two of us. Research, it seemed, could be done on an absentee basis. Detachment was mirrored repeatedly: The respondents had absentee researchers, and the project had an absentee codirector. Research was beginning to look like a business rather than an intellectual pursuit. As any marketable commodity, the research document was planned for production at the end of the assembly line of our divided labor.

Because conflict is painful, we generally strive to reduce it. This striving can be a creative force transforming the disintegration of the individual or social system into reintegration. My conflicts propelled me to reflect on methodology and the sociology of sociology. The discrepancy between the actual and the expected forced me to articulate a model of research procedures. I suggest that before beginning a project, all of the elements of the question "How will who study whom?" should be specified. This question asks who will do the study (and why); how will the study be done (and why); who or what is going to be studied (and why); and what do we want to know (and why). With this framework, reflective researchers can examine *the politics* inherent in the choice and definition of the topic, the manner of studying it, and the intended results. Our failure to ask these questions demonstrates that in our project we had no wider perspective than the study itself. We did not look beyond the study to see its context. We did not recognize the questions we were not asking. If such questions are not posed, research begins to have the quality of a knee jerk rather than an intellectual pursuit. These questions represent a first step in overcoming alienation and meaninglessness, namely, the ability to metacommunicate (see Bateson and others, 1956). Without reflection, action becomes meaningless behavior.

The research process in which I participated had many qualities of a ritual: "the emphasis passes from content to form, from substantive questions to procedural ones, and virtue comes to be localized in the proper performance of fixed act sequences" (A. Kaplan, 1964, p. 146). The virtue of strict adherence to scientific procedure was distorted into mechanical repetition.

Rather than a series of careful decisions dealing with emerging issues, the project reenacted a procedure followed countless times, in different research institutes, on different subjects, with different objectives. In all of these research projects research assistants, like midwives, eased the process along, smoothed out the wrinkles, guided the delivery of the product. Nowhere was there an invitation for creativity except perhaps in subtle issues of style.

> There is a lot of misery in surveys, most of the time and money going into monotonous clerical and statistical routines, with interruptions only for squabbles with the client, budget crises, petty machinations for a place in the academic sun, and social casework with neurotic graduate students. And nobody ever reads the final report. Those few moments, however, when a new set of tables comes up from the machine room and questions begin to be answered; when relationships actually hold under controls; when the pile of tables on the desk suddenly meshes to yield a coherent chapter; when in a flash you see a neat test for an interpretation; when you realize you have found out something about something important that nobody ever knew before—these are the moments that justify research [Davis, 1964, pp. 233-234].

The exact following of the ritual protects researchers against colleagues' criticisms of procedural errors, an overriding concern. From my perspective, however, ritualized activity belonged in the religious world where precise, unquestioning replication of acts demonstrated faith and brought serenity. Social science, I thought, had the obligation to alter the status quo, to create new meanings and methods, to stretch the boundaries of patterned thought, to break new ground. To add insult to my injury of disillusionment, the ritual in which I was involved was only imperfectly enacted.

A second function of research ritualism is to protect researchers against the criticism of sponsors who are potentially dissatisfied with the results. The researchers' ability to show that they abided by scientific research canon, used only mathematical (rather than valuative or even logical) analysis, and always remained detached and aloof is their insurance policy against a sorry customer. Similarly, nurses record their patients' progress not only to better treat their ailments but also to protect themselves by documenting their meticulous adherence to detail.

To familiarize me with the Washington, D.C., public school system and with congressional reasons for financing the study, the project director provided me with a booklet (House of Representatives, 1966) written for a congressional committee that Congressman Adam Clayton Powell, Jr., chaired. (Perhaps here lies the reason this grant was offered to a New York-based group.) This booklet was all the reading that was done by the team for the project before we began to work on "the instrument." From reading it, I was amazed to learn that much basic information was already known before the study had even begun. Would our project be an exercise in redundancy? Not only was the information already assembled, but the basic issues were commonly understood features of contemporary American urban life. In addition, the political battles surrounding specific school policy questions were not suspended while we "scientifically" settled the issues; instead, they continued unabated in the nation's capital. The project that was about to begin, therefore, used an exorbitant amount of the taxpayers' money to duplicate existing information for the doubtful consideration of supposedly interested parties and the unlikely intellectual stimulation of the researchers themselves. My familiarization phase consisted less of exploring the subject matter of the teachers than acknowledging these conditions.

The Instrument

Since there was no real preliminary stage, the project began with the codirectors sitting down with me during the first week of my employment to construct a questionnaire. The sources of our questions varied: Most reflected our personal interests. Each of us had a chance to include a favorite concern. Some questions were designed to yield basic face-sheet data;

some were taken from other studies of teachers so as to create comparative data. A few stemmed from reflection about the goals of the project, that is, questions relating to the policy issues that the study was supposed to answer. It was satisfying to participate in this process and to be given the freedom and trust to include my own questions. Later, when I became completely disillusioned with this method, I sensed that the pride and personal investment researchers have in successfully obtaining answers to their own questions can make them lose a critical perspective on the overall purpose of the project.

The question-composition stage involved some intellectual exchange about what we were trying to measure, but it saddened me to recognize that everything we would learn would be limited to this questionnaire. As the only source of our data, it concerned me that its construction was so arbitrary and artificial. There was no careful translation of a highly conceptual interest into a question that could be measured and counted. I knew that we would later forget the rationale behind particular questions. There was no testing or questioning of the questions themselves. We merely assumed that anything we asked would yield responses we could count. Although no one on the research team denied that our analysis would be confined to responses to written questions rather than including observed behavior, we frequently lapsed, both during question-composition and response-analysis stages, into references to the respondents' actual, observable, or experiential behavior. With each question we *created* rather than *reflected* reality because we asked the teachers to respond to our questions rather than to describe their experience. The questionnaire was a mirror of the researcher's world, not a vehicle for expressing the teacher's world. The distance from the teachers' reality imposed by using our questions was increased by compelling them to use our forced-choice answers.

My description does not claim to be the only or true version of the research project; it is the retrospective account of a research assistant. There is no single true account but only a collection of various perspectives varying with time and interest. The multiple definitions of the project include at least those of the principal investigators, the project directors, Congress, the people of the Washington, D.C., public school system, the computer personnel, the coders, the bureau personnel, and the manuscript readers. There are as many perspectives as there are participants and audiences of a reality or event. An event's meaning is the coalescence of as many points of view as there are relations to that event. With each additional perspective, the meaning changes. Meaning is thus in continuous flux. My description of this project as a disillusionment reflects my needs, my relation to the project, and my conceptual perspective as much as it does the project itself.

Returning to the questionnaire, I now appreciate a deeper conflict. It is impossible to know which questions will be relevant for understanding a situation until information has already been obtained from other questions. This drawback of the one-shot questionnaire can be overcome by conducting a pilot study, but then the population to be studied with the improved questionnaire is no longer naive, or a new population must be used that might be dissimilar to the first. The time elapsed between asking the original questions, analyzing the questionnaire, and requestioning affects the population. If one population is pilot-tested and another seriously tested, the two populations must be identical. In any case, the unique attributes of the pilot group are lost. Questions pulled out of the air are less worthwhile for understanding a population than those grounded in the population's experience. If questions are not so grounded, then they must be grounded in the reality of other research. Given these constraints, what could I ask the schoolteachers of Washington, D.C.? More important, what would they like to be asked and why? All that I could learn would come from the items in the questionnaire, but I did not know what to ask. Had not Merton defended sociology against its detractors by claiming that "[Sociologists,] at least the best of them, know that, whatever the worth of one or another tool of inquiry, it is the questions put into the inquiry that determine the significance of the results. If the questions are trivial, then the answers will be trivial" (1976, p. 183).

We lacked fundamental questions to ask the school system and a means of translating such questions into measurable items of a questionnaire. With no grounding we could not judge our relevance, so we simply guessed and focused our energies on practical problems. Since we had no time or inclination to gain actual on-site experience, our *questions reflected stereotypical thinking*, and on this our eventual analysis was constructed. Such practice subverts the very function of research-based expertise in contemporary society, which is to introduce pluralistic definitions of reality. "Pluralism encourages both skepticism and innovation and is thus inherently subversive of the taken-for-granted reality of the traditional status quo" (Berger and Luckmann, 1966, p. 115). We never grasped the teacher's perceptions or experience, nor did we allow our a priori assumptions to be challenged. In the beginning I rebelled and said I could not compose questions for people whom I could not even picture in my mind. As I recognized that the project would continue despite my protest, I conformed by throwing in my own questions devoid of an experiential base. I concluded that even if naturalistic field techniques are not considered a valid social scientific method, some experiential techniques must be used to ground quantitative measures in reality.

The questionnaire-construction procedure was as mechanical as the computer that analyzed the responses. Everything was mechanized. Even the teachers' responses were transformed into checkmarks and then mere holes on IBM cards. The study lacked organic qualities. It did not stem from an attempt to get the whole truth but rather from an attempt to extricate from people something that had the appearance of meaning. We pretended that we had asked the teachers real questions; we pretended that they had answered us; and we pretended that anyone cared. We accepted everything at face value, never examined our own motivation, and always assumed that our questions and the teachers' answers were intelligible and sincere. We never asked how we could actually learn something meaningful and/or useful about the teachers of the Washington, D.C., school system. We did not treat them as human beings but as objects of our project—to answer questions with forced choices is dehumanizing. We were operating within a behaviorist paradigm, which assumes that a question elicits an answer, just as a stimulus is followed by a response. The social science term *respondent* reflects this dehumanization—a respondent is not a person but a producer of a response to a questionnaire stimulus. But is this response-stimulus set analogous to the responses of individuals to other stimuli, to spontaneous behavior in natural environments, to self-perception? What sociologists can think of themselves as respondents? Unless sociologists accept this view of themselves, they are being either inconsistent or elitist when applying it to others.

Parallel to my dismay at the relatively arbitrary choice of questions was my bewilderment at the use of indexes from other questionnaires. Although this practice might have reflected a directive from "above," it seemed premature to make comparisons with other populations before understanding the target group. Did the use of another researcher's index or question cluster reflect our dependence, unimaginativeness, or the routinization of our work? Was this primarily a time-saving, corner-cutting technique? Did we have confidence in national norms, or were we striving for replication, one of the hallmarks of scientific research? Did this questionnaire's orientation toward comparisons with other teachers detract from its ability to gather data that illuminated the qualities of these particular teachers? Should we use someone else's index if we do not know its value? The indexes themselves were irritating: What was the relation between a "Pollyanna" scale that we included and how a person actually felt or usually acted?

Stein (1964, p. 214) describes a fantasy that was acted out in our project:

> One of my favorite fantasies is a dialogue between Mills and Lazarsfeld in which the former reads to the latter the first sentence of *The Sociological Imagination*: "Nowadays men often feel that their private lives are a series of traps." Lazarsfeld immediately replies: "How many men, which men, how long have they felt this way, which aspects of their private lives bother them, do their public lives bother them, when do they feel free rather than trapped, what kinds of traps do they experience, etc., etc., etc.?"

My doubts were mirrored by Stein's "strong negative reaction to the prevailing ethos which proclaimed survey research and survey logic as the major ways of developing significant sociological generalizations" (1964, p. 214).

Questionnaires often reflect the unwillingness or inability of researchers to personally encounter their subjects. These instruments stand between the researchers and their respondents. The researchers assume that truths can be discovered by use of a question-answer model rather than through lengthy, complex exploration and interaction. Our work required massive self-deception. We pretended we could write a question that could tap an existing basic attitude (as if it were a thing the respondent had that we would get). But attitudes are not context-free; they are time bounded and socially situated. When researchers ask for attitudes in a questionnaire, one social setting is being substituted for another. Questionnaire answers reflect the social situation of being questioned about attitudes. They are not necessarily correlated with the respondent's attitudes in another social situation. For example, "There is reason to believe that opinions on such issues as a president's popularity or the desirability of entering a war cannot be accurately reflected in a social survey. Such opinions, tied as they are to small social networks, are often not clearly formed, perhaps not even existent. The forcing of a response into a *yes, no,* or *no opinion* continuum distorts the uncertain reality that opinion occupies in the symbolic world of the respondent" (Denzin, 1970a, p. 183).

More disconcerting than the presumed relation between responses and behavior was our interest not so much in the actual response but in inferences that we could make about these individuals from their responses. Their answers were only partial reflections of the questions; our interpretation of those responses was only partially a reflection of the actual responses. We deceived ourselves by taking the responses at face value and deceived the respondents by patently asking one question while really exploring another. The questionnaire seemed especially inappropriate when I tried to answer the questions myself, for I could not answer these questions seriously. My feelings and thoughts were not translatable into codable responses but were issues to be explored in conversations with trusted friends or during quiet introspection. Did this questionnaire mock the teachers' reality?

The myth prevails among social scientists who use self-administered questionnaires that the typical respondent's intention is complete honesty and that attitudes and feelings are stable and accessible. Respondents are presumed to be able to make decisions, to be unambivalent, to have excellent recall, self-awareness, and ability to follow instructions, and to have a cooperative attitude toward social science research. Social scientists assume that respondents understand the gist of every question, and they rely on their respondents' docility and willingness to answer if asked. Social scientists assume respondents are not suspicious and do not question the motives of the questioners or the value of the research. The imagined respondents are willing to divulge private thoughts and expose deviant behavior. Respondents believe questionnaires will benefit either themselves as individuals or "society," "science," or "the future." They see no contradictions between anonymity and truthfulness.

Social scientists have recently become concerned that these assumptions might be unfounded. Perhaps real respondents do not fit this ideal image. Critics urge that researchers observe real behavior rather than responses to forced choices about behavior. In the case of a questionnaire, the actual behavior is the *mode of responding* rather than the response's content. Studies have been designed to compare respondents' replies with other data about the same issue. The hypothesis is that questionnaire responses reflect factors other than question content. Data derived from questionnaire responses are frequently discrepant with data derived from other sources. Several studies show that people reported having voted although records indicate that they did not (Bell and Buchanan, 1966; Parry and Crossley, 1950; Calahan, 1968; Clausen, 1968; all cited in Phillips, 1971, p. 23). People reported not knowing about contraceptives although according to clinic records they participated in a birth control program (Green, 1969). In a study of ex-patients, "58% of the respondents gave inaccurate reports concerning their length of stay in the hospital, 23% were inaccurate with regard to the month of discharge, 35% with regard to diagnosis, 25% with regard to type of surgery, and 10% were inaccurate in their reports as to whether or not surgery had been performed" (Cannell and Fowler, 1963, in Phillips, 1971, p. 23). People have underreported their deviant behavior relative to criminal records; they have exaggerated their amount of education and downplayed their poor grades; they have minimized their divorces; they have overreported possession of a driver's license and exaggerated their contributions to charities; they have misrepresented their sex life and use of narcotics as determined by polygraph tests and urinalysis (Phillips, 1971).

Researchers, too, have been known to distort reality in their responses: "We frequently found that an interviewer's account of how he had conducted an interview bore little resemblance to the actual recorded interview. This raises some question as to the validity of the generalizations suggested in the literature by experienced interviewers that were based only on recollections of their performance" (Richardson, Dohrenwend, and Klein, 1965, pp. 1-2).

Although self-interested responses are expected of taxpayers, researchers tend to expect their respondents to be accurate and honest rather than motivated to protect their self-esteem. The inaccuracy of official reports might explain the discrepancy with self-reports, but another plausible explanation is that the imperfect memory or self-esteem needs of respondents lead to discrepancies with information obtained in other ways. In what other social situation is it so naively assumed that questions have accurate answers that are so easily tapped? Inferences about behavior based on these reported attitudes are even more questionable. Researchers project their wishes for accurate responses onto their respondents because of their own need for self-esteem. The respondents' ability to deceive would undermine the researchers' methodology and work. Similarly, the researchers' needs to hide their own misdeeds in the research process (to be explicated below) prevent them from recognizing the inaccuracy or dishonesty of their respondents.

While I participated in the Washington, D.C., schoolteachers' study, I was unaware of the source of my vague discomfort with the methodology. I felt as if we were characters in a Kafkaesque novel. The three of us sat in a small room on the Upper West Side of Manhattan, pulling questions out of the air or out of other manuscripts, questions directed at people whom we would never meet, people who were sitting in their schools in which they had worked for many years or for only a few weeks, schools which they hated or loved or felt apathetic toward on some days and felt otherwise toward on others. One day, in the midst of the daily round of frustration and elation that might make up a teacher's world, a directive came commanding all teachers to sit at their desks and give respectful attention to a thick booklet. On this booklet were large-type INSTRUCTIONS telling the teacher to be honest and candid and do exactly as told. Throughout the booklet little numbers and coding notations floated on each page, reminding these people that they were going to be converted into IBM cards. Throughout this booklet that requested their sincerity and respect were bizarre questions asking them to rank, according to their preference, groups such as blacks, Jews, Ku Klux Klan, and Peace Corps volunteers, and questions that asked them to tell us how happy and how prejudiced they were. Miles away from us, they would make little marks and scribbles that would become extremely significant, more significant to us, in fact, than they themselves. How distant was their subjective experience from the act of making a mark on the anonymous questionnaire? What was the relation between their paper-and-pencil rank ordering of those emotionally charged groups and their behavior toward members of these groups? After finishing the questionnaire, the teachers would relinquish them to our scrutiny. The markings would be converted into a report suggesting policy changes to the school board. While working on the questionnaire, pondering its probable absurdity and remembering all the other questionnaires and forced-choice questions I have endured, I vowed never again to participate in or accept the results of an attitudinal questionnaire.

Particularly irritating was the solemnity of our cover page instructions:

This questionnaire is being given to staff members in the Washington Public Schools. It is part of the Washington School Survey, a comprehensive study which Teachers College at Columbia University is making to secure information needed for improvement of the schools from the viewpoints of teachers, pupils and parents.

We ask your cooperation in filling out this questionnaire as frankly, honestly and completely as you can. Your personal opinions are important to help us arrive at reliable conclusions about the opinions and attitudes of the staff of the schools.

This questionnaire will not be seen by any person connected with the school system of the District of Columbia. Its contents will never be associated with you as an individual. When you have completed the questionnaire, enclose and seal it in the pre-addressed envelope provided and deposit it in the designated place. Your responses will be combined with the responses of others and tabulated with them for the research report.

The questionnaire has been designed to take as little of your time as possible. Most questions can be answered with a check mark. However, we urge you to write in any qualifications or comments you want to make in order to fully represent your views.

Please check when you have finished to make sure you have skipped no pages.

Thank you very much for your cooperation.

On this page we directly addressed the teachers. What did we say to them? First, we identified ourselves and explained the questionnaire's rationale. We did not solicit their cooperation but merely announced the fact that the questionnaire was going to be administered. The smooth language disguises the invasion of privacy and the assumed right to expect compliance. It also invokes a norm: Since all teachers will be given this questionnaire, to not respond is deviant. The term *staff member* attempts to win compliance with a prestigious euphemism for teacher.

Another compliance inducement mechanism is our statement that the information will be used to improve the school. How many times has this promise of eventual improvement been fulfilled? Particularly disturbing is the paternalistic, conservative attitude toward social change that underlies such a promise. If something needs improvement, we implied that the solution is to hire a research organization to survey the participants and make recommendations. Other models of change that are less alienating include reinforcing the teachers' ability to organize, formulate ideas, and shape changes grounded in their experiences or to demand power from those in control. We condescendingly implied that since the teachers could not change their school system, we would change it for them.

The term *improvement* similarly implies that something is wrong and needs to be improved. Had we said the information would serve as a basis for a model school system to be used in other cities, the teachers might have fulfilled this expectation and given us a positive evaluation of the schools. We were frankly interested in problems that we would overcome *for* the teachers. We defined our relationship with the teachers without their participation and without their acknowledgment that the school system needed study or improvement. Questionnaires depend on respondent compliance, which hinges on the researchers' identification and stated purpose. These, in turn, divulge expectations that influence responses. A miniature social system is thus established.

In an atmosphere of great seriousness we solemnly asked complete strangers for cooperation, frankness, honesty, and precision. On what grounds did we deserve the respect and frankness we were requesting? Were we being honest with them? The entire set of instructions was a hard sell on many different levels: *utilitarian*—this questionnaire will help improve the school system; *coercive*—you are going to fill this out because special time has been set aside by the administration; *beseeching*—we ask your cooperation; *intimate*—your personal opinions are important to us; *praising*—you can help us; *protective*—no one else will see these; *practical*—rather than ask whether you will comply, we explain what to do with the completed questionnaire;

apologetic—we hope this is no trouble. We appealed to the "inherent characteristics of the respondent that facilitate participation" in interviews or research, including:

> "altruism"—the desire to help one's fellow man can be manipulated so that the respondent will participate if he can be made to feel that the research in which he is a participant will be of help to mankind; "emotional satisfaction"—the opportunity to express opinions, to experience identification with the researchers, to cooperate with science; "intellectual satisfaction"—for respondents who enjoy discussion and the exchange of ideas but whose daily lives lack intellectual stimulation, the opportunity to be questioned, to think about and respond to new or different topics, can be highly rewarding [Richardson, Dohrenwend, and Klein, 1965, p. 62].

The assurance of confidentiality, although standard practice in contemporary research, also reinforces paranoid thinking. "We won't show this to anyone else" implies that the respondent has something to hide, that we are asking dangerous questions, that we can protect the respondent, and that the respondent is not willing to own up to his or her opinions. We assume that anonymity is useful not only because of our concern with confidentiality but also because of our disinterest in the uniqueness of the respondent. What could we possibly do with their names if we had them? Between the lines is the notion that whereas people dare not be truthful with one another, they will welcome the opportunity to unburden themselves in an anonymous questionnaire. Sealing the envelope symbolizes the secret pact between the respondent and the researchers. The reference to taking as little of the teacher's time as possible implies that we do not expect them to care about or to spend much time improving their schools.

Our efforts to construct unambiguous questions frequently resulted in stilted, childish, or even humiliating language: "There are many groups in America and we would like to get your feelings toward some of these groups. Here's something we call a 'feeling thermometer.' Here's how it works. If you don't know too much about members of a group or don't feel particularly warm or cold toward them, then you should place them in the middle at the 50 degree mark." The wording we used in no way communicated familiarity with black language or teacher terminology. In our New York offices, several hundreds of miles away from the teachers, much time and tension were expended in phrasing the questions, compiling the questionnaire booklet, dealing with the press, and meeting deadlines, rather than in exploring Washington, D.C., or thinking about the problems of urban education.

While putting the finishing touches on the questionnaire, we were informed of the ever-changing political turmoil of the District school system. With this news, I developed an appreciation of the problem's complexity and the contrasting triviality of our research. The continuous flow of news created an image of a school system in a state of transition, trying to cope with population changes and trying to clarify its identity and organization. To my amazement, we were attempting to capture this flow by utilizing the most static research instrument available— the one-shot massive questionnaire, best used to study stable, persistent social structures!

When the questionnaire was completed, I wondered if we had asked any of the right questions. What were we going to do with all the contrived data we had created? What difference would this study make to anyone? The positive reinforcement from outsiders temporarily assuaged my doubts. For example, the superintendent of the District school system dismissed all the students two hours early from school one day so teachers could fill out the questionnaire during school time. This unusual action lent our study an aura of significance and respectability. We were complimented on our ability to be on schedule. Everything was proceeding according to plan, even if the research assistant was convinced that the study was meaningless. The one ray of hope I saw in this massive exercise in absurdity was the final page's open-ended question soliciting a short paragraph on the strengths and weaknesses of and recommendations for the school system. In that space, in which the teachers could express themselves in their own words, I believed I would learn something.

The day following distribution, the questionnaires returned to us in a station wagon—carton upon carton of slightly crumpled but very familiar pamphlets that had been in the hands of the people whose behavior and attitudes we were going to assess. What had these strangers confided to us? What was their experience as respondents? What did they think of our questionnaire and of us? I looked for scribbling in the margins, for the human protest of graffiti, for differences in handwriting, for signs of life. But there were as few such signs from them as there were from us. An insulting twist deepened my frustration —when a graduate student removed the pages containing the open-ended paragraphs on the last page of the booklet. He conducted a separate analysis, which was never communicated to us. There was never an opportunity for our team to read these open-ended remarks.

The Respondent

The questions that this experience raised remained with me throughout my graduate work. What is the experience of the subject or respondent as a person being studied by a sociologist? What is the phenomenology of "being studied"? Is it as well defined a role as that of the researcher? Is the behavior that the researcher observes or measures an artifact of the role of research subject to a greater extent than it is a reflection of the subject's behavior in other social situations? Do researchers in essence create what they observe? In other words, do researchers create not only the questionnaire but a "respondent mentality" that produces results contingent on being a respondent and dealing with questions constructed by a researcher?

I formulated such questions retrospectively, since I was mystified by the study process while engaged in it. As I continuously worked through the experience, I extracted methodological questions that captured my uneasiness at the time and shaped the subsequent work I undertook. For example, most of the respondents in our sample were black women. Absolutely no consideration of this fact was made in the construction of the questionnaire. Nor did we entertain the idea that responses might have reflected the black women's attitudes toward being questioned by the Bureau of Applied Social Research, which they might have accurately perceived as a white, male-dominated organization.

The influence of the experimenter's or interviewer's race on the research subject has been documented repeatedly (Banks, Berenson, and Carkhuff, 1967). Studies have also shown that blacks and whites are more likely to give socially acceptable responses when interviewed by a member of the opposite race and more likely to give an honest answer when interviewed by a member of their own race (Hyman, 1954; Athey, 1960; Summers and Hammonds, 1966; Williams, 1964). This dynamic may account for the response elicited by our job satisfaction question: About 80 percent of the teachers said their job was satisfying, approximately the same percentage thought their students liked school, and most were at least somewhat satisfied with the quality of their students' schoolwork. Does this positive evaluation reflect their true feelings about jobs and students or their desire to present the researchers with socially acceptable responses? What does a response mean? Pettigrew has argued that blacks in white America are always acting, transforming their behavior to conform to white prejudices and to avoid white punishment.

'Got one mind for white folks to see, 'nother for what I know is me . . .' go the lyrics of an old Negro folksong, and white social scientists have repeatedly learned the truth of these words when conducting research on Negroes of all ages. Similarly, public opinion surveys using both Negro and white interviewers have obtained sharply diverse results with equivalent samples of Negro adults, particularly in answer to questions concerning the race issue. . . . So effective is this impassive facade, many white Americans have long interpreted it as proof that Negroes are happy and contented with their lot [Pettigrew, 1964, p. 50].

Other studies cited by Dohrenwend (1966, p. 19) indicate that the response style of blacks favors positive self-appraisal more than does the white response style with regard to reporting illnesses or educational and occupational aspirations for their children. The existence of response styles should dissuade survey researchers from accepting responses at face value or out of context. The response style that has been shown to characterize interracial interaction prevents the automatic generalizing of information from interracial to single-race research situations. The existence of a response style invalidates conclusions that did not take this response style into account, even if interaction is completely attenuated, as was true in our study.

Another social category that influences interaction is gender. Is it not reasonable to assume that an explicitly black female social research organization would have elicited different responses from the teachers of our study? Women and men respond to the opposite sex even while considering other matters. Goffman (1971) has suggested that gender's impact on interaction is pervasive, while race is sometimes irrelevant. Since the instructions for our study were signed with a male's name, it is plausible that the women respondents were producing responses influenced by their definition of what men want or what women should say.

The problem of responding in a particular fashion regardless of the content of the question has been shown to be more typical of certain personality types than of others (Couch and Kenniston, 1960) and to be elicited by certain types of questions. The more ambiguous the question, for example, the more likely the respondent will produce a yes or no answer that does not reflect the content of the question (Christie and Lindauer, 1963). The more significant the relationship between researcher and respondent, the less likely that the respondent's answers directly reflect the questions, and the more likely they reflect the respondent's perception of their relationship. In the case of interviewing, "it might be difficult for a young male investigator to interview women on aspects of their menopausal experiences or for a young woman to interview soldiers about their off-duty recreational patterns with the risk of distorting the responses" (Richardson, Dohrenwend, and Klein, 1965, p. 31). Similarly, "there is often a suspicion that refugees tend to flatter Western inquirers by telling them what they think will please them, rather than the truth about the Soviet system" (Field, 1955, p. 674).

Another identifying tag on the questionnaire was the connection with Teachers College of Columbia University. Since relative prestige affects interaction, it will affect responding to questions as well. If the teachers perceived the researchers as distant colleagues facing similar problems but affiliated with a university, they could respond in ways that inflate their own teaching abilities and satisfaction. However, if they identified our institution as prestigious relative to the public school system, they could feel humble and exaggerate their deficiencies or express their envy. In analyses of interviewing interactions, university affiliation was found to be a factor that affects the respondent's willingness to participate:

> His preconceptions of, or prior experiences with, research or the sponsoring organization will color his initial [sic] perception. Some persons regard social research as "nonsense," as manipulative in a sinister way, or an invasion of privacy. Others regard with hostility or indifference the sponsoring university or the research organization, which the interviewer may mention in the hope of encouraging the respondent to participate. Although for some respondents a university affiliation enhances the interviewer's prestige, others regard a university as a collection of "long-hairs," "leftists," or "absent-minded professors" [Richardson, Dohrenwend, and Klein, 1965, p. 66].

Laboratory experiments, like interviews and surveys, have been shown to be influenced by expectations that subjects and researchers have of one another. "For example, the 'real-life' relationship between subject and experimenter was found to make a difference in the subject's behavior in the experiment. In one investigation it was found that a faculty experimenter induced higher performance levels in subjects than did a graduate student experimenter" (Proshansky and Seidenberg, 1966, p. 16).

Factors that influence interviewing also produce response

sets toward the imagined researcher. All of these relationships between respondents and researchers must figure in the clarification of the data's meaning. These features of interaction are not sources of bias but are the particular social forces at play in the form of interaction known as social research. Respondents respond to the context in which a questionnaire is presented (in this case, the classroom), to their expectations about the researchers' values and hypotheses, to their previous experiences as a research subject, to the form of the question, and to more than just the question's content. The ability of human beings to act in terms of more than one stimulus at a time and for responses to be overdetermined must be reflected in our survey data analyses. The questions themselves are only one of many triggers to an answer. To understand the response styles operating in our survey would have required knowing the respondents' perceptions of the researchers and of the study itself. Not only did we overlook the need to pose these questions to our respondents, but we ignored thinking about them altogether. Without this information I could not accept our data.

No matter how detached or removed experimenters, surveyers, or researchers attempt to be, they cannot prevent people from interacting in terms of an "observing other," or a "looking-glass self" in the famous phrase of George Herbert Mead. The act of taking others into account is similar to the "audience effect" in experimental social psychology. This effect characterizes interaction in general, not only interaction in experiments. Nevertheless, social psychological experiments show that having an audience increases motivation, distraction, moderation in judgments, common associations, and cautiousness, and decreases idiosyncratic thoughts. In general, the anticipated reactions of the audience are taken into account by the actor. Over time, adaption to being observed tends to occur and the audience effects tend to decrease (Deutsch, 1968; Kelley and Thibaut, 1954). I claim that this audience effect does not depend on an actual audience but is part of taking into account the generalized other in everyday interaction. There is no way to avoid the subject's responding to the idea of being studied unless deception or unobtrusive measures are used. Respondents act on the basis of their definitions of the research situation, the researcher, and the research task, at the very least.

Why did the respondents answer our questionnaires? Which individuals comply and cooperate and which do not? Under which conditions do subjects respond or participate willingly in the researcher's design? Much literature in social research is concerned with subject compliance. In the Milgram (1963) experiments, for example, professionals expected that his experimental demands would produce minimal compliance, but instead the subjects endured severe discomfort in order to comply. In these experiments the researcher expected less compliance than the subjects were willing to give! The King and Henry (1955) research on stress similarly demonstrated that people were willing to undergo experiments that induced great discomfort. When placed in a situation of acute frustration and little opportunity for tension reduction, the subjects in these studies underwent physiological changes, expressed anger toward the experimenters and toward themselves, and became anxious or devoid of all affect, but they nevertheless continued to participate.

The compliance of many individuals when confronted with "science" obligates researchers to understand the impact of these attitudes on subject behavior and to not exploit this subtle form of coercion for unethical ends. "The mere existence of consent does not exempt the social scientist from the moral obligations of respect for another's privacy" (Shils, 1959, p. 124). In this instance of victimless crime, as in all others, both parties are willing to participate. The degree of the subject's cooperativeness with the research is a clue to the subject's perception of the researcher. This perception is reflected in the behavior of the subject during the research, whether it be in the form of responses to a questionnaire, willingness to comply in an experiment, or cooperation in an interview. The cooperativeness of some subjects reaches uncanny proportions. Subjects produce what they think the experimenter wants, even if the experimenter does not want it. For example, in medical research "on the common cold, it has been found that whereas many of the volunteers who are given infectious material develop a cold, a significant proportion of the control group who are given non-infectious salt water also develop a classical cold, indistinguishable from the infectious type" (Cassell, 1970, p. 61). The existence of placebo effects illustrates the suggestibility of subjects (patients and respondents) in the social psychological setting of science (medicine and research). Just as respondents' behavior is becoming increasingly understood as a function of the social setting and of their perception of the researcher, so too in medicine is the patient's response to treatment becoming increasingly understood as a function of the doctor-patient relationship and the patient's expectations of the situation.

One of the reasons for the patients' suggestibility in doctor-patient interactions is their discomfort or distress. The nonroutinized quality of the research experience, whether as innocuous as an anonymous questionnaire or as provocative as a laboratory experiment in which electric shock is administered, creates sufficient emotional arousal to increase the subject's openness to the researcher's influence. The questionnaire's request to examine the self, the forthright discussion of problematic issues, the disruption of the taken-for-granted attitude with which daily life proceeds, and the mystification of science contribute to the respondents' suggestibility, compliance, and response set. "Schutz [claimed] that we experience a special kind of 'shock' when suddenly thrust from one 'world' . . . to another" (Goffman, 1974, p. 4), as is true when shifting to the role of respondent.

The classic experiments of Asch and Sherif demonstrated not only that individual perception is altered by group norms but that groups pressure individuals to voice opinions they do not hold without the individuals even recognizing this collusion. The important implication is that different situations produce different perceptions and definitions of reality rather than there being a *real* response that contrasts with a *biased* response. The human experience is varied, not a dichotomy between real and biased. Behavior can best be accounted for in terms of all the possible impacting conditions in which it is imbedded.

Although social psychological experiments have revealed

the phenomenon of subject compliance, researchers frequently desire even greater cooperation from their subjects or respondents. Researchers assume a right to know, which is underscored by expressions of annoyance when subjects refuse to comply with research demands. Researchers lament a high rate of nonresponse in survey studies and devise remedies for this problem rather than questioning why people bothered to respond at all. Researchers plan constraints and follow-up techniques to retrieve lost members of their sample because a lost member represents a failing on the researcher's part. Researchers' ideal subjects are compliant, cooperative, obedient individuals with a respect for the researchers' work. Sociologists are more likely to notice their subjects' unwillingness to respond than their proclivity to acquiesce.

Nonresponding is not necessarily a blight on a study; rather it could be interpreted as the respondent's meaningful statement concerning the wish not to be placed in the role of respondent, the irrelevance of the questionnaire, or the unattractiveness of the research purpose. A nonresponse is a meaningful statement and a source of understanding for the researcher just as is the actual response. In field studies some participant observers have used their rejection by the studied group to understand the subjects' or the community's perceptions of them or the research objective. In the study of mental health education in a small Saskatchewan town by Cumming and Cumming (1957), the rude, hostile treatment of the interviewers by the townspeople lent credence to the hypothesis that the layman's tolerance for mental illness behavior is greater than the tolerance of the professional attempting to liberalize the citizen. The "closing of ranks" was an act of noncompliance with the research design by the townspeople that helped the researchers evaluate the educational program.

In my conversations with members of various research teams employing questionnaire, interview, or panel techniques, one of the most frequently mentioned sources of concern was the possible loss of sample members or research subjects. I was frequently told that the sign of failure for an interviewer is the subject's unwillingness to grant an interview, complete the planned schedule of questions, or follow through on repeated sessions. Nonacquiescence, however, might elucidate precisely the underlying attitudes of the subject that are concealed by a polite facade. As the interviewers themselves acknowledged, their own concern with the subjects' cooperation permeated all of the interviews.

In other words, not only are subjects compliant when agreeing to undertake immoral or illegal activities or to modify unwittingly their statements to fulfill the researcher's projected expectations, but researchers themselves are compliant for the sake of retaining the subject's cooperation. The subject's willingness to cooperate with the researcher's wishes fluctuates throughout the process. During the interaction between researcher and subject, each member's attitudes feed back into the questions and responses. Each sizes up the other and evaluates the costs and benefits of continuing the activity.

Although the teachers in our study might have been a compliant group, or one that was favorably disposed to research in general, or one that considered this questionnaire to be in their interest, it is clear that the constraints on our respondents were very great. The superintendent had dismissed the students early so that the questionnaires could be completed during school time. The forms were distributed, monitored, and collected on the spot so that we could achieve as high a return rate as possible. Our artificially high response rate reflected these constraints. What were other effects of these constraints? A nonresponse, which was almost impossible, could have indicated attitudes toward the research that would have been valuable information.

Consider, for example, the nonrespondent in a different study who submitted this poem in lieu of a questionnaire to express his attitudes:

A Note from the Underground,
by non-respondent No. 5542.

The little men in untold legions
Descend upon the private regions.
Behold, my child, the questionnaire,

And be as honest as you dare.
"As briefly as possible, kindly state
Age and income, height and weight.
Sex (M or F); sex of spouse
(spouses—list)
> *Do you own your house?*

How much of your income goes for rent?
Give racial background, by percent.
Have you had, or are you now having
Orgasm? Or thereunto a craving?
Will Christ return? If so, when?
(kindly fill this out in pen)
Do you masturbate? In what style?
(fill and return the enclosed vial)
Do you eat or have you eaten
Feces? Whose?
> *And were you beaten?*

Was your mother? sister? dog?
(attach descriptive catalogue.)
Have you mystic inspiration?
Our thanks for your co-operation."

Distended now with new-got lore,
Our plump and pleasant men-of-war
Torture whimsey into fact,
And then, to sanctify the act,
Cast in gleaming, ponderous rows,
Ingots of insipid prose.
A classic paper! Soon to be,
Rammed down the throats of such as we.
> Anonymous, 1972

The social constraints on responding prevented me from determining the teachers' perception of the usefulness of complying with our research request. These were some of the circumstances that provided a context for the particular responses we received.

Hughes (1960) has argued that a successful investigation requires the confidence of those being studied. This confidence must be deserved and is contingent on the respondents' understanding the future of the findings. Unless the meanings imposed on being a respondent are understood, the research findings are meaningless.

Deception

Some sources of subject compliance are naturally occurring artifacts of the research situation, but another significant source, specifically designed by the researcher, is deception. The history of deception in research is long and rich:

> In recent years there have been a great many experiments and investigations reported in which deliberate falsification has been introduced. Instructed stooges have been directed to deny sensory evidence, or to mimic pain that they did not feel, or to obstruct situations planned by their peers. Investigators have posed as possible converts to flying-saucer cults. Under the guise of "participant observation," various forms of "cover" have been developed for social investigators, which have later been revealed to the public in the reports on the experiments [Mead, 1970, p. 374].

An entire subdivision of social psychological research could be entitled "stooge," "false pretext," or "false information" research. The ethical and intellectual implications of operating under these interpersonal conditions have been analyzed elsewhere (*Daedalus*, 1969; Sjoberg, 1967). One of the deleterious effects of utilizing deception in research, in addition to the effects on the subject, the investigator, the study itself, and the general culture, is the possible spread of deception throughout the research enterprise. The maze of complicity could become highly complex: The sponsoring agency could be deceived in the grant application; one's colleagues and research partners could be misled; and results could be misreported.

Although deception was minor in our teachers study and consisted primarily of promising improvement of the school system and burying sensitive questions within the questionnaire, these features alerted me to the potential for greater deception in sociological research. Where were the checks on our relations with subjects? The American Sociological Association's Code of Ethics ("Toward a Code of Ethics for Sociologists," 1968) contains rules to protect individuals from sociological investigations that decrease their dignity or infringe on their privacy. These rules have been criticized by an appeal to values higher than privacy and dignity, such as law and morality (Galliher, 1973). To confine research to those from whom voluntary consent can be obtained is to confine research to the powerless and the compliant. Should individuals be protected from investigations or should researchers be protected from noncompliance?

Deception enters the research design when researchers cannot create conditions of direct questioning or observation for their study problem. Since the subjects' knowledge of the research purpose affects their participation in the research, deception allows the researcher to retain the subject by presenting more attractive purposes. This technique expresses researchers' omnipotence, control of the environment, and distance from the subject. Deception is a by-product of the secrecy and suspense built into research, in contrast with a possible alternative structure of open, collaborative exploration. The assumption of deceptive research is that better knowledge can be obtained from a naive subject than from an informed collaborator. Deception stems from the application in social psychological research of a natural science model that does not require informing the objects of study (usually inanimate) of the research purpose. This application relies on contempt for individuals, which is disguised as obeisance to scientific procedure.

When the interests of subjects are ignored or denied, researchers must deceive their subject. The conflict arises between retaining the subjects' cooperation and obtaining data concerning behavior not in the subjects' interest. The academic community urges researchers to keep open the doors of the towns, institutions, or groups for future researchers by not alienating subjects. Preserving the goodwill of subjects and the good reputation of social research is an added responsibility for the researcher.

Subject compliance can be obtained, however, by redefining the research topic into matters of intrinsic interest to the subject. In the Schwitzgebel (1964) case, for example, juvenile delinquents not only were paid and given special bonuses for their participation but were also treated as experts in the field of juvenile delinquency; they were allowed to quit whenever they wanted; and experimenters shared meals with them. "We had no legal or political power to force or coerce prospective subjects into attending. They could only be invited, encouraged, and rewarded for their attendance" (Schwitzgebel, 1964, p. 19). The combination of encouraging autonomy and offering compensation provided the experimenters with cooperative subjects and also had a humanizing, therapeutic impact on the boys. In the juvenile delinquency study the investigators' interest in gathering data was matched by the subjects' interest in participating.

How do social scientists decide whether to deceive or, more generally, how to relate to their subjects? Relations in the field or in the laboratory are reflections to some extent of the individual researcher's personal values held in check by research ethics committees. In addition, however, researchers neutralize or rationalize their guilt when the demands of science conflict with their values:

> These include such questions as whether full honesty about his purpose is practicable (it may take more time than is available to explain, or require specialized knowledge the informant lacks; and, when gathering information, the investigator may not even know the use to which it will later be put) or compatible with that purpose (if personal sympathy with an informant is necessary to elicit honest information, by the same token that information becomes a form of affectionate response and its subsequent use in an "objective"—i.e., depersonalized —context can constitute a kind of emotional betrayal) [Orlans, 1967, p. 21].

In Orlans' discussion, dissonance is diminished by references to "full" honesty (there is no need to be fully honest so long as I am partially honest), practicality (I can only do what is practical), efficiency (it would take forever to explain everything), the subject's lack of interest or lack of adequate education (he wouldn't understand my explanation anyhow), and rationalization (he doesn't want to know anyhow).

The rationalizations researchers use to get themselves off the moral hook of deceptive research can lead to their own self-deception, particularly when dealing with the subject's resistance to being studied. For example, Spiegel (1969, p. 128) discusses the difficulty of studying people who do not wish to be studied:

> We *constantly have to deal with this problem* in the ghetto. That is, our clients, let us say, in the ghetto say: We need research like we need a hole in the head. And what are you going to do with the things that you are learning? Are you going to help us, are you just here to stamp out violence and so forth. We usually *get around this* because of their own ambivalence; that is, it is not as if the majority of the people in the ghetto were so enamored of riots. They sympathize with the kind of response that gives rise to a riot, but any kind of knowledge that can help—after all, they are the ones who are most hurt—any type of knowledge that can give rise to changing conditions which would make riots unnecessary is in their interest. When they come to see that this is *what we are interested in doing,* not in stamping out riots and violence, but in helping by testifying before all sorts of audiences, by helping to change conditions in the ghetto, then the *resentment toward what we are doing* dies down [emphasis added].

Spiegel's labeling the ghetto residents' attitude to riots as "ambivalent" might be accurate, but he does not confront their unambivalent attitude toward his research or toward him. His rationalization resolved the problems of dissonance, or subject resistance, so that the scientific research design could remain intact.

Creative methods are needed to produce knowledge without infringing on the privacy, autonomy, or dignity of human beings or resorting to the researcher's rationalizations. One solution is to examine reflexively the very processes that occur in the attempt to study. All eventualities are possible arenas for understanding social processes and the self in relation to them. Being prevented from carrying out a research plan is a ripe learning opportunity. For example, Rodman and Kolodny (1964, p. 175) report, "In one case we know of, the only recourse left to the researchers was to shift their interest from a comparison between experimental and control patients to a study of the resistance of the practitioners to the research project." The natural events that surround a research project can become data worthier of sociological analysis than the contrived data of the research design itself. The fundamental problem is the researcher's assumption of a *right to know* that serves as a carte blanche for activities that contradict other values. The right to study human beings cannot be taken for granted by the educated elite or protected by deceptions and rationalizations if a noncompliant subject balks.

Research is frequently conducted on a rape model: The researchers take, hit, and run. They intrude into their subjects' privacy, disrupt their perceptions, utilize false pretenses, manipulate the relationship, and give little or nothing in return. When the needs of the researchers are satisfied, they break off contact with the subject. An alternative, which might be called humanistic research, would transform this aggressive model. The optimal outcome would be a redefinition of researchers and subjects into collaborators with mutual interests and potential mutual benefit. A study would be conceived and desired by both parties and designed to provide helpful information that would be used by both to effect change. Each party would agree to participate openly and to reserve the option of withdrawing. Each would have a vested interest in the success of the enterprise, and the motivation of each party would be recognized and accepted by the other. Each would be willing to openly acknowledge and discuss the grounds for continued participation in the relationship.

Recognizing the motivations behind participation in research is an essential element in the rehumanization of both the researcher and subject. When researchers see themselves as the unembodied instrument of science, they are likely to see the subject as a data container that must be manipulated to divulge its contents. But if researchers acknowledge their personal interests—humanness, desire for money, publication, prestige, insight, adventure, or whatever—and attempt to understand the other's motivation, then the two will gain meaningful knowledge about one another. What motivates your subjects to allow you to study them? How does that motivation become a part of the self that is presented to you? What motivates you to study them? How can these be combined to preserve your dignity and goals?

My preoccupation with the respondent's perception of us as sociologists and researchers was not only motivated by my concern with understanding the ethical and sociological blind spots of research methodology. These concerns were also related to my ambivalence about my emerging identity. In other words, I projected my negative and positive self-images onto the respondents' conception of us and imagined that they saw us in those terms. Subconsciously I wanted the respondents to tell me what they thought of my chosen profession, to shape the parameters of my emerging identity as sociologist, to determine the respect I could give myself as a professional sociologist in this society. But without any data or way of knowing how respondents perceived us (aside from a few outraged remarks written on the questionnaires), I had to rely on my imagination.

I believe that this process of seeking the subject's perception of the researcher is not a neurotic shortcoming but a necessary component of meaningful social research. First, one cannot understand the statements or behaviors of another person without understanding their perception as to who they are answering, being observed by, or responding to, or their definition of the situation in which the researcher plays a part. Only in the context of that imagined or real interaction do the subjects' behavior and statements make sense. Statements are not merely *made*, they are *made to* someone. Who are you to the respondent? How are you stereotyped? Parties to social interaction create meaningful contexts in which to interact. If this context is simply imagined because there is no face-to-face interaction, then the meaning becomes more difficult to ascertain. Fortunately, while working on the teacher study I was unaware that eventually I would ask these questions, for if they had been my concern from the start, I would not have been able to undertake the study. Excessive self-consciousness would have precluded action, but I suspected that insufficient self-consciousness rendered activity meaningless.

Disruption

The face-value attitude considers responses to questions within a questionnaire as reflections of the respondent's thoughts about the subject matter of the question. The critical attitude, in contrast, considers responses to questions as reflections of the respondent's feelings about being put in the role of a respondent. Some people feel threatened by questioning. The special relationship of schoolteachers with the public causes them concern about investigations into their work. The defensiveness of any group is aroused when questionnaires are imposed on them that they did not request. Defensive responses need not be less useful to the researcher than undefensive responses; they merely arise from the participants' perception of being questioned as threatening to their self-esteem. The particular set of contingencies under which the respondent is operating must be understood to evaluate the responses. Questionnaires and interviews make issues salient that the respondent previously might not have noticed. When previously unexamined issues are considered, the respondent can be suspicious or intrigued. Clues as to the researcher's real intent are sought in the language and form in which the questions are posed. In our case, I believe the irritatingly condescending language of the questionnaire reflected the condescending attitude of the university researchers toward the public schoolteachers.

Even the researcher's so-called objective, or neutral, question can disrupt the respondent's assumptions or daily routinized activities. The researcher can innocently insert a ques-

tion that is taboo within the subject's milieu. This disruptive research quality can free the respondent to reformulate a belief:

> Espers believe in reincarnation and they also will
> acknowledge the fact that the human and animal popula-
> tion of the world is increasing. Juxtapoxing these two
> beliefs, I asked several Espers where more souls for the
> greater number of living bodies come from. The Espers
> recognized the inconsistency and admitted they could
> give no answer. My main informant became so interested
> in the question that he read books on Eastern religions
> and asked a good many of the other Espers what they
> thought. (I may have thus unwittingly started a chain of
> events that will produce innovations in the Esper belief
> system.) [Simmons, 1969, p. 101]

Disruptive ramifications of research can become so severe that
the research kills the thing being studied. There is most likely a
saturation point for research of a social system, which, if ex-
ceeded, leads to the system's collapse. This strain is especially
evident when research is performed on small, socially unstable,
deviant groups or organizations. One case of this occurrence is
the invasion by the news media of the residents of a "cooperative housing unit near the University of Michigan where 29 men
and women moved into each other's rooms for a three-week experiment to see if they could break down some of the barriers
between the sexes." The "barrage of news articles, radio interviews, and television news films" culminated in the ending of the
experiment and the closing of the house to newspeople. There
was "a feeling among many residents that the press 'wrecked'
what might otherwise have been a noble venture" ("Test of
Coed Living Ends in Michigan," 1972). Not only were participants in the experiment distressed at "what they called inaccurate and misleading news accounts" that sabotaged their project, but the endless investigating and reporting left little time
for residents to do anything without constant inquiries from the
media. The outsiders' need to know about the social system

deprived the insiders of the time, energy, and privacy to stabilize and maintain that system.

Another way in which research can be disruptive is when researchers embed themselves in a social system, participate and strengthen it, and then pull out. In the participant observation research described in *When Prophecy Fails,* researchers comprised a significant proportion of the fledgling group's population. Swelling the ranks served to strengthen the group in its formative stage, while abandoning the group after the prophecy's failure reinforced the failure. Just as research can bring about a social system's demise, so too it can help establish social groups. Research can lead to group formation by exposing the common plight of individuals who are unaware of one another.

Research is a social activity that influences that which is being studied. A questionnaire or other data-gathering device causes repercussions that change the social system. The system concept by definition states that multiple repercussions occur when one factor has been altered in a set of mutual contingencies. Even research as removed as our survey led to the early closing of an entire school system. More important are the disruptive consequences that follow from drawing people's attention to the basic assumptions on which their social system rests. Basic assumptions provide the meaning and underpinning for social systems precisely to the extent that they are unquestioned. When they are challenged, the possibility of replacement arises and the system is thereby changed. For example, "men who teach psychotherapy in a mental hospital talk about people who do research in the mental hospital and see them as disrupting the authority and essentially destructive" (Ekstein and Wallerstein, 1958, p. 7). The disruptive effects of questioning include the destruction, change, jeopardy, and creation of new social systems.

The social psychology of a survey project is the study of an encounter in which one party is usually absent. In the initial stages, the researchers project an image of a typical respondent and posit questions to be answered. During this phase, the researcher and the respondent have no contact. In the data collection phase, if self-administered questionnaires are used, the researcher is absent. The respondent projects an image of the questioner or of project goals and provides responses. The features of communication among strangers characterize the attenuated interchange between respondent and questioner. Researcher-respondent communication is a form of stranger behavior, but since interaction is minimal the social processes of self-presentation, control, embarrassment, guilt, anger, face saving, manipulation, deception, negotiation of reality, seduction, and departure occur in the imagination of the researcher and respondent while preparing and filling out the questionnaire. Since neither party can test reality, however, the data that are generated are not grounded.

In a noninteractive questionnaire study such as ours, respondents are influenced by factors in their immediate questionnaire-completion environment more than they are influenced by the researchers. For example, our study's connection with the superintendent of schools, or with the particular individual who proctored the questionnaires, or with the particular time of the workday when the questionnaire was completed, or with the room in which it was completed can affect the responses. How did the teachers interpret the early dismissal of school? Did their delight with this vacation spill into the pages of the questionnaire? Did they resent disrupting their teaching schedules or depriving their students of valuable class time? Despite our reassurances, did they fear repercussions on their jobs if they answered critically or truthfully? Did they express their anger at having an additional piece of paperwork to complete? Similarly, what did it mean to the respondents to be given a questionnaire at that particular point in the year? From their perspective, what time was it in the history of their setting? Was it politically dangerous to complain? Was it a period of acute tension or change? Our study did not attend to these time dimensions. It was completely ahistorical. The proper interpretation of survey results rests, to my mind, on a parallel study of the research context.

My discomfort with our project stemmed partially from

our complete disregard for the contexts in which the responses were created and collected. These contexts are composed of intrinsic factors, in contrast with the traditional extrinsic factors, or independent variables. Factors within the research process itself affect the product, which reflects not only the content studied but also the act of studying. Intrinsic factors must be reported for results to be meaningful. The problem exists in participant observation as well:

> Only rarely do we find the investigator reporting just how he set about his work. How long was he in the community and during which seasons? Was he alone or accompanied by his wife? Had he visited the community previously? Did he know anyone there before his arrival? How, and where, was he housed? What local help did he hire? Who collected the basic material? The local situation the observer has to cope with is always important. It is usually more or less structured by the stranger's presence. The mere fact of knowing they are being observed may produce a change in the people observed. Their reactions towards the visitor must both be distinguished from their community life and interpreted through it [den Hollander, 1967, p. 12].

The best research reporting describes both the intrinsic and extrinsic features by presenting research as a social psychological activity with attention to personal and social system details. "Every researcher is obligated to report the effects of the following variables upon his causal propositions: the situations of observation; the attitudes and definitions of the interviewers as these pertain to the interview process; variations in definitions and meanings observed among respondents or subjects concerning the research act; unique aspects of subject-observer interaction; time and its passage" (Denzin, 1970, p. 166). Attention to these intrinsic features of research is very low. The list of possible intrinsic factors is infinite, limited only by practical considerations. Research consciousness should search continuously for additional relevant factors that shape meaning. What are the exact components of this research activity that can

influence behavior? What is the effect of the particular research
sponsor? Of the physical appearance of the questionnaire? Of
the degree of formality with which the questions are phrased?
Of the respondent's attitude toward the imagined cost of the
research? This search for specific features of the project con-
verts research into the dynamic process of discovering the way
people impose meaning on their environments.

Dishonesty

When the teachers' questionnaires returned from the
field, our small team was suddenly enlarged by additional persons with new tasks. The pencil scratches the teachers made in
the questionnaire booklets had to be transferred to coding
sheets and then punched onto computer cards. Even though all
the questions had been composed in terms of their future coda-
bility and the coding scheme was printed in the booklet itself, I
quickly learned that numerous complications arise when trans-
ferring responses into IBM card holes. This transfer process,
which merely translated one language into another, consumed
much energy, time, and money. It was also one of the most disillusioning aspects of the study. Several individuals were hired
temporarily to help in the massive job of handling the 2,200
questionnaires. These individuals had no commitment to the
project whatsoever. They had no sense of the project's history,
no appreciation of its goals, no personal stake in its success.
Compared with them, I considered myself highly dedicated to
the project. To make their dull jobs less boring, the coders engaged in a lot of joking and humor, with much of the laughter
directed at the respondents and their "absurd," "deviant," or
"contradictory" answers. The respondents became objects, de-
serving as little respect as the crumpled pamphlets that represented them.

Worse yet, in my view, was the coders' desire to "save the
sample," that is, to fill in missing answers so that the questionnaire could be included. If a respondent did not indicate race,
for example, coders took it upon themselves to skim the questionnaire, guess the race, and fill in the blank. Not only does

this practice blatantly distort the data, but it disregards the intention of *not* indicating one's race on a questionnaire. Through the joking banter and the filling-in-the-blanks game, coders used their own common sense to construct plausible identities for the respondents. From the data the respondent did provide, coders inferred sex, race, school level taught, and more. The interaction of the coders had the quality of a jury deliberation with the verdict in this case being the respondent's identity features. The coders' behavior puzzled me, particularly when I did not share their inferences. But even more painful was the dissonance I increasingly sensed between the attributed and experienced meaningfulness of this study. Whereas until this stage I had thought, "If it does not mean anything, at least it is accurate within its own definitions," I now saw that "the data are not even clean!" With each passing day, we seemed to be moving further and further from the reality we were supposedly studying.

In addition to filling in the blanks and reconstructing respondents from inferences, many other coding decisions altered the responses—decisions that reflected the coders' image of the respondents. Interpretations, discretion, discounting, and other personal judgments were imposed on the supposedly objective statistical data. Our whole set of amassed materials, the questionnaire itself with its particular questions, and the data punched onto the cards reflected the researchers and the research process more than the world of the teachers in Washington, D.C.—a world that we never saw.

The coders were not acting out of malice but out of practical necessity. They had no time to ponder meanings; they had to make decisions. It was their self-assigned task to resolve the ambiguity of experienced reality as expressed in the questionnaires in order to produce unambiguous scores. Ambivalence is not accommodated in survey questionnaire studies but is labeled "inconsistency" and discarded. The coder's transformational work is functionally similar to other relatively low-level work that translates into practical terms the less pragmatic notions of higher-level persons in the organization. For example, the task of aides in a psychiatric hospital is to implement the treatment recommended by psychiatrists, but the aides must also cope with the patients' daily problems. Aides find a way of interpreting theory to fit practical necessities. The difficulties of this translation are compounded by the discrepancy between the upper echelon's ideal and the implementer's recognition of limits. When there is insufficient communication upwards and inadequate power to protest the order openly, coders (or aides) engage in extricating behavior to lift them out of the scene, such as doing minimal although generally appropriate work. X tells Y to do something to Z but is not present to realize that the order is impossible. Y does not agree with X but is relatively powerless. Deviant behavior occurs that saves Y's self-esteem and avoids a confrontation with X. Since Y's behavior is undetected, it appears secretly powerful, particularly against Z, the ready target for Y's frustrations.

The year preceding the teacher study, Julius Roth (1966) published cases of research assistants reporting on their work. In his cases, as in our project, deviant behavior helped the assistants to transcend their alienation. I was amazed to read that this coping behavior took the same form among Roth's low-level researchers as it did in our study. The cases he presented are of a paid observer, a coder, and an interviewer. For the sake of comparison with the coder behavior in our project, the following is an excerpt from the coder's statement in the Roth (1966, pp. 190-191) article:

> There didn't appear to be too much concern with the possibility of inconsistency among the coders. Various coders used various methods to determine the code of an open-ended question. Toward the end of the coding process, expediency became the keynote, leading to gross inconsistencies. The most expedient method of coding a few of the trickier questions was to simply put down a "4" (this was the middle-of-the-road response on the one question that had the most variation). If the responses were not clear or comprehensible, the coder had two alternatives: on the one hand, he could puzzle over it and ask for other opinions or, on the other hand, he could assign it an arbitrary number or forget the response en-

tirely. In the beginning, many of us, when in doubt about a response, would ask the supervisor or his assistant. After a while, I noted that quite often the supervisor's opinion would differ when asked twice about the same response and he would often give two different answers in response to the same question. One way the supervisor and his assistant would determine the correct coding for an answer would be to look at the respondent's previous answers and deduce what they should have answered— thereby coding on *what they thought the respondent should have answered,* not on the basis of what he *did* answer. . . . I feel questionnaires should be used to see *if* consistent patterns of views exist among respondents and it is not the coder's job to put them in if the respondents fail to. A few [of the coders] would discuss the respondent's answers as if they took one political or social standpoint as an indicator of what all the responses should be. They would laugh over an inconsistency in the respondent's replies, feeling that one answer did not fit the previous pattern of responses. The final problem leading to gross inconsistency was the factor of time. The supervisor made it clear that the code sheets had to be in to the computation center by Saturday. This meant that on Saturday morning and early afternoon the aim of the coders was to code the questionnaires as quickly as possible, and the crucial factor was speed, even at the expense of accuracy. The underlying thought was that there were so many questionnaires coded already (that were assumed to be coded consistently and correctly) that the inconsistencies in the remainder would balance themselves out and be of no great importance. I found myself adapting to this way of thinking, and after spending two or three hours there on Saturday morning, I joined in the game of "let's get these damn things out already." It did indeed become a game, with the shibboleth, for one particularly vague and troublesome question, "Oh, give it a four."

The similarities between the coder behavior in the Roth article and in the teachers study include saving the data by filling in the blanks, resolving ambiguities and making the work

easier, constructing an image of a respondent and molding the
questionnaire in that image, mocking the respondents, having
contempt for the questionnaire, being concerned with the deadline rather than the work itself, being concerned with technicali-
ties rather than meaning, being alienated from higher-level
personnel, establishing cohesiveness among low-level personnel,
and having an interest in getting the job done rather than in
doing the job well. C. Wright Mills (1959, p. 205) summed up
the issue succinctly: "Now I do not like to do empirical work if
I can possibly avoid it. If one has no staff, it is a great deal of
trouble; if one does employ a staff, then the staff is often even
more trouble." Coder deviance is coping behavior that is systematically generated from conflict-ridden tasks. Roth's coders
led him to conclude that the coping behavior that decreases a
study's validity is reduced more effectively by modifying the
grounds of alienation rather than improving the policing. If the
research activities and the research organization were designed
to utilize the workers' curiosity and creativity rather than their
mechanical uniformity, then such behavior would be minimized. "If it were possible to structure the research activities so
that they would provide payoffs for all concerned, then the
organization would operate primarily in terms of voluntary
cooperation, and those with the chief administrative responsibilities would be relieved to a large extent from the tasks of detailed supervision, inspection and policing of activities" (Whyte,
1969b, p. 36).

Once the cards were punched (an activity in which discretion was exercised and simple errors committed) the fun began
for the statistically oriented researchers. Our cards waited on-
line with thousands of cards from other projects, and then,
since we were able to pay, they were fed into a computer,
according to programs that we had requested from the professional programmers of the bureau's permanent staff. Tests of
significance were adopted from standard statistical methodology. We used these tests automatically (Skipper, Guenther, and
Nuss, 1967). All 0.05 correlations appeared on the computer
printout with an asterisk. Whenever one did appear, we set to
work to explain the correlation. Never did we ask how much

variance was accounted for, because our success was defined in terms of these asterisks. Success was determined by statistical significance, not by understanding or accuracy of our explanation. The technology of research overshadowed both the human subjects and the subject matter. Each asterisk we produced reinforced our sense of doing something significant, important, and scientific.

From my perspective, this search for asterisks and explanations of correlations was a fishing expedition in a lake that we had stocked ourselves. When we had an idea for a correlation, we ordered a program to retrieve the data, studied the computer printout, had another idea, and ordered more printouts. We began with a simple plan to determine the basic characteristics of our sample. Immediately, however, we encountered problems, few of which were interesting but all of which buttressed my dismay. For example, for some reason our sample contained more teachers than were registered in the selected schools we studied. Such a discovery is not so unusual, and researchers are now suggesting the double-checking of raw, tabulated, and keypunched data: "Comparisons of such information items as date of birth and age or highest degree and years of education are quite often most illuminating and indicative of data quality" (Bryant and Wortman, 1978). We explained away all these problems rather than question what they might mean or if they invalidated the study. Our investment was too great to undermine our work at that late date. But more than that, we were enacting a research ritual whose very nature prevented us from questioning our behavior.

With the arrival of each new computer printout, there was an air of suspense. We developed an unconscious dependency on the computer's magic to do our thinking, to explain and almost *do* the research. We were its tools rather than vice versa. But the computer could only correlate race with age with sex with experience with attitudes with . . . with . . . , ad infinitum. In his critical, provocative thesis that explicates the process of "victim-blaming," Ryan (1971, pp. 44, 47) criticizes the well-known, massive, and expensive Coleman Report for precisely this kind of "conclusion": "His data are correlational;

he reports only what characteristics of children and schools go along with, are found together with, differing levels of achievement. . . . His findings cast little light on the causes of differing levels of achievement. . . . [He] has managed to disguise as findings what amounts to nothing more than an enormously inflated statement of the problem!" These correlations were based on comparing aggregates that were not actual groups but were created by the administration of the questionnaire. These aggregates were not natural groups and therefore should not have been considered sociological entities. In survey research "the individual remains the unit of analysis. No matter how complex the analysis, how numerous the correlations, the studies focus on individuals as separate and independent units. . . . As a result, the kinds of substantive problems on which such research focuses tend to be problems of 'aggregate psychology,' that is within-individual problems, and never problems concerned with relations between people" (Coleman, 1958, p. 28). The questionnaire is addressed to individuals and inferences are made as to how the group would respond and behave.

From the correlations that the computer delivered, we spun plausible explanations and began to believe in them. We constructed a reality peopled by individuals who could not negotiate with us. No longer did we deal with teachers as individuals; at this stage we spoke in terms of groups—"black female elementary schoolteachers tend to view Ku Klux Klan members . . . ." Although my project directors' statistical skills mystified me at first, I was quickly able to pick up their pattern of scanning printouts for trends or deviant cases. As my mastery of this demanding task increased, I, too, became more interested in technique than in meaning. Our ease in using relevant statistical procedures deceived us into believing we had mastered reality.

A low point in this excitement of technical mastery was my chance discovery that one or two printouts were filled with errors that reflected mechanical problems. How many of our other analyses were based merely and perhaps erroneously on what the computer produced rather than on what the teachers wrote, let alone what they wanted us to think or what they actually believed? After that blow to my admiration for the computer, I greeted each new printout with more suspicion than awe. After taking so many steps away from the reality we were supposedly studying, I could give these tables little credence. Since these flaws did not distress the project directors, who were content to rectify errors that they caught while treating all the other data as accurate, it became clear that our study did not have to succeed and that there was no way of determining success. Although there might have been a standard of elegance or clarity in exposition, there was no way of being wrong. Even if the data did not reach the accepted level of statistical significance, we did not have to say that anything was wrong. We could still make comparative statements or proclaim that no differences existed among these groups with respect to these variables. Observing the process of data analysis led me to conclude that anything can be considered data and any data can be interpreted. The mere ability to devise an interpretation is the criterion of success. As long as research is designed to create data, as long as there are no clear-cut differences between data and real findings, and as long as having findings is the criterion of a successfully completed research project, then it is nearly impossible to fail. The only failure would be to not write the report. Our commitment was to getting the job done, and since we were not accountable for anything else, we persisted with this limited criterion of success. The inability to fail threw doubt on the possibility of success, a condition characteristic of rituals. We employed no pragmatic or action-based test of our results but used merely the criterion of making some sense of our figures, which is dangerously similar to mere confirmation of our expectations.

I became deeply distressed over the energy I had expended in the project and the prospect of continuing to invest months of work in the study of people with whom I would never come into contact or understand. The paradox of science jarred my consciousness: the more intimate one's acquaintance with a subject, the less scientific one's knowledge; the more detached the observer, the more credible the knowledge. Experiential knowledge is discounted as "mere subjectivity," whereas lack of experiential knowledge is almost an index of respectability. Human contact and influence are labeled "contamination." In this age, when the senses and reason are mistrusted in favor of statistics and technology, deep personal immersion as a method of study is either heresy or at least profoundly suspect. There is an inverse relationship between distance from the subject matter and the academic community's trust of results. Sociologists run from social reality to embrace truth; they do not want to get their hands dirty by plunging into the buzzing, blooming confusion; their professional prestige is a function of their ability to provide unexpected, distinctive, noncommonsensical theories, for otherwise their notions could not be differentiated from those of Everyman. Sociologists pride themselves on not being naive, on not accepting their perceptions as truth, on relying only on hard data despite their questionable manufacture. Sociologists do not actually mistrust their perceptions as much as they rely on their professional vocabulary to define reality. They debunk the apparent social facade by positing another latent reality. They remove themselves from the flow of life to stay immune from commonsense explanations. The optional venture "into the field" occurs early in a career before the student becomes entrenched in the norms and life-style of the academic world.

Experience has fallen into disrepute. Sociologists have designed their own alienation while decrying the alienation of contemporary society. Perhaps the alienation they see is a reflection of their alienated perspective on the world, a world in which they never fully arrive but only peer at from a great distance, which they tabulate but do not appreciate except as nonprofessionals. What kind of a profession is this after all?

Peter Berger (1963, pp. 9-10) poignantly sketched the relationship between the kinds of studies that sociologists produce and the kind of social world they inhabit:

> A goodly part of the sociological enterprise in this country continues to consist of little studies of obscure fragments of social life, irrelevant to any broader the-

oretical concern. . . . The political and economic structure of American academic life encourages this pattern. . . . Colleges and universities are normally administered by very busy people with little time or inclination
to delve into the esoterica produced by their scholarly
employees. . . . They cannot be expected to read what
their professors write, having no time for such activities
and, especially in the more technical disciplines, lacking
the necessary qualifications to judge the material. The
opinions of immediate colleagues of the professors in
question are suspect a priori, the normal academic institution being a jungle of bitter warfare between faculty fac-
tions, none of which can be relied upon for an objective
judgment of members of either his own or an opposing
group. To ask the views of students would be even more
of an uncertain procedure. . . . [Thus they] fall back on
the criterion of productivity as used in the business
world. . . . This forces scholars to concentrate on work
that can easily and speedily be converted into a respectable little article likely to be accepted for publication in a
professional journal. For sociologists this means some little empirical study of a narrowly confined topic . . . [but
since the] ritual requirements are so well known to all
concerned . . . the sensible person reads the sociological
journals mainly for the book reviews and the obituaries,
and goes to sociological meetings only if he is looking for
a job or has other intrigues to carry on.

Berger's sociology of knowledge approach to the sociologist's consciousness fits the model of reflexive sociology that
Goulder (1970) advocated. Reflexive sociology is possible only
after transcending the normative alienation of mainstream
sociological work. In this cycle of dubious work described by
Berger, studies are often produced in order to be tallied by ad-
ministrators; their publication is delayed and typically un-
assimilated by colleagues. Where is the substance beneath these
forms? The fragmented world of the sociologists' imagination is
a partial product of the kind of labor they engage in. Since their
labor is counted in units of fragmented articles, they ponder
larger issues at their risk and on their own time. People in the

sociologists' universe are too busy managing their careers to stop and explore ways of asking important questions or finding new ways of gathering knowledge. Although Gostkowski (1974, p. 23) presents a compendium of suggestions for the "empirical humanization of mass surveys," he despondently acknowledges that his proposals

> will probably not meet with any objections. . . . In real life . . . researchers [will not be] implementing the postulates of the humanization of survey-based sociological research . . . [because of] certain criteria of evaluation of research achievement . . . [namely] the quantity of published works and articles—and not their quality. . . . [The] bureaucratic and superficial quantitative approach in the sphere of institutionalized procedures of evaluation of scientific achievement is the *main ally* of methodological shortcomings of survey-based works in sociology.

Demands of production (such as time allocation) govern the methods used to acquire knowledge. Since time is money and the clock is always ticking against the worker, time-consuming, exploratory studies have no place in American sociology. Studies must be accommodated to fast-clipped, complex schedules. If research topics must be collapsed into their least time-consuming dimension, then the following model emerges: Ask some people a question, give them a list of answers from which to choose, count the responses, and make inferences based on statistical manipulations. Ironically, in the long run this method consumes more time in data manufacture and inspection than does observation in a field setting from which much can be learned quickly. If a picture is worth a thousand words, how much is observation of an ongoing event worth?

The distrust of experience in social science is closely linked with the issue of bias, because the knowledge derived from experience is supposed to be distorted by selectivity and vested interest. This tradition derives from Weber's notion that sociologists' work should be removed from their values and personal preferences and guided only by the canons of scientific procedure. This distinction between the experience-based or value-laden sociological investigation and one that claims to be strictly scientific is greatly overdrawn. Personal values creep into all the components that are supposed to be regulated only by scientific procedure, from the definition of the research topic to the preparation of the report. The sociologist guards against this intrusion and usually believes with Durkheim that sociology must be an utterly objective science:

> Durkheim's point of departure is that we do not know, in the scientific sense of the word *know*, what the social phenomena which surround us, among which we live, and, it can even be said, *which* we live, really are. . . . This does not mean that we do not have some idea of them; but precisely because we have a vague and confused idea of them, it is important to regard social facts as things, i.e., to rid ourselves of the preconceptions and prejudices which incapacitate us when we try to know social facts scientifically. . . . Precisely because we have the illusion of knowing social realities, it is important that we realize that they are not immediately known to us. . . . [There is] a misconception that we can understand social phenomena in terms of the meaning we spontaneously assign to them, (but) the true meaning of these phenomena can only be discovered by an exploration that is objective and scientific [Aron, 1970, pp. 69-70].

In other words, since our knowledge gained from the experience of everyday life is "vague and confused," the purpose of science is to demonstrate the paucity and erroneous nature of that knowledge. Reliance on our experience, it is claimed, is an obstacle in the scientific pursuit of knowledge. Similarly, we do not understand the world in which we live; our experience is erroneous.

Durkheim's paradigm of the empirical method enabled him to collect what he considered value-free data that rendered his biases irrelevant and forced appropriate interpretations. This heritage has led to an unhealthy mistrust of our selves, our values, and our experience, while the demand for increased production of knowledge remains high. In this paradigm of the definition of knowledge which is socially organized to produce alienated labor, research can easily become a mere means to an end (money, academic advancement, or professional prestige) rather than being concerned with intrinsic ends.

If personal experience and values invalidate research, it follows that sociologists should study only that in which they have no possible interest (as in the teachers study). But we know that laborers who perform alienated work also create shoddy products, commit acts of sabotage, and become dessicated. The self becomes dehumanized, mechanized, and remote. Practical concerns and our unrecognized value of being value-free in the teachers study kept us from looking at the teachers' lived world, from drawing on our own experience, from making judgments, and from making suggestions to help the school system. Our reliance on numbers consumed our energy. The tension between the "ideal" of experience denial or value freedom and the impossibility of achieving that ideal produces deviousness, ritualism, and evasiveness within the research process. Polanyi (1958) demonstrated that the physical sciences, too, are not value-free but that subjectivity is an important element of each stage of the scientific process. If subjectivity is a factor despite the ideal, it would seem rational to encourage the social or physical scientist to utilize subjectivity to enhance the study rather than to deny its intrusion.

The underlying value of empirical sociology implies the control and destruction of the sociologist as a human being. Sociologists are supposed to control their desires and values, to suppress and repudiate their experience. In this framework sociologists destroy their uniqueness for the sake of replicability; that is, any sociologist should be able to produce the same results as any other. In other words, the goal of scientific methodology is to deny the researcher's and subject's uniqueness so that they may be replaceable and interchangeable as in modern forms of bureaucracy or production. In Maslow's (1966, pp. 10-11) view, the dehumanization of the scientist is matched by the dehumanization of the subject:

> Practically all scientists proceed on the tacit or explicit assumption that one studies classes or groups of

things, not single things. . . . Each one is treated as a sample of a species or of a class, and therefore as interchangeable. . . . Any one sample is just that, a sample; it is not
itself. It stands for something. It is anonymous; expendable, not unique, not sacred, not sine qua non; it has no
proper name all its own and is not worthwhile in itself as
a particular instance. It is interesting only insofar as it
represents something other than itself.

Maslow rejected this model for the study of persons and relationships. Instead he recognized his unique contribution to his
studies and the necessity of approaching the people he studied
as the "unique and peculiar, the sole member of his class." He
suggested that if you are to study something, then *you* must be
there, involved, alive, invested in the study.

In physical and social science, the value of self-control in
suppressing biases is coupled with the fantasy of control over
the other (the subject). The wish is for reality to stand still long
enough for the scientists to capture it. "Laboratory experiments
are not designed, McGuire (1973) argues, to test carefully formulated, theoretical hypotheses but to demonstrate the experimenter's ability as a stage manager. . . . 'What the experiment
tests is not whether the hypothesis is true but whether the experimenter is a sufficiently ingenious stage manager to produce
in the laboratory conditions which demonstrate that an obviously true hypothesis is correct' " (Mishler, 1978, p. 10). This
wish for control steers social scientists away from studying
action over time or the ambiguity of change. The world nevertheless refuses to stand still, refuses to accommodate completely to science, although modern forms of bureaucratic
organization have almost succeeded in making most life processes conform to the needs of data gathering and processing.

Respondents answer questionnaires with dubious seriousness and respect, responding frequently to the interviewer's
characteristics rather than to the schedule. Respondents sometimes "contaminate" the field by telling prospective interviewees what to expect; they sometimes refuse to participate or
attempt to manipulate the interviewer. In other words, the subjects' uncanny ability to continue to act like human beings can

interfere significantly with the research design. These methods do not capture their subjects' humanness, nor do they tap that of the sociologists, for to do so would destroy the myth of a generalizable, value-free social science in which findings were free of specific contexts, of either the theory studied or the study process. The process of professionalization, moving in the opposite direction, attempts to convince students that the sociological perspective is unique, powerful, and distinct from everyday understanding. The pursuit of conformity within the scientific model as a guard against idiosyncracy becomes an end in itself, leading to ritualism and the suppression of individuality. "I am sure that you have all had the experience of having students and younger colleagues complain about how they can't find methods to study the problems in which they are interested. All too often we help them reshape their problems so that available traditional methods can be used. In the process, the original problem is often lost. . . . Science . . . need not add to other alienating forces in the society" (Mishler, 1978, p. 28).

The social science model has become codified into a set of rules that are revered unscientifically. Other models such as philosophy or art rescind the claim of generalizability as they lift the controls from the researcher and the subject. These models do not attempt to inhibit the researcher's creative powers, but rather draw on the insights of human beings who seek to understand themselves as they explore problems. The scientific model depends on selective inattention to all that is not measured. The teachers study presented me with a model of research without confrontation, contact, or passion, a model increasingly dissatisfying.

Disillusionment

Despite my increasing alienation, I continued to work on the project for several reasons: I had been involved in the study since its inception; I was caught up in the momentum of deadlines; I felt an obligation to the directors; I needed the money; I wanted to continue learning about the study process and the source of my alienation; and my dissatisfactions were incoherent and I was therefore unable to justify my departure. In this late stage my gravest concern was our lack of discovery. We reinforced common knowledge without demonstrating that our prodigious efforts produced new knowledge. The discovery of the obvious raised serious questions about the project's value. Was sociology the discovery of the obvious? Our findings can be interpreted differently, however, by apologists of such research rituals: The reaffirmation of the obvious implied that our questionnaire and interpretations were accurate reflections of reality. In this sense our study was validated. As a counterargument, nevertheless, we could be accused of building our stereotypic views into the study to such an extent that we never quite transcended them.

The steady flow of obvious conclusions led me to seek and seize the surprising case. This feature of the phenomenology of conducting survey research most likely influenced the project director to recommend that the Washington, D.C., school board observe its deviant 'schools (in the sense that some schools defied common expectations) to discern ways in which a school overcomes an environmental pull toward failure.

My alienation increased when outsiders joined our project for a few weeks to use our data for a secondary analysis. First, I doubted that they could analyze our data in a valid manner unless they understood the context of their production, but this context had not been recognized, analyzed, or conveyed to anyone. These outsiders were unaware of our procedures and oblivious to all the problems, defects, and irregularities I had observed. Instead, they accepted the data at face value, undisturbed by the issues I have raised. Second, I believed the teachers were being used once again in ever distant ways to enhance the goals of others. Was it not unjust that their data were being restudied without their consent or knowledge?

A final blow came from Washington. Several weeks *before* our study was completed, the school board decided to implement a new educational policy, which our study was originally to develop. The decision had been made without reference to or help from our project. The ritualistic intent of the sponsor mirrored that of the researchers (see also Berk, 1977). James

Davis (1964, p. 227) reports a similar experience of policy being decided before his findings were reported: "The Fund for Adult Education received the report and must have been clairvoyant, for they gave Great Books a large-scale grant about a month before they saw the results, such being the crucial role that social research plays in decision-making in Modern America." Obviously these studies are undertaken for purposes other than producing findings. Absurdity compounded absurdity. I learned that the discrepancy between the commitment to funding sponsors and their commitment is the source of much frustration and miscommunication between researchers and sponsoring organizations. Despite this blow, we were so embedded in our work momentum and time schedule that we never considered quitting. We, too, were concerned with completion rather than implementation; the report had become an end in itself devoid of other meaning or uses. The completion of this task with its own time structure and life almost completely divorced from the events in the Washington, D.C., school system propelled us forward.

Writing the manuscript was the final stage. This activity was performed in bits and pieces; each set of computer printouts was translated into verbiage; no overarching idea was developed in the report. The linguistic mode was technical precision mirroring the assumed precision of the data. The director used a general scheme of presenting the teachers in terms of race, sex, age, and income, followed by the attitudes of several subgroups to racial, educational, or community problems. The findings were always presented in comparative terms, such as group X was more something than group Y. The report was divided in two sections: the first concerned teachers, the second concerned schools. I quickly grasped the technique and could easily create a topic on the basis of one or two questions in the questionnaire. I would then write out the relevant correlations in a paragraph or two and claim that these were findings. Since research assistants can easily perform this job at the culmination of a project, they are frustrated if not considered coauthors of the resulting manuscript. The question arises in the research hierarchy as in any other work hierarchy as to who has done the work and who deserves the credit (that is, profit).

Our project's final manuscript should be seen as a report about the questionnaire rather than a report about the teachers' perceptions of their lives and jobs. Our language is so careful that it becomes awkward in its disclaimer of knowing anything other than responses to the questions we posed. The stiff style is also a result of the content: We translated numbers into words rather than writing an account of the teachers. Theoretically, we could have presented only tables and omitted all language, but our verbiage served to read the tables for the reader. The report was a straightforward presentation of the raw data with some translation. Did our hesitancy reflect a lack of sociological imagination to explore the meaning of what we had asked the teachers, or were we instead acting appropriately by not creating the appearance of meaning where there was none?

The codirectors knew our translations were deadly to read, as they periodically tried to liven the "sociologese" by injecting statements about what the data might mean. This liberation from strict statistical interpretation spoke to the readers' probable need to make a composite from the fragments. What was the relation between the tables and reality and how should tables be bridged to create a whole? Phenomenologically, readers were left to construct the whole by filling in the gaps with their own imagination, just as the coders had done. To omit detailed description, therefore, was to invite readers to exercise their own preconceptions and prejudices in the understanding of quantitative research results. The results, therefore, reflected the researchers, the questionnaire, and the readers rather than the people questioned.

This study did not presume to be more than instant research, a one-shot deal produced by professional survey manufacturers for the bountiful federal government. Instant research is a contradiction in terms, a sham and pretense at research, which requires reflection and care. Levine (1977, p. 1) put the issue more mildly: "Contract research differs considerably from grant research in that the scientific investigator's scientific freedom and independence not only are not guaranteed, but are not even desired by the government agency letting the contract. . . . It goes, however, by the name of research, whatever its uses, and thus reflects on all of us." Time is a significant component of the phenomenology of researching. It is either something to be rushed through or an envelope of creativity. My experience on the teachers project revealed the dangers of adjusting the research method to the schedule devised by outside agents rather than to the natural, unpredictable processes of discovery.

My work on this project demonstrated the paradoxical relation between interest and research. Those who believe (subjectively) that objectivity is furthered by the sociologist's detachment consider interests detrimental. Values are assumed to bias the perspective of the knower on the known. However, we might also ask about the detrimental effects of researchers' *lack of interest*. A court judge should be disinterested in a case without being uninterested. This norm of disinterest will likely be corrupted into a lack of interest in instant contract research in contrast with researcher-generated projects. The driving, compelling need to find answers to the researcher's questions provides a productive condition for unprejudiced research unlike the remoteness and detachment that go hand in hand with noninvolvement. The study will suffer if the researchers do not care personally about the results, just as a product's quality diminishes with the worker's lack of incentive.

If researchers are to care, they must work on issues of personal concern. In our study the results were personally inconsequential: It made no difference to us that certain correlations were significant, that certain trends developed while others did not, that certain policies were appealing while others were disliked by the respondents. How would the research process have differed had we been accountable for improving the school system on the basis of our policy recommendations? How would our study have changed if we had to justify our activities to the teachers?

At the completion of our study, I knew little more about the teachers of the Washington, D.C., school system than I did before the study. I was unable to make policy recommendations, since the whole did not emerge from its tiny parts, and none of the tiny parts were meaningful from my point of view. The directors, notwithstanding, made two major recommendations: (1) The school system should examine and follow its own unusual cases (for example, an excellent school in a depressed neighborhood could be a more useful success model than examples from other states), and (2) an intensive study should be done on these deviant cases. Denzin (1970a) noted that the basis for the frequent call for more research found at the end of many reports is the shortsightedness of the survey itself. Since "few investigators think beyond their own work to future studies . . . the analyst often concludes that his survey has raised more problems than can be answered" (Denzin, 1970a, p. 174). The request for additional research is typical in static research designs, such as survey questionnaires, which cannot be modified retrospectively to investigate emergent hypotheses. The parameters of a survey are defined when least is known about the subject matter, that is, before the study has been undertaken. Only after data collection is under way, however, are the important questions unearthed, but at that late date the feeble suggestion can only be made that those questions be investigated in future research projects. Since much research is not that of cumulation or replication, however, it is unlikely that these requests for more research will be heeded. Researchers also urge more research in order to further their livelihood and protect their interests, just as tobacco growers urge us to continue to smoke. Which social science report calls for the phasing out of research in a particular area? The investment of energy, time, and money leads to justifying these expenditures by insisting the rituals be continued.

My intent is not to criticize the personalities or capabilities of the project directors, but rather to uncover the assumptions underpinning this particular research project and the manner in which it was organized and in which it elicited patterned ways of defining the situation. I recognize that my position as a research assistant was conducive to developing a critical perspective. Because research assistants are not held responsible for carrying through a research project, they feel free to criticize it. They are employed typically on large projects that require the work of many hands or on small projects in which the director is too busy to assume complete responsibility. Research assistants are by definition less well trained, less experienced, less advanced in their careers, and usually younger than their directors. For these reasons, research assistants are less concerned with the successful completion of the project or careful about its rigorous administration. Only under unusual circumstances will their definition of the project coincide with the perception of the director; conflict is likely. The possible targets of the conflict are the other team personnel, the research assistant's self, research in general, the particular research project, or an outside object. To this extent, therefore, my critique reflects my project role, age, experience and cultural environment.

While participating in the study, I focused on two scapegoats for my disillusionment: First was the project directors themselves, whose attitudes seemed unimaginative, apolitical, and uninformed; second was the methodology. Following my examination of the researcher-at-work literature and unsystematic, informal interviewing of other members of survey research teams, I have abandoned concern with the first target and focused entirely on the second. I have come to believe that the method presupposes a set of assumptions and creates a social psychological process that permits and reinforces the kind of work I witnessed and engaged in. The method or research design would likely seriously limit creativity of any sociologist who strictly adhered to it.

Perhaps all research projects terminate with some pangs of regret among the team. With hindsight, flaws and gaps in the acquired knowledge are uncovered no matter which method was used. But in the research project described here, the backward glance was particularly frustrating. Not only did I recognize that we had not asked meaningful questions, but the teachers had been prevented from communicating with us. At the end of the study, we had statistically manipulated forced-choice answers to questions asked in a vacuum. My work in this project placed me, or encouraged me to place myself, in a double bind. We worked very hard to create a product that was obsolete before completion, that was not grounded in reality, and that no one wanted. We labored in a mirage of learning whose only tangible products were a report, IBM cards, printout sheets, and paychecks. I tried to pretend that we were actually trying to learn something as my training had taught me, but the academic description of research clashed with my actual experience, just as in a double bind the victims must avow a definition of the situation discrepant with their experience. Similarly, I was unable to communicate. With whom should I have spoken about this disillusionment? My loyalty to the research team inhibited me from asking others if they concurred with my suspicion that this research was a sham. With such little experience, could I trust my own perceptions? The actions of the other team members did not seem to indicate that my alienation was shared. Before friends or teachers, I would be ashamed to admit all the time and energy I expended in alienating work if I planned to continue. These inhibiting forces locked me into the conflict between what the profession I was attempting to enter defined as real and what personal experience had shown. At the end of this journey, the choice remained to accept this mainstream work or to search for alternative methods based on alternative assumptions. A way of doing sociology was needed in which the objections to this experience could lead to a new foundation. I wanted to do a kind of sociology that began at the experiencing self and slowly developed from the firm, solid base of actual, personal, undeniably experienced situations and sentiments.

My work on the teachers study has become a private symbol of a negative image of sociology. It represents the rejected past, which in the process of being rejected released creative energy to seek new methods and certainties to fill the resulting void. Because my rejection of this prototype was confirmed by my graduate school environment, my criticism crystallized and led to projects using a different research method. In this way rejection became a positive source of growth.

There appear to be two ways of advancing a field of study: The first is the traditional mode of accumulation or extension within the framework of previous discoveries; the second is advancement by metacommunication, or analysis of the very framework in which existing knowledge has been accumulated. Critical self-consciousness about the activities labeled research, reflection about the epistemological status of truth claims, and moral assessment of the value of sociological projects lead to breaching the confines of established ways. Knowledge can be extended either by asking more questions within a framework or by asking questions about that framework, thereby reducing its possible constriction of thought. The spiral of potential metacommunication is endless: Frameworks encompassing frameworks encompassing frameworks propel the mind into a bog of relativism. Applied without limit, this process is as unproductive as not analyzing the assumptions underlying one's method at all. Short of these extremes, however, is a broad range of questions about the meaning of the sociologist's activities for others, the sociological nature of sociological work, and the contrast between sociological and other ways of knowing.

What began as a private defense against the dissonance between the ideal and the real in the teachers study became a personally useful educational tool. This phenomenological stance toward my experience allowed me to fuse cognition, interaction, action, and unconscious processes for the sake of understanding. I discovered the significance of asking first-order questions in a substantive area while at the same time asking second-order questions about the study itself. This approach combined intensive self-consciousness, critical awareness of the method used, and exploration of the substantive issues. The findings of such an approach would be presented in three categories: description of and discoveries about the self, the method, and the substantive questions. My goals for any search for knowledge (research) became tripartite: insights into *the person, the problem,* and *the method.* Since each is a component of the study, each should be a component of the product. Each reflexive study is an occasion for personal growth, potential illumination of existent or new methods, and presentation of new conceptual frameworks, information, theories, or correlations.

The final task of an ideal study would be to interrelate the three components: For example, how do the substantive findings relate to the investigator and the conditions of investigation? With this kind of information we could explore the relation between a particular account and a particular researcher, so that the relationship between the sociologist's and the subject's perceptions could be understood. "The account which the agent gives of the intentions and goals implied by his behavior is not the only account which it is possible to give; and there are some awkward questions to be asked about the relationship of two different accounts, say the agent's and the social scientist's" (Ryan, 1970, p. 17). The increasing recognition that the sociologist's perspective is one of many and is grounded in a particular set of circumstances deflates the pretentious social science claim that its hard data "tell it as it is." Introducing the tripartite model serves to rehumanize sociology by bringing the researcher's consciousness into the arena as one element of the context of research. Different products and perceptions can be evaluated in more finely grained contexts. In the following chapters, two additional research projects are described in which I used this framework to analyze my struggle with these problems and to resolve them.

CHAPTER 3

Dilemmas of Participant Observation

The Researcher of This Project

This second case study deals directly with the relations between person, problem, and method and represents an experientially defined second phase of my socialization process. For ease in presentation, the discussions of person, problem, and method are separated, although they constantly interact. The person undertaking this research project was a graduate student enrolled in a particular school of sociology; the problem studied was a feature of patient life in a mental hospital; and the method used was participant observation. All three factors had bearing on one another. The analysis of this participant observation study is concerned with its *experienced* dimensions in contrast with its idealized or generalized description. Through

126

experiential analysis, untreated features of the participant observation research process are uncovered. Instead of attempting a comprehensive analysis of this method, my focus is on its dilemmas and value as an opportunity for self-analysis. The substantive problem of this study is mentioned in passing where relevant.

My hope is that by vividly describing and accurately labeling these blocks and dilemmas, I will assist others in confronting them effectively and perhaps in discoursing more. Although researchers must learn from their own experience, our shared discipline-culture of sociology should provide published warnings so that some difficulties could be avoided merely by reading about them. Miller (1952), for example, wrote of his regret that insufficient fieldwork descriptions prevented his knowing about pitfalls in field research, such as the problem of "overrapport." Although I believe the dilemmas I will discuss are generic to participant observation, some are highlighted or aggravated by the specific fieldwork setting of a mental hospital. Levinson (1957) argues that research in that setting is beset with dilemmas in every stage: problem selection, data gathering, achieving a role, interpreting, writing, and publishing, even if the researcher is a staff member of the hospital. To document the generic nature of the dilemmas, I will refer to published accounts of other researchers' experiences.

I entered a mental hospital as a graduate student interested in carrying out a participant observation study on friendships among patients. I left the hospital eight months later affected by its milieu, its people, and its conflicts. This experience prompted changes in my attitudes toward myself and toward methodology, just as fieldwork had done for Wax (1971, p. 79): "I also had changed, in the sense that by undergoing this gradual process of instruction and resocialization I had found out things about the Japanese Americans and their situation which made it impossible that I ever again approach or talk to them in the way I had approached and talked to them three or four months before. In this sense I had become a different person, a person who could never go back to being what she had been before."

This chapter continues my search for a viable identity as a sociologist after my abandonment of survey research. By tracing the social psychological processes of participant observation research, I hope to illuminate the problematic dynamics.

In the first chapter's discussion of the difference between method as ideal and method as practice, I described how the discrepancy discovered in training can be resolved only by direct experience. In the second chapter I presented the case study of my initial research project, which made me aware of the gap between the ideal and real in social research. By examining my experience, I conceptualized some problematic aspects of that form of research in practice. Continued study of survey research would probably show me that some of these problems are now resolved, that other problems were idiosyncratic, and that survey research can be more sophisticated than its employment in the teachers study. The timing of that experience, however, makes these ameliorations irrelevant. As a formative socialization event, the survey project led me away from further inspection of the method rather than closer to examine its inadequacies. More precisely, this model of sociology caused me to revolt and search for an alternative. I did not want to become the kind of student Znaniecki (1934, p. 234) described:

> The statistical method might be simply dismissed as a scientifically useless, but inoffensive amusement of the type of chess or crossword puzzles, if it were not for the social harm it is actually inflicting. Firmly entrenched in institutions of higher education and even more so in institutions of research, it exercises a highly undesirable influence upon the younger generation of students in sociology and neighboring fields. This influence consists in substituting tabulating technique for intellectual method, and thus eliminating theoretic thinking from the process of scientific research.

Nor did I want to be included among those sociologists characterized by Clinard (1966, p. 405) as lacking firsthand experience:

The sociologist may claim to be an expert on minorities, political sociology, industrial sociology, urban sociology, criminology, mental disorder, social change, or social stratification, with little, if any, firsthand experience with the data. He may never have talked with a lower-class Negro in Harlem or in Mississippi, met politicians, experienced at first hand an industrial plant or a slum, interviewed many delinquents, criminals or mental patients, or, if in social stratification, personally studied individuals from various social classes and occupations.

Just as the "negative" research design became the impetus for exploring methodological alternatives, so, too, did the negative role model in my socialization become the springboard for locating new sources of identification. The socialization process relies on negative as well as positive models, and at this stage my identity was being shaped by rejecting the negative.

The concept of negative role models provides a framework for discussing briefly the problems, conflicts, and identity formation issues in the socialization of sociologists. Feelings of identity originate in the self but are also shaped by others' confirmation of behavior that they consider successfully role related. Some behaviors are more critical than others for communicating that one possesses a certain identity. For me, the significant attribute of sociologists was the adequate performance of sociological research. Therefore, although I had directly observed role models as teachers and indirectly as published authors, only in the survey research project did I have the opportunity to watch a potential role model at work. No matter what the place of my project directors in the sociological profession, for me they were central during my identity formation, especially since one codirector was a woman. These role models, which ideally could have provided an opportunity for identification in the socialization process, became negative role models, and I became a rebel. By the time the survey research project ended, I had already formed a commitment to sociology based on the idealized version presented in the classroom. For this reason, I reacted to the survey project not by abandoning the discipline but by searching for an alternative method. Diesing (1971) has also observed that commitment to discipline is stronger than commitment to method, and that the discipline rather than the method is the source of personal identification. Switching fields is a personal risk, considering the investment in the original identification.

The survey research project became an intellectual and personal puzzle: Was it deviant or representative? In this phase of partial socialization and budding commitment to the discipline, the only method I had actually witnessed troubled me. My youthful enthusiasm as a student led me to believe I could change everything. With this transitional identity of critic, I sought a setting that would fit my needs.

Entering graduate school was an extension of habit and an act of faith. As a creature of academia I could hardly imagine myself functioning in another milieu. Moreover, I refused to accept that sociology depended on the alienation and seeming fraud I had witnessed and experienced. Was it not possible to transcend the ritual and pseudoresearch of massive questionnaires? Were there not other methods useful for explaining social life, and other selves I could develop as a sociologist? Graduate school held the promise of a reference group that would confirm my values and help me formulate the next step.

Brandeis University was my unwittingly fortunate choice. Not only was the faculty in basic agreement concerning the need for alternatives to survey research, but it demonstrated interest in the socialization process of the students. Studies of departments of sociology characterize the Brandeis faculty members as critics of the profession. Friedrichs (1970, p. 127) labeled the work of several of them as "sociology of the prophetic mode." He referred to Everett Hughes (then of Brandeis), who advocates the coupling of the sociological imagination with a utopian one. In Horowitz's (1968) scheme, the faculty of my time would have been labeled "antisociologists," in contrast with the "professionals, the occupationalists, and the unsociologists." In condensed form, Horowitz's anti-sociologist:

1. Is critical of sociology from a perspective outside of sociology, such as the humanities; views sociology as parochial and of questionable value; is philosophical, alienated from sociology, and polemical.
2. Is critical of society as well; is frequently politically radical; is alienated from society; identifies with marginal groups; is deeply committed to social change.
3. Is productive.
4. Proselytizes with views that contrast with those of the "organization men of the field."
5. Is cosmopolitan and aware of and concerned with basic issues rather than transient ones.

The Brandeis antisociologists socialized students into an identification with sociology based on a critique of sociology that verged on rejection. Some of the faculty were severing ties with the discipline and were deeply engaged in developing clinical work or engaging in non-Western religions and consciousness. In addition, many of the faculty deliberately suspended even these concerns as political crises rocked the nation. The values that the faculty communicated to their students might be summarized as follows:

1. A multidisciplinary perspective: Sociology as a discipline must be permeated with history, art, psychiatry, philosophy, and anthropology, among other orientations. Students should be well read in many of these fields.
2. A multifaceted approach to reasoning: Sociological reasoning must build on the evidence of fieldwork, utilize theory, provide examples from history, literature, and phenomenology, and develop a critical perspective.
3. Close interpersonal relations between faculty and students: From these relationships will develop significant research topics reflecting mutual concerns.
4. The personal development of students: Through self-reflection, analysis of their own motivation, involvement, and the exploration of new, even exotic experiences, the students'

personal boundaries will be expanded. Self-motivation and
the ability to rely on one's own initiative are to be encouraged.
5. A critical perspective on formal sociology and an ameliora-
tive relation to society: Applied work is valued and trivial
research rejected.

Brandeis also nurtured one of sociology's public rebels,
Martin Nicolaus, who condemned the profession at an annual
meeting of the American Sociological Association and launched
the short-lived "sociological liberation movement" (Nicolaus,
1968). Some Brandeis students and faculty were active or side-
line supporters of this position.

If Brandeis was a "school of sociology," it could be characterized by the critical examination of the assumptions on
which social institutions, social interaction, and knowledge are
based. By definition, this perspective demystified those assumptions as it exposed them. If this perspective was applied to sociology itself, the student was left with little to take for
granted. Since no single paradigm was urged on students, all
were prodded to discover and form their own.

The transition to graduate school involved a change from
excessive to minimal structure and direction. Sociology became
not a body of knowledge but a debunking perspective that still
remained humanistic. As intellectuals, the faculty were interested, as was I, in changing the definition of sociology and in
creating innovations for teaching procedures, course content,
and research techniques. As individuals and as a group, this
faculty had acquired fame as representatives of nonquantitative
sociological methods, one of which was participant observation.

Participant observation held the promise of answering my
need for direct contact with the subject of study, for natural
interaction rather than instruments as the source of data, for
access to nonverbal communication, for accountability to study
subjects, and for involvement with the significant institutions of
our social order. I sought experiences outside the university for
opportunities to test ideas and interact with other professionals.
Since I was interested primarily in an antidote to my previous

research experience, my substantive research questions were secondary to the objective of learning participant observation. At first glance, participant observation was the ticket to real learning and fascinating places. Subsequent training in this method; an openness to historical, psychological, and political concerns; the almost limitless definition of what constitutes an appropriate sociological research problem; and the interest in fusing knowing with doing crystallized into a new identity available to me as a future sociologist.

Socialization into this new identity was aided by rejecting the former model and by the Brandeis faculty's self-image as underdogs with a cause, or prophets with a message. Our emotionally charged seminars and guest lectures became opportunities for expressing opposition to and transcendence of the "Establishment." As a student searching for a professional identity, I tried to comprehend this model and its requirements. The emphasis on nonauthoritarian teacher-student relationships and respect for individual growth resulted in few demands on students and limited formal instruction. Students were supposed to be independent thinkers, pursuing their projects, conferring with the faculty, engaging in lively seminar discussions, venturing out on their own, and even reversing roles with the faculty from time to time. Although faculty offered guidance in fieldwork when requested, students were primarily on their own to cull the literature for guidelines and attempt to create new knowledge by firsthand investigation of a site. Nader (1970) and Landes (1970) describe similar milieus as appropriate for methodological training in anthropology, while Richardson (1952) advocates a more didactic approach.

Initially, participant observation met my criterion for honesty since statements could not be made unless the phenomena were witnessed. The supportive Brandeis faculty inculcated self-confidence in my ability to master the method with ingenuity. The students were urged to be themselves, to be "anti," and to learn what the faculty had to offer but to reject everything if needed. In this strangely permissive atmosphere, students were left with the unspoken fear that one day traditional demands would reappear that we would be unable to meet.

A few years had elapsed between the teacher's study and the mental hospital project. My personal circumstances had changed: No longer an unmarried undergraduate discovering the Columbia traditions, nor a hired hand performing the mechanics of survey research, I journeyed beyond the preliminary stage of professionalization and embarked on a search for a positive identity. After a few semesters of theory and orientation to Brandeis sociology, I became impatient to plunge into the field, to enter the "real world" beyond academia and to make my contribution.

Molding the Substantive Issue

The psychological distress I observed among some of my closest acquaintances led to an interest in the sociological, psychological, and psychiatric problems of mental illness and patienthood. Social psychology and social psychiatry became my areas of specialization. I adopted as mentors the faculty members most expert in these issues and began my investigation of the pertinent literature: family dynamics, labeling theory, etiology of mental illness, sociological descriptions of mental hospitals, and psychological theory. As a participant observer in a psychiatric setting, I could continue my mentor's work (Stanton and Schwartz, 1954), building on his findings and thereby providing myself with a sense of continuity with the "body" of sociology, a relevant feature of the sociologist's identity. My reading was directed both to learning about these topics and locating lacunae in which I could make my contribution. This reading pointed to two areas that merited further investigation.

First, most of the mental hospital literature dealt with relationships between psychiatrists (or other staff) and patients, rather than with relations among patients. However, since most patients occupy beds in state hospitals that are underfinanced and have low staff-patient ratios, the amount of time that patients can spend with staff (Devereux and Weiner, 1950), let alone with psychiatrists, is relatively small. For this reason, patients probably spend most of their time relating to, or at least in the presence of, other patients. But relationships among patients were barely treated in the literature. As a special group, hospitalized mental patients could be informative for sociology since the persons involved in the relationships are unable to sustain normal life outside the hospital. What do they do with one another inside the hospital? Do they develop the friendships and animosities that are found in all social groups? If so, how does this affect the patient's condition? Does a patient-friend represent an escape from the realities of the mental institution, or do other patients comprise the nightmare of being there?

The second relatively untreated issue in the literature was statements and analyses of the patients' perceptions of their own experiences. The lack of concern with the patient's perception contrasted with the sociological perspective I was studying in graduate school. This perspective sought to understand meaning in terms of actors' definitions of situations, to grasp the "interpretation of social phenomena from the point of view of the persons under study" (Wagner, 1975, p. 179). The patient's definition of the reality of the mental hospital interested me not as a manifestation of illness but as one of several definitions of reality maintained by staff, relatives, observers, community members, and others. If the psychiatrist's and sociologist's perspectives on patienthood are suspended, how do patients view their hospitalization? Is there a means of discovering what becoming and being a patient mean to patients? What is significant in their experiences? The written statements of patients had to serve as my source of data since I had no experience of patienthood. Applying the patient's perspective to the issue of patient interaction and then comparing staff and patient perspectives on patient interaction would yield a well-rounded understanding of the phenomenon. Ultimately this understanding should be useful for shaping social environments within hospitals to enhance the beneficial components of patients' communal living. These theoretical problems converted into research questions were grounded in personal interest and guided by sociological imagination, methodological interest, and relevant literature. This step in the research process contrasted vividly with the survey research project that had lacked these three components: personal relevance, an introductory formulation of the problem, and familiarization with pertinent literature. In addition, since I was working alone and not in a team, I could follow my own imagination and needs.

Having isolated an interesting topic, I returned to the literature for a more careful examination. Second only to one's personal experience is vicarious knowledge of patienthood available through reading patients' published reports. To learn about their experiences, I compiled a bibliography of nearly 300 autobiographical statements written by formerly hospitalized mental patients. These documents ranged from brief essays to lengthy monographs. This literature made it possible to combine my two questions: Did the patients who published accounts of their experience mention that other patients were significant to their well-being? And how did patients evaluate the influence of their fellow patients?

I discovered two types of published accounts: narratives of the author's psychological processes and descriptions of the hospital social world. The second type indicated awareness of and concern with the welfare of fellow patients. Other patients were second in significance only to the internal experience of the writers. Sometimes the two factors were combined, for example, when other patients were incorporated in the delusions, paranoid fantasies, and sexual desires of the writers. Fellow patients were socializers—they taught newcomers how to be patients, how to survive the institution, and how to relate to staff. Patients feared the fellows with whom they were incarcerated but ironically also relied on them. Even those patients whose comments about or relations with other patients were minimal seemed to have entered a delicate mutual agreement in order to maintain their aloofness. The self-selected group of patient-writers uniformly devoted a great portion of their documents to descriptions of patient subcultures and to explanations of mutual assistance among patients.

These autobiographical statements revealed that patients form an informal social structure parallel to the formal social structure of the hospital hierarchy. Within their own group there are those who are labeled "healers" and those who are "sick." These healers constitute a potential therapeutic resource in the mental hospital; if these people are unrecognized, a useful reservoir of peer assistance is wasted and these patients' self-esteem is deflated.

The discrepancy between the relevance of interactions among patients and the relative lack of attention granted this issue in the professional literature led to my definition of a research topic suitable for participant observation research. If patients do affect and relate to one another in typical relational forms, then in any ward of a mental hospital I should be able to observe patients engaged in friendship, hostility, competition for leadership, ostracism of the deviant, and more. From the general topic of interaction among hospitalized mental patients, my focus became patient liaisons, or friendships. The task was to locate these friendships and then determine what they mean to participants, to staff, and to me as a sociologist-observer. Following my formulation of these questions, I wrote a paper outlining the social structural and ideological features of psychiatric hospitals that encourage or discourage the formation of strong bonds between patients, as discussed both in professional and autobiographical literature (Reinharz, 1969).

The sociological literature on hospitals and mental patients mentions patient relationships in the context of the general social structure of the hospital. These comments do not always support one another. Sullivan (1964) was the psychiatrist who discovered the importance of understanding mental illness within the context of an individual's social environment. This perspective led to his close association with social scientists and his attempt to integrate the insights of psychiatry and social science. *Psychiatry*, the journal that he established in 1937, became the vehicle for communication between the two fields. In addition, his hospital began to open its doors to sociological investigations. At the same time, a sociologist (Rowland, 1938, 1939) sketched the patient roles and patterns of interaction that are shaped in state mental hospitals.

But it was Schwartz who, in his doctoral dissertation and in his study with Stanton of the private, psychoanalytically oriented ward, laid the groundwork for the systematic study of hospital life. "Inter-patient relations on the ward are not amorphous. Even on a disturbed ward informal structuring does arise, sometimes developing into a form of group life. This fact poses some questions about the organization and effects of inter-patient activity. What are the interpersonal conditions that permit a group to emerge, develop and die out?" (Stanton and Schwartz, 1954, p. 189).

Other sociologists considered the patient's capacity for group formation to be very limited. "There is no evidence that mentally ill people are capable of the effective group action of delinquents and criminals, whom society isolates partly to prevent formation of subsocieties. In short, there is danger of criminals banding together to perform dangerous criminal acts, but there is no danger of psychotics banding together to perform acts of lunacy" (Cumming and Cumming, 1957, p. 126). However, Stanton and Schwartz documented the existence of stable patient groupings in their case history of the informal social group known as "the sewing circle," which encompassed relationships ranging from "chummy intimacy" to "intense competitiveness." Goffman (1961) maintained that because of the nature of total institutions, all interaction is charged with extra meaning toward the institution itself. In his view hospital personnel undermine trust among patients to prevent their forming strong coalitions. Patients "contaminate" each other with the stigma of patienthood but also collaborate to form an "underworld" so they can "make out." Types of "fraternalization processes" are enumerated that result in "special solidarities," such as cliques, courtships, and buddies. Private relationships are used for mutual support and to express hostility to staff.

Whereas Stanton and Schwartz (1954) concluded that the amount of patient interaction varies with patient type, Goffman (1961) suggested that interaction is correlated with the particular stages of a "hospital career." Considerable ambiguity exists, however, as to the extent of interaction in "continuity relationships." On the one hand, Goffman claimed a "relative lack of group formation among inmates in public mental hospitals," while on the other hand he spoke of "informal peer-group pressure." He reported cases of patients who, although quite ill themselves, regularly helped other patients who were worse off but who did not interact with them socially when help was not needed. Caudill (Caudill and others, 1952; Caudill, 1958) testified to the existence and importance of patient groups and patient mutual aid. In an applied study, Jones (1953) manipulated the social life of patients to enhance their recovery, labeling this form of hospital treatment "social psychiatry," "therapeutic community," or "milieu therapy."

After reading the autobiographical statements of formerly hospitalized mental patients as well as sociological and psychiatric literature describing and analyzing the operations of a psychiatric institution, I concluded that a significant difference between patient writings and professional studies was the patients' emphasis on the significance of other patients and the professional emphasis on the staff. Patient friendships emerged as a feature of the setting worthy of further attention. But its prior, even if limited, treatment in the literature led to my subsequent feelings of superfluousness and to a defensive possessiveness about "my topic."

Having *defined a general problem* and *examined some literature*, I was now able to perform the third step—*problem refinement*. Essentially this meant selecting a specific population to study. There were several reasons for my eventual choice of adolescents. Their absolute and relative number was increasing significantly in psychiatric hospitals as a result of their increase in the general population and of hospital policies to expand adolescent admissions. In addition, this age group was likely to have a wealth of patient relationships since peer relationships are so significant in the adolescent developmental stage.

Adolescence is a period of burgeoning, vibrant interest in heterosexual contact and diminishing constraints on autonomy and infantile fantasies of dependence on parents and parent surrogates. In American culture, adolescence is a period of identity experimentation or of a moratorium that delays the final identity formation until early adulthood. One avenue of identity expression is friendship. Adolescents experiment with values, life-styles, and ideologies by adopting various kinds of friends. Adolescence is the period when for the first time and with great urgency the individual asks, "Who am I, where am I going, and

with whom do I belong?" Peers compete with parents for providing guidance, support, intimacy, and wisdom. The family is
replaced by peers and heroes who become an alternative source
of a sense of self. Even if adolescents who become hospitalized
mental patients have deficient peer relations, I expected friendships to be more visible, significant, and dynamic among adolescent patients than among patients in other age groups.

In the psychiatric hospital, however, adolescents' identity
problems are increased since a major source of identity, their
patienthood, is unsatisfactory. Their ties with the family are
severed or strained, and their opportunities for sexual experimentation are limited in a total institution. Do they handle
these problems by forming friendships and cliques that differentiate between "them" and "us" and thereby help the adolescent discover who the self is? Do they displace the distance they
feel between themselves and the older generation onto the patient-staff dichotomy? Erikson (1963, p. 262) claims that
"adolescents not only help one another temporarily through
much discomfort by forming cliques and by stereotyping themselves, their ideals, and their enemies; they also perversely test
each other's capacity to pledge fidelity." Given this theory, my
problem was to determine whether adolescent mental patients
turn to each other for friendship and peer-group identification,
and if so, how? This focus within the general problem of inter-
patient interaction seemed so benevolent—how do adolescent
patients help and harm each other? Yet there was one major
difficulty. The problem had been formulated before I entered
the field rather than arising from the research process in the particular field setting. It was an intellectual problem that had been
imposed upon the special requirements of participant observation.

Person and problem overlapped in my unconscious wish
to use the study of a mental hospital to vent my liberal attitudes and my "unprejudiced" beliefs, which were significant
features of my developing identity. Little did I realize that my
so-called lack of prejudice was really a strained willingness to
perceive the patient as victim and the staff as unenlightened.
Nor did I understand at the time the importance of coming to

terms with such prejudice before, rather than during, fieldwork. I protected myself slightly against this predisposition to take sides by taking a staff role (dance therapist) and therefore having to disparage my own behavior whenever I negatively stereotyped the staff. Not only should I have recognized these attitudes, but I should have dealt with them directly by examining their roots. My commitment to the study of mental hospitals overrode the caution that my bias required. My belief in the necessity of studying a psychiatric setting through firsthand experience overpowered my ability to recognize my own prejudices. Rather, I defined myself as a novice, value-free sociologist and did not attend to the fact that as a human being I had many feelings, values, and views. I reveal these problems retrospectively to illustrate the sociologist as a human being and how this humanness is partner to sociological imagination.

My choice of setting and subject matter also reflected the insecurity of a young student. I wanted to study a limited space, a place I could define and manage, with people (patients) who did not have the power to obstruct my plans. Although some people might think the study of mental hospital life requires great effort, strength, and courage, the opposite held in my case. For me the hospital represented a safe, secure, circumscribed place in which I could establish competence. In the subtle matter of selecting a research problem and site, the researcher's unconscious and conscious needs seek fulfillment. What can the researcher learn about himself or herself from selecting a particular topic? Out of the whole realm of human affairs, why did I choose to explore a mental hospital? One answer is that I plunged into the study of a mental hospital in a kind of counterphobic manner, to grapple with the personal pain of having friends of my own recently hospitalized for psychiatric problems. Unconsciously I probably attempted to subdue this horror by studying hospital life.

As time passes, increasing insight is gained into the motivation behind the selection of research topics. Precisely in this stage of problem selection there is room to exercise personal needs and idiosyncracies. Do we formulate research projects from questions or needs? These multiple sources of our motivation influence all the subsequent stages of the research process.

Initial Dilemmas and Blocks

Although researchers are warned not to be biased, they frequently mistake this advice to mean they should avoid commitment. Research without personal commitment lacks an essential source of motivation and is likely to be deprived of experiential insight, but personal interest can unwittingly translate into taking sides and thereby coloring perception. Useful antidotes against such bias are to assume the role of a member of the group for whom one has antipathy or to analyze the sources of one's antipathy by working with a partner who favors a different group. The "dilemma of commitment" to an outcome or a subset within an organization is an aggravated physical and emotional strain during the research process if the researcher attempts to discount or suppress these feelings. Although always defined as crucial to the research, impartiality also represents a constraint against acting genuinely. Contrived neutrality is difficult if not impossible to sustain in social settings. This dilemma of commitment, which is a barrier to research completion, deepens with the identification process that methodologists have noted between researchers and their subjects.

Geer (1964, pp. 328-329) entered a field site expecting to be bored by studying freshmen college students, as others had expected, including a dean:

> I expected to find evidence of this unfavorable adult bias toward adolescents. But on the third day in the field I am already taking the students' side. . . . I have fallen into empathy. . . . My reaction to the dean's question suggests not only anger at his failure to understand my job but also anger on the student's behalf: why call them children? I am taking up cudgels on their side. Perhaps the rapid development of empathy for a disliked group does not surprise old hands at field work, since it seems to happen again and again. But it surprised me.

Stein (1964, pp. 208-209) wrote, "My main point of attachment to the study was my identification with the gypsum miners." He went so far as to talk like a miner, adopt their contemptuous attitude toward surface workers, and even dream their dreams! Finally Becker (1967, p. 240) has generalized, "In the course of our work and for who knows what private reasons we fall into deep sympathy with the people we are studying, so that while the rest of the society views them as unfit in one or another respect for the deference ordinarily accorded a fellow citizen, we believe that they are at least as good as anyone else, more sinned against than sinning."

My partiality toward the cause of the patients not only helped formulate the research question but also led to my being unaware that I was taking their side. My delineation of the topic in terms of friendships among patients was intended to avoid issues such as staff-patient conflict but led to a certain myopia. By spending time with patients, I tended to see things from their viewpoint while calling it *my* viewpoint. Awareness and acknowledgement of my predispositions would have safeguarded against confusing the two. I entered the hospital bent on changing it before I even understood it.

The issue of commitment reveals the historical period and the values among social scientists at the time this study was done. During the period of the hospital study (1969-70) most students had causes of their own and had repoliticized American society with regard to opposing the Vietnam war, speeding the process of black civil rights, and liberalizing the educational institutions. Youth is generally the time when commitments are tested by deeds and rhetoric. With increasing age, researchers become increasingly committed to the professional identity.

There is probably some positive relationship between youth and low professional status, on the one hand, and the adoption of an underdog perspective on the other. Correspondingly, I would also expect that as sociologists get older, as they become increasingly successful, more likely to live next door or to associate with those who are also successful, or themselves become involved in the practical management of public affairs, they

too will come increasingly to adopt overdog standpoints
despite their continued public professions of liberalism
[Gouldner, 1968, p. 103].

Sympathy is extended to the group being studied by perceiving
them as underdogs:

> [Albert Reiss] describes an instance in which one
> of his observers, playing the role of a plainclothesman, ac-
> tually threatened a suspect with a night stick. The ob-
> server had forgotten his many hours of training and had
> adopted the police role with a "vengeance." Another ob-
> server, on duty in a police lockup, adopted a measure
> police officers used to humiliate the prisoners. In addi-
> tion, he gave vent to race hatred that even shocked the
> very officers he was supposed to be studying. Over all,
> Reiss notes, the observers tended to become pro-police.
> Observers often saw the men as caught up in a difficult
> system [Glazer, 1972, p, 69].

The likelihood that propinquity will lead to identification
with the subject and distortion of comprehension is aggravated
by the specific dictum in participant observation that descriptions of the situation should be presented from the perspective
of the members. To achieve this, no effort should be spared to
understand, to participate in, and to share their views. Being
socialized into the setting by its members produces for the researcher acculturation in their perspective. When the members'
perspective is not adopted, the researcher appears indifferent,
hostile, or ignorant and will be tolerated only briefly. Their investment in assisting the researcher's work diminishes if the study
is perceived as unsupportive of their perspective. Since people
are interested in convincing others of the merit of their position, it is unlikely that researchers can entirely avoid the subtle
confirmation that is intrinsic in interaction.

My unrecognized anticipation of identifying with the
people I would study also influenced my selection of an adolescent population. Some of my first field notes express my felt
distance from the geriatric group and affinity for the adoles-

cents. As time progressed and my identification with the adolescent patients took root, both their patienthood and their youth became significant sources of commitment. My emotional attraction to this age group was related to personal issues that were unconsciously worked through on this project.

The methodological stages discussed thus far include (1) definition of the problem and (2) preparation for entry into the field by way of library work, which combine into (3) problem refinement. Within the phase of problem definition the dilemma of commitment and the related issue of identification begin. The next stage brings the "dilemma of preparedness."

As preparation for fieldwork, anthropologists typically urge learning the language of the culture to be investigated, obtaining appropriate letters of introduction, making adequate transportation and survival accommodations, studying the literature that has accumulated on the culture, developing tools of investigation, and more. Strauss and his colleagues present the sociological point of view: "The field worker usually does not enter the field with specific hypotheses and a predetermined research design. He does have general problems in mind, as well as a theoretical framework that directs him to certain events in the field" (Strauss and others, 1964, p. 20). Whereas researchers might come to the field armed with information, they are advised to avoid well-formulated hypotheses that encumber observation. Predefinitions function as undesirable prejudgments or prejudices.

In a different vein, Hughes sees preparation not in terms of preconceptions but as help for meaningful interaction with setting members. He writes, therefore, that information opens doors, not that expectations close the mind:

> The time came when I had to desert statistical reports and documents and fare forth to see for myself. It was then that real learning began, although the knowledge gained in advance was very useful; in fact, it often made possible the conversations which opened the field. One who has some information and asks for more is perhaps less likely to be refused than one who has no advance information; perhaps the best formula is to have

advance knowledge, but to let it show only in the kinds of questions one asks [Hughes, 1960, p. vi].

The dilemma of advance knowledge is not settled once and for all upon entering the field, because fieldwork is composed of myriad situations, each of which can be entered with or without information and preconceptions.

In contrast to the Strauss group's notion of "mixed preparation" (general rather than specific hypotheses, and directing frameworks rather than predetermined designs) and Hughes' notion of the informed observer, Wolff (1971) considers essential the utter suspension of everything that bears on exploration in the field. Wolff uses the term *surrender* in presenting this extreme point of view. Anything that precedes entering the field is completely inappropriate and harmful to the process of study, because it is grounded in other circumstances or other observers. Since each researcher and each research experience is unique, nothing can be borrowed. Wolff strives to achieve a tabula rasa mind in which the situation produces concepts. However, it is impossible (except in certain religious systems) to strip the mind of all preconceptions, to enter a state in which everything is suspended.

Bruyn (1966) addresses this problem in an outline of the phenomenological method, which includes participant observation. The phenomenological procedure entails approaching the subject with "no structured expectations of how an object should be described. . . . He must have no hypotheses to direct him as to what he should find in his investigation. The investigator goes into the situation to be studied with a totally open mind—open, in fact, to all the stimuli that impinge upon his consciousness. He admits only that which is immediately experienced as he concentrates on the object of his inquiry" (p. 272). Bruyn admits this is impossible and urges a policy of *minimizing* preconceptions and rejecting the prepared attitude of traditional empirical studies.

The desirability of avoiding preconceptions is grounded in the basic tenets of the sociology of knowledge, that is, that people perceive the world through the concepts they utilize, and that expectations of what reality is tend to be fulfilled by the way we act on reality. In order that the phenomena under study not be relegated to a reflection of the researchers' way of looking at the world or to a realization of their expectations, these preconceptions must be suspended as much as possible, leaving researchers open to the field that impinges on them. This kind of research requires mental discipline to suspend and strip preconceptions, to free oneself from the "scientific" pattern of preparation. Without grounding in existing literature, subsequent research is not cumulative and can rediscover what has already been reported. Discovering for oneself replaces concern for building on precedents.

My defining a limited research problem in the mental hospital study—the examination of patient friendships—predisposed me to attend to only those interactions labeled "friendships" by the members. It also prevented me from studying other interesting problems that came my way. If people in the hospital did not use the word "friendship" to describe a particular relationship, I bypassed it in search of one that fit the category I brought to the setting. This perspective of searching for data to fit predetermined categories led to frustration and wasting time that might profitably have been spent examining the relationships that did exist, whatever their nature, whatever their label.

My expectation of an explicit "friendship" label created additional difficulties, such as recognizing that to a great extent patient friendships are classified as deviant behavior or covert activity by mental hospital staff who seek to regulate the dynamics of patient life (Huesler, 1970). The sociological study of patient friendships as deviant behavior requires particular techniques that differ from the study of friendship as an acceptable form of patient interaction. In addition, the private nature of friendship behavior required active overhearing or snooping, which left me very uncomfortable.

I am sitting in the cafeteria trying to casually overhear conversations. If any of the patients would know what I am doing, they would really freak out. Here is their paranoid fantasy come true! *

*The material in italics in the case study chapters is excerpted from my field notes of those projects.

Similarly, the transitory nature of friendships in the hospital led to my doubting the value of including those shifting relationships that lasted a day or a week. Selecting incidents or instances that fit my categories created problems that would have been avoided by constructing categories appropriate to the interaction patterns I observed. Participant observation research only partially derives its concepts during the study itself.

In addition to the tendency of research tradition to promote the problematic process of developing expectations (especially those beyond awareness), another factor making "blind entry" risky is the funding process. Agencies grant funds for the purpose of obtaining particular results. Can the methodological position of surrender match the perspective of a granting agency? This is but one way in which forces unrelated to the conduct of inquiry reinforce conventional patterns. Riesman and Watson (1964) point out, however, that concern with the stipulations of the funding agency is frequently a matter of projection rather than reality. For example, "NIMH policy is explicit that a research proposal is not a contract and that grantees have discretion to change it as the work develops. Retroactively, it would appear that the proposal at times assumed undue *hegemony* over our thinking simply because it was 'there,' an apparent authority to which appeal could be made. It is probably not the first time that NIMH or other donors will have noticed efforts to escape freedom in this fashion" (Riesman and Watson, 1964, p. 317).

Pressures to utilize specific hypotheses also come from setting members. The rationale presented to gain access to the setting must make sense to the setting members in terms of the researcher's plans to look at certain issues. If explicit hypotheses are shared, there is pressure to remain committed to that particular study and even to become rigid for the sake of fulfilling the obligations made when gaining access. To avoid these problems requires converting setting members into collaborators in the research process. Such collaboration poses its own constraints, however, such as the difficulty of freeing members' time to participate and sustaining their enthusiasm.

The foregoing description of the dilemmas of commit-

ment, preparedness, specificity, and rigidity yields a larger problem—blocked research—which is developed throughout this
chapter. In general the term *blocked research* is intended to
convey the irreversible interruptions of the research process or
the diversion of energy from the original intentions. This jam-
ming results from problems in a particular setting, problems of
the method itself (which on site appears to be inappropriate to
the subject at hand), or problems with the researcher-as-person.
Using the term *blocked* rather than *failed* underscores the fact
that research as a process can be corrected or transformed to
yield results different from the original purpose. *Blocked research* also indicates that the setting influences the process after
the researcher defines the original thrust.

My first field experience followed much preentry preparation, leading to various blocks discussed in this chapter. I
blocked myself from experiencing the "field as it was" because
of the demands of formulating a grant proposal, because of
anxiety about entering the field without a structure to order my
observations, and because of my viewing participant observation
as a version of scientific empiricism rather than an utterly different approach. Since I had not yet worked in this new modality, I remained grounded in the tradition of control—controlling
the self and the study process. Only after this mental hospital
research experience ended could I label and understand these
assumptions, thereby freeing myself to employ a more fully
"unprepared" approach in a subsequent study. By that time
(see Chapter Six), the method of grounding myself in prefield
perceptions, which had burdened me in the hospital study, was
replaced by general intellectual curiosity and critical reflection of
ideas that I tried to suspend. By removing specific questions I
was free to explore the field as it presented itself to me and to
relate it to the literature retrospectively.

The dilemma of preparedness—the balance between being
informed and simply having one's expectations fulfilled in the
research process (Rosenthal, 1966)—is related to the looseness
of the problem definition and to methodological flexibility. On
the basis of the project described in this chapter, I suggest that
researchers minimize expectations of the setting, formulate and

reformulate problems only in the field, and remain open to change as the setting impinges on the sociological imagination. To operate at the extreme of these values is unrealizable, and continuous redefinition is chaos, but with experience the dilemmas are tested and personal resolutions are forged.

In the example of patient friendships, naturalistic observation made it clear that patients were confined not only by their illnesses but also by the structure of the hospital. Their friendships were not solely an extension of their own attitudes but represented behavior regulated by the hospital. No physical contact ("p.c." in the hospital terminology) between patients was permitted. Patients could be restricted to their room or their ward and could be banned from having phone conversations and from participating in activities with other patients. In addition, during individual psychotherapy and ward meetings, and in all private or group discussions with staff, the milieu therapy perspective that the hospital had adopted legitimized probing into, squelching, or otherwise interfering with patient interaction. Since my prefield definition of friendship consisted of reliable spontaneous interaction in shared time, I was discouraged to find that patient friendships could not typically possess these qualities. It turned out that friendships were instances of regulated behavior and could be studied only in the context of staff attitudes toward patients. A flexible approach toward my research problem would have led to a redefinition of the topic, such as "How, why, and with what impact do staff members attempt to regulate patient interaction?"

Why did I not change topics? As a novice participant observer I was experientially unaware that "in the field, the research design serves as a place to start, an initial focus of attention, and perhaps as a point of reference or departure for later explorations. In any case, unless it is very general, it is usually transcended, supplemented or left behind as the developing field work suggests new topics and hypotheses" (Diesing, 1971, p. 143). Because of my commitment to the topic outlined in my grant proposal, I would have felt very guilty if I had abandoned it. Knowing intellectually but not understanding experientially that fieldwork is an unfolding, ever-changing process, I retained rigid concepts of problem formation, data collection, and data analysis that I had gleaned from the literature and transferred from my survey research experience. "Little record exists of mistakes and of learning from them, and of the role of chance and accident in stumbling upon significant problems, in reformulating old ones, and in devising new techniques, a process known as 'serendipity.' A lack of theory, or of imagination, or overcommitment to a particular hypothesis, or a rigidity in personality may prevent a field worker from learning as he stumbles" (Powdermaker, 1966, pp. 10-11). Changing topics seemed irresponsible and dangerously unprofessional to a person forging a professional identity. Subconsciously I believed that I should act in accordance with the unknown set of rules for performing participant observation research. This belief led to various forms of behavior, including rigidity and anxiety. When in my subsequent study (Chapter Six) I developed a greater sense of identity and trust in myself, I was able to ignore the mythical rules and work according to an inner set of guidelines that permitted flexibility and change.

My experience of blocked research in the hospital study resulted from my looking for certain problems in only certain ways—I was blind to the possibility of studying what I was *actually experiencing* and observing. I differentiated my study from my experience rather than integrating them, an approach that would have reduced the dichotomous pulls and enhanced the holistic qualities of the research enterprise. If I would have permitted myself to let go of my predetermined research topic and perspective, alternative foci drawn from examining my own experience would have included the "definition of an event in a mental hospital," or the "creation of a new profession—dance therapy," or "sources of conflict among activity therapists." My access to such issues was immediate because I had adopted the role of activity therapist and spent much time executing its duties. The consuming nature of that role-related work added to the difficulty of researching a tangential topic. I prided myself needlessly on my ability to keep the so-called bias inducing role perspective (therapist) separate from my research activities.

Similarly, Whyte (1971) was disappointed in retrospect

because he had separated his recreation from his research activities in Cornerville, thereby losing quantitative data concerning the relation between a gang member's bowling scores and his social position in the gang. Instead, Whyte reported,

> I had been looking upon Saturday night at the bowling alleys as simply recreation for myself and my friends. . . . I was bowling with the men in order to establish a social position that would enable me to interview them and observe important things. But what were these important things? Only after I passed up this statistical gold mine did I suddenly realize that the behavior of the men in the regular bowling-alley sessions was the perfect example of what I should be observing. Instead of bowling in order to be able to observe something else, I should have been bowling in order to observe bowling. I learned then that the day-to-day routine activities of these men constituted the basic data of my study [Whyte, 1971, pp. 37-38].

The point is that everything should be recognized as potential data, particularly since the meaning of an activity for the researcher is not necessarily the same as for the member. Even that which the researcher thinks of as "time off" or "interruptions" can represent exactly the regularized activity patterns through which the observer acquires insight into the setting dynamics. The role of dance therapist through which I chose to study patient friendships was also (perhaps even more) conducive to studying staff attitudes and behavior. Ignoring the data that accrue from the researcher's own role-related behavior is analogous to peering around rather than through a pair of "role glasses" needed to participate in a setting. I was afraid to look straight through my setting's role lens lest it distort the "real" image.

I reported to my [academic] advisor the difficulty of always trying to study something other than that which I was experiencing and wondering whether or not I lacked the control to do participant observation research. [He] encouraged me to stop fighting this war within myself and to explore instead what was happening to me. He asked me to acknowledge the experience as worthwhile, valid data. But I cannot follow this advice. Years of education have taught me otherwise, that such an investigation would be mere subjectivity.

To me research still meant control rather than letting go. I was suffering from an effort to control my curiosity and to channel it where it was not going. Advice is effective only when the recipient is ready to receive it and has experience that gives it meaning. I needed to traverse and review the entire research process in the hospital before I could understand or accept such recommendations. I could break the traditions of procedure only gradually, as my frustrating experience accumulated.

I now recognize that all research findings, particularly those involving participation, are grounded in the natural or adopted role of the researcher. All interaction infers role attribution that in turn is coupled with a perspective on defining reality. For this reason all participant observation research must include at least the study of the researcher's experience grounded in the researcher's adopted role.

I spent eight months at the hospital. Its culture of authoritarian benevolence and mystification impinged on every experience, but I did not allow myself to study it. By trying to split my observations from my "irrelevant" feelings, I hoped to confine myself to a neutral perspective on the relations between patients. One source of the relentless energy I poured into my dance therapist role was this blocked flow of research energy that sought alternative outlets. The relation between experience and examination is the crux of the participant observation method. One person both participates and observes by being simultaneously on two levels, in other words, by communicating and metacommunicating. Participant observation is not unlike everyday social interaction, which also is characterized by self-consciousness and environmental awareness, and therefore includes both communication and metacommunication. If prolonged, however, this combination is difficult to sustain. The consciousness of being a researcher interferes with the requirements of spontaneous interaction. This is so because while participating the researcher thinks about being an active listener, noticing other behavior, recording, interpreting, and correlating.

The unique feature of fieldwork is that most of the raw material is a product of sharing experiences with the people studied. Participant observation in its pure form as a data-gathering method is nothing more than experiencing a setting, overcoming the difficulties of multidimensional, multipurpose interaction, and recording one's observations. The difficulties are diminished if after entry and participation, the researcher forms a research problem from the collected data. Having the research intention, however, leads the investigator to engage in activities other than spontaneous interaction so as to explore the potential for study. The range of activities includes the range engaged in by setting members plus observation, participation, interviewing, collecting and reading documents, making enumerations and counts, and other forms of systematic data collection (Zelditch, 1962). From these activities a research problem emerges that is grounded in what is experientially and methodologically possible. Whyte (1961, p. 305) provides fine examples of unobtrusive research methods used to collect data for *Street Corner Society*:

> At one time I was nominated as secretary of the Italian Community Club. My first impulse was to decline the nomination, but then I reflected that the secretary's job is normally considered simply a matter of dirty work —writing the minutes and handling correspondence. I accepted and found that I could write a very full account of the progress of the meeting as it went on under the pretext of keeping notes for the minutes.

However, Whyte (1951, p. 503) missed the opportunity to do the same with the bowling activity:

> I suddenly discovered that the individual's bowling scores were closely tied in with his position in the gang. However, I awoke to this at the end of a bowling season. Had I sensed this possibility, I could have kept a record

of hundreds of strings of bowling scores that would have provided a rich body of statistical data for further analysis of the relationships.

The three components of the dilemma of preparedness are (1) the tension between entering the research project with no preconceptions (which is impossible) or with predetermined definitions, (2) the degree of generality (or specificity) with which the research problems are posed, and (3) the degree of rigidity (or flexibility) with which the topic is maintained. An additional problem concerns mastery of the literature. Simply put, it cannot be mastered. It is frustrating to recognize that there is always more to read within a discipline or in related fields. The sociological imagination can be stifled by overexposure to the works of others and by too little investigation of personally defined directions. The wish for thorough grounding in the literature delays the beginning of a project, but inadequate reading increases the researcher's vulnerability to the pitfalls, errors, and obstacles of the research process. I had internalized the students' norm of attempting to review all the literature before entering the field, while knowing that this was impossible. Not having read everything about participant observation, patienthood, and friendship before beginning the project raised nagging guilt and insecurity. My stage in the socialization process is reflected here, for with time the student is concerned less with having read everything than with making a contribution.

Selecting a Stance and Role for Fieldwork

My preparation for entry into the field culminated in locating a specific site with my advisor's assistance. A previous student had worked successfully as an activity therapist at a nearby psychiatric hospital at which my advisor had many personal contacts. Access to the hospital as a field site was thereby available to me, requiring only an interview with the director of the activity therapies department to determine the fit between my skills and the department's needs. This mode of entry coincided with my final preentry concern, devising a manner to present myself to the hospital, which is referred to as role selection in the participant observation literature.

The selected role reflects both the self the researcher wishes to present and the particular definition of participant observation being used. Together these form the researcher's "stance" (see also Schwartz, 1971). Participant observation includes various ways in which researchers present themselves to the members of the setting. Many commentators have pointed to the variety of styles within the method (Junker, 1960; Gold, 1958; Schwartz and Schwartz, 1955).

Participant observation was defined originally by Florence Kluckhohn (1940, p. 331) as the "conscious and systematic sharing, insofar as circumstances permit, in the life-activities and, on occasion, in the interests and affects of a group of persons. Its purpose is to obtain data about behavior through direct contact and in terms of specific situations in which the distortion that results from the investigator's being an outside agent is reduced to a minimum." A later definition states that the "observer participates in the daily life of the people under study, either openly in the role of researcher or covertly in some disguised role" (Becker and Geer, 1957, p. 28).

The stance through which the researcher gathers data in the field has become more complex. The researcher can choose any position on the continuum from complete participant to complete observer. Complete participants do not reveal their research intention to the members of the setting and therefore rely on pretense or disguise. They study the setting by adopting an available role and hiding their research identity. Cases have been reported of such research in psychiatric hospitals (Caudill and others, 1952; Deane, 1961; Goldman, Bohr, and Steinberg, 1970; Rosenhan, 1973), in an apocalyptic movement (Festinger, Riecken, and Schacter, 1956), in the army (Sullivan, Queen, and Patrick, 1958), and in a self-help group (Lofland and Lejeune, 1960). They have also aroused ethical concern among other sociologists (Coser and others, 1959; Davis, 1961; Lofland, 1961; Roth, 1962; Erikson, 1967; Shils, 1959). The complete observer, in contrast, minimizes interaction with members and openly employs observational devices or relies on unobtrusive measures or techniques similar to spying. The complete observer eschews participation.

These choices were experientially unknown to me as I embarked on the adventure of participant observation fieldwork. Without previous experience I could not know which stance would be most suitable for the study. Naive about the complexities of the method, I designed my own version by simply making decisions about problems as they arose in the field. For this reason, this fieldwork was as much a discovery about method as it was about substance and about self. Although I had intended to focus only on substantive issues, my first field trip caught me in the web of person, problem, and method.

The issue of stance, or the balance between participation and observation in a setting, is complicated by two additional factors. First, different positions can be adopted at different times. Second, different stances can be adopted with various groups in the setting, although this causes its own difficulties in role definition (Barnes, 1963). Janes (1961) described five successive redefinitions of the participant observer's stance from the point of view of the community members: newcomer, provisional acceptance, categorical acceptance, personal acceptance, and imminent migrant. With each phase researchers engage in activities that match the community's perception of them at that time. Similarly, Strauss's group that did psychiatric hospital fieldwork makes the following claim:

> [The fieldworker's] identity shifts when he spends an extended period of time interacting with the same people. . . . Initially we presented ourselves as sociologists doing a study of "how a hospital works," and this identification was maintained throughout the research. The qualities encompassed in this identification altered, however, with familiarity. In particular, when we approached participants during early stages of the research, we assumed a high degree of naivete. We played learners (often genuinely), inducing participants to instruct us in the ways of the hospital. . . .

When first we appeared at each work setting, we came prepared with statements about our "identity and purpose." For days—sometimes for weeks—we found it necessary to restate our identities and purposes. . . . Eventually as we had to abandon the naive role, so the observed ceased making direct queries about our presence. . . . As we became increasingly active in the field, we used more interview tactics with participants [Strauss and others, 1964, pp. 26-27].

In my own case, I was taken by surprise at the immediate necessity of establishing a reason for being in the hospital. Blau (1964, p. 26) similarly states:

At the very start of the intensive observation of Department Y, I was introduced to all its members by a senior official at a meeting and given an opportunity to explain the study briefly. I realized that an observer must explain at the outset who he is and what he wants to do. But I failed to realize that what I defined as the beginning of the actual observation was not the beginning for these agents. I had been seen around for two weeks, and my failure to explicitly clarify my identity earlier gave rumors about me that much time to circulate.

I had not yet decided my self-presentation when I was queried by the first person I met at the hospital, an adolescent patient sprawled on the lawn tanning, who was curious about me, the stranger.

The proper timing for entering the field and preparing a self-presentation are the relevant issues here. The mode of self-presentation should be worked out before entry into the field, but the specific problem to be studied should be worked out in the field and not vice versa. In that first encounter, during what I had defined as the preentry phase, I discovered that I was uncomfortable admitting to patients that I was interested in studying them. A few minutes later, however, during my job interview for the dance therapist position, I found myself talking about my research intentions. These first encounters forced me to offer a truthful, inoffensive, and not overly hesitant rationale for my presence much sooner than I had expected.

My reluctance to be forthright with patients about my research intentions reinforced my decision to take on a staff role behind which I could hide. Could I possibly form relationships with patients if I would tell them of my research interests?

What kind of explanation do you give to another of what you are doing? Do you always know what you are doing anyhow? How do you not deceive and yet maintain your integrity and your access into the situation? What would have happened if I would have said, "I'm here to study your friendships?" I was afraid to ask. What should you explain? How much? How little?

I was uncomfortable with what Shils (1959, p. 125) calls the historically unprecedented intrusion "into privacy solely for the sake of a contribution to the general understanding of man's nature and society." If I avoided telling patients I was interested in studying them, then I denied them the fundamental right of saying no. I circumvented the problem of gaining cooperation by not letting patients know I had research intentions. This covertness did not represent contempt or disregard for research subjects or for mental patients but stemmed from a feeling of benevolence—since I had no harmful intention, and since raising the issue was disruptive, there was no need to be direct. This lame excuse was reinforced by the bureaucratic structure of the hospital. Because the director of activity therapies gave me permission, I imposed myself on patients without their consent. I abided by the power structure of the hospital, which did not require obtaining consent from each patient.

Can a mental patient decide whether or not he will be a research subject? Is this an unnecessary burden on him to decide? Is it fair to the patient? What am I doing this research for anyhow? Who is this going to benefit? Are mental patients a trapped sample or do they have the same civil and human rights as anyone else to deny my studying them? I can't bring myself to say to them that I am studying them for fear they would feel like guinea pigs. But I do and will continue to tell staff. This difference in the way I present myself implies that I want to establish different relationships with staff and patients.

Maybe this is a typical phenomenon. You don't tell the people you are studying them, but you do tell their bosses. This way I am able to play out both sides of my ambivalence—to tell and not to tell. I solved the problem by telling some and not others.

Concealing my research role for the sake of reducing patient self-consciousness or not disrupting friendships was part of an assumption that researchers have a disruptive impact on their environment. Nowadays, the requirement to obtain approval from a human subjects review committee would compel the researcher to justify all strategies used in obtaining data.

Schwartz and Schwartz (1955, p. 347) claim that the behavior of patients changed in response to being observed:

> *During the early stages* of our research [there] was a great amount of feeling aroused in both patients and staff by the investigator's presence. The patients were curious and, at times, hostile to the investigator; they watched him closely and sometimes attacked him verbally, insisting that they did not want to be guinea pigs. The ward staff was covertly, then sometimes overtly, suspicious of his intentions and role—sometimes they used him as a scapegoat—in general, they were interested but wary. However, these feelings *gradually diminished,* and *at the end of six months* the observed no longer reacted to the observer with strong negative feelings, and responded to him much as they would to a regular ward staff member" [emphases added].

In my eight-month study, six months could not be spent in getting used to being observed, so I tried to bypass this problem by not informing the patients of my research interests.

The assumption that social environments are relatively unstable leads to research strategies that minimize the disruptive effects of the researcher. Conversely, one could assume, as did Henry (1967) after living in the homes of families with psychotic children, that personality structures and social environments are stable and resistant to change. Custom and organizational structure perpetuate behavior patterns, the alteration of which requires great effort and usually meets with resistance. In addition, to the extent that behavior patterns are unconsciously derived, they are not amenable to conscious change. One drawback of not disclosing my study purpose to the patients was the difficulty of maintaining my research focus while with them, which meant I was changing rather than they.

My stance became "covert researcher" in most settings within the hospital, but "overt researcher" in others, particularly those exclusively designated for the activity therapists. It was not problematic to present myself as both researcher and dance therapist to the activity therapists because I was not studying them. They were used to people performing research in the hospital and adopted an introspective, analytic outlook in their own work as well. To my knowledge, the activity therapists did not inform patients about my research interests even though I had not requested them to avoid this.

In a complex social system, one can be a complete participant in some settings and a balanced participant observer in others. Although these multiple stances optimize access to the social system, the researcher feels fragmented and inconsistent. One of these varied stances becomes the needed escape from the strain of the other, but the researcher can lose touch with the "real" self. Merton (1947) suggests avoiding the problem of multiple self-presentations by gaining multiple sponsorship, which allows multiple entries into the setting. Unless the researcher is very familiar with a setting, however, detrimental support could be obtained; for example, the support of a director could be the "kiss of death" in working with the staff. "Were members of the research staff observed to have frequent access to the management offices in the early stages of the inquiry, they would at once have been tagged as agents of management. Later disclaimers and explanations would scarcely alter the convictions of those who preferred to believe the testimony 'of their own eyes' " (Merton, 1947, p. 305). What would be the most appropriate sponsorship is unknown before a researcher enters a setting. Sponsorship or trust from a competing group can be denied because of the researcher's original identification. A successful example of multiple sponsorship is Jaques'

(1952) Tavistock-sponsored study of a factory, which ended when the manuscript was reviewed by all the parties involved. Concealing my research interests from the patients prevented me from engaging them in any explicit research activities, such as formal interviewing. To not identify oneself as a researcher places the researcher in a passive role "unable to take command of the situation. The observers were forced to maintain constant alertness for relevant data that members of the group spontaneously brought forth and had to be extremely tactful and skillful in following up leads so as not to appear too inquisitive" (Riecken, 1956, p. 211). Not all problems can be studied in this manner.

The activity therapists to whom I disclosed my research interests cooperated in informal interviews and assisted me in my work, while the uninformed patients could not do so. As time passed, however, the activity therapists forgot my real purpose and related to me as a fellow activity therapist. In order to keep my researcher identity alive, I went to pains to behave or talk in ways that would remind them I was both an activity therapist and a sociologist. The director's announcement of my intentions in the first activity therapies staff meeting was quickly forgotten under the weight of the staff's various concerns. Efforts to reassert and reconfirm my researcher role continued during activity therapies staff meetings, which consumed four hours per week. Most of the twenty members of the activity therapies staff expressed their views in these meetings, and I also casually shared my observations and growing theories.

My adoption of the dance therapist role was based on the rationale that the stance of a complete observer would deny me access to the spontaneous interaction of members of a natural setting. My resolution of the interwoven demands of selecting both a research stance and a role hinged on my ethical concern for avoiding exploitation of the setting members. I hoped to accomplish this by sharing my dance talents in return for observing them. My survey research experience led me to believe that researchers use human subjects primarily for their professional gain, secondarily for their possible contribution to knowledge, and lastly (if at all) to benefit the subjects themselves or future generations. Social scientists writing on research ethics have warned against exploitation of subjects, but I wanted to engage in exchange (see also Glazer, 1972) or reciprocity between myself and the people I studied.

As I began the third study (Chapters Six and Seven), I sought a higher level of reciprocity than in the mental hospital study—engaging in studies only upon client request, encouraging the client's active collaboration, and sharing findings and reports with the setting members. In the hospital study, my relationship with the patients was shaped by a developing definition of ethical considerations in research. At this stage of my socialization, my ethical concern was operationalized in my wanting to give the patients something to justify or pay for my using them. This primitive solution of exchange was a form of barter, however, in which only one partner was aware of the transaction and set the terms. Nevertheless, my belief that I was not exploiting the patients or staff because I was providing them dance therapy assuaged my ethical concerns. Through dance I could give to those from whom I was taking. Being a dance therapist thus resolved my ethical and self-presentation doubts. True, it was a viable role, but the stance problems were not resolved. I did not understand at the time that I not only had to adopt a viable setting role, but I also had to find a way of defining the relation between my research and setting roles.

Another way of looking at the issue of role selection is to examine the roles I did *not* adopt from among those suitable for the resarch topic of friendships among patients. Theoretically, like Caudill (Caudill and others, 1952) and some others, I could have disguised myself as a hospitalized patient, but this seemed distasteful, time consuming, and requiring acting skills too great to make the ruse viable. By contrast, in a role of complete observer or obvious researcher I could have conducted noninteractive observations. Such work was at that time being carried out by the hospital's department of social science. But this kind of work suffered from many criticisms I had made of positivist sociology in my survey experience. The other available roles included psychiatric aide, maid, or research assistant in the social science department. All of these options required either an excessive time commitment or unattractive work. These "open entry" roles could have been adopted without the previous training required for the professional roles in the hospital.

The fact that my options were extremely limited (Goffman's study and Caudill's restudy utilized participation in the activity therapies departments) leads me to wonder if the issue of role selection is distorted. Given the methodological stance the researcher wishes to adopt, the choice of roles is limited. Despite this determinism, however, throughout my research experience at the hospital I believed I had selected and adopted the activity therapy role for moral reasons.

By coincidence, when I started to work at the hospital, a young man who wanted to make a film about the adolescent patients was conducting preliminary participant observation research, using the complete observer stance. The hostility he elicited from the activity therapies staff members at their meetings and the resentment they felt for the amount of time "wasted" discussing whether to allow him to participate in their meetings reinforced my preference for participation. The difference in the activity therapies staff's response to complete participation and complete observation was striking. Because the meetings that decided acceptance or rejection were conducted by consensus decision making, they permitted a relatively open expression of feelings. But the filmmaker's self-definition as an "observer only" put him in a closed-communication role while everyone else was relatively open to express and to receive feelings.

I used the staff's feelings about the prospective filmmaker to reinforce my own acceptance (having arrived two weeks earlier entitled me to make comments as if I were already an old-timer or socialized staff member) and to open the way for his acceptance.

Went to the hospital at 12:30 to attend activity therapies meeting which is known as the "other" meeting for want of a better word to substitute for what is essentially an encounter, training, or sensitivity group. Almost all of the meeting hinged around the question of A's [the filmmaker's] presence as a par-

ticipant observer. The conflict about the firing of B that was troubling everyone since last week was avoided by talking about A and perhaps using him as a scapegoat.

I made a few contributions, expressed myself clearly and got a good response. N said I deserve applause. I said that research should not be prejudged. Research can be harmless, useful or become exploitative. Some have likened it to rape. In order to absolve themselves from this ethical problem some fieldworkers have fed back the money they received from a book into the situation, or they have at least given the participants the benefits of their research in some kind of exchange.

My field notes reveal my attempt to gain acceptance as a member of the activity therapies staff while expressing my role as researcher. The problem of A's participation was resolved only after several other intense meetings. Finally some staff members proposed that he be permitted to observe if he shared his own thoughts and feelings at the weekly meetings. Since a vote was not taken, A did not have to abide by this plan, but after a few more meetings he did not return. I learned that this group did not tolerate easily the stance of neutral observers, so I was strengthened in my participant stance. A's case also demonstrated the importance of not having partisan allegiances when trying to secure entry. A had entered the group through his connection with a party to a troublesome staff conflict. He was a victim of poor timing, close alliances, and an unacceptable stance. The initial stage of my involvement as a staff member was shaped by reflection on this coincidental event. A's situation was different from mine, of course, in that he was filmmaker and not a sociologist. Nevertheless, an excerpt from his log, which he shared with me, indicates the similarity of our experience:

> Talking to J over lunch. He takes me by surprise because he thinks I am trying to interview him in the usual manner, what he does, what he is in charge of. At this point my sense of identity returns and I feel a bit more secure. At least I have a name of a thing I do. FILM MAKER. More confidence. About this confidence itself I feel ambivalent, as if by its very presence it makes me a

liar. Anyway, the Liar asks the Therapist what does he feel about his work.

Although I sought acceptance from the activity therapists by adopting an active participation stance, I was also removed from them because of certain characteristics: my part-time schedule and explicit plans to leave after eight months, my concurrent status as a full-time student, and my not yet being "burned out" as an activity therapist in contrast with many of my colleagues.

Competing Identities in the Field

My selection of the dance therapist role was intended to solve both the ethical and stance issues; however, only a pseudo-resolution had been achieved. How would I express my researcher self? Was the dance therapist role a vehicle or a cover? Did this role give me maximum access to patient friendships? Because I did not ask these questions at the time, my resolutions of the myriad methodological dilemmas were laden with other implications. The dance therapist role became a way of escaping from the difficulties of the research task. This enjoyable, nonthreatening role reduced the sense of being an outsider, while at the same time providing relief from the strain of fieldwork activities, commonly acknowledged as exhausting or fatiguing (McCall and Simmons, 1969). Although the dance therapist role required considerable physical exertion, its immediate results—concreteness, opportunity for emotional release, and aesthetic nature—were all compelling features, affording relief from the complex psychological concerns of the staff and patients and the intellectual demands of my research project. The compatibility of the dance therapist role for me as a person, its fulfilling qualities, and the positive feedback I received from those who used my services almost precipitated my "going native" and abandoning the whole research enterprise.

In his description of the effects of the Crestwood Heights study on the research personnel, Seeley writes of identity crises that were expressed by going native but that really signified a career change. The impending crisis can be the impetus for going into the field in the first place.

> We walked the brink of a crisis or a succession of crises of identity, individually and collectively, and we led and were led in so doing. The crisis focused on the operation and its aims, the nature of the "team" (or whether indeéd it was a team), the division of labor, the intended product, the nature of our sciences "pure" and "applied," and actually, for some, who we were and what we were doing here. Interpersonal conflict, overt and covert, increased, and so did intrapersonal stress, for some of us, to the point of threatening or breaching habitual defenses. Hardly one of the senior personnel involved failed to show a sharp career break, objectively visible as well as subjectively palpable. Two of the senior authors ceased to be practicing social scientists, and one retained the definition but played a then largely anomalous or unconventional role [Seeley, 1971, p. 170].

Seeley's experience prompted his decision to undergo psychoanalysis. The dilemma of socialization for the participant observer is to achieve adequate socialization into a setting for active and natural participation without becoming a complete member who has abandoned other identities, including that of researcher. The dance therapist role was more compatible with my personal needs than with my researcher needs. "Going native is most likely to be a problem when the complete participant stance is used" (Gold, 1958, p. 220), or when the researcher engages in "prolonged direct participation, loses his detached wonder, and fails to discover certain phenomena that the relatively uninvolved researcher would observe" (McCall and Simmons, 1969, pp. 63-64). Vidich (1955, p. 357) sees going native as a consequence of the participant observer's search for "genuine experiences," tempting the researcher who "unqualifiedly immerses and commits himself to the group he is studying." In such circumstances researchers cannot detach themselves from their experiences, which become precious and cannot be analyzed.

A few cases of researchers who profoundly moidifed their identity can be found among anthropologists: "Curt Nimuendajú, took his name from the Indians of Amazonia with whom he lived for decades and among whom he died. To a degree he 'went native,' but he shaved every day in the jungle and became an ethnographic authority on the area" (Baldus, 1946). The man who goes completely native participates fully in native life, but in so doing he ceases to be an observer and can no longer be counted within the fold of anthropology. Frank Cushing did not become a Zuni, but he became so emotionally identified with the people that he refused to continue publishing his Zuni data   (Paul, 1953, p. 435; see also Rosen, 1968; and Stock, 1973).

Other commentators understand going native as analogous to overrapport (Miller, 1952) and talk of "overidentifying with the participants' viewpoint" (McCall, 1969) or "becoming identified with the ideology of the dominant faction in the organization or community and framing the questions to which his research provides answers so that no one will be hurt. . . . He unwittingly chooses problems that are not likely to cause trouble or inconvenience to those he has found to be such pleasant associates" (Becker, 1971, p. 276).

Despite these references to the problem of going native, there are few published accounts of the phenomenon, since those who have gone native cease to publish or omit discussion of the problem in their publications. It is difficult to evaluate one's own personal experience with this category, or even to know if going native is irreversible or merely a transitory phase. In my own case, the pull toward going native stemmed from the compatibility of the setting role and the weakness of my contrasting identity of sociological researcher based on negative role models or an antisociologist ideal. This weak sociologist-researcher identity made me vulnerable to the attractiveness of the situational roles, first of dance therapist and later of covert therapist.

Polsky (1962) portrayed similar tension in his study of incarcerated adolescents: "The values of the subculture are contagious. Even the investigator felt their pull and might have been sucked into the system, . . . had he not had a firm footing in his middle class culture on the outside" (Witmer, 1963, p. 202). Part of the hazard stems from working on the turf of a close-knit social group or a profession with a powerful identity. Clausen has warned sociologists to overcome doubts of their profession's value, adding that sociologists "working in a psychiatric setting need not, indeed must not, try to 'make like a psychiatrist' " (1965, p. 43).

Perry, conversely, claims that the therapist feels overwhelmed by the skills and paraphernalia of the social scientist: "The psychiatrist may experience difficulty maintaining the necessary self-picture as a researcher because (1) he does not have certain research tools of high social value that are available to him and/or (2) he has no individual tools, no tools peculiar to his own profession at his disposal. . . . A threat often appears to him to come through the superior power of the social science techniques" (Perry, 1966, pp. 457, 461). In my pull toward going native, my ambivalence about participation quickly gave way to my search for real action, real joy and suffering, and real experience, in contrast with the "ivory tower" of the university. The guilt of abandoning my researcher identity, however, kept my going native in check. My graduate school sponsors and those who provided access to the hospital on the basis of my self-presentation as a researcher became internalized constraints against complete abandon. Hughes (1956, p. 86) mentions the double loyalty "to those who have admitted him to the role of confidante and to his colleagues who expect him to contribute freely to the accumulating knowledge about human society and methods of studying it." The goal is to utilize these loyalties to prevent being seduced into going native. Since the patients were unaware of my research interests, their expectations of my behavior worked against my commitment to research.

My weak identity as a sociologist hid behind the easily assumed identity of a dance therapist when I began to present myself to the hospital's staff and patients. Only among the activity therapies staff did I regularly share interpretations of what was going on from a sociological perspective, but these remarks did not differ noticeably from the continuous analysis of the hospital environment by everyone connected with it. For the patients, I was a dance therapist; for the activity therapies staff I was also a researcher whose extra role was forgotten with time. Only when I had to request access to a situation or when I wanted to conduct an interview did my research identity surface. In addition I was accountable to no one in the setting as a sociologist but to many people as a dance therapist. Gold (1958) stresses that fieldworkers who use the complete participant technique have trouble with either the assumed role or the research role. The strength of one overrides the other.

Even Wolff's (1971, p. 247) discussion of surrender contains a warning against forgetting the research task and becoming lost in the research site:

> If I surrender to a community or any other social phenomenon, I must as a man and a student eschew two dangers. . . . I must not forget that I am a student who wants to find out and report as objectively as he can—if I do forget this, it means either that I was not in control of my private needs or wishes (in a fashion that ranges all the way from simple distortion to "getting lost," in various senses of this term, including the "going native" mentioned before) or that I have neglected features at work in it that man shared with nonhuman phenomena, including nature, other communities, society at large, the economy, the political situation, the historical moment—and, once more, in myself.

If the research role is sustained with difficulty, the assumed role becomes part of the researcher's self-concept. As a remedy, "the field worker needs cooling-off periods during and after complete participation, at which times he can 'be himself' and look back on his field behavior dispassionately and sociologically" (Gold, 1958, p. 34). Not expecting this problem, I made no such provisions.

Hughes' (1960) discussion of the dialectic tension between the complete observer and complete participant concludes with the following solutions: be a part-time participant and part-time reporter, be a private participant and public reporter, or be a public participant and a secret reporter. My stance was largely the last—public participant, secret researcher. Its pitfalls can be described in social psychological terms. The self is presented in a setting in terms of a role that is confirmed by others and thereby loses its "as if" qualities for the researcher. If the presented self is compatible with the private self-concept, then it becomes incorporated into the self-concept and shapes subsequent behavior. The discrepancy between the way one is perceived by others and one's self-concept is a form of cognitive dissonance that seeks resolution. The difficulty of maintaining an unconfirmed private self-image, particularly in an authoritarian social structure with explicit rules, is made clear in Reynolds and Farberow's (1976) study of patienthood, which led to a suicidal attempt by the pseudopatient researcher. Avoiding the hostility of the research subject by concealing the research intention forfeits the help the research subject can render. The negative research image I developed during the survey project made me anticipate only poor outcomes from informing others and guilt for not being forthright. Gans (1968, p. 315) cleverly linked researcher guilt and overidentification with the subject in a vicious cycle: "Deceiving people and catching them unaware make the field worker both guilty and sorry for the people he is studying, and in partial recompense, he identifies with them, taking their troubles to heart, sometimes even accepting the validity of their causes." Guilt compels abandoning the research effort in certain cases and joining the community for some purpose. An instructive example can be found in the introduction to Lifton's (1967) *Hiroshima* study:

> Despite the seventeen years that had passed since the bomb, no Japanese individual or group had carried out a detailed or systematic study of its general psychological and social effects. The few scholars who had initiated such studies had cut them short, and had either reported their findings in fragmentary, exaggeratedly technical form, or else had been so struck by the human suffering encountered that they ceased their research and dedicated themselves to programs of much-needed social welfare [p. 4].

Here the guilt of surviving and identification with the survivors overwhelmed the researchers' identity, making it impossible for the researchers to initiate or complete research.

The problem of maintaining my weak researcher identity was compounded by the demands that my job as dance therapist made on my time, both on the job and in preparation at home. Occasionally my activity therapies supervisor obliged me to perform extra tasks, such as conducting tedious, lengthy interviews concerning patients' activity preferences, which consumed my research time for several weeks. As a regular role member, I was expected to perform all the duties of a part-time activity therapist. The activities director who hired me on the strength of my psychology, dance, and teaching experience was not concerned with my lack of formal dance therapy credentials. The newness of dance therapy work for me, however, meant that much preparation was needed before arriving at work each day and some consultation was needed at work to deal with problems that arose. Because of these constraints and the attractiveness of the dance therapy role, at times I suspended my research activities altogether—my form of going native.

These factors impeding the development of my research identity and activities were intensified by other time constraints. Simultaneously I was a full-time graduate student and teaching assistant, a married woman, a daughter, a granddaughter, a friend, an observer in another setting, and a student of yoga and folk dance. These commitments prevented me from observing at the hospital during certain hours. Satisfactory participant observation requires freedom and flexibility, but life's circumstances do not typically permit total immersion in a single activity. Dance therapy required approximately ten hours per week with participant observation remotely related to this work requiring another ten. Whenever several hours or an evening became free, I rushed to the hospital in order to do more observation. Time spent at the hospital was limited by outside commitments and consumed by inside ones and commuting, and I discovered the strain of squeezing participant observation in among other duties.

I would recommend that such research be a less interrupted activity. Time must be available for the unconstrained researcher to "hang around" the site for long hours and at odd times to follow up leads whenever and wherever they occur. This kind of work demands relative freedom from outside obligations and suspension from other parts of the self so that the researcher can cut off one world and enter another. Unless these obligations are suspended, the researcher is distracted, but who can so readily break these bonds? In my third research project (Chapters Six and Seven), I did what was necessary to divorce myself temporarily from all but my fieldwork, avoiding the hindrance of time constraints and conflicting obligations, which left me a happier, more productive person. Both the amount of time in the field and the time available for writing and analyzing field notes suffer from outside commitments. The dilemma soon emerges that the more time spent in the field forming relationships and gathering data, the less time available for recording. Junker (1960) suggests the following ratio for participant observation fieldwork: observing, one-sixth; recording, one-third; analyzing, one-third; and reporting, one-sixth. To record for two hours each hour of observation was impossible, so I found myself reducing observation time in order to record, and vice versa. Time constraints also impinged on my research by making it impossible to obtain comparative observations in other hospitals. How did patient friendships differ in hospitals that did not serve wealthy patients or boast excellent facilities and a high staff-patient ratio, as did the hospital under study?

A reason my time in the hospital was consumed by the dance therapy role was that I plunged enthusiastically into work that was so compatible with my needs and outlook. The philosophy of the activity therapies department matched my own, and the role reinforced my predilections rather than challenging them. Because of this fit, my role became not only a source of identification and an escape, but engaged me with my departmental colleagues in challenging the psychiatric establishment. In staff discussions among activity therapists, traditional psychiatry was usually questioned or rejected. One student activity therapist completed his training by writing a paper that revealed the values he had acquired as a member of the group. Our common goal, he claimed, was to relate to the patients' humanness rather than to their pathology. We were the "good guys" of the hospital who did not pay only lip service to milieu therapy, but truly appreciated the patient's potential for growth within an appropriate psychosocial environment. Our task as activity therapists was to

> design situations which accepted the patient to be of unconditional value as a human being; situations which allow her/him to be and feel her/himself. When the patient realizes s/he is experiencing a reality in the form of activity, s/he is potentially capable of experiencing and defining her/himself. . . . S/he is able to grab another handle of reality. A.T. [activity therapies] provides activities in such a way that the patient can accept the participation as hers/his, as being completely "normal" and therefore being harmlessly real [Hardesty, 1970, p. 3].

My propensity for seeing patients as underdogs became coupled with the notion that traditional psychiatric practices reinforced their oppressed condition. By contrast, the consensus of our countless staff discussions as activity therapists was that our attitudes and work were beneficial to patients. The activity therapists believed their treatment of patient needs was more enlightened than that of other hospital departments. The seductive philosophy of the role I had adopted diminished the chance of my viewing other staff and patients in their own terms, for every group was busily concerned with labeling the others.

Despite my feelings of righteousness regarding my ethical, nonexploitative, reciprocal relations with patients, I know now that I deceived myself by confusing my role toward the patients with my research intentions. After adopting the patently nonexploitative dance therapist role, I still had the problem of how to operationalize my research interest. Because I had tackled the problem obliquely—how should I relate to patients—rather than directly—how should I do research with the patients—the research stance was not resolved unless I assumed that simply being a dance therapist was doing the research. That strategy would have been appropriate for certain topics, but for studying patient friendships it was deficient and deceptive.

Because this issue was inadequately resolved, it recurred repeatedly. However, after establishing myself in the field, I believed that changing my stance was not permissible. As time passed and my research interests still were not known to the patients, I felt like a coward and was perplexed that I was engaged in research according to principles that I condemned. I rationalized my disguised participant observation in the following ways: First, the patients were free to reject my company; second, my research activities of observing and recording patients' behavior were already being done by nurses and psychiatric aides. I hid my research intention from the patients lest I acknowledge this guinea pig aspect of the relationship. Was it necessary to inform every patient that I was observing friendships when my behavior did not impose on them in any way? In this way I gradually neutralized my guilt and accepted the inevitability of a certain amount of secretiveness.

My setting role as dance therapist satisfied the criteria of meaningful participation, viable exchange, and access to the study of patient relationships. But my research role was problematic. First, a mental hospital, especially a prestigious one such as I was studying, employs many different kinds of professionals. According to its annual report, the hospital employed psychiatrists, physicians, clinical physiologists, neurologists, dentists, radiologists, neuropathologists, biophysicists, biochemists, sociologists, social anthropologists, psychologists, psychiatric social workers, activity therapists, teachers, vocational rehabilitation counselors, nurses, and others. All of these trained individuals were contributing to the patients' welfare or to the advancement of knowledge. Where did I fit in and what could I contribute that the staff could not? Were there any niches left in the hospital for a novice sociologist? Was there any hypothesis that had not yet been explored? In this initial research phase I attempted to carve a research identity but was overwhelmed frequently by feelings of being superfluous. The hospital was saturated with so many researchers, what could I do that was unique? Sociological research had already been done on the mental hospital, so why had I come? Was sociological research different from all the thinking, observing, and investigating done in the hospital? What was a sociologist?

Glaser and Strauss (1967, pp. 30-31) remark that sociologists are prone to feelings of inadequacy when they define their task improperly:

> [The task] is not to provide a perfect description of an area, but to develop a theory that accounts for much of the relevant behavior. The sociologist with theoretical generation as his major aim need not know the concrete situation better than the people involved in it (an impossible task anyway). His job and his training are to do what these laymen cannot do—generate general categories and their properties for general and specific situations and problems. . . .
>
> Sociologists who conceive of this task as their job are not plagued (as are those who attempt to report precise description) by thoughts such as "everybody knows it, why bother to write a book" or feelings that "description is not enough." Sociologists who set themselves the task of generating theory from the data of social research have a job that can be done only by the sociologist, and that offers a significant product to laymen and colleagues alike. . . . The distinctive offering of sociology to our society is sociological theory, not only researched description. Indeed the market, corporate, and government fact-finding agencies can easily outdo any sociologist in researched descriptions through sheer resources, if they care to.

What do you do, however, if the practical activity of the studied setting is theorizing?

The feeling of superfluousness almost overwhelmed me when I visited the social science department chief, who kindly handed me massive completed reports describing months of observation in the wards (Longabaugh, Dummer, and Forster, 1968a and 1968b). The director of activity therapies likewise had prepared many papers on adolescents in the hospital. His long, complex guides, intended as helpful for formulating a psychosocial diagnosis of a group member, almost completely discouraged me from the attempt to describe a patient's psychological condition. In addition, since all of the necessary information desired by these guides could not be gained solely by participant observation, I wondered if the method was appropriate to my problem. The reports from social group workers whom the activity therapies director supervised also seemed to deal with the very matters I wished to investigate and contained successfully designed interventions. For example, one wrote that "a primary concern is the therapeutic potential patients have for each other and how one can use ward group interactions to enhance this potential" (Glotfelty, 1966). Had my professional identity been stronger and my research anxieties weaker, this groundwork could have been used productively. Instead I perceived the work that had gone before me as preemptive and threatening.

My overidentification as a hospital staff member led me to question my contribution as a sociologist. This problem is linked directly to doing research in a setting composed of articulate, observant, reflective members. As a novice sociologist, it was almost impossible to differentiate my observations from those made by setting members. To overcome this lack of a sense of identity as a sociologist, I could have engaged in highly visible, blatantly sociological research activities, but participant observation as a method does not rely on such pursuits.

One technique I used to overcome this identity confusion was applying specific sociological theories that I was studying concurrently in graduate school to my work in the hospital. For example, we studied the labeling theory of deviance, which suggests that behavior is not inherently sick or bad but is so labeled by people in the environment who perpetuate this behavior to fulfill their labels. Thus, for weeks I eschewed the labels "mental patient" and "mentally ill" in the hospital, and with each encounter with patients I actively engaged in behavior that communicated expectations of normalcy. I developed relationships with patients who I thought would respond to these new expectations, and I reported amazed discouragement to my advisor when this method did not produce the anticipated outcome.

The doubly disappointing results "proved" to me the hopeless nature of the person's problems and the bankruptcy of sociological labeling theory as an intervention guide.

My training as sociologist was leading me to believe that hospitalized patients were being wronged, that the medical model of mental illness was wrong, and that my progressive Brandeis education freed me from all the misconceptions under which hospital personnel labored. I clung to sociological theory to retain my identity in the face of other powerful conceptual frameworks such as psychiatry. In the hospital under study I sought evidence of the findings of Goffman and of Stanton and Schwartz so as to vindicate sociology.

Despite these mental games, however, my predominant existential state during the first phase of my hospital stay was one of superfluousness. Each unique activity of my sociological researcher identity was already being performed in the hospital: The nurses and psychiatric aides took copious notes to record patient behavior, the staff gathered in countless meetings to share and analyze observations, and small groups met informally in the hospital coffee shop to air their latest theory about the nature of mental illness, the dynamics of milieu therapy, and so on. Each week professional papers were presented by renowned scientists and therapists, and numerous researchers were conducting studies in the hospital. Had mental hospitals in general been saturated with research, and was it therefore unnecessary to attempt yet another study? Conversely, no one was conducting dance therapy as I was. Dance therapist was an acceptable, efficacious identity that fit in the huge bureaucracy of interdependent roles that were linked together to form the hospital. In that role I could feel part of the whole, in the sense of contributing to common goals, relating to other role incumbents, and having clear-cut boundaries that prevented me from feeling swallowed by the hospital complexity. As a dance therapist, my image of hospital life was clear, but as a sociological researcher, the hospital became an undifferentiated mass of concepts, ideas, and hypotheses.

The issue of researcher role identity was aggravated also by my working alone without an inside support to whom I could report my findings and vent my feelings. I am responsible for not having arranged for an inside support, but its necessity was not known to me, nor did I want to burden anyone with this task. The notion of burden reflected my view of the hectic schedule maintained by the hospital staff and the low priority I assumed my research had. I especially felt it would be a burden since my study was self-initiated rather than commissioned by the hospital. From time to time I used the friendships I developed among staff in the hospital to share my ideas and feelings. But these spontaneous friendships were needed also for relief from working and studying. With them I could be the researcher only on occasion.

These professional and personal insecurities were not easily shared with my advisor. Could I speak freely of events in the field that I feared were inappropriate? Could I expose my mistakes and shortcomings if I was attempting to establish professional attitudes and behavior? Our debriefing sessions therefore focused on matters of content. In addition, many of these thoughts and feelings were vague and became clear only after the project was completed. At the time I experienced merely persistent feelings of uneasiness as the "researcher" and satisfaction as the "dance therapist." I feared I had gone native.

What were the consequences of having a situational identity stronger than my researcher identity? First, it created a certain research confinement, or passivity, in me.

> The researcher may be able to get himself a job in the plant and enter in the role of a worker. In that case, total immersion may be possible, for the stranger has a job to do and does not have to explain why he is hanging around. If the researcher conscientiously writes up a work diary on the events of each day, he may put together valuable data on the social system of the plant. . . . The participant observer in such a case may be able to penetrate deeply into problems whose existence is overlooked by the interviewer.
>
> On the other hand, the role of a worker is a confining one from a research standpoint; it provides little scope for asking unusual questions and for following up

leads. The disadvantage can be overcome to a certain extent after the researcher has gained acceptance into the work group. Then he can begin to confide in other workers, to tell them that he took the job in order to learn from first hand experience what factory life is like, and that he will appreciate the help they can give him, based upon their much longer experience. This enables the researcher to fit some interviewing in with participant observation [Whyte, 1951, pp. 500-501].

The limited number of interviews I conducted with staff (none with patients) reflected my reluctance to assert my researcher self and to modify or complicate my relationship with others. I was also ambivalent about muddying the purity of participant observation with the "unnatural" act of interviewing. But primarily it was my public dance therapist identity that blocked me from using other research procedures. Furthermore, those interviews I did conduct among staff showed them idealizing their conceptualization of hospital ideology and presenting formal views, just as Becker (1956) had found among medical students. My interviews were useful primarily for gathering basic information and for sifting between the staff's ideal attitudes and actual behavior with regard to most topics, including patient friendships.

I did not know then that both my adopted and my continuing roles—dance therapist and sociological researcher—could be equally significant. I did not want my satisfying, even exhilarating dance therapy role to be trivialized as "only" a means of access to my research problem. In a short period I had become protective of and committed to my setting role. The need to obtain endorsement from the upper echelons of the hospital administration to do research was obviated by adopting the dance therapist role and observing from it. Since I did not appear to be doing anything other than dance therapy, I did not need additional sanctions. This rationalization reflected the intimidating effect of the hospital on me, especially when one considers my low prestige. Levinson (1957, p. 641) indicates that this intimidation is characteristic even of experienced social scientists working in mental hospitals, not only novices.

The research observer is ordinarily allowed to intrude only into the daily life of patients and lower-status personnel. We know very little about the sociology and social psychology of top-level hospital administration (or of other institutional elites), in part because investigators have not had sufficient status to enter the more secluded domain of the upper echelons. Such high status is of course not merely to be "given"; it has to be earned.

I understood the hospital well enough, I thought, to know I was a "low-caste stranger" (Daniels, 1967). Because I was intimidated, I mistakenly assumed that the powers-that-be would only set up obstacles to my research interests rather than providing assistance. If a covert stance is taken, the possibilities of cooperation and assistance are indeed limited.

Staff Member/Researcher Role Conflict

Since I believed that participant observation's distinctive value was access to the insider role, I became an insider (even if part-time and low status) and lost the benefits of the outsider stance. Schwartz's discussion of the insider/outsider tension mentions some benefits of not being a regular insider: "Some patients felt they could talk to me because I was not paid to listen to them, as was the staff. They objected strenuously to, as they put it, the 'paid friendships,' offered by the staff. Since I was not in the formal role of therapist, a 'paid listener,' some patients felt they could talk to me more freely than they would to a therapist" (1971, pp. 100-101). Kluckhohn, however, believes that the uninvolved stranger is offered critical information simply because there is no consequence to such unburdening (Trice, 1956). Merton (1947, p. 305) agrees: "Informants will not hesitate to make certain private views known to a disinterested outside observer—views which would not be expressed were it thought they would get back to management. The outsider has 'stranger' value." The balance I struck between insider and outsider in this project diminished some of my "stranger" value for patients but might have alienated those patients reluctant to interact openly with staff members.

Being a staff member with outsider features was close to being "special," a taboo status which implied staff alliance with patients for "neurotic reasons" or as a consequence of being manipulated by patients. The staff assumption was that patients were trying to "split" staff for their benefit, such as by bending the rules regulating patient life. It would have been interesting to ask those staff whom patients trusted to question the patients about whether I was manipulated and how open patients allowed themselves to be with me. This would have been a check on my observations. Hughes (1956, p. 84) believes that "each observer, himself a member of society, marked by sex, age, race, and the other characteristics by which people place one another in various roles or relations, must find out not merely what the significant kinds of people are in the groups and situations he wants to study; he must also learn to perceive quickly and surely what role he has been cast in by the people he is studying." Patients appeared to be forthright with me at some times and manipulative at others. Whatever they feared about staff, they might have feared about me. Even when I was not acting in my staff role, evidence was probably always there in my mannerisms, posture, and reference to the world outside the hospital that I was a staff member. Erikson (1967, p. 370) argues that signs of one's covert roles can never totally be suppressed: "It is impossible to avoid arousing at least a subliminal suspicion." One barrier that might have prevented patients from expressing their private views to me as they might have with a disinterested outsider was that as an insider I inevitably gave off signs that I was rule abiding. Also some of the specific characteristics of spontaneous patient interaction might have been forfeited when I inadvertently communicated that I was researching.

My field notes indicate that I represented both staff and outsider to some of the patients:

Nighttime; walking past the two-storey building housing the male adolescent unit on the bottom floor and the female adolescent unit on the upper level. Windows are on top of each other. Guy in room beneath girl has window open and is talking

*with the girl above him. I walk past them looking at him but
not seeing her.*

*I wonder what he is doing with his window open and
leaning out and am puzzling over whether or not I should go
around and tell a staff member on his hall that it looks like he's
trying to climb out the window.*

He asked the girl, "Who walked by? Shula?"

I said, "Yes, it's me," and walk back.

He said, "Don't worry, I'm not an escape risk."

I said, "I thought you were trying to split."

"No, I'm just talking to Linda."

It was only then that I saw Linda above him.

*He said, "I can't see her but you can see us both, what
does she look like?"*

*I described her hair-do. They were laughing and happy.
He said, "Don't tell anybody about this."*

"Why?" I asked, "Is it illegal?"

"No, but it's stretching things a bit."

*I said good night and walked off. I heard him call, "Hey
Linda, what did Roberta say to. . . ."*

My immediate response to the situation (to evaluate patient behavior in terms of hospital rules) was as a responsible staff member. This is what the patient expected if he believed he had to
prevent me from acting like a staff member reacting to an
escape. But I also allowed myself to be special (by not reporting
the open window and by asking the patient what the policy was
rather than informing him) in an attempt to remain an outsider.
Although the origin of my response might have been identification with the patients against the hospital, reinforced by a research need to gain their trust, I learned that outsiders threaten
the staff's control over patients. This small incident illustrates
the confusion and ready manipulation engendered as the researcher tries to establish an insider/outsider balance.

This interesting issue of patients' differentiation between
staff and outsiders was overlooked since it did not coincide with
my research topic. It would have aroused more of my attention
if I had encountered practical difficulties communicating with
patients. As I became more familiar with the patient culture,

my staff role, which had been a convenient way of becoming integrated in the environment, was becoming an increasing burden. When I walked into a room full of adolescent patients and someone said, "Here comes the folk dance lady, everyone!" I wished they could have forgotten my obtrusive role. The role suited to entry is not necessarily the best one for the requirements of later stages in the research process.

The crucial dilemma of my adoption of a staff role was the concern that if patients perceived me as a staff member, their communication with me or in my presence would become what I came to call "stylized." A vivid example of stylized behavior was contained in a conversation overheard between two female adolescent patients. Nancy was initiating recently admitted Susan into patienthood by instructing her in the norms of patient culture, particularly how to manipulate staff members into lifting a general "restriction" on patient freedom which is frequently imposed on the group in response to one patient's rule infraction. Susan asked Nancy what she should say to staff members because she felt she was supposed to talk to them but didn't have anything to say. Nancy explained how as the restriction wears on, people con the staff and say the things they want to hear, like that restriction is really doing them good: "How clever of you to have imposed a restriction at that particular moment" [Field notes].

The norm of staff members at this particular hospital was to uphold the ideology of the hospital and of their profession. Although the formal rules in which I was personally instructed were limited to "keeping patients safe by locking up all sharps," a general ideology of patient-staff interaction was transmitted continuously during staff meetings and informal discussions in which we discussed and evaluated what we were doing. The staff and patients spent most of their time strategizing how to deal with one another and socializing newcomers into the appropriate attitudes. As a researcher on a mental hospital ward, Schwartz (1971, pp. 92-93) underwent the same process of making "important accommodations to certain critical values and norms held by the institution's staff":

One of these values required that persons interacting with patients manifest "sensitivity to the patient." The expectation was that the patient would be accorded respect and not demeaned in any way; that one should become aware of the patient's peculiar sensitivities and respond so as to minimize the possibility of upsetting him or in some way injuring his self-esteem. . . .

Another norm, related to the one just discussed, was that personnel should avoid responding to the patient in kind if he manifested assaultive, abusive, or demanding behavior.

A value almost universally accepted and acted upon that played a dominant role in the institution was the interpretative-analytic mode.

At the hospital in which I worked and conducted my research, the social science department studied staff ideology and defined certain values, labeled "the givens." They are expressed in abbreviated form, as follows:

1. Patients are unable to serve their own and/or the society's interest effectively; therefore society (by means of the hospital) confines and attempts to change them.
2. Staff is oriented toward action rather than passive waiting for spontaneous remission; the action involves manipulating the social environment and the patient.
3. The hospital is responsible for not letting patients hurt themselves and should attempt to prevent patient deterioration even if patient improvement is not possible. The hospital is completely responsible for the patient 24 hours per day.
4. Patients do not always know what is good for them, how they should be treated, or if they should be treated. Patients sometimes act contrary to staff's best judgment. "Patients must be monitored continuously to prevent their impeding the treatment program."
5. We do not know how to cure mental illness, and there is only minimal consensus among the staff responsible for this work (Longabaugh, Dummer, and Forster, 1968a).

In the initial phase I learned and accommodated this set of givens, but in subsequent phases I experienced conflict between my personal and work-related attitudes and the predominant staff ideology. The conflict was kept in check. However, by acknowledging that "minimal consensus among staff" exists, there was no reason to be concerned with rejecting some of these givens, as long as my role was not jeopardized. In addition, could I really pass negative judgments on this hospital, which claimed to be one of the country's best? Had I worked there long enough to judge it? Could I gain sufficient insight in my low status to obtain a clear understanding of hospital policy?

At the same time, however, my graduate courses were teaching me an alternative set of assumptions that could be used to understand patient behavior and to provide patient care. Most persuasive to me was the work of Ronald D. Laing (1971, 1972), especially the theory of the dis/confirmation of experience and its role in the etiology and maintenance of mental illness. On one occasion I did challenge a staff member in terms of these alternative assumptions, questioning her treatment of a patient who was lying in bed screaming and thrashing her limbs. The nurse on duty ignored the patient on the principle that "she only wanted attention." After this patient's exasperating behavior continued in the face of the nurse's calm attention to other matters, I lost my distance and sat at the patient's bedside until she calmed down, then encouraged her to become active in something constructive. The nurse dismissed my bewilderment and distress as "part of the typical pattern." This response increased my distress and made me further question the staff ideology.

This incident enraged me. The nurse apparently disconfirmed the patient's experience and my response. This disconfirmation gradually renders people incapable of remembering their own intentions, of trusting their own reactions, and of containing their aggressive impulses toward the source of the invalidation. I wanted either to flee the confusing situation or to fight the participants. Fighting would have involved urging the patient to make demands of the nurse or directly challenging the nurse myself.

Being a staff member automatically meant I had to assume responsibility for patient safety and power over patient behavior. The staff is analogous to police in monitoring behavior, which is reported to the judges (psychiatrists) who control punishment (restrictions) and rewards (passes or freedoms) and who can be bribed (by engaging in "therapeutic communication"). On certain occasions, staff described their own role with labels such as "being security" to indicate the regulation of patient behavior and traffic. A staff member is never truly off duty while on hospital grounds because all patient behavior that is witnessed is potentially meaningful or dangerous. Staff differed, however, in their readiness to assume responsibility for patients beyond the staff member's formal care.

The police analogy holds also in that the function of police is to be citizens' friendly helpers, not only the agents of control; so, too, the staff is oriented both toward the prevention of rule infractions and assuaging patients' distress. As a staff member specializing in an activity rather than assigned to a particular patient unit, I could leave the odious monitoring tasks to staff members responsible for particular groups and engage in the "higher" purposes of therapeutic interaction with patients. But during those times when other staff were not present, I felt the obligation to police patient behavior. I use the word *felt* rather than *knew* to indicate the ambiguity and confusion surrounding staff responsibilities. The only way to determine if the felt obligation was a real expectation from the hospital structure would have been to check with each psychiatrist concerning each patient regularly, as many activity therapists did:

Meeting of administrative psychiatrist and ward staff on B hall for severely disturbed male older adolescents and young adults. Also attending is another activity therapist specializing in music. Purpose of meeting is to discuss each patient on the hall who participates in activity therapies so that activity therapists can share with staff what they are learning about patients and so that staff can aid activity therapists in their work by let-

ting them know what patients are like on the hall and in other forms of therapy. . . .

As meeting ended there was talk about a couple of patients meeting surreptitiously. Greta, the other activity therapist, asked if they were allowed to meet and the doctor said they were "not supposed to communicate." Another therapist said they don't really talk to each other, just touch a lot. Greta said she would appreciate it if she would be informed when people were not allowed to be together so she could enforce this decision and not let patients manipulate her ignorance. No method was devised at the meeting, however, to provide her with this information.

Activity therapists expressed frustration formally during staff meetings and informally on other occasions over the following issues: They resented having to play the police role incumbent on all staff, being uninformed of the restrictions pertaining to a particular patient, and having their work undermined by other forms of therapy or ward policy. As an activity therapist, I was caught up in a staff role that generated these attitudes and feelings.

As a staff insider, the opportunity for spontaneous interaction with patients diminished not only because of my monitoring responsibility but also because of the responsibility "to be therapeutic" at all times. I was certainly not opposed to being therapeutic. Rather, the problem was that the process was never clearly defined and was constantly changing. Being therapeutic meant engaging in professionally rule-guided rather than spontaneous and intuitive behavior. In the midst of the confusion as to what is therapeutic for whom, staff members learned to rely on their private theories of mental health and illness, which is precisely what the hospital's ideology of coordinated milieu therapy did not intend. Although the various wards strove for a unified, consistent therapeutic philosophy, there were no specific instructions for communicating with each patient under all circumstances. We were left on our own, therefore, to decide matters charged with great significance. For example:

At the morning meeting between Dr. Bender [hall admin-istrator for female adolescent patients], Sylvia and Nina [fellow activity therapists] and Jill [my activity therapies supervisor], Dr. Bender informed us that the patient Susan had cut off all her hair. Somehow she had gotten a "sharp" from a patient who had gotten it out of the nursing station, although that patient had not gotten it out for that purpose.

The next evening when I walked into the patients' kitch-en, the first thing I saw was Susan's new "hair-do." It was just chopped off in clumps as close to her head as she could get, extremely uneven, but to me she still looked beautiful. My im-mediate reaction was to recall what Dr. Bender had reported to us the morning before, and to wonder if I should remark about her hair to her, but I decided not to because I couldn't under-stand at the time and cannot remember now what his attitude towards it was other than that it was a significant gesture. I stood there probably staring at her head without saying any-thing and feeling that not only was my spontaneity tarnished but that I was made to feel ridiculous.

The issue of spontaneous vs. considered reactions burdens my interaction. I find myself weighing whether or not I should say something, what I should say, etc., instead of merely talk-ing. This reflects the assumptions that seem to be operating around here that everything one does has an impact on the pa-tient and since everything matters, it is important to make the right decisions and say the right things.

Being a staff member meant I could not interact with patients strictly according to my sense of what was best.

In addition, as a part-timer with limited responsibilities because of my peripheral activity therapies role, patients were able to manipulate the confusion and lack of staff consensus:

Susan [adolescent patient] asked me to unlock the ward door so she could leave. I said, "Can I?" She said in a very cocky yet straightforward enough way that I could not mis-understand her, "I have full towns and grounds" [that is, she was not restricted to the hospital and was allowed to go out]. So I said, "Just a minute, I don't have my keys, I'll go and get them." I turned around to get them from my coat pocket. At that moment I felt overwhelmed with conflict and suspicions about whether or not Susan was telling me the truth about her privilege status or merely conning me into letting her out. Why ask me? She could have asked another staff person. But I was in her presence when she wanted to go. I also felt awful to have to be in a social system in which suspicion is generated in me from time to time, where I come to mistrust the statements of a whole category of people [patients], and it is by my constant mistrust that I am doing my best duty. I remembered how staff berates patients for not trusting and rewards them for trusting, but this trust is not reciprocated. Caring and trusting are at odds here. The staff must care enough to try their best to keep patients safe, yet they don't trust them to keep themselves safe.

I walked down the hall, torn inside, not knowing what to do. Should I just get the key and let her out or ask someone? Happily, Nina [a group worker, activity therapist, and friend of mine] was standing near my coat. I asked her if Susan had towns and grounds because she had asked me to let her out. Nina said she didn't know either although she was the group worker for the ward. She would ask one of the aides. Nina said to me that Susan should have asked someone "on checks" [aides and nurses checked patients' presence and general demeanor every 5 or 15 minutes]. Nina went to the nursing station and learned that Susan cannot go off the hall until her room is cleaned up. She then told one of the aides about Susan's request. I walked up to her and said that I had been told she could not go off the hall until her room had been done. And then she exploded. I felt extremely unhappy walking back toward her, having to confirm that I did not trust her, that I was suspicious, that I was unable to satisfy her request, etc. She yelled about not even having the chance to get off the hall, and how she cleaned up her room so that she could go off and then she gets told she can't go off unless it's cleaned (I think she meant the aides didn't know that she had cleaned it). She screamed that she was humiliated, walking out, stomping and screaming all the time. I felt stupid, impotent, sorry, standing there. How did I let all of this happen to her and me? This was not the way I wanted to act with patients, with people. Why did I have to be put into these boxes, binds, mazes, despite myself? I felt controlled, manipulated, forced to be an instrument of someone else. I also feared that Susan had lost trust and faith in me, didn't like me, and wouldn't want to speak or let me work with her.

I didn't want to hurt her, especially since I knew her a little. I also have a sense that she is an important person on the hall, surrounded by friends and isolated from staff. I felt that I had betrayed her trust, that her anger was healthy and that her environment was cruel. Perhaps this shows that I identify too much with the patients or that she manipulated my guilt in order to feel anger.

As I stood there in the then empty hall with her stamping and yelling, I felt small and alone and thought of the countless times in my life when I was reminded to clean up before doing something I wanted to; and that my protest was normal, part of growing up. Should Susan's behavior be seen as pathological just because it is taking place in a mental hospital? It all seemed very unfair and the feelings were very strong.

I started to walk into the living room where Nina was waiting for me, when Susan came walking down the hall towards me with another staff member. She had probably taken that staff person to her room, shown her that it was neat and was now being let out. I turned around after making a quick decision, got up my courage and said that I was sorry about the incident, that I felt awful. And before I could explain she said that it was not my fault, it had nothing to do with me, and on and on like that. I felt relieved that she was not angry with me, but then guilty that I wanted to remain free from responsibility for patient anger and dump it on someone else's shoulders. If the staff wants locks, they have to suffer the consequences of enforcing them, just as the patients have to suffer being locked in.

I assume patients are truthful with me because I have so little power, but maybe I should assume that they deceive me because I am not fully informed.

Staff and patients are integrated in a pattern of trying not to be manipulated by each other. This self-fulfilling prophecy communicates the expectation of being manipulated, even if manipulation is unintended. The problem of manipulation arises in a closed environment with a caste system of the powerful (staff) and the powerless (patients), in which the basis for granting anything (goods, affection, or freedom) is vague and constantly changing. The problem is aggravated by the fact that staff feel that they are manipulated by other staff as well as by patients. The impact of the hospital's social structure is felt in these moments of emotional upheaval in which the complex hierarchy of roles and functions intersects with the psychodynamics of individuals occupying those roles. The resulting interaction patterns reflected, to my mind, a collapse of all the roles into three major categories—doctors, patients, and irrelevants (all other support staff). Basically, the hospital seemed to divide its members into doctors and all others, the latter being either mentally ill or simply limited in their understanding to some degree. The major characteristic of being perceived as a patient or as not-a-doctor was being treated with massive doubt. The doctors' interpretation of events and meanings was definitive because of the doctors' status, not because the interpretation was proven accurate on the basis of later events or evaluation.

The powerful feelings I had as a staff member made it difficult to sit back calmly and observe patients in their interaction with one another. The physical access to the patients afforded by my role was dampened by the emotional stress that accompanies involvement in a hierarchical work organization designed to produce mental health. My reciprocity in dealing with patients was also more complicated than I had anticipated. In addition to being unique individuals, staff members are utilized by patients to fill symbolic roles in the powerful dramas affecting their emotional lives. There were times when my mere presence upset a patient with whom I was not even interacting because I reminded him of someone or gave him frightening "vibrations." Conversely, when patients became emotionally attached to me, their therapists or the ward staff might decide that we should spend less time together. In other cases, the valuable time remaining for observations after formal dance therapy was consumed by emotionally starved patients with whom, as a staff member, I could not regularly refuse to interact. Since many of these individuals were not adolescents, I became frustrated when their needs blocked me from observing the patient population relevant to my research interests. To avoid these interactions, I resorted to lame excuses (sometimes lies), which did not add to my comfort in the situation:

When Laura [adolescent patient] left to go to school, I sat at the table in the coffee shop waiting for Nina [group worker] so I could conduct an informal interview with her. I sat alone and was afraid to catch the eye of an elderly man who is saccharine and who will sit for hours telling me how nice I am and nothing else. I felt very inhuman deliberately avoiding catching his eye because he was obviously walking around looking for someone to be with.

I believe that my staff role also blocked my research interests in that I felt obligated to relate to patients as individuals whom I should serve rather than understand. The conflicts between the practitioner and researcher perspectives on the client (see also Fox, 1959, for conflicts in the researcher/practitioner role) were embodied within a single researcher/practitioner. As a sociologist one should see the individual as a member of a category about which generalizations can be made. As a person and as a dance therapist, however, I cared for the patients as individuals. I saw their differentiating characteristics despite the pressure of administered hierarchies to treat them as embodiments of diagnoses. My task was to enhance the patients' mental health by designing a dance therapy that would help them individually and within their small groups. As a result I formed different kinds of relationships with different patients. Knowing the patients as individuals made studying them difficult and conceptualizing them categorically rather than individually painful.

Were these the reactions of a responsible staff member or my personal response of overrapport? Schwartz (1971, p. 88) describes a similar response to the patients' humanness: "The flow of life in the ward was such an intensely human experience that theories and conceptions of social organization or interpersonal relations did not seem particularly relevant or important."

My intent to study patient friendships led to my interest

in studying patients not in general but as particular individuals. My need to know weakened when challenged by my respect for other people's privacy; my need to answer predefined research questions weakened in the light of my search for authentic experience. These are the pitfalls of becoming personally involved in a setting and opposing the "doing of research" with the "gaining of authentic experience." In the study described in Chapters Six and Seven, I tried to blend these goals in order to reduce this conflict. In the hospital study, however, I created a paradox by focusing on a nonpatient aspect of patients, namely, their friendships. Recognizing the individuals in their friendships meant respecting their uniqueness and privacy, a hindrance to carrying out observations for the sake of the research project.

This problem in the study of intimate behavior is a nagging concern of all participant observation, since observations depend on the kind of relation that develops between the researcher and the setting member. The research process of this project reflected this conflict by vacillating between focusing on the uniqueness of individual patients and patient relationships and developing generalized conceptual patterns. By the time of the third research project (see Chapters Six and Seven), I was ready to free myself from this problem with the following pragmatic solution: Let the data-gathering process focus on the uniqueness of the phenomena, and share the pattern-generating process with the participants in a collaborative effort.

CHAPTER 4

The Stress of Detached Fieldwork

The end of the preceding chapter highlighted some dilemmas of participant observation resulting from the identity conflicts of the sociologist in the field. In Chapters Six and Seven I present a final, contrasting project in which I resolved the dilemmas and thereby strengthened my identification with the discipline. The meshing of person, problem, and method produces these dilemmas, which arise with all methods.

In the category of "person," a factor relevant in the mental hospital project was that the study represented my first field study and was undertaken with relatively little guidance. I was my own teacher. I had to present myself to setting members as skilled in the method even if I felt like a novice. As a newcomer to the hospital, I thought that only those generalizations that differed from those of setting members were useful. But as a relative outsider, how likely was I to develop new, different, and valid insights? Was my task to learn the nature of the environment for myself or to provide members with new knowl-

195

edge? What constitutes a product if the researcher is relatively inexperienced? Would I find my identity only in obscure topics or in technical measurements? Since I had not developed enough trust to allow myself to "surrender" to the situation and "catch" what it offered, I was intent on mastering, conquering, and subduing the environment. By the time of the third study (Chapters Six and Seven), I could easily allow myself to adopt the role of passive learner open to whatever the field could teach me. Fieldwork was redefined then as a cumulative process extending from study to study and continuously shaping the human instrument.

My product standards as a novice, which derived from famous studies, were unreasonably high and therefore frustrating. How could my part-time, eight-month field involvement match a Whyte, Liebow, Gans, Schwartz, or Lewis? The inexperienced researcher has not integrated the self-concept and the researcher role (Gold, 1958). For the student whose professional identity is unclear, the first field experience can further deepen rather than resolve identity confusion. The weaker the professional identity, the greater the likelihood that fieldwork will be used as an opportunity to go native. The research process becomes the arena for identity formation.

A mental hospital is particularly stressful as the site of a first field experience because of its considerable interpersonal tension. In addition, since nothing is irrelevant, everything is important in terms of security or mental health; all setting members are analyzing everything that transpires. In this milieu the researcher becomes concerned with doing the impossible, that is, capturing everything. The source of greatest difficulty for beginning fieldworkers is the belief that fieldwork will proceed smoothly. However, "*most* anthropologists who have written detailed, descriptive accounts of their experiences indicate that they *usually* had a *great deal* of trouble ... and some were *never* able to establish a professionally adequate working situation" (Wax, 1971, p. 89; emphasis added). Some examples of very troublesome fieldwork efforts are reported by Evans-Pritchard (1940), Diamond (1971), Lowie (1959), and Powdermaker (1966). Fieldworkers believe their peers avoid the extraordinary difficulties that they alone endure. The social psychological concept of "pluralistic ignorance" fits this situation exactly: "the pattern in which individual members of a group *assume* that they are virtually alone in holding the social attitudes and expectations they do, all unknowing that others privately share them" (Merton, 1957, p. 377). Thus pluralistic ignorance, resulting from low mutual observability among fieldworkers, functions to save face for the sociologist encountering trouble in the field but prevents the profession from facing these problems and smoothing the socialization process of its novices. The problems of self, therefore, influence the presentation of method and the socialization of new cohorts. Only redefinition of research reporting in experiential or existential terms will produce accurate norms for participant observation fieldwork. Similarly, the integration of personal, methodological, and substantive analyses will elucidate the differences between the first and subsequent field experiences. The anxieties surrounding the establishment of a professional identity that accompany the ordeal of the first field trip recede in subsequent trips. But the danger that the researcher will enter with received notions increases as each field trip builds on the findings of previous field trips. These chapters on initial research experiences are a contribution to the materials needed to examine these dilemmas.

Junker's (1960, p. 105) study of teaching students the interviewing techniques of fieldwork discusses the specific difficulties of beginners that nevertheless "illuminate some of the basic problems encountered by all social scientists." Students are particularly sensitive to "being rebuffed," "forcing an undesirable topic on an informant," having "inadequate interviewer status" or "inappropriate role," "handling emotional involvement," and dealing with "the ethical problems of reporting." Since these concerns modify students' actions, they also affect project results. In order to reduce anxiety in these research activities, fieldworkers must undergo them and personally resolve the dilemmas that arise for them. It is not uncommon for experienced fieldworkers to claim that the only way to learn fieldwork is to do it.

The first field experience is stressful not only because the student must resolve issues of fieldwork but also because it constitutes the critical phase in the sociologist's socialization process. To become an adult in the discipline, work must be undertaken outside the classroom. In anthropology the stress involved is almost valued as an indicator of the ordeal to be overcome before entering the profession:

> The field experience is the principal initiation rite into the anthropological profession. . . . Anthropological rank is achieved through field work, and at times the rougher the field situation, the greater the rank. Supposedly one grows under stress, and the greater the stress, the more we grow. . . . Anthropologists do sometimes suffer needlessly. . . . Sleeping on a wooden bench is more anthropological than sleeping on a comfortable double bed in the hinterlands of Mexico—the argument being that a comfortable bed would only accentuate the differences between the anthropologist and the people he is living with [Nader, 1970, p. 114].

Important outcomes of enduring the ordeal are an increase in self-confidence (Lortie, 1968) and public recognition of personal commitment, which leads to integration of the anthropologist into the disciplinary community.

The first field experience provokes identity questioning: Who am I, why am I doing this, what am I doing here? Along with introspection, however, the stress of the first field experience is expressed in crying, eating (Wax, 1971), huddling into protective friendships, "taking long solitary walks, going to bed early and reading" novels (Briggs, 1970, p. 271; see also Malinowski, 1961, p. 5), "depression and concomitant inhibition of activities, rejection of members of the culture studied as beyond the pale in certain respects, and paranoid feelings that one is being cheated, plotted against, or laughed at contemptuously" (Fischer, 1970, p. 270)—and plunging into continuous activity, as I did.

Weidman (1970, p. 241) interprets the meaning of the initial field project:

My fieldwork was not simply the fulfillment of a requirement for the doctorate in anthropology. It was not solely a means of escape or a way of learning more about the self. It was not just a convenient way of continuing a most important relationship that grew out of my graduate years. *Most importantly, it represented one of the last hurdles to professional status.* It required the consolidation of a body of knowledge and the utilization of the key method of a discipline in a creative way. It meant *becoming an anthropologist* ... (which) allowed me as a person to relate most meaningfully to others while being at ease with myself. In essence, anthropology helped me to establish an identity [emphasis added].

The student in the field strives to adopt a new identity and seeks ratification. From whom? Setting members cannot be expected to satisfy the sociology student's needs; the mentor is more interested in evaluating outcomes than appreciating the process; family and friends cannot comprehend the problem adequately; and fellow students are working through the problems themselves. The student's socialization through fieldwork is therefore very much a solitary concern.

Students give the first field experience significance beyond the findings to be collected; their enthusiasm is coupled with naivete, their book learning with limited personal experience. In my own case, all of these conflicts as well as ambivalence about my identity as a researcher were expressed in frustration that arose from maintaining control over my activities rather than from being free to explore my personal feelings. That freedom had to wait for the next field trip (Chapters Six and Seven), when my identity became clearer.

Although my dance therapist role began to dominate my identity, my involvement in graduate school and the sharing of field notes with instructors helped sustain a residue of a sociologist's identity. After the initial orientation phase, in which I was accepted by the activity therapies staff and other members of the hospital staff with whom I worked, I refocused on the research question that I had brought to the setting. To gain an understanding of the mental hospital, I continued to present myself to others as a newcomer for the privilege of asking questions and making mistakes even though for all intents and purposes my initiation phase at the hospital had ended. The friendly, ill-informed, newly arrived staff member appeals to patients who can assume the function of host or guide and thereby be more oriented than is the staff member. If the newcomers, however, do not acknowledge their confusion or if they do so in a condescending manner, as was frequently the case with psychiatric residents, they are met with the patient's biting contempt or ridicule. In other words, it is only the humble newcomer who evokes help from the patients.

Because staff and patients were scattered in many different hospital locations, I could repeatedly request explanations about hospital functioning, individual attitudes, and proper responses to certain situations. Although this approach for obtaining information could not be repeated with any individual, the continuous turnover of patients and of staff enabled me to use it repeatedly. The approach is characterized by a somewhat disingenuous naivete (Geer, 1964) and feels manipulative rather than spontaneous, shedding doubt on the emerging rapport. It is likely that this initiation phase is prolonged to delay subsequent stages.

The Dilemmas and Blocks of Gathering Data

The pattern that characterized my eight months of fieldwork consisted of segments of days that could be used to observe, coordinated with other segments devoted to my work as a dance therapist. My responsibilities outside the hospital were combined with time set aside for recording my observations, without arranging a specific regular schedule for this. Such an unsystematic, inadequate arrangement could occur only in a first field experience. An uninterrupted block of time and concentration is required to digest events, record, reflect, plan, and prepare subsequent phases.

Both the close attention used to collect information in the field and the attitude toward recording require great self-control. But even perfect conditions and attitudes require an understanding of likely problems in order to prevent them. At first, my orientation could be labelled "inclusivity." I imagined myself as a tape recorder, recording everything I could hear or see. After this approach proved unfeasible, I turned off the tape recorder so I could "become involved" and later transcribe my involvements at the end of the day. Nevertheless, the pressure to memorize remained because every observation must be grounded in the details of its context. If I controlled my impulse to absorb more than I was prepared to record, I felt blocked in my awareness of a situation.

At first the environment's newness made observation and written description relatively easy. There was no burden of a backlog of unrecorded observations. In the beginning everything impressed me. My field notes of the initial period are filled with physical descriptions of people, places, and events. Attempts at analysis were premature. The focus on the physical setup reflected my attempt to get a lay of the land, to master the space so that I could navigate it. As soon as I focused on the research topic, however, I recognized that the task of capturing intimate interaction was difficult because observation was awkward.

Early in the evening I saw Tom [male adolescent patient] sitting in the library area with a guy from SBI [the male adolescent ward]. They were talking in soft tones to each other. Tom looked very unhappy. I couldn't tell if the guy from SBI was comforting him or causing additional unhappiness. I could not ascertain what they were talking about because I was trying not to look as if I was trying to listen. They were speaking to each other quietly, which made it difficult to hear anything.

Not only did my topic of intimate behavior present particular observational obstacles, but there was also the dilemma of focus inherent in participant observation research. Wolff (1971, p. 239) presents the ideal when he writes of the "pertinence of everything," the flip side of the "suspension of received notions." The pertinence of everything means simply that "all that comes to one's attention is pertinent." My field notes contain phrases such as "Everything fascinates me. Every patient." Wolff concedes that "the great difficulty is to keep pace with 'everything' " while engaged in this "supreme concentration." Junker, too, recognizes the dilemma implied in the attempt to record everything. Theoretically, he argues, " 'everything' should be recorded so that all the facts about operations that are relevant to making the results meaningful can ultimately be reported"; but "it is impossible," so we must create a "balance in field work between recording 'everything' and recording 'nothing' " (Junker, 1960, pp. 15, 18). By necessity, more is absorbed than can be recorded. Ironically, however, recording includes *more than* has been observed, such as ideas, associations, concepts, and questions related to the observation.

When I first tried to observe everything, various difficulties arose:

> *I asked him why he went to a military academy and he said it was his mother's idea, but she did not know what it would be like either, that they would really use rifles, etc. I cannot remember all the details because while he was talking to me I was trying to observe other people in the room. Lesson: if I want to remember a conversation I have to give it my undivided attention and forget about capturing anything else.*

I revised my dictum of recording everything to recording everything about something.

Nader made the same transition:

> During my first field experience I did not work this way [analyzing solid blocks of data, such as conflict cases, proverbs in natural conversation, and coparent patterns]; *I tried to gather all new information.* In looking over my field notes, I discover that much of what I took down as field data has not been of much use to me; but this cannot be known at the time. *After my second trip* to the Rincón Zapotee *I no longer collected everything. I focused* on detailing blocks of data, the analysis of which was to take me again from anguish to exultation" [Nader, 1970, p. 116 (emphasis added)].

Physiologically it became imperative to be selective rather than inclusive in observing and recording:

I was concentrating so hard on what was going on, in addition to trying to figure out what my feelings were and what if anything I should contribute to the group, that I got a terrible headache which it took hours to get rid of. It's awfully difficult to remember what is said in our group meetings because there is no particular focus other than the members and their interaction. By the time the meeting ended my head was bursting with pain.

Observing in preparation for recording is exhausting unless the ideal of covering everything is replaced by partial coverage:

The evening ended with my feeling utterly frustrated for having been in a setting with so much going on that I was unable to observe.

Unless observing attention diminishes somewhat, the researcher's ability to interact in the environment is impaired. Berger's phrase "the imperative of triviality" was coined for a different purpose but fits perfectly the dilemma of the sociologist attempting to capture everything. Berger (1971, p. 4) claims that people are limited in their ability to pay attention: "Social life would be psychologically intolerable if each of its moments required from us full attention, deliberate decision, and high emotional involvement." Since fieldwork is like an altered state of consciousness, in which the researcher tries to become a set of raw nerves, sensitive to the here-and-now of the flow of events, there must be some respite by returning to the normal half-asleep state in which we typically function. Doing fieldwork is being in a state of excessive stimulation. In participant observation fieldwork, full attention is required continuously to uncover significant events and create meaning from the flood of stimuli pouring in. But "triviality is one of the fundamental requirements of social life. . . . Were social life in its entirety to be charged with profound meaning, we would all go out of our minds" (Berger, 1971, p. 4).

In addition, patient behavior is never meaningless if there is a therapeutic intent. Everything can be taken into consideration for patient administration or treatment. As a result, staff and observers are bound in a web of exhausting meaningfulness. Staff members frequently spoke of themselves in terms of burning out or fearing they would do so as a result of this intensity. As a participant observer and staff member I shared their sensation of excessive stimulation and responsibility, but I also found relief from this extensive, almost excessive meaningfulness by adopting certain tricks that staff members used, such as huddling together with staff in the coffee shop or nursing station in ways that discouraged patient interference, arranging numerous support meetings, focusing on specific patients and almost ignoring everyone else, and partying and joking about work to deflate its seriousness, although the latter frequently backfired by making shoptalk pervasive. As a participant observer and staff member, I had to learn to focus on certain items and ignore others in order to be able to observe at all. Conversely, I learned to observe a scene without concentrating all of my attention by developing a kind of peripheral attention (Lee, 1970). The material of this subliminal awareness is accessible during note-writing time, so that the focus utilized during observation is not equivalent to the limit on the subsequent field notes.

Related to the issue of *focus* is another problem—defining a *boundary* for the system under study. If all events acquire meaning in terms of their context, then a context must be selected for any problem studied. These contexts are not inherently limited but are defined by the researcher for pragmatic and theoretical purposes. Contexts, of course, must be placed in larger contexts, and so on. Since the boundaries are limitless, observers can quickly lose control of their study as they move outward, just as they do in the attempt to notice everything. Diesing (1971, p. 271) discusses this problem:

> How large a system should he include in his observations? He wants to study a whole system, not just a fragment, and this requires a continually expanding boundary as he finds his subject matter participating in larger systems. But he also wants a thorough, detailed study of all the important interrelations in his system, and this requires him not to dissipate his energies too

widely. He cannot satisfy both of these contrary requirements fully; no matter which way he turns, his work will
lack something—in comprehensiveness or in completeness
of detail or in both.

In my research project a context was needed for studying
adolescent patient friendships. But which context? The ward?
But the context of the ward is the hospital. The hospital? Since
the ward can only be understood as a component of the hospital social system, I visited each ward, attended hall meetings,
acquainted myself with some patients and staff, and thereby
familiarized myself with the hospital as a whole. The events I
observed were meetings, informal gatherings, activities, and social occasions of various kinds. I also spoke privately with patients and staff as our relations developed. My approach was to
sustain access to settings by forming relationships, to go where
invited, and to avoid requesting entrance to other situations. Although I was not overbearing, I played an active role, asking
questions, making comments, and initiating and responding to
events. This corresponded with my personal style and aided my
familiarization with much of hospital life. But after the initial
familiarization, I vacillated between strictly and loosely marked
boundaries. Sometimes I threw the net wide by participating in
formal and informal conferences with patients and treatment
personnel, chatting with secretaries, sitting in the cafeteria, and
attending an unending stream of meetings. At other times, when
that method dissipated my energy, I focused my attention on a
particular adolescent friendship.

Some of this contextual work was irrelevant to the research but valuable for my dance therapist role. Since the contexts of the two responsibilities differed, their merger was not
convenient. The issue of context should be asked in two ways:
How large a context is necessary, and how small a context is
adequate? Shifting back and forth produces boundaries that are
both appropriate for the problem and manageable for the person. One must remember that all system boundaries are artificial and arbitrary, established for the sake of study rather than
inherent in the social world.

Closely linked to the dilemmas of scope of attention and

defining the boundaries was the issue of *indicators*. Friendship is an abstraction; it is also a label for certain behaviors that is applied appropriately by socialized members of a culture. As a student of friendship, however, what should I consider an instance of this abstraction? What kinds of information will be useful in creating an understanding of friendship and related phenomena? During the data-gathering stage, decisions must be made about the kind of information and the number of indicators that will be available. I learned to not pay attention when the scope became unwieldy and to abandon indicators that were too numerous to pursue. The following excerpts from my field notes illustrate that participant observation brings to the researcher's attention an ever increasing number of ways to gather data related to the research problem. As each new source of data is recognized, the researcher must decide whether this indicator of the phenomenon is worthy of pursuit. With experience, the researcher learns that there are more indicators than can be managed, and many can be listed only as strategies not utilized. During this first field experience I hoped to pursue them all.

Arrived at the hospital at 12:20 this afternoon in the pouring rain. Inside the coffee shop Pam [staff member], a guy from SBI [an adolescent patient William] and Sue [adolescent patient] were seated together. (Perhaps they are friends. I think I am going to spend some time in the coffee shop studying the traffic and seating arrangements. There are probably a lot of clues to friendship right there.)

Staff meeting on B hall [severely disturbed young men] with the administrative psychiatrist, nurses, aides, and group workers following the 8 a.m. hall meeting. Almost every patient was brought up individually for discussion of his specific problems, especially those that need the doctor's attention. One patient has been spending all of his free time with a female patient from C2 hall. The nurse said "They're spending more time together than they should." (I'd like to know what that means, because here is a heterosexual patient friendship that apparently causes some distress in staff and they feel something "should be done" about it. I don't know the history of this "couple." I'll

*have to return to the nurse and ask her to explain her concern
further and learn something about what the staff perceives is
wrong about patients seeing a lot of each other in these kinds of
relationships.)*

*I learned that Tom and Mike [adolescent patients] are on
MES, an abbreviation for mutual escort, which means either
party can go anywhere as long as the other comes along. Being
assigned MES privilege accounts for their being seen together so
much. I guess MES is a product of and builder of friendships. I
have to find out who is on MES with whom, how people get
assigned that status, what they think of it, what staff expects to
accomplish by it, etc.*

*Wendy [adolescent patient], who had acted wildly last
week while I was teaching dance (running around, calling dance
an "international communist propaganda conspiracy," changing
the speed on the record player in the middle of a song, etc.)
asked what we—Marty [staff member] and I—had been doing in
the pool room and I jokingly said, "making out." I said this because of what my advisor had told me about a technique for
handling sexual remarks. I wanted to show Wendy that it was
OK to say what she said because it was obviously a joke, so I
kind of joked in return.*

*I remember wishing I knew of a more "in" way of saying
the same thing, but the only expression I could think of was
"making out." (It's amazing how much special vocabulary is
used here, between patients, between staff and patients, and of
course, among staff. I think it would be relevant to collect the
special words of the adolescent patients because I noticed that
the different cliques use different vocabularies to set them off
from each other and express their unique identities. Some say
things like "meds, spacey, spaced out, wibbly, wobbly, far out."
When I said "making out," another male adolescent patient
said, "yea, that's what we did in high school," which meant that
I hadn't used a contemporary term. I had used an old expression which was one of the many tiny details which made me an
outsider to his clique.)*

Given the proliferation of indicators, a decision must be
made either to follow one or several, or to utilize instead what

Erikson (1959) calls "free-floating attention." I could take the
active stance of selecting indicators from the environment, or I
could be passive and "wait to be impressed by recurrent themes
that reappear in various contexts" (Diesing, 1971, p. 147).
Neither stance is pure in fieldwork.

My comprehension of participant observation methodology was affected by my rebellion against the survey research
methods I had witnessed as a research assistant. Since I equated
survey research with a systematic, mechanistic, detached perspective, participant observation had to be unsystematic, un-
impeded by any mechanical aids, and completely involving. My
need for a survey research substitute made me see detachment
as the hallmark of a science-adoring, self-annihilating world. Detachment was inhuman; involvement would rehumanize society
and reform sociology. To reinforce my views I had only to observe the psychiatric position toward patients, which so frequently coupled unfeeling detachment with professionalism and
patient distress. But my personal methodological quest skewed
participant observation from its accepted definition as a balance
between detachment and involvement (Powdermaker, 1966) to
a method that defined detachment as the researcher's personal
shortcoming. Because I was attempting to reassert social research's human qualities, I needed to diminish what I perceived
as its inhuman qualities. I worked out this internal conflict by
contrasting the two research projects as symbolic representa-
tions of these two perspectives. In the final project (Chapters Six
and Seven) I reinterpreted the issue of detachment altogether.

The interplay between person and method is apparent in
the researcher's resolution of the involvement-detachment dilemma. My moral indignation concerning the detachment that
characterized the teacher study led to a near abandonment of
my researcher stance in the hospital study. This issue cannot be
resolved didactically by reading methods texts but must be experienced so that the researcher can forge a workable, personal
balance. The resolution is also influenced by the particular
problem and setting that are studied. The psychiatric and bureaucratic ideologies espoused in the mental hospital of this
project shaped my resolution of the detachment-involvement

tension as they did for all the hospital personnel. My reaction against the negative model of active data acquisition utilized in the survey research project predisposed me toward a passive approach in participant observation. I attempted to gather my field data from unscheduled, unorganized, unsystematized being in the field.

Passivity in the data-gathering process nevertheless requires activity in the recording and analysis phases. Although free-floating attention is useful for gaining impressions of the passage of time, hypotheses can be formulated and tested only if systematic data are gathered or if the recorded data are analyzed for evidence of hypothesis confirmation or fitness for model building. Only if the model of study is redefined to eliminate concepts such as hypotheses and testing can free-floating attention be used to create a case study involving accurate and adequate description following immersion in the case.

Those dilemmas—the impossibility of attending to everything, defining boundaries, constructing indicators, and a passive or active stance—are not all the methodological and personal difficulties of data collection. Several others remain. One might be called the reality principle—"You can't be everywhere at once." Since the data of fieldwork are the researcher's recorded observations, they depend on the researcher's choices of where to observe and what to do. Each selected meeting or conversation eliminates other data, which are lost forever. All data are continuously being lost except the small amount that can be observed and recorded. When experienced, this disconcerting fact of life has a tragic quality similar to that discussed by Gouldner (1969). Some field note samples illustrate this dilemma:

I feel as if there isn't enough of me to go around, that there's too much going on, that it's all interesting, that I don't have enough time to do everything I want to in order to learn enough, and that it is hard to integrate all this into the rest of my life.

I can't write sufficiently because I am thirsting for "the experience of being there." I want to be there all the time. I find myself driving out to the hospital whenever I have a free hour between anything.

I can never be satisfied with what I am learning, seeing, and doing on the wards. There is always more—more meetings to attend, more people to talk to, more hanging around to do in order to catch the flow of everyday life. I stay long hours at the hospital, inviting myself to as many situations as I dare, not going home til late at night and getting up early again in the morning ready for more. Many times this means that I cannot write all the notes I should in order to keep an ongoing record. Sometimes I just jot down in outline form what I have observed. I end up leaving much to memory or to discussion with others. I know this is a pitfall of participant observation, but I want to minimize my researcher's attitude and be there more.

Gans (1968, p. 312) described the same issue:

> One source of anxiety during research is the constant worry about the flow of research activities: Is one doing the right thing at the right time, attending the right meeting, or talking to the right people? [Since it is impossible to be] in many places at the same time, one must make the right choice of what to study every day, and even so there is always the danger of having missed something and of never being able to retrieve an event that has already become history.

The passage of time makes material irretrievable. By the time certain events have been studied, they have also changed.

Since a researcher cannot be everywhere at once, choices are made consciously or unconsciously, and whatever is not captured is relegated to worry or regret. When the decision is out of the researcher's control, such as when dance therapy duties interrupted my observation of an interesting scene, frustration is inevitable. Reiss (1968, p. 312) suggests that participant observers reduce their concern about missing important events by focusing on "recurring behavior." But if observation time is limited, access is tenuous, or a rare opportunity arises, the researcher's desired course of action can be blocked. Every moment is the precious beginning of a future event or the follow-up of some past event. The fieldworker is painfully aware of the connectedness of events and of finding a means of fitting the observation schedule to the idiosyncratic requirements of following particular incidents or patterns.

The multiplicity of perspectives was an additional difficulty of this research project. I quickly learned that my description of a setting could vary markedly from the description by other setting members. After observing and describing action and sharing my notes with others, I might find I had missed what someone else considered significant. Clearly there is no single correct description of anything in the field, since every description stems from an observational perspective. Unless the multiplicity of perspectives in any given situation can be accepted philosophically, however, faith in any description is hard to sustain. If observations are grounded in perspectives, what was the perspective that underlay my work? Was it that of a sociologist, a naive person, a newcomer with low status, a peripheral member, or a young female? How can the observer trust that his or her perspective is accurate and adequate, since many descriptions are possible? If the multiplicity of perspectives is accepted as valid, then the researcher need not worry that his or her particular perspective is a bias that distorts some perspectiveless description of a given situation.

Diesing (1971) differentiates between observer bias ("Every scientist must perceive and interpret his subject matter from some standpoint and thereby bias his conclusions") and participant bias ("Every scientist must be active with his subject matter in some fashion and must therefore change it as he studies it"). He argues as follows:

> Participant observation *depends* essentially on the *creative* use of bias to discover things that would otherwise not be observable, so the minimizing of bias and involvement would destroy the method. An observer who is *not* emotionally involved will be unable to empathize, to see things from the perspective of his subject, and therefore will miss much of the meaning of what he sees. Consequently he will not know how to ask the right ques-

tions and look in the right places. In personal intimate activities, detachment is a barrier. An observer who does not actively probe and provoke will miss important aspects of his subject matter: its defenses against threat, its reaction to crises and problems, the limits of its tolerance [p. 280].

Doing fieldwork is a process, therefore, of learning to recognize, trust, and use one's own perspective.

The Internal Noise of Anger and Anxiety

The most significant problem I encountered in gathering and recording data was what I call "internal noise." Internal noise refers to the eliciting by the research environment of personal, psychological, and physiological responses in the researcher. The crucial word is response. When I began this project, I believed fieldworkers should not respond personally but should actively observe and record the environment as it is. Of what possible significance is my personal response to the environment? In retrospect, the resolution of this issue was the most useful in enabling me to clarify my methodological position.

At the time of the study I sharply differentiated between what was "out there"—the observed, captured, and recorded environment—and what was "in here"—feelings, responses, and reactions. As a budding sociologist, I was oriented toward noticing the external environment and toward discounting my personal responses. I did not yet understand that all observations were the interaction of the observer and the observed, that each observation inevitably contained some of me. It soon became clear that even unattended personal feelings during the research process would persist and affect my consciousness, eventually interfering with my work. The unwillingness to recognize feelings that I considered irrelevant to the study problem was part of my desire for self-control. But the environment is powerful in producing feelings. These I interpreted as interfering with my work rather than as being data themselves. In a continuous struggle I tried to squelch my feelings and to ignore distress, joy, or fear—in other words, to deny totally the hospital's effects.

The sharpest examples of my internal noise were anger and anxiety. The anger stemmed from what I considered to be the double binds of the hospital ideology. For example, senior staff instructed lower-ranking staff to act in contradictory ways:

> *A very special patient is coming but we should be on our guard not to treat her in a special way [nursing supervisor announcement to ward staff].*

> *Dr. Roth arrived quite late, which made it impossible to discuss every patient. We discussed several, however. The first one's major problem is that "he doesn't recognize that he's really a dependent guy." When all the therapists reported on how well he was doing in their activities, Dr. Roth said, "You see, he keeps on telling us he's normal."*

Staff also manipulated patients with dubious results:

> *My doctor says the reason I'm sick and not getting better is that I don't accept the fact that I'm sick, so he wants me to recognize it and is confining me to my room until I really get sick [female adolescent patient].*

A month later this patient was incoherent and "had to be placed in packs to calm her."

I was also angry with the staff for imposing values on the patients in the name of authority or mental health, such as the importance of neatness, performing chores, eating certain foods, and taking regular exercise. One patient who experimented with a vegetarian diet was said to be "starving herself." In short, the powerlessness of the patients offended me. The contrast between the rules and regulations of the hospital and the current counterculture of nonhospitalized adolescents exacerbated the contrast between social norms and hospital policy. Any rules could be applied in the name of mental health—no freedom was sacred.

Another source of my anger was being assigned a supervisor with whom I did not work comfortably:

In supervision I told Jill [my supervisor] that when I feel my dance activity is superfluous to what is happening on the hall, I think I should cancel it. I cannot remember her response. The reason is that I don't listen when she speaks to me because I find it hard to respect the work she does. She makes me angry by not seeming to respect mine. How can supervision continue on this basis? She doesn't want me to teach yoga unless I am an accomplished anatomist. (I wonder if there are other people I don't "hear" because I don't want to hear them.)

After "forgetting" that Jill had asked me not to offer yoga, I suggested to Dr. Bender [administrative psychiatrist for female adolescents] that I start a yoga program on his hall. I wondered what would happen if my supervisor had the right to fire me. I wondered if she would do it and if such a thing had ever happened.

My exaggerated paranoia stems from the fact that even though we've never mentioned it, I think we both know that we don't care for each other. I try very hard to be pleasant, and sometimes it is torturous. I don't like her ideas or ways of doing things. My relationship with her is one of the few difficulties I am having right now. I wish I could be in a t-group with her and get it out. Anyhow, she is justifiably angry with me now because I unthinkingly undermined a decision she made as my superior not to offer yoga.

Anxiety arose when I consciously violated hospital policy or thought I had done so inadvertently. I worked in an explicitly rule-governed environment that aroused concern lest I break rules unwittingly, be caught breaking rules purposefully, or hurt patients unintentionally because I did not know all the rules. The line of command that existed in the bureaucracy of the hospital contrasted sharply with other environments in which I was involved:

Susan [female adolescent patient] sat on the couch opposite Nina [group worker] and me while the two of us talked. I

*tried to continue the conversation with Nina as if it didn't mat-
ter that Susan happened to be a patient. I couldn't think of any
reason we couldn't talk in front of her, so I asked Nina if she
was crocheting the piece she was working on for John, her boyfriend. Under her breath, half turning to me, piercing me with
her eyes while trying to cover it up with gentleness, she said,
"Drop it." In a flash I realized that she doesn't talk about her
boyfriend with patients present, and that I had "broken a rule."*

*I got a flashback of a time on the hall when the patients
[female adolescents] were angry about being restricted and dis-
placed some of their anger on Nina who happened to be there.
Some of their frustration was concerned with not being able to
have sex. They yelled at her for being a hypocrite and "probably getting knocked up many times a day." Nina walked away
coolly.*

*I sat there thinking: Am I supposed to conceal this impor-
tant element of life? (Am I supposed to ask the ward administrator for permission to discuss sex, boyfriends, etc.) Is it improper, unwise, anti-therapeutic for staff to mention anything
important about their lives in front of, let alone, to, patients?
But don't patients expect staff to have normal lives, and
shouldn't they hear about it in terms of developing models? Are
we improper models? What would have happened if Nina hadn't
been there and I had talked openly to a patient? What about the
times I did do just that?*

At times my staff and research roles seemed to suppress
my humanness. Fears were generated by my research intentions: Was I sure I knew what was going on; how could I manage the overwhelming data; what frameworks should I create?
Surprisingly little of the anxiety stemmed from contact with
people who were ostensibly mentally ill. The elaborate bureaucracy of the hospital regularized life; the high staff-patient ratio
made the patients of the hospital less dominant; the drugs
quieted them; the rules held them in check; the locked "sharps"
made them less of a danger. Much of the craziness was missing
and replaced by emptiness.

Distress gripped me when I was caught in the conflict between patients and staff and when the staff treated a patient
differently from what I considered appropriate on a matter of

vital importance. The staff member might assert authority by pulling rank or minimize my reaction by labeling it the naive response of a newcomer or a part-timer. The staff considered excessive sympathy to be a sign of presocialization or preadjustment to hospital reality before patterned responses had been learned: Newcomers used categories "from the outside" to understand behavior "on the inside."

My anxiety grew out of the suppression of my freedom to act spontaneously, which in turn hinged on the staff's belief that they should present a united front. A wide diversity of opinions might be expressed among staff in meetings, but when two or more staff interacted with patients, staff disagreement was taboo. The staff's rationale seemed to be that patients would become confused if the staff was inconsistent. The staff openly discussed the need to prevent patients from splitting the staff's opinion on an issue or from causing the staff to take sides with a patient against another staff member, both of which supposedly result in chaos on the ward and a breakdown of therapy. The proscription of open disagreement in front of patients had the effect of limiting staff interaction with patients, of leaving individual staff members guessing what the staff point of view was on a particular issue, and of directing almost all remarks to the administrative psychiatrist at hall meetings rather than to whomever was speaking.

Frequently, these ward meetings of staff and patients left me with unexpressed rage since open disagreement among staff was discouraged. If a patient observed the difference between hall meeting statements or behavior and those expressed outside the meeting, then the value of interaction with people during or outside these meetings might be undermined. The dilemma of suppressing disagreements arose particularly in situations having both an administrative and a therapeutic function. From time to time a patient made a direct comment to me in these meetings:

Early morning (8 a.m.) hall meeting on SB2 [female adolescents]. We know that Wendy is under a great deal of pressure because after 5 years of hospitalization, she is not going to be *sent home but rather transferred to another (state) hospital. Her parents and insurance policy can no longer meet the bills (approximately $100/day). She says to the psychiatrist in charge of the meeting, "I know you are sexually attracted to me and that is why I wear sunglasses. If I would take them off, you would not be able to control yourself." Nearly everyone in the room began to giggle because of the blatant reversal of roles in her statement. Wendy happens to see my inadvertent smile and snaps at me, "What are you laughing at?" I don't know how to respond because I perceive there is a "right response" rather than merely "my response." I feel staff observing me to see if I can perform therapeutically or at least "appropriately." I feel patients observing me to see if I will answer honestly or disguise my feelings. I escape the bind by answering literally (one of the known escape routes or symptoms of the double bind)—"I laughed because I thought it was funny." Which of course, says nothing.*

It bothered me particularly that all action was labeled either appropriate or inappropriate, and yet as far as I knew, tests or experiments were not conducted to determine if "inappropriate" behavior had any adverse effects on patients. Furthermore, if the humanness of staff was suppressed, how could they humanize the patients? Instead I felt reduced to employing techniques to manipulate and control patient reactions. Although the internal noise produced in me by the environment deflected my attention from studying patient friendships onto how a doubting staff can best survive in a mental hospital, these reactions unfortunately did not become the actual focus of my study, as I later came to believe would have been methodologically sound. My notes became concerned more and more with problems of hospital ideology and policy:

The staff assumes that they are faced with a technical task rather than a humanizing one. To be therapeutic is to carry out predetermined procedures based on certain theories. According to the technical task orientation, there are right, proper and appropriate ways of interacting and doing things with and for patients. That frame of reference is the criterion against which behavior is judged.

*Even though the hospital is wealthy and progressive, it is
still a bureaucratic, totalitarian structure which is supposed to
provide a therapeutic milieu for the patients. Isn't there a way
fully human individuals could engage patients in a total, complete way, in which role distinctions could be eliminated to provide for the emergence of human qualities such as spontaneity
and self-trust? The design would try to allow and provide circumstances and conditions which would release the human
potential capacity in BOTH the patients and the staff.*

What is best for a patient is not known. Does one reinforce *his problems by* paying attention *to them, or does one,
through attention to his problems give him the opportunity to
relieve himself of them? Should one talk "reality" or talk
"hope"? Does it make any difference what one says or does
with a patient, or is it only the influence of the parents and the
therapist that counts? Do you let the patient know how he
makes you feel, or is it unfair to burden the patient with your
feelings? Do you preserve a relationship at the expense of violating your perception of reality? Do you allow the patient to see
more of you than is prescribed by your role—do you allow your
self to emerge and assume an active part in your behavior in the
hospital? Do you take the patient home with you, literally and
imaginatively? How do you respond to a patient who is complaining bitterly about other staff? There seems to be a real conflict between following institutional expectations and being
human wherever and whenever you can.*

*I always feel as if I have to take sides. It's becoming in-
creasingly difficult to remain the neutral observer. Unfortunately my identification with patients usually means that when
I take sides (which I do covertly), I frequently feel critical of
staff. But the hospital contributes to this by always splitting the
patients and non-patients. Of course those are relevant categories but it reinforces the "total institution" caste system
rather than fostering a sense of therapeutic community. After
all, the patients and staff have much in common. Just today
Ginny [staff member] nearly burst with enthusiasm and excitement when telling me she had been accepted as a psychoanalytic patient in an institute that has a long waiting-list. She
wants, and feels she needs, therapy too.*

I am experiencing massive mistrust of my self. It's as if the rug keeps on being pulled out from under me. The hospital can function to make you lose faith in yourself. You might be having a wonderful time, for instance, and then find out later that someone got upset at what you were doing, or that someone disagreed with what you were doing, and you are afraid for the patient and for yourself.

I wish I had time to do a study on what a "good" staff member is—in the eyes of staff and in the eyes of patients. I feel a pressure to uphold an undefined ideal of the "good" staff member. The good staff member doesn't fit the kind of person I want to be. The good staff are the ones who are manageable just as are the good patients. The whole hospital is concerned with smooth functioning. Like all bureaucracies, the most important thing is that the system should not have its procedures disrupted.

The crucial theme here is the hospital's assault on individual self-trust. This first field experience, which was intended as an opportunity to develop my identity as a researcher, was conducted in a setting that undermined its members' confidence in their own judgments. As I began putting my vague discomfort into words, I sought other staff who might share my point of view. Quickly I found aides, activity therapists, and nurses who had similar viewpoints. For hours we discussed alternative therapeutic settings that put into practice ideas we preferred to those used at the hospital. The constant existential thread in our discussion was whether the hospital should be changed from within or whether it was better to contribute to another, more ideal therapeutic setting in which we could believe. This conflict, shared by many of the young staff, accounted for some staff turnover and involvement in alternative mental health facilities (see Holleb and Abrams, 1975; Chamberlin, 1978; and Jaffe and Clark, 1975).

The issue of abandoning a social institution in need of reform in favor of joining a promising experiment concerned us all:

Olive [activity therapist] began talking of her discomfort with her work in the hospital in terms similar to those with which I characterized my experience: She was tired of "feeding the patients the hospital line" and wanted to develop a personal line. When I tried to probe as to what the hospital line was, she said it was a technique that involved denial of your own feelings, throwing everything back on the patient, and considering everything the patient's problem. As Dr. Bender put it, "It's the patient's burden to account, explain and understand everything."

Life outside the hospital also has its problems; interpersonal conflict and personal doubt are certainly not confined to the hospital setting. The unique quality of a psychiatric hospital, however, is that opinions as to what is normal become matters of *policy*. Feelings as well as actions either conform with or violate those policies governing both staff and patients. No experiences within the hospital are immune from regulatory policy or therapeutic interpretation. But these are never clearly expounded because then their efficacy could be challenged. Policy is made by those with power, which means doctors decide for patients even if structures are established to give the patients the impression that they control an aspect of their lives. When I assumed the role of "middle management" between the powerful and the powerless, I felt obliged to implement ideas that I had not participated in developing, that I might reject, or that I did not understand. Decisions about anything in the hospital seemed to be a matter of rank rather than inherent truth. In staff-patient conflicts, the patient was always wrong or ill, and the staff member was always right. The staff were not supposed to befriend the patient or to care except in a professional way:

Hall meeting on female adolescent ward. Dr. Bender answers Betsy [patient], who has asked him if he cares whether or not she gets out of the hospital eventually: "You'll be ready to go out when you stop worrying about whether or not I care. You have to care about yourself because I cannot."

Because I personally did not accept the merit of these basic assumptions underpinning such responses to patients, I was anxious lest I inadvertently communicate my contrary attitudes to the patients or staff. Without accepting the medical model or bureaucratic organization of therapeutic institutions, I could not very easily feed the patients the hospital line.

Staff members appeared interested in other staff's interaction with patients and invariably evaluated staff-patient encounters. This informal evaluation inhibited idiosyncracies and spontaneity and kept staff members "in line":

> *I am beginning to have problems with the fact that not only is patient behavior always evaluated, interpreted, and used as proof of illness, but so, too, staff's behavior is constantly judged. When I relate an incident in which I was involved with a patient to another staff, that staff immediately puts the story in the framework of "Did you fail or succeed?" This simplistic framework loses sight of the nuances of relationships and the complexities of interaction. It also precludes thinking of people in other than measurable terms of success or failure.*
>
> *What I have found is that when I relate a story and it is interpreted as a success, numerous reactions can follow: The person can be pleased with my success, can be jealous of my success, etc. There seems always to be an emphasis on the person to whom the success "belongs" rather than an attempt to learn from each other's behavior. Everything is evaluated informally and everyone feels threatened about not being successful in their work. I believe this all stems from the fact that everyone is made to feel like a patient, with the only nonpatients being the doctors.*

In addition, staff members were jealous of other staff to whom patients paid much attention. Some staff avoided patients but many competed for patient attachments, a matter particularly evident when conflicts arose in scheduling the patients' time. Patients alone could demonstrate that the staff was efficacious and competent.

The most highly valued prize was a patient's statement that "I've never told anyone about this before but I want to tell you." Such a statement indicated that the staff member had won the patient's trust. Nevertheless, the staff member was supposed to urge the patient to share the material only with the private therapist and not with the ward staff. The personal qualities of the staff member in whom the patient wished to confide were not reinforced, and the material of all staff-patient discussions became public when it was passed on in observational notes. My channeling of patients' confidences to their therapists conflicted with my researcher role, which sought confidential material, particularly about friendships.

In an excerpt from my field notes cited previously, patients were shown coaching each other to interact in terms of policy rather than spontaneously. Such rule-guided interaction was also characteristic of staff. For both patients and staff, this implied an inability to assume responsibility for the self:

> *I met Ed [middle-age male patient] in the library at our usual 10:00 appointment. As we walked toward the chairs he said he had two things to talk about. (He is rigid in his thoughts, his body movement, and maintenance of his phobias.) The two things were his concern with Mary, an activity therapist, and the fact that he, Ed, was supposed to cry. "My therapist told me to cry," he said. I was shocked and saddened. So often I ask a patient something about himself and get as an answer, "My therapist says. . . ."*

As a counterpoint to the patient's dependence on the psychiatrist (for which the patient is blamed for being "dependent"), the following excerpt illustrates the staff's efforts to induce staff dependence on psychiatrists:

> *I met Margaret [group worker] for our informal interview in the coffee shop. She apologized for being late but she was being "bawled out" for something on the hall. She has some responsibility for a patient who had asked me to find him a Hebrew tutor. Margaret apologized for getting me all confused about the tutoring. I cannot figure out whether or not to get involved in it, except that the patient asked me if I would help him find the tutor and if someone asks me for help I usually try to offer it. So why not for him?*
>
> *She said I should alter this staff-patient relationship. I should not say "yes" right away. I should say, "I'll talk to your doctor about it and then we'll decide if it's good for you. If so, I'll be glad to help." I thought to myself that this response undermines the patient's sense of self in addition to the staff's*

ability to make decisions. I felt that if I actually did start talking to patients in that way, no one would ever want to waste their time talking to me. I was afraid to share these thoughts with Margaret. Somehow I had to publicly share the "staff way of doing things."

Some communication was allowed and some was not, leading staff to wonder what was permissible to say to patients. Such confusion stemmed from the controls on communication and the sense that everyone was being observed. Eventually staff and patients did not know what they should say to each other, while at the same time they were embedded in a highly emotionally charged environment. There seemed to be so much feeling in the hospital of which both staff and patients were aware but which they felt uncomfortable discussing together. Under the facade of openness there were areas of taboo and confusion: escapes, intrigues, friendships, plans, new rules and regulations, and new therapeutic programs. There was an actual proscription against informing patients that their case history was scheduled for discussion in an upcoming case conference.

These observations were also noted by Caudill (1958, pp. 332-333) in his extensive study of a psychiatric hospital:

> The conflicts between individual staff members, or between role groups in the staff, are often as important for the understanding of the nature of a problem in the hospital as are the actions of particular patients. If the goal of a therapeutic community is to be reached, there must be a greater openness among staff members than is usually the case at present. . . . Changes in the organization and atmosphere of the hospital must be made so that neither staff nor patients are punished for their efforts at greater openness and understanding.

The following is an example demonstrating the anxiety engendered by the social organization of the hospital and the undermining of my self-trust:

I entered the female adolescent hall to prepare for the dance session I would conduct this evening. Before beginning, I decided to use the bathroom and have a cup of coffee. I asked one of the patients where the nearest bathroom was, took off my coat, and tossed it onto a chair. When I did that, the keys in my pocket made a clanging sound.

I walked to the bathroom knowing that I shouldn't leave unattended keys in my pocket especially after the patients could clearly hear the sound. I didn't know what to do. I wanted to demonstrate to the patients, in case they did hear it, that I trusted them not to steal the keys. I wanted to be nonchalant and not suspicious. I did not want to turn around and blatantly take the keys out in front of them. I acted in favor of preventing humiliation and violating a rule (that keys never be left unattended) even if it presented a risk and temptation.

In the bathroom I became anxious. I thought that if someone took the keys I would be fired, but realistically it would be difficult for a patient to take the keys unnoticed, let alone use them. Numerous scenes flashed through my mind, e.g., the hospital policy (or is it a myth?) that when someone loses his keys, he loses his job; and every key and lock in the hospital must then be changed.

I left the bathroom and saw my coat lying on the chair, untouched. I scolded myself silently for being so suspicious of patients, but I felt so shaken I had to sit quietly before I could begin my work.

In this section I have presented several illustrations of the way the hospital impinged on me as a person. This internal noise was noticeable in terms of the powerful emotions it engendered—anger, anxiety, disorientation, and fear. These emotions were reduced to noise in the sense that I attempted to direct my attention away from these distractions to the substantive focus of my study. Since these personal responses to the environment could not be suppressed entirely, they became a kind of static interference with my real work. These infringements on my personal, research, and work roles were noticeable particularly in terms of assaulting my self-confidence and inhibiting my spontaneity. Together they contributed to a general feeling of suppressing my humanness. These responses to my environment clashed with my efforts to continue my work.

I later read that my pejoratively labeled "internal noise" is considered useful data by some methodologists:

If the system is small, the researcher can gradually turn himself into an analogue of the system, so that he reacts as it reacts, feels as it feels, thinks and evaluates as it does. The next step is to make this implicit knowledge explicit. . . . Self-observation is a special source of evidence that is sometimes overlooked. When the observer has been well socialized, his own reactions are part of the system he is studying. Consciously and intellectually he is still the detached observer, but emotionally and subconsciously he has become an active part of his subject matter. Consequently his intuitive reactions provide evidence as to the covert meaning of actions or statements. . . . Evidence from self-observation is reliable only insofar as the observer is really a socialized part of his subject matter [Diesing, 1971, pp. 5, 151].

Fortunately, this internal noise did make its way into my field notes. Only after the fact, however, did I develop the methodological insight to recognize that I was creating an unnecessary obstacle by not utilizing my personal responses to the environment as the very avenue for learning about that environment. Those which I considered irrelevant, even illegitimate feelings and tried to push out of my way were in fact valuable sources of understanding. This insight led to my "decriminalization" of such data and the reformulation of problems of method, which I crystallized into experiential analysis.

Devious Behavior in the Field

Anxiety about my potential and deliberate deviousness extended beyond my actions to my very thoughts. In other words, I thought I would be found out for having the wrong thoughts. "Does the organization of a mental hospital inculcate mental illness among staff?" I wondered. At the same time, I felt committed to acting in the service of what I considered would abct patient improvement even when such action did not conform with my perception of the norms. It became clear that "subversive action," "devious behavior," and "illicit relationships" (or leaving) were ways of coping with the stress (referred to as "burn-out") of being a staff member and a researcher in the mental hospital.

An important devious attitude that a staff member can hold is known as "the messiah complex." Many staff members informed me that new staff frequently develop this attitude, which is a belief in their personal ability to cure patients. Caudill (1958, p. 282) noticed something similar in his discussion of first-year residents: "They frequently refused to admit the extent of the patient's illness . . . [and had a] desire to grant a good deal of individual latitude to patients and to chafe under the rules and regulations of the hospital." Such attitudes are considered inappropriate even if they stem from the resident's having made good contact with the patients. I was warned that the desire to cure is actually derived from a neurotically based and inappropriate "need" to cure. The other major warning was to not be misled by patients who appeared normal but were really sick. Staff frequently evaluated a group of patients informally in terms of their relative sickness, apparently to demonstrate that the more normal in appearance, the sicker in actuality. The new staff member was socialized into believing that to fail is inevitable, ostensibly to be protected from disappointment.

But an additional effect of the warnings against the messiah complex was to prevent the newcomer's potential success from discrediting the work of other staff. I experienced the conflict between the socialization process of the hospital and the motivation that led people to work with patients in the first place. I could not suspend my desire to help patients even if this attitude was inappropriate for a researcher (Clausen, 1965) or smacked of the messiah complex.

My solution to the dilemma of wanting to help patients without being ridiculed as a false messiah was to form special relationships at the periphery of my work at the hospital. In these private relationships that were free from scrutiny, I could allow my messianic fantasies or humanistic inclinations full sway. When these special relationships did not escape the staff's watchful eye, they were described as "patterns" that patients developed with a certain type of person, such as a young woman or a new staff member.

Because veteran staff labeled the patient attachment a "pattern," they devalued the staff member's contribution. The need to form these relationships was explained in terms of the structure of the hospital. Since special relationships are clandestine, there is no supervision over them. Without supervision these private therapy relations cannot benefit from being discussed and thus remain private, exclusive, and prone to fantasy.

Special relationships formed only if the staff member's schedule contained some free hours and the patient was free to move about the hospital. Also, the hospital ideology that the formal therapist alone was responsible for the patient had to be challenged. Special relationships implied that a particular staff member possessed special attributes permitting special trust. This kind of relationship was particularly attractive to those staff who overidentified with patients or were overcommitted to their work roles. The difference between being responsible and being overzealous was not clearly defined in the hospital, but those staff who were felt to have trespassed the boundary were socially pressured to conform.

All institutions that care for a client class (schools, hospitals, and nursing homes) develop norms that govern their staff's level of care:

Sandy [female adolescent patient about to be discharged] returned to the hall from her trip to the city after being promised a job as cashier at a downtown men's clothing store. I asked her if Mr. Fisher [occupational rehabilitation counselor] had gotten her the job and she became very animated saying, "Mr. Fisher is no help at all. There's a joke going around about him that you can go to many sessions with him and he'll never mention the word job. He doesn't know a thing about jobs. He's a frustrated person who wanted to become a psychiatrist but couldn't make it, so he dabbles around in it and really tries to get into your head." She felt this was really dangerous because she thought he couldn't handle it. She has seen him 4 or 5 times but his efforts to establish a "special relationship" have not succeeded.

The staff's rationale against developing special relationships was that the formal therapist's influence should be powerful and exclusive. Special relationships by staff could undermine the patients' relationships with their formal therapists. In addition, special relationships could lead to jealousy if one special patient discovered that his or her special friend had a special relationship with another patient. For these reasons, it was thought that special relationships harmed the therapeutic milieu by fostering distance between staff and patients.

According to the hospital's ideology, the staff were most effective if communication with other staff occurred outside of patient contact, so that all environmental influences were coordinated. Regardless of whether this belief helped patients, it unquestionably enhanced administrative control over staff members, which was operationalized in nursing notes, supervision, and countless staff meetings. Occasionally I violated this principle by engaging in devious activity, finding ways to be with a patient as a human being rather than within a staff-patient relationship.

Researchers must decide in the field whether they can engage in illegal or socially deviant behavior:

> From the outset, I had decided that I would never shoot crap, pool, or play cards for money, or bet money in any way (numbers excepted, since playing numbers is safely impersonal), and would meticulously avoid the slightest suspicion of a personal involvement with any woman. These self-imposed restrictions to some extent did underline my marginality. My explanation that I couldn't afford to chance a fight or bad feelings because of my job was usually accepted, and I was generally excused from participating in these activities rather than excluded from them [Liebow, 1967, p. 253].

Whyte, however, regretted his illegal activity of casting several votes in an election:

> When I discovered that I was a repeater, I found my conscience giving me serious trouble. This was not like the picture of myself that I had been trying to build up. . . . I had to learn that, in order to be accepted by the

people in a district, you do not have to do everything just as they do it. . . . I also had to learn that the field worker cannot afford to think only of learning to live with others in the field. He has to continue living with himself. If the participant observer finds himself engaging in behavior that he has learned to think of as immoral, then he is likely to begin to wonder what sort of a person he is after all. Unless the field worker can carry with him a reasonably consistent picture of himself, he is likely to run into difficulties [1971, p. 35].

In my case I drew the line at not giving my home address or phone number, even to those patients with whom I had established a special relationship, until I finished my work at the hospital.

The danger of devious staff activity was jeopardizing the patients' therapy, according to staff ideology. Moreover, staff were never to express criticism of the hospital, so that the patients' trust in the hospital would not be challenged. This meant "towing the line," an attitude whose therapeutic implications were not examined. Open communication by staff to patients was discouraged as a sign of a patient's manipulation of the staff. Both as a researcher and a staff member, I was not to get too close to a patient. Throughout my hospital fieldwork I was troubled by these undefined differences between involvement and overinvolvement, between being honest with a patient and expressing my neurotic needs as in a countertransference reaction. In light of these issues, how could a researcher express care and empathy in the hospital? Could I allow myself to be human?

My propensity to engage in rule-breaking behavior followed the demystification of psychiatry, which occurred in response to three factors. The first was my attendance at the "doctors report," in which the clinical status of patients about to be discharged was announced. Only half of the patients were discharged at least "moderately improved"; the other half were merely slightly improved, unimproved, or worse than when admitted. Surely this record cast doubt on the efficacy of hospital policies. Second was that each ward functioned autonomously and generated its own policies, some of which contradicted those of other wards and therefore threw doubt on all of them. Third was the fact that many rule makers were psychiatric residents with limited experience, who "knew little about mental illness as a category of illness" and "lacked detailed knowledge about their patients" (Longabaugh, Dummer and Forster, 1968a, p. 13).

The therapist's relation with the patient was the factor used to discourage other staff from forming special relationships with patients. The implicit operating norms of communalism in this hospital stated that all ward staff were responsible for all patients and all patients had access to all ward staff. In addition, all patients were to be treated equitably with no favoritism or prejudice. Democratic administration of care, however, did not take into consideration the specific affinities that developed. The dictum that a staff member should be available equally to all patients on a ward made it difficult for patients to understand and differentiate their psychosocial environment.

These norms contributed to patients' referring to staff involvement as "paid friendships." Patients and staff, among themselves and with each other, discussed at length the nature of friendships outside the hospital and how these differed from relationships between staff and patients. If staff became too friendly with patients, prohibited behavior typical of outside friendships could develop, such as providing phone numbers and addresses, exchanging gifts, sharing secrets, being interdependent, and meeting regularly. Similarly, staff attitudes to patients' relationships with other patients were contradictory: Interaction was encouraged as a sign of mental health, but deep involvement was discouraged since important confidences should be shared with the therapist only. In both staff-patient and patient-patient relationships, knowledge about forbidden behavior, such as taking drugs or "splitting," was not to be guarded by "the friend" but reported. Friendships were mistrusted as were all private behaviors that evaded hospital controls.

Egalitarian treatment was particularly pronounced in the adolescent wards, which functioned according to the principles of milieu therapy: All patients were punished for the infractions of a single patient except when there was voluntary confession. As a consequence, patients of an entire ward were frequently restricted to the ward for lengthy periods because a single patient had escaped or used drugs. All staff were supposed to relate to the patients as if they all were guilty. Collective punishment complemented collective care. My researcher self in the relationship with patients was problematic, but my staff role contributed many additional difficulties.

"The most serious ethical problem—and the one for which there is no permanent resolution—is the fact that friends in the group studied may be displeased or discomfited when research reports reach publication state. . . . One inevitably approaches all relationships with informants from the specialized perspective of one who eventually will withdraw. . . . [There are insoluble] difficulties involved in the growth of friendships between the observer and the studied" (Daniels, 1967, p. 290). What should I tell my patient friends about the outcomes of my research effort, particularly about what I was finding in hospital life, such as the significance of "special relationships" among staff and patients. The problem was minimized by the fact that it was only after I left the geographical area of the hospital that my formulations took shape. By that time most of these relationships had faded, and my guilt could be easily neutralized.

The compulsory egalitarianism of staff-patient relations contributed to the patients' interest in forming genuine friendships among themselves. Nevertheless, the staff attempted to regulate these patient relations in line with the staff's concept of a therapeutic mandate. The therapist's relationship with the patient was not manipulated in this way. Because the ward staff could not observe the therapists in their therapeutic hours, they observed the therapists' behavior in the public hall meetings. The hall staff used this behavior as a model for their own.

Ironically, although I attempted to avoid the deviant behavior and attitude patterns of which I was warned by staff, they developed nonetheless. I believed I had unusual curative abilities; I sided with the patients against staff and others and saw them as victims; I felt competitive with other staff; and I experienced the internal noise of anger and anxiety. I also became firmly socialized as an activity therapist and occasionally was caught up in activity therapy politics with other departments. These conflicts usually concerned whether doctors should deny patients the right to participate in activities as a punishment. If we were providing valuable therapy, surely the patients should always have access, as was true of their therapeutic hours. I restrained myself from active involvement in these conflicts to protect my access to particular wards as a researcher. As a participant observer, I developed the same definitions of the institution as did members of the role I had adopted; I was subject to their pressures and emotions.

The hospital was a stressful work environment for staff and a stressful living environment for patients. Staff stress manifested itself in the following ways: secrecy concerning work, griping, forming special relations with patients, rule breaking, and a high turnover rate. In my case, the stress was aggravated by an unsatisfactory on-site relation with my supervisor, who did little but police me and assign work. Staff stress was reduced when they felt respected by powerful insiders. Such respect produced a sense of competence and usefulness. But such respect was infrequently expressed because patient outcome was so vague and because the powerful insiders were too busy to work with the ward staff.

Undeniably many staff members derived satisfaction from their own perceived efficacy with patients. However, this intrinsic satisfaction was dampened by pejorative reference to the messiah complex. The chief source of stress for the caring staff members was the nature of work in the bureaucratic institution, which involved extensive administration, a proliferation of rules, compliance, docility, and cooperative behavior by patients and staff. Such an organizational form produces stress, regardless of the wealth of the setting (Huesler, 1970). Rebels are cooled out: Patients are considered mentally ill and staff are considered unprofessional, naive, immature, or neurotic.

The stresses that I introduced because of my research project added to those inherent to the hospital. If the setting had been characterized by trust and openness, I might have been better able to enlist cooperation for my study rather than experience fear and guilt. Similarly, a more open setting would have allowed me to utilize my supervisory and other close work relations for debriefing my feelings and thoughts. Had I not been concerned with jeopardizing the research project, however, and thought of my work merely as a job, I might have challenged the system more to test its values. Since my research endeavor was proceeding with the hospital's permission, I was afraid to risk overt nonconformity. I compensated for the stress by committing much energy to patients in my work as dance therapist. As a result, my research effort was eclipsed by the pressing concerns of mastering the work within the organization. My hours in the hospital were filled with frustration, pain, and the intermittent joy of my dance therapy and special relationships. The hospital continuously dredged up questions about the nature of reality, the standards of society, and visions of a better world.

As time passed, my research project as originally defined seemed less significant and less feasible, particularly since I needed unconventional techniques to study intimate behavior, which in this mental hospital was deviant and largely hidden. I began to appreciate the difficulty of understanding "the other's" experience, but I was too guilt ridden by my own devious activity and attitudes to acknowledge my own experiences in the hospital. I had not yet accepted the legitimacy of a reflexive study, let alone appreciated its inherent value. Whereas I had hoped to master the hospital, it was actually mastering me.

Drawing Conclusions: Final Dilemmas and Blocks

Just as the preparation and on-site stages of participant observation fieldwork have their characteristic dilemmas and blocks, so, too, are the concluding phases beset with problems—validity, proof, generalization, and publication—many of which are discussed in the literature (Vidich, 1955; Vidich and Bensman, 1971; Fichter and Kolb, 1953; Colvard, 1967; Becker, 1958, 1971). During the final phases, the researcher must organize the data within a *framework* that has emerged in the field and that is flexible enough to adapt to additional data. In this case, as the internal noise increased, the focus on patient friendships receded, becoming part of the larger problem of the coping patterns of staff and patients within the hospital structure and ideology.

The methodological difficulties were sometimes overwhelming. I never resolved the ambivalence about the covert quality of my work. When the time came to prepare a report about the effect of the hospital's social structure and ideology on staff and patients, I needed courage to expose the institution that had let me in. Even with time I remained reluctant to reveal my real attitudes and means of coping with the hospital. The self-doubt and mistrust that the hospital engendered made it difficult to study the mistrust itself. Similarly, my understanding of participant observation methodology blocked the focus on myself in favor of studying external reality.

With time, however, I understood the place of this research experience within my professional socialization. It became a vehicle for exploration, for testing new ideas, and for experimenting with an untried method. I discovered that I was still developing my sociological identity and research skills in the field. At the end of the eight months in the hospital, I properly prepared myself and the patients for my departure and wound down the dance therapy activities. The research problem and the personal lessons to be learned, however, were not so neatly finished. Gradually I perceived one of the cardinal dilemmas of participant observation research—it is never finished (Glaser and Strauss, 1967). Conclusions are temporary and reflect the current coming to terms with the research experience.

While in the field, data continue to come into the researcher's awareness. Once the researcher has left the field, the data can be reworked in innumerable ways. With each new situation, the preceding work takes on new meaning. Fieldworkers have published reanalyses five, ten, and fifteen years after they left the field as their previous experiences took on new meanings. The crammed time schedule of this project did not leave much time for reflection, but in the light of later projects and less hectic agendas I made sense of these experiences. Because participant observation relies on the uniquely human qualities of the observer, it is not surprising that it benefits from hindsight. This lack of clear-cut completion distinguishes this method from surveys with their delimited samples and instruments.

I embarked on this research project with zest to replace my negative experience as a survey research assistant. I selected participant observation fieldwork in order to become thoroughly familiar with my subject matter and to resolve the superficiality and distortion of survey research. To my surprise I discovered that participant observation contained its own dilemmas, most of which had to be resolved by the researchers themselves as a function of their personal and sociological identity. I had to experience these dilemmas to forge my own solutions. Just as participation in a natural setting is "necessary to provide us with reactions of our own which will help us to properly understand the reports and behavior of others" (Phillips, 1971, p. 152), so, too, was a participant observation project necessary for me to understand the reports of others who had used this method and to uncover additional dilemmas. This research experience represented the stage of my socialization in which I recognized the necessity of assuming personal responsibility for the development of methodology.

At the start of the hospital study, I adhered to the notion that research must not be influenced by the researcher's self. And yet the psychiatric hospital, as a bureaucratic organization for the care of emotionally disturbed individuals, engaged my self. Anxiety, delight, fear, anger, and compassion welled up inside me as a response to being socialized into this environment. While in the field, I suppressed acknowledgement of this internal noise for the sake of the study. Only after leaving the field and allowing time to pass could I recognize and analyze what happened to me as a researcher (as a *person*), how the setting and its members were organized (the research *problem*), and the emerging dimensions of participant observation (the research *method*).

The result can only be described as an understanding of the process of studying patient friendships in a mental hospital from the perspective of a part-time dance therapist and part-time participant observer and should not be considered an objective or perspective-free analysis of hospital phenomena. This specific perspective illuminated patient friendships without pretending to be timeless or universal. Having broken through the resistance to self-examination in this first field study, I could benefit from a freer research attitude in subsequent studies. As an outcome of this participant observation field experience, I dared to challenge the conventional notion that the substantive problem can be studied alone as if no context is provided by the researcher as a person. In a subsequent project discussed in Chapters Six and Seven, I further abandoned this person-free attitude and became more radical in my conception of method. In that study I converted what had been internal noise into the major source of fieldwork data. The acknowledgement of my own experience in this later study did not compel me to go native as was largely the case in my dance therapist role in the hospital study. Going native had been an escape from the stress of the researcher role and a response to the internal noise of the staff member role. The conflict between competing identities characteristic of fieldwork led to fluctuation in my role commitments. A rigid problem definition exacerbated these difficulties because I struggled against changes emerging in the field. Because of this rigidity, my field experiences seemed like intrusions on, rather than contributions to, my fieldwork.

I had yet to conceptualize method as the creative product of the researcher and the substantive problem, rather than it being a fixed technique. The rules I thought could serve as a guide to fieldwork did not dissipate the dilemmas I had to discover and resolve for myself. To follow fieldwork techniques is to work with received notions or predetermined expectations, which in turn affect perceptions of the field. Familiarity with these problems is necessary, but each site demands a reinterpretation of fieldwork. The creative product results from the researcher's suspension of method prescriptions, of probable findings, and of fixed definitions of personal identity before entering the field. Instead of discipline, the researcher can follow the "drift" produced by the setting. While in the setting, which phenomena are encountered? Which feelings are experienced? Which self did the setting evoke and what kind of action followed? If the researcher's self and the properties of the setting are expected to surprise the researcher, then fieldwork is the occasion of personal growth, especially when coupled with disciplined reflection. By not separating experience from research, the amount of available data is increased and must be accounted for. If the research method includes the research experience, then conflict, alienation, and internal noise can be reduced.

Participant observation fieldwork is a frustrating, anxiety-provoking, yet personally fulfilling process that is experienced; it is not a technology. If participant observation is routinized like other stressful work, it

> [does not have to be] a continuous bout with anxiety. Sometimes it becomes just another job ... [but] more often than other research methods and other jobs, participant-observation provides great satisfactions: discovering new facts, coming up with new ideas, watching people act by, and put life into, the concepts of sociological theory, and knowing always that, in contrast to any other method of social research, participant-observation puts one about as close to real data and the sources of real data as is humanly possible [Gans, 1968, p. 309].

The product is a reflection of the researcher's involvement, observation, and self-consciousness about participation with subjects in their natural environment. To do this the researcher must develop sensitivity to observe the environment and the self, as well as analytic sociological skills.

Diesing (1971, p. 241) suggests researchers should learn to probe their subconscious in order to understand and explain "why one reacted in a particular way and why one reached a particular conclusion. The manifold interrelations between observer and subject—mutual expectations, shared understandings, shared experiences—have to be brought into the open; the implicit values, beliefs, and commitments underlying one's reasoning have to be made explicit." Within this definition of method, sociologists can "own" rather than deny their experience. The hospital study revealed hitherto unexamined aspects of my self and my developing identity as a sociologist. I concluded that the setting in which I should express my personal commitment should not be a setting in which my role is researcher. Competing identities in the field can characterize the first field experience, but the subsequent projects should reduce the dilemma of commitment. The interest in being socialized as a member of a setting has to be differentiated from the wish to critically understand that setting.

These past two chapters have described one participant observation research enterprise. This self-disclosure is not free from pain but is one of the necessary multiple foci of a research project. In the narrative account or descriptive chronology, the dilemmas and their social psychological explanations are interwoven—the interplay of person, problem, and method. The reticence of fieldworkers to discuss their experience and the arbitrary definition of "findings" belie the actual process of participant observation. "The experiences of field workers have not been systematically reported—and as a result a whole area of methodological skills—the human relations skills which go with the social researcher's role—has remained relatively uncodified" (Mann, 1951, p. 341).

The chapter is intended as an analysis, not as a confession. Many of the difficulties were specific to a first field trip, some were generic to working in a total institution, and others were dilemmas inherent in the participant observation method. Because I defined research unidimensionally during this project, I tried to focus exclusively on matters of substance, and let matters of method—ethics, procedures, relationships, and a search for identity in the field—remain peripheral. With time my perspective became multidimensional.

Field data analysis is similar to therapy in that the material repeatedly needs to be reworked. The conceptualization stage seeks categories to match the observed phenomenon. Until the phenomenon has been labeled, there is a nagging, incomplete understanding of it.

Fieldwork as a method of self-discovery is cumulative.

The first field experiences begin the processes of exploring the self and method, and in later projects problems specific to a setting or to sociological theory have greater sway. During this project I understood very little about what was wrong, and I blamed the methodology of participant observation. Only later did I reformulate my experience in terms of the three major variables: who I was at the time, the substantive issue I was trying to study, and the notions of method I brought to bear—that is, person, problem, and method. Nevertheless, since I did attribute problems to participant observation research, particularly the suppression of the researcher's self-awareness, I continued my search for yet another method that would bring me closer to the truth.

CHAPTER 5

Reclaiming Self-Awareness as a Source of Insight

An outcome of my experience with survey research and participant observation was my private discovery that the reflexive attitude could illuminate the dual problems of seeking a sociological research method and developing a personal identity as a researcher. Solutions to these problems would emerge from honest and careful examination of my experience as a researcher. A crucial component of an alternative direction for sociology, therefore, was precisely the concept of self, particularly the researcher's self, which is suppressed in mainstream methods. The use of the reflexive researching stance is the first step in uncovering the basic assumptions in sociology. In addition, this stance reduces the self-imposed alienation of supposedly objective methods. "The academic social sciences are the social sciences of an alienated age and alienated man. . . .

240

The 'objectivity' of the social sciences is not the expression of a dispassionate and detached view of the social world; it is, rather, an ambivalent effort to accommodate to alienation *and* to express a muted resentment of it. . . . The dominant expressions of the academic social sciences embody an accommodation to the alienation of men in contemporary society, rather than a determined effort to transcend it" (Gouldner, 1970, p. 53). Experiential research products, by contrast, are written from the perspective of research-as-process, in which a specific researcher assumes responsibility for all actions. The self becomes the medium of acquiring knowledge. Such reports define knowledge in terms of explicit descriptions of experiences, behavior, and observations.

Instead of avoiding self-revelation (in Gouldner's terms, "self-obscuring methodologies"), the reflexive stance exploits self-awareness as a source of insight and discovery. The self can be used in research not only as an observer (as in participant observation), but also as a receiver and receptacle of experience that is to be explicated, as I learned in my subsequent project. Social science's camps are split between those who wish to depersonalize the process of knowing in the hopes of obtaining universal, "pure" knowledge and those who acknowledge that since the self of the observer is always implicated, it should be converted into an invaluable tool. The hesitance of Freud mirrors how social scientists feel about self-disclosure. However, Freud (1931, p. 17) overcame these doubts:

> I must, therefore, resort to my own dreams as a source of abundant and convenient material, furnished by a person who is more or less normal, and containing references to many instances of everyday life. I shall certainly be confronted with doubts as to the trustworthiness of these "self-analyses," and it will be said that arbitrariness is by no means excluded in such analyses. In my own judgment, conditions are more likely to be favorable in self-observation than in the observation of others; in any case, it is permissible to investigate how much can be accomplished in the matter of dream-interpretation by means of self-analysis. There are other difficulties which

must be overcome in my own inner self. One has a comprehensible aversion to exposing so many intimate details of one's own psychic life, and one does not feel secure against the misinterpretation of strangers.

In his discussion of the restrictive impact of scientific norms on his research and identity, Mann (1973, pp. 15, 34) cries out:

> I will no longer cringe at being called unscientific. I will no longer hide my subjectivity in order to pass by the guardian at the portal of science. Anyone who deviates from the official code is prone to think that he or she is utterly alone. That's one reason there's so much furtiveness, dissembling, and self-doubt abroad in the world, even in the world of the researcher. If the official code sanctions the search for regularities which are generalizable across a range of comparable conditions, one feels deviant if in fact he thinks it quite sufficient to understand one particular person or one particular group.

Without the processing function of the human observer, only objectlike interpretations can be made of human events. If it is acknowledged that the researcher's social and personal contingencies do affect the research, we can redefine the research task as the attempt to describe and utilize rather than obliterate the researcher's self. When scientific instruments are used instead of the human observer, we learn only about reality as it appears without personal involvement or interpersonal dialogue.

Self-utilization and self-revelation in psychology, sociology, and related fields are typically dismissed as unscientific. But this reaction is relevant only if the scientific model is accepted. Studies involving the self are labeled "merely subjective," impressionistic, arbitrary, or journalistic. Some philosophical schools, however, claim that rather than being arbitrary, such studies are the *only* truth. Kierkegaard, for instance, opposed the "pursuit of objectivity" and suggested instead that "truth lies in subjectivity: true existence is achieved by intensity of feeling" (Wahl, 1949, p. 3). Kierkegaard presented a model of an individual thinker striving for simplification and attempting to approach pure experience: "Someone who is in an infinite relationship with himself, has an infinite interest in himself and his destiny—always feels himself to be in Becoming with a task before him, in a state of sustained effort —he is impassioned, inspired" (Wahl, 1949, p. 4).

Kierkegaard was not unidimensional but suggested that different ways of knowing are appropriate for different problems. The subjective approach is appropriate for matters concerning society, values, religion, and human life. Truth is not merely a matter of the intellect but of the whole person. Subjective truth, he claimed, is not a truth that I *have*, but a truth that I *am*. Kierkegaard began to formulate a connection between commitment and knowledge. Subjectivity is not by definition arbitrary. Instead it can reflect the deepest possible connection between the individual thinker and the world. If we think of social life not as a set of elusive fixed laws but as a process of becoming, then our participation in events will assist our comprehension. This is the assumption on which participant observation and anthropological fieldwork are based. For example, James Agee (Agee and Evans, 1972) became an existential, subjective reporter of the conditions among southern U.S. tenant farmers. His subjectivity was not arbitrary, but passionate, committed, and enlightening. Similarly, the phenomenological school that developed from the works of Husserl claimed to be creating a program for establishing "certain knowledge" obtained in an immediate vision. To achieve these intuitions, Husserl proposed a method of reduction, that is, eliminating presuppositions and translating images to ultimate essences. Phenomenological knowledge is claimed to be more basic than scientific knowledge since the latter derives from assumptions beyond the realm of experience, whereas the former attempts to rid itself of presuppositions and strictly excludes assertions inaccessible through intuitive experience. What emerges from the phenomenological approach, then, are "elaborate and painstaking descriptive analyses" (Kockelmans, 1967, p. 43), the product of adopting the proper reflexive attitude, which yields the facts of immediate experience.

A vivid model can be found in Descartes (1960, pp. 38-39), whose intellectual pursuit specifically avoided arbitrariness and ambiguity. In his search for certainty, he too was reduced to the knowing self:

> Books formed my education from childhood, and because I had been induced to believe that, with their help, I might acquire a clear and assured knowledge of everything there is of use in life, I felt an intense desire to learn from them. But, no sooner had I completed this whole course of study, at the end of which it is customary to take one's place in the ranks of the learned, than my opinion changed entirely. For I found myself hampered by so many doubts and errors that the only benefit of my efforts to become an educated person seemed to be the increasing discovery of my own ignorance. . . . And so, in the end, I allowed myself the liberty of taking my own predicament as universal, and of concluding that nowhere in the world was there any knowledge professed of the kind I had been encouraged to expect.
>
> And so, for all these reasons, as soon as my age freed me from the subjection to my tutors, I entirely abandoned the study of books. And, resolving henceforth to seek for no other knowledge than the knowledge I might find in myself, or else in the great book of the world, I spent the rest of my youth in travel, in visiting courts and armies, in seeking the company of men of varying character and rank, in gathering experience, in putting myself to the test in the encounters that come to me by chance, and in reflecting always and everywhere in such a way on the events with which I was confronted as to draw some benefit from my reflections. For it seemed to me that I should find more truth in the reasonings which a man makes with regard to matters which touch him closely, and of which the outcome must be to his detriment, if his judgment has been at fault, than in the reasonings of a man of learning in his study, whose speculations remain without effect, and are of no further consequence to him than he may derive all the more vanity from them the further removed they are from good sense, because of the greater skill and ingenuity he has to employ to make them seem plausible.

> However, after I had spent some years in the study of the book of the world and in the effort to acquire experience, I resolved one day to study my own nature as well, and to employ all the resources of my mind to choose the paths which I ought to follow.

Descartes's (1960, pp. 42-43) search for certainty concluded with the isolation of the reflexive attitude:

> Now, however, that I intended to make the search for truth my only business, I thought it necessary to reject as absolutely false anything which gave rise to the slightest doubt, with the object of finding out, once this had been done, whether anything remained which I could take as indubitable. . . . But then, immediately as I strove to think of everything as false, I realized that in the very act of thinking everything false, I was aware of myself as something real—and observing the truth: I think, therefore I am, was so firm and so assured that the most extravagant sceptics were incapable of shaking it, I concluded that I might have no scruple in taking it as that first principle of philosophy for which I was looking.

Descartes recorded a process that includes the following stages: defining the search; seizing a method enthusiastically and carrying it through; evaluating the outcome and finding disillusionment, doubt, and uncertainty; abandoning the method but retaining the problem; repeating this process with increased focus on the problem; reduction; and discovery of the self. These stages also characterize the reflexive search for sociological method and identity, which results in a focus on the self.

The contemporary exponent of the view that all knowledge (including science) is a fusion of subjectivity and objectivity is Polanyi (1958, pp. vii-viii):

> I want to establish an alternative ideal of knowledge, quite generally. Such is the personal participation of the knower in all acts of understanding. But this does not make our understanding subjective. Comprehension is neither an arbitrary act nor a passive experience, but a responsible act claiming universal validity. Such knowing

is indeed objective in the sense of establishing contact with a hidden reality; a contact that is defined as the condition for anticipating an indeterminate range of yet unknown (and perhaps yet inconceivable) true implications.

Polanyi addresses directly the two criticisms most frequently raised with regard to nonobjective methods: arbitrariness and bias. His views on subjectivity gain additional weight from his background as a distinguished chemist. As do the phenomenologists, Polanyi demonstrates that so-called scientific knowledge reflects particular assumptions.

The very striving for a scientific, logical, empirical quantitative ideal is as much a product of subjective bias, I have argued, as is the repudiation of the intuitive, imaginative, personal, self-disclosing ideal. The efficacy of science is partially due to the fact that a belief system has been established which allows us to trust and therefore to suspend doubt. "Science is a system of beliefs to which we are committed. Such a system cannot be accounted for either from experience as seen within a different system, or by reason without any experience. Yet this does not signify that we are free to take it or leave it, but simply reflects the fact that it is a system of beliefs to which we are committed and which therefore cannot be represented in noncommittal terms" (Polanyi, 1958, p. 171).

Rules have been organized to prevent blatant deception, and we trust that they are upheld. Nevertheless, there are numerous cases of scientific hoaxes and frauds, and there are probably lesser perversions that have gone undetected. Only recently it was reported that data of published reports are relatively inaccessible (Bryant and Wortman, 1978).

If science relies on a certain amount of trust, then we can consider trusting other sources of knowledge as well, such as the knowing self. Polanyi (1958, p. 249) wishes us to "reappraise our capacity to acquire knowledge . . . and credit ourselves with much wider cognitive powers than an objectivist conception of knowledge would allow . . . because knowledge is existentially dependent." In my view, Polanyi has resolved the inherently contradictory charges of arbitrariness and bias with his notions of passion and commitment. Passion and commitment turn the problem of bias on its head by acknowledging the root of knowledge to be within the unique individual. Polanyi rejects any knowledge or claims that cannot be attributed to the experience of the individual. He proposes the methodology of commitment as an alternative to the methodology of detachment. Since in this view detachment is impossible in practice and undesirable as an ideal, commitment involves an open avowal of one's research activities; it substitutes freedom of exploration for control. The validity of the products depends on the critic's perspective. Polanyi (1958, p. 303) provides a diagram to illustrate the problem:

> Epistemology has traditionally aimed at defining truth and falsity in impersonal terms, for these alone are accepted as truly universal. The framework of commitment leaves no scope for such an endeavor, for its acceptance necessarily invalidates an impersonal justification of knowledge. This can be illustrated by writing down a symbolic representation of the elements joined together within a commitment and contrasting these with the same elements, when looked upon non-committally from *outside* the commitment situation. We may, for example, represent a factual statement from within as:

personal	confident	accredited
passion	utterance	facts

> and from without as:

subjective	declaratory	alleged
belief	sentence	facts

Polanyi differentiates between passive and active knowledge, which is the difference between experiencing and making sense of that experience.

All knowledge is personal in the sense that meaning is created by the speaker/writer/researcher. Bias becomes nothing more than being human and socially situated. What would be left if a person were to remove all biases? If it is accepted that knowledge is situationally located in configurations of social,

temporal, and physical relationships (that knowledge is a sociological product), then a knowledge claim must always be confronted with the question: What are all the circumstances under
which this knowledge was gained?

Statements must be put back into their natural environments—into their contexts (Mishler, 1978). Meaning is derived
from statements in context. Divorced from context, they are
divorced of meaning and therefore lose their truth value. Thus
meaning emerges when the behavior or statement is matched
with its proper context. This relocating and meshing is a substitute logic for chronological causality. The researcher's claims
can be evaluated only by experiencing the account of the processes through which experience was converted into knowledge.
For example, the very data on which studies are built belie the
multiple possible definitions of social reality:

> The use of diagnoses that appear on hospital case
> records without further examination of the underlying
> diagnostic procedures is completely inadequate. Studies
> that include standardized and evaluated diagnoses of
> cases as part of the investigation are ideal but this is not
> always feasible or economical. Faced with someone else's
> diagnosis, investigators should at least try to find out
> 'who' this someone else is—a first-year psychiatric resi-
> dent, a senior psychiatrist, a staff conference; and the
> basis on which the diagnosis was assigned—a half-hour ad-
> mission interview, psychological tests, a month's observa-
> tion on the psychiatric ward" [Mishler and Scotch, 1965,
> pp. 283-284].

Similarly, Glaser and Strauss (1967, p. 5) contend that "the
adequacy of a theory for sociology today cannot be divorced
from the process by which it is generated."

The generation of knowledge includes the reader's experience as well as the researcher's. Homans (1950, p. 10) calls this
process "extension": "No one will make progress with this
book who does not train himself to extensionalize, who does
not habitually catch himself as he mouths one of the big ab-
stractions and ask: What does this mouthful mean in terms of

actual human behavior that someone has seen and reported? Just what in human behavior do we see?" Knowing is a human process, even if the human element is obscured behind mechanical instruments. Wherever the human element enters, there the knowledge remains situated. As a scientist or a sociologist, a particular perspective obtains. There is no escape from the humanness or the social attributes of the researcher. Polanyi (1958, p. 327) says, "I must understand the world from my point of view." Gouldner (1970, p. 54) says, "The sociologists' claim to autonomy entails a contradiction" of sociology's assumption "that men are shaped in countless ways by the press of their social surround."

The Sociologists' Perspective

As a budding sociologist, I had difficulty articulating my criticism even after rejecting the mainstream assumptions that the sociologist's perspective is autonomous and unique and transcends everyday reality. I could never accept the claim that sociologists are aware both of latent and manifest meanings of events, that they transcend the conditions that brainwash or shape Everyman. In my view, sociologists should be considered removed from much of social reality if they are confined to academia. They rarely go native. They suspend pity, passion, and remorse while they work:

> Professional sociologists often show an interest that is obligatory rather than spontaneous and irrepressible. On the whole, it seems to be activated, directed and nourished by particular assignments, by the desire to take an academic degree or by professional literature, rather than by an insatiable curiosity about the undigested social reality that surrounds us. As a rule they have neither an extensive nor an intimate knowledge of the everyday world around them, often not appreciably more than scientists in other fields, and less than a lot of people with everyday experience like general practitioners, rent-collectors, district nurses or social workers. . . . They sometimes display a staggering ignorance with respect to

their own society [Jongmans and Gutkind, 1967, pp. 10-11].

Sociologists have one primary identification (which I was supposed to be developing), whereas they attribute multiple roles to other members of society. Their commitment is to a paradigm that treats society as if it were the subject matter of a physical science. Sociologists appear to believe their special floating consciousness can tap the feelings and attitudes of the common folks, then produce reports without their getting involved or being affected. They believe this is not only possible but desirable.

Few social scientists describe themselves as "simply human" rather than as exceptions to the laws that they create. For example, Gouldner (1970, p. 496) writes, "There is not as great a difference between the sociologist and those he studies as the sociologist seems to think, even with respect to an intellectual interest in knowing social worlds. Those being studied are also avid students of human relations; they too have their social theories and conduct their investigations." The sociologist cannot and therefore does not have a radically detached perspective. To believe otherwise is to believe in unembodied researchers. Garfinkle, too, criticized the

prevailing claim that one cannot be doing cogent studies without there being the accompanying assurance that present company is excused. That is to say, suppose I furnish you an account of the organization of a hospital. The question may then be asked in return: Did you take in account the ways in which you were knowledgeable about those arrangements, and did you use as a resource your own grasp of those arrangements so that what you did was to engage in an explicating procedure in which something otherwise familiar was made visible once more?

There is the assurance that research undertakings which are delivered were made by someone already knowing what he is looking at, and making use of what he knows, in order to make the thing that he will have delivered a cogent or believable report.

What we are proposing is that all such attempts to excuse the present company, to propose that one can do practical sociological accounting while reserving that privilege, makes use of unexamined practical devices to assure the cogency, the recognizability and the visibility of that claim [Hill and Crittenden, 1968, pp. 111-112].

Presuppositions cannot be entirely stripped. Try as you may, you cannot suspend them because they are imbedded in your very language; they are your epistemology. They can be altered by experience, they can change over time, but they cannot be suspended. Membership in the human race and one's social origins cannot be suspended for the sake of pure observation. The activity of observation requires a sense-making individual who uses categories that are grounded in certain contexts. Sociologists are necessarily part of what they are studying; they are present in their statements. We cannot completely divorce ourselves from our work, nor our work from our selves. Whereas Homans urged sociologists to let "man" back into their notion of sociology, I urge that sociologists themselves appear, that they liberate themselves from the faulty pursuit of detachment.

Sociologists do not stand outside the one-way mirror of life, devising notions that are truer than those of the actors. Rather, the sociologists' notions are different. They are their own notions reflecting the sociologists' embeddedness in particular perspectives. Sociologists do not transcend the insight of the sociology of knowledge. There is no such thing as scientific privilege or license. It is contradictory to claim that statements about the social world are valid while exempting the process of acquiring that insight. The act of discovering must be explained by the same rubric as that which is discovered.

Failure to include the scientist, the research process, and the reporting under the same set of contingencies has opened the way for unethical acts to be performed in the name of science. Science was to have provided scientists with immunity from the ethical constraints to which mere mortals (their subjects) are bound. However, when science mystifies, norms can be altered and deliberate scientific catastrophes can ensue.

If scientific privilege is suspended, then social scientists are part of the studied world, subject to its consequences. Knowledge is not given in nature but is created by individuals as thinkers acting through their individual personalities, intellects, experiences, and passions. The person does not disappear while doing science.

Implied by these statements concerning the humanness of sociologists is the recognition of the traditionally under-socialized concept of the sociologist (to complement the over-socialized concept of man). My attempt to reclaim sociologists as social actors is done partially to provide me with a viable identity. This attempt compensates for the alienation I experienced in denying my beliefs and awareness for the sake of being scientific. Instead, sociologists as actors can find within their own experience the starting point and checkpoint for social knowledge. Sociological perspectives will then be as varied as individual sociologists. Like Parsons, some will see order, while others like Goffman will see an embarrassed world engaged in countless miniature dramas. Some will see chaos; others will find cause for despair or for joy. The sociologists know and interpret everyday life precisely because they are social members. They have access to the "inside track" and are capable of *verstehen*. Use of the researching self, of personal involvement, and of the unique perspective in interpretation is repudiated in mainstream social science, which defines the self as a source of error rather than as a source of knowledge, or an impediment rather than a conduit for discovery.

Bennis (1968, pp. 231-232) advocates abandoning the fear of the subjective:

> The reflexive process can be an advantage, for it provides an "inside track," a "within-ness" that other sciences lack, although to be sure, it can be at times crude and terribly misleading folk wisdom. Because of this fear, social scientists often (and unwisely) either ignore or eschew the rich insights of the inside track rather than use them for theory development and for testing hypotheses. And in the last twenty years or so, the "outside track"—that of using instruments external to the phe-

nomena under investigation—has been considered the only reliable mode of truth.

Tiryakian is another methodologist who has argued that the sociologist use the distinctive tool of personal knowledge, which can be extended to knowledge of others, of groups and of society. He says, "Since the observer is a human being studying other human beings, he has access to the inner world of experience. This direct access is 'sympathetic understanding' and 'intuition' by means of which the observer can view cultural phenomena 'from within' " (Tiryakian, 1965, p. 678).

These writers criticize the use of instruments that stand between the observer and the studied object and advocate instead a more direct knowing grounded in self-awareness. Social phenomena can be both observed and experienced. To understand these phenomena, it is reasonable to utilize both other- and self-observation. Uniquely human avenues are required to understand human behavior in contrast with the alternative scientific perspective of objective instruments, detached observers, and quantification, which miss the experiential phenomena.

Scheler's position on the viability of experiential knowledge was most radical. He believed that knowledge of others is not necessarily indirect, analogizing, or empathic. Rather, people have "direct knowledge of the psychic lives of our fellow-humans because ego and non-ego have both emerged out of a common stream of life-experience" (Scheler, 1954, p. xi).

We do not have to build up a picture of other people's experience from the immediately given data furnished by our own, and then to impute these experiences, which have no intrinsic marks of "foreignness" about them, to the physical semblances of other people. What occurs, rather, is an immediate flow of experiences, undifferentiated as between mine and thine, which actually contains both our own and others' experiences intermingled and without distinction from one another. . . . Our claim is that so far as concerns the act and its nature and the range of facts appearing within it, everyone can apprehend the experience of his fellowmen just as directly (or indirectly) as he can his own [Scheler, 1954, pp. 246, 256].

The sociologist's task, then, is to become aware of experiences of the self and others. Self-awareness, self-utilization, and self-revelation are, for Scheler, the starting points for an adequate understanding of social life.

Inclusion of the self in sociological research is not without attendant problems. Modifying the scientific stance with a relativistic, personal, truly sociological perspective depends on relinquishing a certain arrogance and accepting our inability to control the social world. The application of most positivist methods depends on the control of subjects or at least the pretense of control. Acknowledgment of the limitations of social science methods and the dependence of truth claims on particular perspectives on a given situation compels the use of "I believe" rather than "It is true." This reformulation requires an expository style that conveys exacting honesty. Beginning with the question "Why am I doing this in the first place?" reflexive studies continuously demand self-assurance so that the sociologist can share publicly his or her self-awareness.

Seeley (1971, pp. 164-165) discloses the difficulties of the self-revealing sociologist:

> This is not the place for some sort of psychodynamic self-exposure. Not that it would not be scientifically apt, but that it would be socially inept. It would be seen as in bad taste. It might create pressures on my friends and colleagues to do the like. It might embarrass me later or put me at a "competitive disadvantage." (In any case, self-disclosures at any depth have to proceed like disarmament negotiations, each step on each side making possible the next step on the other. What could be done by social agreement and in mutuality, therefore, is not even instrumentally effective as a lone, quixotic, rather than heroic, act.) In any case, detailed psychodynamic stories may involve and damage living persons, a consideration that raises social, emotional, and ethical problems, which go beyond the purview not just of sociology but also of available codes of personal conduct.

If complete forthrightness is required in all phases of research, who is capable? The protection of one's self-image or self-esteem competes for primacy with the ideal of completeness or candor. Researchers, too, must manage the impressions they create in their various audiences. It is therefore socially and emotionally complex to deal with the self in print. The second problem is how to assess the relevance of all one could report. According to the empirical model, "the investigator is expected to function as a data-collecting machine and, theoretically at least, another machine would obtain the same results. Thus, whether the data-collecting machine is male or female, young or old, black or white, Jew or gentile, should not influence the results obtained. Nor should it matter whether the machine operates in one setting rather than another, whether the machine has certain expectations, needs, desires or beliefs" (Phillips, 1971, p. 142).

If we are not machines, then what about ourselves is specifically relevant to the discussion? Phillips (1971) focuses on the need to make explicit one's implicit theories and "models of the actor." If we know that attributes of the researcher affect the research process, which attributes are significant? What shall I tell you about myself? Who am I? Is it relevant that I am female, thirty-two years old, married, Jewish, a mother, from the East Coast, middle class, born in Holland, a periodic resident of Israel, or slim? Is it significant that I am professional, feminist, socialistically inclined, energetic, talkative, a leader, a follower, open-minded, sensitive, gullible, overextended, accepting, flexible, friendly, inquisitive, self-doubting, searching, hard working, and demanding of others? I am also melioristic, sympathetic to the underdog, concerned with injustices, moralistic, and tend not to blame persons but systems. My attributes have influenced my study processes and formed my preconceptions. Objectivity should thus be redefined from the elimination of the influence of the investigator's personal features to a clear understanding of their influence.

To search for this understanding is to blatantly ignore sociology's traditional phobia of being "reduced to psychology." Durkheim (1964, pp. 124-125) introduced this concern in *The Rules of Sociological Method*: "Since social facts' essential characteristic consists in the power they possess of exercising, from outside, a pressure on individual consciousness, it must be that they do not derive from individual consciousness and that accordingly sociology is not a corollary of psychology." Sociology is not hereby reduced to psychology but instead acknowledges its partnership. The legitimization of self-awareness will yield a fuller documentation of research processes and a greater awareness of the nature of social processes. It will ground sociology in experienced reality. I propose this perspective as an alternative to the search for disembodied objectivity.

The following section examines how subjectivity can be developed into a method by applying the sociological imagination to the researcher's experiences, using these experiences as an avenue for creating meaning in the social world. Once the self is reclaimed, experience is accessible.

Discovering Experience

An outcome of my comparative analysis of participation in research projects is the argument for reestablishing experience as the foundation of social research. Toward that end, the outline of what I call an "experiential method" for social research is presented in the last part of Chapter Seven. As background for the later discussion, the controversy surrounding experience deserves some attention. My survey study was a chronicle of "experienceless research." The participant observation method seems ambivalent toward experience. Chapters Six and Seven focus on a project in which my search for method resulted in a reliance on experience. My discovery of the salience of the sociologist's rejection of experience came from my participation in experienceless research. This personal discovery might become a group discovery for the discipline of sociology if there is a shared readiness to uncover this procedure.

When sociology aspired to become a science, its tradition of interweaving experience and reason fell into disrepute. The redefinition of truth in mathematical terms has undermined the claims of thinkers. Knowledge is suspect until measured and verified statistically. The experiencing self can merely intuit, describe, and perceive subjectively. Scientific knowledge requires suppressing the self and treating the humanness of the researcher as an obstacle. The experiencing self has been redefined as a source of bias standing between pure reason and the phenomenon waiting to be captured and measured. The experiencing self has been reevaluated as worthless in establishing truth, as simplistic when compared with quantification, and as deceptive and misleading.

A frustrated, divergent reaction has also persisted. Polanyi (1958, p. 64) wishes to "tear away the paper screen of graphs, equations and computations, [and] lay bare the inarticulate manifestations of intelligence by which we know things in a purely personal manner." Earlier, Dilthey and Weber articulated how our understanding depends on our experience. Dilthey believed that "the unit of investigation in the social sciences is given in experience" (Kress, 1970, p. 79). Like Weber, Dilthey was primarily concerned with the process by which meaning is created. Dilthey posited an outer world of empirical facts and an inner world of cultural meanings. The social scientist's task was to develop "a disciplined awareness of the inner life of man as experienced in its immediately apprehended form" (Bruyn, 1966, p. 114). This duality in ontological realms requires dual methods and the development of a model for social science different from the natural science model, which is concerned only with the external world. The social science model must begin instead with experienced reality guided by rational systems of explanation: "To reject natural science is not to invite merely a welter of subjective impressions, but requires a genuine intellectual discipline" (Hodges, 1944, p. viii).

Weber proposed that sociology's tasks are both the *verstehen* of social action and the construction of causal explanations. He essentially defined two kinds of interpretations: logical-mathematical and emotionally empathic-artistically appreciative. Whereas the "highest degree of rational understanding is attained in cases involving the meanings of logically or mathematically related propositions," another valid form of understanding is interpreting "facts of the situation as experience has accustomed us to interpret them" (Brodbeck, 1968, p. 22). The problem lies in trying to understand phenomena or concepts that are not experienced. Since Weber defined sociology as a science, he exposed himself to criticism about the unscientific nature of *verstehen* (Abel, 1967; Wax, 1967; Hempel, 1965). In other words, Weber claimed that personal experience can be used to understand behavior observed in others by parallel inferences, just as inferences are made on the basis of tests that measure the behavior of others. Explanations and actions are evidence of *verstehen.*

Znaniecki's (1934) methodology posits experience as the unit on which social theories are constructed. He utilized the concept of immediate evidence, which was derived from St. Augustine, Descartes, James, Bergson, and the phenomenological school. The unique feature of Znaniecki's phenomenological sociology was that the truths "are intuitively apprehended as self-evident" (1934, p. 219) without formal scientific proof. Znaniecki defined experience as the foundation of knowledge about reality, but he differentiated between natural and cultural reality. Nature is the appropriate area for impersonal study, while cultural knowledge is never unbiased because of the observer's embeddedness in a group's perspective. Znaniecki's two realities demanded two ways of knowing: the naturalistic and the humanistic. Humanistic knowledge is gained by action and experience. "The humanistic approach is the experience of the agent" (Znaniecki, 1934, p. 56). This forms the basis of all valid sociological materials:

> The sources from which sociology actually draws its materials can be classified into: (a) personal experience of the sociologist, original and vicarious; (b) observation by the sociologist, direct and indirect; (c) personal experience by other people; (d) observation by other people; (e) generalizations made by other people with or without scientific purposes. . . . [Despite the availability of other material,] the scientist's personal experience is the primary and most reliable source of information in sociology. The sociologist must claim for his own social experiences the same objective validity as students of nature claim for their methodical observations [Znaniecki, 1934, pp. 156-157].

Znaniecki's humanistic alternative to the natural science model was grounded in the personal experience of the sociologist. After experiencing, the sociologist reflects, analyzes, and reconstructs the experience as knowledge. The data of experience are reorganized as sociological knowledge. The sociologist must differentiate between what is actually experienced and what is not. Only that which is explicitly recalled as "part of his active experience can be treated as fact" (Znaniecki, 1934, p. 160). Retroactive distortion, however, blurs the differentiation of fact from explanation. Experiences are replicable if described in sufficient detail. Sociological knowledge derives from activity, particularly the activity of creating a society. "Whoever wants to know a thing has no way of doing so except by coming into contact with it, that is, by living (practicing) in its environment. . . . If you want to know the theory and methods of revolution, you must take part in revolution. All genuine knowledge originates in direct experience" (Mao Tse-tung, 1954, p. 282). Sociological knowledge can refer to its subject matter from the outside as a finished product or from the inside as an ongoing process.

Redfield (1948) and Nisbet (1963) reviewed sociological classics and our most influential concepts and concurred that they were not produced from the application of scientific method but from a holistic image grounded in experience: "If there is evidence that any one of these ideas (mass society, alienation, anomie, rationalization, community, disorganization) as first set forth in the writings of such men as de Tocqueville, Weber, Simmel, and Durkheim, is the result of problem-solving thought, proceeding rigorously and self-consciously from question to hypothesis to verified conclusion, I have been unable to discover it" (Nisbet, 1963, p. 69). Whereas these thinkers utilized experience for direct knowledge, scientific sociology generally repudiates this form of knowledge as "subjective." The indirect knowing of scientific procedures manipulates reflections of objects in preference to engaging the phenomenon on its own terms. Expertise is the degree of proficiency in interpreting those reflections rather than the degree of intimacy with the issue at hand.

There is a tension between the qualities Redford isolated

in his study of sociological excellence and the contemporary social definition of research. Phillips (1971, p. 149) writes, "It is possible for us to achieve understanding from consideration of many of our everyday, on-going social involvements"; Riemer (1977, p. 469) suggests "that sociologists rely upon their own unique biographies, life experiences, and situational familiarites in doing research" as if it were a novel approach.

Few sociologists have published studies of their "everyday, on-going social involvements" within an "experiential analysis" framework (for examples, see Riemer, 1977, and his references). Many investigators planned certain experiences in order to study particular problems using the participant observation method. An early instance is Nels Anderson (1923), who lived the hobo life for his participant observation study of homeless men. In these cases, even deep involvement is only temporary. Purely experiential research would not possess this "as if" quality. For example, Hughes (1970) examined the experience of teaching, Whyte (1969b) analyzed research administration, Rose (1968) studied his experience of political victimization, and short reflexive pieces appear periodically in the *American Sociologist*. Using an inductive approach, these experiential analyses traverse both micro and macro levels. The reflexive analysis uncovered both inner felt states and the "objective conditions under which the experiences are had" (Dewey, 1954, p. 34). The sociologist's task is to describe those states, conditions, and connections in relation to a social level of interpretation. This unconventional definition of the task of sociology is my personal resolution of a search for method.

Phenomenological examination of everyday reality via personal or shared experience complements other ways of knowing. But these other methods must face scrutiny as to the experiential basis on which their information is obtained. This scrutiny can only proceed under two conditions: (1) the description of method and research process are described in enough detail to enable the reader to examine the experience, and (2) the general meaning of methodological terms is not assumed to be experientially accurate.

Studies that strive to enter the experiential world of their subject matter encounter problems in converting such experience into data. In the scientific paradigm, data are conceptualized as fixed and unambiguous so they can be manipulated and a relation can be established that is "certain" until amended by further research (Gadamer, 1975). The knowledge obtained from engagement retains its human character if it relinquishes the claim of scientific certainty by substituting personal or human authority. Bion (1961) has demonstrated the clinical and Barrett (1962) the philosophical ambivalence people have to the development of experiential knowledge. Experiential learning repersonalizes the foundation of knowledge. Knowledge is organized from experience rather than from decontextualized verbal behavior or observed activity that is measured or counted. Experience knows no boundaries and includes a potentially painful awareness of fantasy, imagination, and bodily states. Experiential analysis includes rational and irrational phenomena rather than only rational scientific assumptions:

We do not know how to move in a chaotic reality, do not know how to handle it, and when we describe it we do so as if it were organized. Conditioned by a culture which worships reason like no other, and moulded in a sequence of educational institutions which inculcate the high values of logical thought, clarity and a sense of order, our mind habitually looks for order where chaos reigns, longing to discover a pattern and a structure, preferably a coherent one with an inner logic. Our passion for neatly smoothing out a disorderly social reality, again, fails to do justice to the complex variety of all social life [den Hollander, 1967, p. 20].

Experiential study does not predict its outcome except for its distinctively human quality. The descriptions and meaningful discussions it creates are founded on irreducible, immediately apprehensible elements that are not evaluated in terms of their measurability. Experiential research or learning is not confined to passive contemplation but derives from active engagement and involvement:

What we want for our future activist is a large experience with field studies that enable him to confront directly some of the phenomena of life in all their complexity and immediacy. . . . The fieldwork of a student would be bound to have implications for the welfare of individuals or groups he studied, and that would lead him to ask questions not only about the nature of what he observed, but about what he ought to do.

It would be precisely the student's concern about what to do in a practical way that would give him experience in synthesizing knowledge. Forced to consider the various possible consequences of any action he might take on a human or social problem, the student would begin to gain an understanding of some of the ways in which things cling together, and of the ways in which they can be brought together intellectually [Sanford and Krech, 1969, pp. 252-253].

The experiential foundation is elusive and requires continuous examination of the fit with language. To deal with lived experience is to remove anything that interferes with direct apprehension. When the intention overwhelms the effort, the researcher is left with nothing but method.

Experiential study is linked closely with the arts and humanities (Bruyn, 1966), which utilize preconceptual phenomena and diverse media of expression. Even if the medium of sociologists is confined to the printed page, language of explication can differ from the nonexperiential language of science. Experiential language affects the reader's cognitive and personal understanding. This language can "bring others to full consciousness of their experience" and "enable us to make sense of a multitude of inchoate feelings" (Dawe, 1973, p. 38). The purpose of such language is to extend the experience.

Language can destroy or explicate experience. Words do not correspond to experience but are of a different functional order "which carries forward the very experiencing they explicate" (Gendlin, 1965-1966, p. 2). Experiential explication, therefore, draws on *preverbal* experience and creates a sensation of *response* to that experience. "This felt response is a shift in feeling, in experiencing, in how we are in the world" (Gendlin, 1965-1966, p. 4). Such explications are not evaluated on the basis of certainty but on the basis of response and evocativeness, which are functional rather than static criteria.

The function of language for the sociological research process differs for the scientific and the experiential models. The former is concerned with objective precision, which flattens affect and conveys control of the environment. The latter is concerned with evocative precision, which includes affect and conveys immersion. The socialization process of sociology students is characterized by a reshaping of their language. Studies based on the explication of experience provide a model for a professional identity that is compatible with my personal values and identity. Their assumptions are not limited to the unidimensional values of science: "Sociology is the total response by the sociologist to the world around him, a response which is a complex unity of thought, feeling, fact, and value" (Dawe, 1973, p. 43).

CHAPTER 6

Analysis of the Team Fieldwork Experience

Presentation of the Final Case

In this chapter, the selected theme parallels that of the preceding case studies—the integration of person, problem, and method in the process of research. By allowing participant observation to reveal further ramifications in the field, this chapter represents my deliberate attempt to resolve previously encountered dilemmas and describes a fortuitous set of circumstances that made this possible. This project not only led to my personal sense of methodological discovery or refinement but also laid the foundation for further socialization steps. It clarified my desire to move' from mainstream sociology as I knew it in two different directions: phenomenology for the explication of lived reality and action research (which I labeled "clinical

264

sociology" at the time) for the application of data-based problem resolutions in particular field sites. As a result of this project, my professional identification became less tied to an academic discipline than to a method that could be affiliated with diverse disciplines. The label that I applied to my emerging method during this project was "experiential analysis." It resolved both my intellectual and identification concerns and became the capstone of my subjective experience of socialization as a sociologist.

Following the phases of initiation, alienation (in the survey research project), and reevaluation (in the participant observation study), I reached a stage of resolution and innovation. I also redefined the socialization process (for myself) as one that goes beyond any defined endpoint (such as the awarding of the Ph.D.) and becomes instead the continuous process of growth and change. Becoming a sociologist does not seem to terminate abruptly, followed by "being a sociologist." Rather, there is a continuous search for an integration of three factors: the evolving sense of self, the succession of problems to be addressed, and the progressive refinement of method.

The study described in this chapter took place in Israel in 1970-1971. It concerns the impact on family life of intermittent shelling by terrorists' rockets in a particular town. The first problem in presenting the case is to determine how much to inform the reader. I solved this by providing an exact description of the research process, beginning with the level of informedness of the researcher and ending with the final resolutions.

Pre-Field-Entry Learning Opportunities

At the end of the 1969-70 academic year, Tamar,* a social worker employed in public health, gave a guest lecture at the Hebrew University's School of Social Work in Jerusalem. This lecture described and analyzed Tamar's work as a consultant on community mental health problems encountered by

*The names in this case study are fictitious.

towns subjected to shelling. In response to the lecture, several students offered to volunteer their services in one of the towns during the upcoming summer vacation. To accommodate this offer, Tamar conceived of the idea of a small research project for the students. Her next step was to gain the sponsorship of the Histadrut (Workers' Council) in the town, since that body had expressed interest in projects that might strengthen the town's neighborhoods and locate indigenous leaders. Tamar succeeded in meshing the Histadrut's stated needs with the students' desires and produced an agreement for a study of the physical, social, and psychological coping strategies of one neighborhood within the town. Six second-year social work students were to be employed at a cost of 400 Israeli pounds per month for two and one half months to cover living expenses. The students were to coordinate their work with the neighborhood's public health nurses, the Histadrut committee for neighborhood affairs, and civil defense, under the direction of Tamar. All of these parties and their supervisors were notified of the agreement.

When the summer vacation began, four students withdrew. At the same time, Tamar and I were introduced by a mutual friend at a conference in Jerusalem. It was then that I first heard of the upcoming project. My academic advisor, who was in Jerusalem at the time, supported my filling one of the vacancies in the project. Tamar then revised the agreement with the Histadrut, offering three participants who would work ten days in the field to determine the family- or neighborhood-related problems in dealing with the shelling. The team consisted of myself (referred to subsequently as SR), Dvora, and Sara (the three fieldworkers) and Tamar, the project coordinator. The fieldworkers were to be provided with an apartment in town and with meals at the health center. Because a minor outbreak of cholera had occurred in Israel at the time, the notified health officials asked that the neighborhood responses to this problem be included in the study project. The project agreement called for a debriefing meeting with the Histadrut representative and the neighborhood committee, followed by a summary report. Before the project entered the field, therefore, it was imbedded in numerous social systems.

Preentry raised the perplexing question of who was the intended beneficiary of this project: the residents of the town, myself, the Histadrut, Tamar, or social science? The possibility that the project might be useful to many audiences was encouraging. Perhaps this complexity would prevent my forming alliances as I had done in the mental hospital study.

My response to the invitation to participate was mixed. The potentially valuable and undoubtedly challenging project involved physical danger, a test of my less than fluent Hebrew-language skills, and teamwork with strangers. Sensing my hesitancy, Tamar invited me to a daylong symposium on "the social effects of the security situation" at which she presented a paper (Gruschka, 1970) that revealed her approach and values in dealing with communities under fire. The 150 sociologists, psychologists, educators, social and community workers, and students attending the symposium hotly debated the claims of each presentation and conveyed a sense of urgency. The professionals expressed frustration in being unable to meet the towns' needs, in working at cross-purposes, and in not obtaining sufficient rewards for their work. Newspaper accounts of the symposium emphasized the following points:

1. The burden of coping with the dangers was unequally distributed between those who lived on the frontiers and those who lived in the rear, creating a situation of debtors and creditors.
2. The level of security-related tension in the general population fluctuated with events, but some stability in attitudes had been established. According to a study conducted in large cities and not in the areas directly affected by shellings, anxiety varied between men and women, among ethnic groups, between parents and single adults, and with level of education.
3. Tamar was identified as a sensitive and intuitive observer who produced relevant facts without the benefit of surveys and statistical evaluation. She termed the population's reactions to the shellings "psychological self-defense." She claimed the attacks produced emotionally charged fantasies, explanations, and attitudes. Some irrational responses she

identified were fatalism, passivity, wishing to absorb all danger so as to protect children, believing that children cannot
experience fear, interpreting the terrorist acts as punishment
for sins or for one's death wishes against others, forcing
oneself to stay awake, staying out of the shower or bathroom and other "dangerous" places, becoming irritated by
noise, developing psychosomatic problems, believing that
surviving the Nazi holocaust provided immunity to future
danger or created special vulnerability, defiance, and an urge
for revenge. Taboos arose around the families of victims.
There was perpetual questioning of why particular individuals were hit and not others.

4. People suffered the conflict of wanting to move away from
danger in order to protect their families while recognizing
the national priority of staying put. The reporter was likely
conveying a national sentiment when he wrote that "it is
gratifying to observe the vast number of those willing to
hold out deliberately" (Ardon, 1970).

5. In order of priority, the border towns' residents were concerned most with shelters, security rooms in their homes,
first aid, street lighting, and related items. Next were matters
indirectly linked to security: health services, population dis-
persal to outlying areas, and strengthening of existing buildings. Ordinary local affairs—political, economic, and educational—took third place.

6. Outside help from the rest of the country usually concerned
needs that were low on the list of priorities (such as entertainment or clothing); the local authorities and the security
institutions were left to deal with the significant problems.
When the local authorities were equal to the task, things
went well; when not, outside help was often a hindrance, at
best useless. "Some people take advantage of the security
problems for their own benefit. But generally, danger brings
out the best values in a community. . . . Danger creates opportunities. . . . It provides an unstructured social situation
that enables persons and groups to perceive the possibility of
introducing desired innovations" (Ardon, 1970).

The Hebrew-language newspapers stressed that voluntarism was not welcome in the form of ostentatious generosity but was appreciated when outsiders assisted the local population by joining them temporarily or permanently. The greatest boon to psychological self-defense was a sense of solidarity with others. This solidarity was sometimes marred by interethnic strain, which erupted during moments of stress. The symposium reinforced my sense of the project topic's national and human significance, revealed the disagreement that attended many issues, and convinced me that I would enjoy working with Tamar. My personal need to work only on meaningful projects with persons I respected appeared to be satisfied.

I used the brief period before entry into the field to continue studying Hebrew and to gather basic information. I was not concerned about prestudy expectations, because from the start I was exposed to multiple points of view, and time was too short for me to form any firm convictions that could influence my field observations.

Since my decision to participate in the project initiated my data collection phase, I informally began to question all my acquaintances about the town. I wanted to understand what this particular town meant to people in Israel. What was its social meaning? I had neither visited the town nor did I have any mental associations. Newspapers provided information about its shady political intrigues. From casual conversations, I developed an image of a poor, ugly town full of immigrants who had not learned Hebrew and maintained bizarre customs. I imagined the residents as mostly aged and infirm, and the town as exposed to continual attack. Army personnel informally commented that the town should not exist since it drained the army and the economy. A professional community worker believed that the town residents who packed their bags and left were acting rationally, and that social workers who encouraged them to remain should reexamine the situation and their own values. A young American tourist told me that the town was beautiful and that he was completely unaware that it was defined as a problem area.

Many acquaintances could only say it was a dangerous place. At the time, however, the newspapers stressed the relative quiet of the region, probably as a result of Israeli army intervention into "Fatahland," the southern Lebanese area from which the terrorists operated. In subsequent reading and interviewing I learned the following: Before the establishment of the state of Israel in 1948, the site of the present town was an Arab village, notorious as a breeding ground of Moslem violence—first against Christian Arabs and later against Jewish settlers. "It was from Khalsa that, in the spring of 1920, thousands of armed Arabs set out against the French forces and pro-French Christian villages in East Galilee to prevent the area from being included in the French mandated territory of Syria. The inflamed Khalsans and villagers of Upper Galilee soon turned against three isolated Jewish settlements in the region, Metulla, Kfar Giladi and Tel Hai, the latter only three kms. from Khalsa. Metulla was evacuated, but the members of the other two settlements decided to stand fast" (Ardon, 1973). The Arab village was almost completely destroyed during the Israeli War of Independence (1948), and its inhabitants fled. The town took its Hebrew name in commemoration of individuals who died defending one of the kibbutzim, and was founded the year following independence as a settlement camp for immigrants, who were arriving at such a rate that Israel's population doubled in the first three years.

After that the town was categorized as a "development town," designed by the Israeli government to receive large numbers of immigrants. The thirty development towns of Israel had two other purposes: the physical settlement of the land and the creation of regional centers throughout the country, thereby preventing the concentration of population in the few major cities by dispersing incoming immigrants. In an interview an official of another development town characterized the concept of "development town" as having no ideological meaning for the immigrants who were placed there. These immigrants brought little experience in urban affairs and had strained or minimal contact with native residents. Rather than becoming regional centers, development towns remained isolated and their institutions developed minimally. In the view of this official, the agencies responsible for their development were poorly coordinated, uncooperative, and duplicated each other's services. The population in development towns was unstable: The upwardly mobile left, and those who had nowhere to go remained. The cultural and educational level remained low, since teachers were not attracted to these towns. Poverty was common. Successful development towns, such as Eilat, Beersheva, Ashdod, and Arad, had special features that compensated for these problems, while the town under study had the double distinction of being a border town and a development town. Each kind of town had its special problems.

Some people with whom I shared my plans criticized "sociological research on suffering." They imagined my running up to a dying victim and asking him how he felt. This feedback raised questions for me about the usefulness of such research. Was this tiny project ridiculous in light of the circumstances of the townspeople? Would I be seen as superfluous or affronting? Later, I was to confirm a statement in the disaster literature: "Persons experienced in disaster field studies report that disaster victims usually want to talk, to tell their stories; and there is quantitative evidence to this effect. Interviewers are seldom refused" (Killian, 1956, p. 30), although researchers who initiated interviewing too early after attack, rescue, and cleanup operations were seen as callous and unsympathetic to the interviewee's sensitive state. Unable to predict the residents' reaction to our project, I could enter the field satisfied at least that we were focusing on their strengths and coping abilities.

Tamar's lecture to the students had closely followed dramatic terrorist incidents in the study area. She speculated that these events triggered a "survivor guilt" reaction among Israelis living in safer areas, which was expressed in their desire to learn about the affected area. Increasing terrorism during the summer months, including several airplane hijackings, daily fighting at the Suez Canal, and intermittent shelling of the border towns heightened both the feelings of danger and survivor guilt. We speculated that survivor guilt separated the students who withdrew from those who remained in the project. As was mentioned at the symposium, such reactions were most powerful immediately after an event. Understanding the multiple motivations of the four project members who remained became an ongoing concern for the project. Various motivations emerged and were clarified during the process. One of Tamar's motivations, for instance, was to set a precedent for establishing and supervising projects such as our own as part of her role as consultant. To this end she kept her own institutional base fully informed of the project's development. Similarly, I pondered the motivation of the two social work students. Tamar believed their motivation was emotional, whereas mine was intellectual and adventure seeking.

The most disturbing social phenomenon mentioned at the symposium was the interethnic strain that sometimes emerged at the time of shelling. A story was told of a group of Indian Jews who were denied entrance into a shelter occupied by families of another ethnic group. My interest in this incident led to a desire to study a neighborhood of Indian families. After obtaining Tamar's consent to study these families, I questioned my acquaintances and consulted the media and libraries for information about Indian Jews (see Strizower, 1959). Immediately I learned that the Indian Jews were surrounded by controversy. Only recently and after a long and bitter struggle had their claim to be Jews been found acceptable by Israel's rabbinical courts. Chief arguments against the claim were the Indians' practice of polygamy and the discrepancy between their method of divorce and Jewish ritual law, which bred disputes about bigamy and illegitimacy. The Indian Jews' practice of polygamy was rooted in Biblical tradition, whereas its prohibition represented, in their view, an effect of assimilation. Some informants attributed the difficulty of the Indian Jews' integration into Israeli society to their peculiar food habits. Others mentioned that Indian Jews maintained low social status among Israeli ethnic groups. The *Encyclopedia Judaica* (1971) and other material published after my study (Mandelbaum, 1975) contained an account of the socioreligious crisis of the Indian Jews (known as Bene Israel) that confirmed the information I had at my disposal.

The project was delayed by bureaucratic problems that I encountered in obtaining a work permit while holding a tourist visa. During this delay Tamar and I met twice. In terms of the subsequent group process, it proved significant that neither of us had preentry meetings with the other two team members. During our meetings Tamar shared her perceptions of the town's problems and major personalities. Although I sometimes felt steered in particular directions, I was no longer a research assistant who would merely carry out the interests of a project director. Rather, I had learned to negotiate my interests with the project's demands. In addition, preparatory information gathering in this project contrasted favorably with the preparatory vacuum of the survey project and the unexamined assumptions and accepted definitions of my previous fieldwork. If the researcher can differentiate information from expectations, then a resolution can be found for the dilemma of preparedness that I had encountered in the previous study.

These meetings also helped me differentiate the perspectives of the insider with vested interests (Tamar) from those of the temporary researcher. That differentiation sharpened my identity as a researcher even prior to entry. As the project unfolded, I discerned new advantages in the collaboration of an actively participating insider and a temporary researcher from the outside. In the survey study of the Washington, D.C., teachers, our research team was composed entirely of outsiders, contributing to the probable meaninglessness and low utilization of the report. My participant observation study in the mental hospital developed no explicit collaboration and left the researcher torn between the roles of insider and outsider.

I arranged one prefield meeting with Tamar to question her as an informant about the town. She had spent several years working in the town in various social service roles but had never lived there. A relatively small percentage of the population knew her, and many could not specify exactly what she did. She saw herself as a bridge between various interest groups and a commentator on social processes. She believed that this bridging function depended on her marginality and neutrality. In response to my questions about the Indian families there,

Tamar mentioned that the group living in the town did not stand up as well to the shelling as did Indian Jews in a nearby "moshav," or partial collective. Tamar's criteria for "standing up well" were that people continue with their everyday life, such as jobs and schools, and that their security arrangements in terms of shelter be satisfactory. She believed, therefore, that to "stand up well" was to acquire physical safeguards and then to live as if there was no danger. In this sense, "standing up" to the situation meant neither fight nor flight, but rather staying put and making do. Staying put represented an act of defiance against aggressive acts. This issue of holding on versus abandonment was highly charged historically, not only for border settlement residents but for many Israelis:

> The terrorists would perhaps have thought twice about attacking civilians had they been able to predict the consequences. "In adversity, defiance," Churchill said of the people of Britain under the German blitz. The border population in towns . . . , in kibbutzim and moshavim, stood up to recurrent showers of mortar, Katyusha and heavier artillery shells and were hardened into the same spirit of defiance. They gritted their teeth, buried the dead, repaired the damage, and held on. The few who left . . . during the period when the terrorists controlled Fatahland in South Lebanon have since regretted it and would go back, were it not for the housing shortage" (Ardon, 1973, pp. 8-9).

Supreme victory over both danger and the pressure to leave was manifested in subduing one's fear and leading an everyday normal life. To be normal was a goal, not a given.

I asked Tamar, as a project director, to advise me about presenting myself to the families I would be observing. We would not be using formal consent procedures, and she suggested I introduce myself as a sociology student who was part of a project concerned with people's ways of managing during shellings and who was also affiliated with the Health Center. She emphasized the need to specify my sponsors because suspiciousness pervaded the town. "People continuously ask themselves—what makes it worthwhile for someone else to come here? They assume some selfish or underhanded motive. It is important, therefore, to explain one's motivation in positive terms." In addition, she believed my sponsorship had to be visible to the friends, neighbors, and relatives of the study families to quell any fears that I might represent a welfare or tax authority. The Department of Health would be an asset in establishing trust, since these families trusted the public health nurses.

When I asked Tamar how to avoid offending the families, she suggested dressing simply and accepting food they would offer in their role as host. To compensate for their cooperation, she suggested I offer to babysit. Throughout our discussion, Tamar emphasized her unfamiliarity with the Indian Jews. I also asked Tamar to evaluate the security of our living arrangements. As she saw them, they were "slummy but adequate." Although the building had no shelter or reinforced rooms, there was a reinforced wall near the staircase to protect us during a shelling. She would continue to sleep in the Health Center, although it was completely unsafe. She assessed paradoxically the danger I was about to face: The chances of being hit by a rocket were very small, but the chances of being killed if hit were very great.

Since Tamar had been to the town recently, I asked her to assess the mood regarding the current shellings. She reported more concern about the possible spread of cholera. She denied being frightened herself. Asked about the experience of a shelling attack, she responded, "It was not frightening when the shells flew over your head and exploded. What was frightening was when something was happening to someone you know." This reaction was also expressed by a kibbutz member whom Tamar and I visited while the project was in the field. Located on the mountain hovering above the town, sitting directly on the Lebanese border, this kibbutz had been the object of the most recent attacks in the area. The kibbutz member to whom I spoke, a mother of three young children, showed me where the last shells had fallen a few meters from her bedroom window. I could see the effects of the explosions on the ripped tree branches, the shattered trunks, and the shrapnel gashes in the walls of the house. When I asked her if she had been frightened, she replied, "Why should I be frightened if I know my children are safe in their underground shelters?" This response seemed untenable, a fearless boast. Had she no concern for her own safety? Was this response her defense before a stranger, or was it real?

After this visit I weighed whether one fears for oneself or for others:

SR: "When I am afraid as I was yesterday and today— really I'm afraid all the time—I am fearful for my own life. I thought this is natural, how everyone feels. But I asked the woman I was visiting today, 'What actually are you afraid of?' She answered, 'When I hear a katyusha, I think, who got hurt, maybe it is my neighbor.' But I don't think that way, I think, maybe it will hurt me.

Tamar: "It is as if she has invested part of herself in another person.

SR: "It doesn't even have to be her family, just 'who was it, who could it have been?' "
[Transcript of field meeting.]

I felt guilt for my concern with my own welfare. But could I be expected to care for others if I knew so few townspeople? Did anyone else feel guilt for concern with themselves? Did anyone else doubt other people's alleged lack of fear? Did unexpressed guilt and doubt produce strained interpersonal relations and therefore a strained community? I began to use my own feelings as guides to issues concerning the town.

In the course of the project I discovered some discrepancies with the information provided by Tamar as informant. This discovery reduced my sense of dependency on Tamar and encouraged my autonomy. (I mention these discrepancies to illustrate the methodological insights I derived from them.) When the project narrowed its focus from an examination of a neighborhood to the study of a few families, all the fieldworkers needed to create a context for the families. I wanted to take a "census" of the neighborhood and to do a "geneaology" of the families, although I did not apply these labels to my spontaneous activities of asking an Indian mother to list all her brothers and sisters or asking an Indian child to tell me something about the occupants of the houses standing between hers and her grandfather's. As children gathered to play this "game," I learned that the neighborhood Tamar believed to be homogeneously Indian was actually inhabited by Druze families (non-Moslem Arabs, some of whom were Israeli citizens) and Jewish families of Iraqi, Moroccan, and other non-Indian origins. One house was occupied solely by a non-Indian, apparently psychotic hermit. Another house was occupied by a native Israeli (sabra) from another city, who was studying the local factory prior to establishing a similar one elsewhere.

The cause of the socially perceived homogeneity of a heterogeneous neighborhood provoked many debates during our fieldwork phase, which a complete community study would have resolved. Our study was not, however, a community study but an exploration of a problem. I was "an active sampler of theoretically relevant data, not an ethnographer trying to get the fullest data on a group" (Glaser and Strauss, 1967, p. 58). Since each piece of information could have led us in new directions, it required self-restraint to stay focused while watching the methodological and substantive insights emerge. This simple discrepancy about the neighborhood homogeneity also reinforced the necessity of evaluating preentry information in the light of experiences in the field.

A second significant discrepancy concerned the expected suspiciousness of the families. The three families with whom I stayed appeared completely unsuspicious of me or my purposes. They allowed me into their homes, spoke freely, and let me tape-record their conversation and spend time alone with their children. They even corrected my improprieties rather than withdraw. They appeared to be relatively open, trusting people. In no household was an ulterior motive sought for my presence or was I asked to reiterate my rationale, with the exception of one blind man who thought I was a campaign worker for a political party and would not change his mind despite my protests. Each family seemed less concerned with who we, the researchers, really were than with placing us in a framework meaningful to them. Another team member reported that one mother was convinced her boyfriend had sent the researcher to communicate with her, while her son believed the researcher was a representative from a distant school that he had been anxiously awaiting to enter.

Had I not been told before entering the field that the townspeople were suspicious, I would not have been so cautious in the field nor so impressed with the families' openness. Geer (1964, p. 328) remarked that this unfounded concern is common: "Developing empathy with informants as a group often presents more of a problem to field workers planning a study, at least in anticipation, than the adoption of an interaction-facilitating role."

Although some anticipated problems such as developing rapport, did not materialize, some unanticipated problems did.

Tamar's suggestion that I offer to babysit as a way of reciprocating the families' assistance seemed inappropriate to me in the field. Each family had already resolved this need by using a grandmother next door, an invalid parent, or older children, or even by leaving the youngsters unattended. My offer to babysit might have been taken as a criticism and would have made sense only if the parents had leisure time and spent it outside their homes. However, the families had limited entertainment opportunities in the town, and they preferred to receive visitors if they were not working a night shift at the local factories or staying home because of the shelling. One mother of nine complained to another team member that the babysitter who enabled her to accompany her husband to the movies once a week was afraid to babysit because of the shelling. Since our need to reciprocate with the families was not resolved by babysitting, it became a nagging problem. Superficially, we wanted to repay their kindness; on a deeper level we wanted to give something of ourselves that would be meaningful to us all. One such positive example was Cora DuBois' training local students as researchers and clerical assistants (Golde, 1970, p. 226).

The discovery of these discrepancies—inaccurate descriptions, exaggeration of anticipated problems, and preparing inappropriate reciprocity—demonstrated that outsiders could offer new perspectives, even on unquestioned assumptions of insiders. Since this format of contrasting insiders' and outsiders' information or interpretations was satisfying to us in the field, we used it to structure our final debriefing reports. We saw that everyone's knowledge was rooted in a perspective and was potentially valid if it could be explicated. The form of consultation we developed at the end of the project followed smoothly from the process of participant observation, which provides the researcher with a grounded perspective. Feedback consultation became its applied form.

Finally, the project coordinator and I expended much time and energy before entering the field arranging for life and health insurance coverage during my stay in the town. These tedious precautions made the potential danger more alarming. The frustration of all the delays intensified my desire to be able to undertake the project. By contrast, the arrangements for the survey project were made before I joined, and the administrative details of the participant observation study were simple once I obtained a job and the approval to observe. Only in the shelling study did I appreciate the bureaucratic entanglements that can affect a research project. Delays, changes, and unexpected external problems are part of the social environment that envelopes and sometimes frustrates the research process (see Wax, 1971, for a harrowing example). Good administrative skills are essential for researchers who must manage these details. Some of these skills are identical with those of personnel management in bureaucratic work settings and pose particular problems if the tasks are distasteful. A project director is not only (or primarily) a researcher but also an administrator of research procedures and a supervisor of research personnel.

Approaching the Field

Following the guideline of the "pertinence of everything" (Wolff, 1971, p. 239) that had become personally meaningful in the previous projects, I began my observations on the bus journey from Jerusalem to the town.

I packed my simplest clothes and other necessities, plus paper for notes and books which I thought might be helpful, and went to the Jerusalem bus station, nervous but proud. [My husband] was very supportive. As soon as the bus departed, I could almost feel the role transitions from wife to observer. I began to scrutinize everything, taking notes, both mental and written, even trying to generate hypotheses. I saw many interesting things on the bus—the underlying suspiciousness and fear when a man in Arab dress got off the bus in the middle of the airport, creating a roar of conversation behind him; the general talkativeness of the passengers. . . . I had made the transition from Jerusalem, Anglo-Saxon middle-class society to another world of peoples gathered from Africa, Asia, and the Middle East. The transition helped to heighten my sensitivity and concentration. I had entered a world which seemed truly exotic, and I was only on the bus getting there!

My field notes then reveal that I was ready to identify with these remote individuals:

In front of me sat an aging couple, Americans by dress, with cameras and coats (despite the 100° temperature), and reading an English-language newspaper in a way that seemed to me to deliberately block interaction with their intrusive co-passengers. At one of the bus's periodic stops, I talked to this couple. The woman complained bitterly about the primitive conditions, the bumpy ride, the heat, and the uncomfortable seats. It was her first trip to Israel. She admired the courage of the Israeli people but she had a hard time tolerating being here. She was almost nauseated watching a young, sloppy-looking man eating pumpkin seeds and spitting the shells on the ground. While she was criticizing, I noticed myself becoming defensive. Instead of agreeing with her, I identified with the people about whom she complained. I was one of them, rather than one of her kind. I tried to explain things to her. . . . When she asked where I was going, I found myself talking about the town in the same stereotyped terms as I had heard—dangerous, poor, undesirable. I chided myself for repeating these slogans without knowing if they were truly descriptive.

To prevent myself from entering the field with expectations that might then be unwittingly fulfilled, I tried to be aware of them, to consider multiple views, and to use my lingering preentry notions for an initial orientation that could be quickly discarded if disconfirmed.

When we changed buses for the last hitch up to the northernmost extremities of the country, I sat in a group of benches at the bus stop among passengers waiting for the bus to the town. I wondered what these probable residents of the town were doing in this city (Tiberias). The women looked strong as they sat among their bundles and children. Some were wearing what I would call "party dresses," light blue satin covered with lace with V necks and very tight fitting. I wondered if they had come to "the big town" for some important purposes and had dressed for the occasion. Or perhaps they merely liked gaudy clothes. I was beginning to stand out in my very plain attire. People were staring at me, perhaps as curious about me as I was about them. The American tourists continued complaining to me in loud, whining English. Most of the other waiting travelers seemed to know each other. I would have to get used to the idea that in field work, the people will study you, just as you are studying them. Luckily, I got the last seat on the bus, the middle one on the back bench, after climbing over boxes, suitcases, live chickens, etc. I squeezed between two teenage girls and two teenage boys. The girls were giggling. They had bought candies and pumpkin seeds which they jammed into a small piece of newspaper which was progressively disintegrating. The candy continuously tumbled into their laps. After they offered me some sweets, I felt entitled to get involved and tried to help them arrange their packages better. Neither seemed intelligent; both were exceedingly friendly. The girl sitting next to me started talking about having gone to Tiberias to see a doctor because of pains in her lungs. Her uproarious laughter with her girlfriend didn't seem to fit this explanation, and made me wonder if maybe she saw the doctor because she was pregnant. (At the same time I disliked myself for not believing her). In order to make the trip, she had taken a day off from school—8th grade.

This phenomenon—the interruption of primary responsibilities for the sake of good health practice—kept recurring. Enough examples arose in my interviews with the families I studied that I could suggest a pattern of attitudes and behavior related to health care among this population. Although the expense of medical care for most Israelis is minimal, medical care users take other costs into consideration, particularly the time taken from other functions. In one family I studied, the cost of the mother's lost wages of an hour or more was seen as so high that she waited until several of her eight children were ill before taking any of them to the doctor, a system rational to her but irrational to the medical personnel. If professionals want to modify health services utilization, they should consider these intervening factors. When our team presented this phenomenon to the public health nurses in our feedback consultation, they devised creative, nondefensive ways of dealing with the matter.

This chance encounter with the teenagers on the bus lay the foundation for a method of organizing data by recording incidents or statements, watching for recurrences, and trying to formulate patterns. The next step was to challenge the pattern by testing if it covered the next related incident and if members of the setting considered it meaningful. This pattern building became a technique for making sense of my disconnected observations. Since I was working in a team, I had the opportunity to describe my way of organizing data to my teammates faced with the same task, to find a label, and to receive reinforcement.

Another significant comment emerged when I asked one of the girls what she thought of the town I was going to study:

It was a good town, she liked it. Why? Because there is a movie house there! This answer helped me clarify several points. First of all, the town obviously must mean different things to different age groups. Some groups might feel their needs are adequately met, while others do not. Second, life must be quite dull, even according to my undemanding standards, if a town's entire reputation can rest on its possession of one movie house. How much more entertainment-poor must a town like hers be? I have to understand the town in terms of relative assets and relative deprivation. To people of this area (Upper Galilee), the town is perceived as a "center" (even though the people of the town talk of themselves as living in the outlying area as opposed to the "center" of the country, that is, the Tel Aviv area). But most important, her quick response indicated that I could ex-

pect some people not to link the town with its intermittent shelling, but with other long-lasting factors such as the need for entertainment.

Here again was an indicator of things to come. Although I could not generalize from the girl's remark, I became suspicious about the significance of shelling in the experience of the families we would study. In contrast with the experts' remarks at the symposium and my great concern, the townspeople with whom I later spoke ranked shelling low on their list of concerns.

My freedom to consider alternative problems represented a personal maturation beyond the guilt-laced loyalty to my original aims of the hospital study. Instead of being stuck on a level of project definition, I would watch the process of aims unfold as fieldwork responded to the increasingly clear delineation of the population's real concerns. Our topic shifted from "How do the people cope with shelling?" to "What concerns the people most and how do they cope with it?" This redefinition underscored the value of gathering data about everything. Whereas formerly I might have defined participant observation in terms of gathering data about predetermined categories such as "friendship" or "shelling," I now allowed myself to study the setting as it presented itself to me.

The boys on the bus rode with me all the way to the town and directed me to the Health Center, where I was to meet the project team. As I stepped off the bus, I was struck by the intense heat and the beauty of the town, in contrast with my drab expectations. Some fieldworkers consider descriptions of scenery and weather a desperate last resort when other data fail. To me, this attitude reflects little appreciation for the significance of the physical environment on the experience of the setting members. The climate, terrain, and appearance of an area are a subtle, pervasive source of data. To convey the "feel" of living in the town's climate and physical setting, I spent a single day during the same time of year as the study on a later visit recording weather data.

Early morning starts with a cloud bank overhead, trapping the foggy mist that has collected during the night. . . . The

*mist is joined by the smoke of fires lit by street-cleaners, who
have gathered small piles of loose papers scattered on the
ground. As the sun rises, the clouds are also burned away, beginning at the top of the cliffs and slowly making a clearing over
the valley. There is no wind but the air is delicate. The fragile
morning gives the illusion that the day will be cloudy and gray.
But as usual, the sun quickly vanquishes the cloudy vapors, and
with no obstacle remaining, it bears down hard on the valley.
This narrow strip, wedged between the Lebanese mountains and
the Golan Heights, is a triangular box in which the heat is
trapped. The sun presses on, the heat accumulates. . . . Indoors
the rooms are heat traps within the larger heat trap of the valley.*

*All my clothing seems excessive. Eventually, I am in my
underwear, barefoot, hair gathered off my neck, sitting at the
open window, which, because of the hour does not permit the
sun's rays to enter although it cannot block the heat. By the
time lunch is over I give in completely to the enervating climate
and fall asleep. . . . I awaken deeply tired. Both the weather and
I are spent. But I know that in this deepest, stillest of heats,
something new is beginning . . . the winds.*

*The Lebanese mountains have caught the sun. A pale
shadow covers the land beneath the mountains, and the sun is
only brilliant on that part of the valley which the rays can
reach. The sky becomes bluer as the disappearing sun removes
the glare. The previously white clouds are beige, as is the ground
below. Trapped beneath the blue and the beige is a very distinctive band of pink. The valley of farms is quiet, the same restful
solidity of farms anywhere. The moon is already out, hanging in
a daylike sky. The wind whips the branches around, and papers
in my room fly in all directions. . . .*

*What was a heat trap during the day has become a wind
tunnel in the evening. The fishponds of the nearby kibbutzim
are like plastic sheets spread out to dry. The pink band becomes
yellow. In this town the weather is something to talk about; it is
constantly changing, and with the open spaces, there is always a
lot of weather to see.*

*The wind is whistling, shrieking like a natural siren. The
heavy gusts rumble through the valley. Our building acknowledges its inferiority by heaving slightly with each major
blow. . . . The moon slowly gains brilliance while the sad cry of
the wind increases my fear of the inevitable NIGHT. All signs*

*point to a storm, but since there are no natural storms at this
time of year, I wonder if the signs indicate a different kind of
upheaval. All is in readiness—for what? The lethargy of the
morning has been swirled into quick scurrying. Am I projecting
my fear onto nature or is this a foreboding atmosphere?*

*... The sounds of the town are much easier to hear—
voices, radios, singing, conversations. Is it because everyone's
windows are open or because the work noises have disappeared?
All the lights are on. At night I can see much more clearly
where people live than during the day. . . . Now there are two
dominant colors: the black mountains reach halfway up the
sky. Apartments ooze a golden honey yellow light and stars pop
out over the valley.*

*The earth rotates away from the sun, rolling, rattling into
its future. What will it bring? A maiming katyusha? I'm on the
alert, sniffing the weather for signs. What is everyone else
doing? The mountains are disappearing, blending into a single,
primeval blackness of the sky void. The town is also a black
emptiness through my window save for the golden apartment
lights, white street lamps, and streaking headlights. Voices bark
out of the emptiness. The wind is cooling, as light as the day
was sultry.*

*Indoors the bugs emerge from their daytime hideaways
and begin their journeys criss-crossing the walls. Outdoors in the
wind, my skirt blows casually over my head, my hair flies apart.
The cool air is like a shower of wind and I am as exhilarated by
its sensuousness as I am terrified of its howl.*

*The last North African yodeling has ceased. What remains
are merely a few distant infant cries. The fearful alertness suc-
cumbs to the combined power of the day of heat and the day of
wind as I sink into another foreign sleep in preparation for
tomorrow's deceptive mists.*

When asked why they stayed, the family members invariably mentioned the scenery, the climate, and the quality of the
water. Their physical surroundings figured greatly in their experience. Part of my work during the project was to cope with
the heat; part of my pleasure, to enjoy the environment. My
subjugation to the environment increased my sense of community and of sharing the town's fate, if only for a short time.

The town's geographical location is a major determinant

of its quality of life. The town, wedged under cliffs beyond which Lebanon lies, is more densely populated at the bottom of the steep slope and spills into the valley. A few kilometers east begin the slopes of the Golan Heights. The two elevated areas merge north of the town, just south of Fatahland, the area from which the terrorist rockets were launched.

My first sight of the town was its sheer cliffs and large, concrete, oval movie theater. With the aid of my fellow passengers, I located Tamar, Dvora, and Sara, who were waiting with their baggage after having met with a town official. Tamar, a woman approaching fifty, with the solid look of an Israeli veteran, greeted all who passed her in the busy center with warmth and a professional air. The two students, women in their early twenties, were both native Israelis who had completed their army service and were preparing for their careers as social workers.

Our first task was to set up living quarters in our rented apartment. The owner, Mr. R., an aging, tall, erect, strong-looking man with white hair, greeted us enthusiastically and showed us the little apartment, which compared favorably with the slum I had anticipated. In his attempt to make us feel at home, he described exaggeratedly how wonderful the apartment was. The lack of hot water would be fixed "tomorrow." He recommended that we either close or secure the windows because of the wind. To alleviate our unexpressed concern, he explained that this particular neighborhood had never been hit. Our more relevant concern, he warned, should be the people in the neighborhood "who aren't the greatest." If we wanted to watch television, we should go to his place because he had "approximately five." Perplexed, we asked him to explain this abundance and learned that he had been referring to his children's sets, to which he had access. Almost everything Mr. R. said warned me to expect different habits, values, and attitudes from those I had typically encountered.

Team Fieldwork

Pressure To Conform and Tolerance of Individual Differences. Shortly thereafter both Mr. R. and Tamar left, and I was alone in the apartment with the two social work students.

How do I feel this minute? Frightened to the core to be where a rocket can fall on me any moment. Completely disoriented. Where is the danger coming from? Inadequate, because of my language deficiency. It is nearly impossible to understand Mr. R.'s Hebrew. He has some sort of speech defect, speaks very fast, has a strong accent, and aggravates my comprehension difficulties. Will everyone here speak this way? Very eager to learn, to observe, to remember every detail.

Who are these two girls that I am here with?

The apartment layout: one large room and, running alongside it, a narrow hall, on the other side of which is a kitchen, a bathroom, and a small bedroom. Off the large room is a tiny porch. Everything is very sparsely furnished, but livable. There are two beds in the small room, but I thought it would make more sense to have two beds in the large room. The two girls said they'd just leave it the way it was and share the small room.

We started unpacking. There was a standing closet with three hangers in it, so each of us used one on which to hang all our clothes. We shared the two shelves. Then the two girls started cleaning and spraying for bugs. They were disgusted by the lack of cleanliness. I didn't think it was so dirty. I didn't know what to do with myself while they were cleaning so vigorously. I didn't want to do something that I felt was unnecessary or to begin changing my ways right away. So after a few minutes, I sat down and began writing about the two problems that concerned me most—fear about the shelling and concern about how I would introduce myself to the "suspicious" families. A little while later my fear manifested itself in slips I made while trying to read a book—I read "protection" for "production," and was generally unable to concentrate. The act of writing helped allay my fears because it allowed me to express myself. Perhaps like Bettelheim, observing and analyzing enabled me to cope with what was an extreme situation.

I am very excited about this opportunity to do fieldwork in an interesting site. I want to make the most of it, to take good notes, to formulate worthwhile ideas. But I am beginning to feel the impact of not doing this project alone. I can feel a certain pressure as I write and they clean. Should I stop writing? What is more important to do—accomplish my purposes or accommodate the group?

Just before Tamar returned to pick us up for a wedding

to which she had invited us as her guests, the three of us were
getting dressed. I felt awkward having to admire clothes of
theirs I didn't like. The girls seem very sweet and friendly but I
feel different from them.

     This excerpt reveals my initial difficulties in becoming a
team member. The alienation and tension I experienced regarding cleaning was my first clue that the team itself would become
a significant factor in our study. This minor incident also
sparked my discovery of experiential analysis. The group's interpersonal relations continued as a private concern in my field
notes and gradually emerged as an issue in the team's deliberations. The project eventually focused on two topics: problems
and coping behaviors of various groups in the town and the
problems and coping behavior of team members in the group
project.

     To elucidate the group dynamics of team fieldwork, I
have culled certain themes from my field notes and meeting
transcripts. Their discussion necessitates breaking the chronological presentation of the project.

     My feeling that the team was threatening my autonomy
was a forerunner of subsequent themes. The conflict between
the unrestricted thinking required for creativity—the independence of the research mentality—and the interdependence of
group structure is similar to the "conflict between research
functions and bureaucratic functions" discussed by Vidich and
Bensman (1971). The conflict was first expressed in simple
housekeeping matters, which posed the question: Was I going to
live the way I was comfortable or the way the group collectively
decided? Thereafter, the chronic problem arose of whether to
type my field notes at the end of the day if my teammates
wanted to sleep after finishing their briefer notes. To me the
production of field notes was the purpose of fieldwork, yet
establishing good team relations was also important. I was willing to be a stranger in the town but not in my own home.
Nevertheless, should I risk tension with the fieldworkers? With
no prior knowledge of the differences between individual and
team research, I lacked the foresight to avoid these conflicts and
the skills to master them.

Vidich and Bensman's (1971) discussion of the conflict between research and bureaucratic functions includes the pressure to homogenize the project members' disparate views. Specialized views might reflect the specialized functions of different members of a research organization, but they can simply reflect different individuals studying different people. We pressured each other to reduce our perceptual discrepancies to a shared view of the substantive issues. This group pressure on perception paralleled the group pressure to create a common life-style or use of leisure time and a common housekeeping style. We retained our individual differences at the cost of subtle group disapproval.

When ideas were discussed, team members would support or disagree until one point of view prevailed. If the pressure to conform was overbearing, the minority view might silently withdraw. Consensus was achieved by convincing or overwhelming others. The need to maintain viable working relations led to the sacrifice of autonomous thought. Norms developed as to how much argument and compliance was acceptable.

The cognitive process of working out an idea was converted into an interpersonal process in which each team member represented a point of view. As soon as I identified the conflict between my independence as an individual researcher and my subjugation to the team's decisions, I noticed the phenomenon everywhere. For example, the group decided to meet with a town official even though one of us could not attend. Another example was that, on behalf of the group, the coordinator accepted an invitation to a wedding at a nearby kibbutz, leading me to understand that she believed the project should combine work with pleasure. I had expected to operate under the "all work, no play" principle, since the project was brief and each minute in the field seemed valuable. Did leisure activities indicate a lack of commitment to the project? (The reverse became true, since joint leisure activities contributed to effective work relations.) Nevertheless, a major prerequisite of this project was to become a team member, accept the project coordinator's guidance, and struggle with my restless independence. The unique demands of teamwork should be considered before entering the field, and the particular expectations of team members should be negotiated in advance. If not, then some team members will use the research project to resolve intrapsychic and interpersonal issues to the possible detriment of the project or other team members.

In addition to the forced consensus of project organization, a second characteristic of group projects is the suppression or encouragement of individual data-gathering styles. In our case, tolerance for differing data-gathering approaches contrasted with the pressure to reach consensus on data analysis or generalizations derived from the data. We encouraged autonomy in the field but preferred unanimity in our debriefing sessions. The project coordinator either established or reinforced these group dynamics.

Vidich and Bensman (1971) characterize bureaucratic and group fieldwork by the rigid commitment to a " 'fixed' statement of the project problem" (p. 318). In the mental hospital study, I learned the necessity of flexibility. My suspicion that coping with shelling was not the population's primary concern led me to reevaluate the project's focus and to consider a larger framework of coping with problems. Since research projects always gather more information than is contained in the initial project definition or funding proposal, there are opportunities to pursue additional avenues. Vidich and Bensman call these peripheral issues the informal or personal project. Such an informal study became the subsequent independent study on which their *Small Town in Mass Society* (1960) was based.

Each of us had a private agenda to work out in the field. After we had clarified our true interests and had tested the expectations of the project coordinator, we agreed that there would be no standardized formats for interviewing and we would each be free to establish a relationship with the families. The debriefing meetings were thus used to review our individual work, share feedback, and plan our next day's work. A few meetings were needed in order to clarify the function of the meetings, the role of the coordinator as limit setter and meeting facilitator, and the team members' roles as data gatherers and analysts.

Our autonomy as data gatherers was highlighted by the

fact that the other two team members never met the families that a team member observed. In addition, each fieldworker developed a protectiveness about "her" families, which the other team members left unchallenged. Although we questioned each other's interpretations, to criticize the quality of a team member's relationships with "her" families was taboo. This autonomy and protectiveness made our group feel less like a team and more like a set of individuals pursuing parallel tasks.

Our team developed a routine for its work. Each morning the three fieldworkers went to the home of a study family, observed, interviewed and interacted, took notes in the field or shortly thereafter individually, and later returned to the apartment. We usually chatted over a light supper and were then joined by the coordinator with whom we reviewed our day, our findings, and our questions. These debriefing sessions of sharing and review proceeded informally, allowing the group's informal social structure to shape our discussions. Each of us raised topics as needed, and together we sought common themes in the collected material. But we did not direct ourselves to search for these themes in our next day's work. Since each of us expected to receive reinforcement or support, each of us was expected to offer it. This led to difficulty distinguishing support of a person from support of her ideas. Inadequate reinforcement preceded withdrawal, resentment, and pairing behavior. The opportunity for obtaining reinforcement in a group comes at the cost of providing support to the other team members. Since the ideal mutuality is elusive, the real balance can become a source of stress. Team membership requires a contribution to team maintenance and is an additional task in the research process.

The underlying conflict between conformism and autonomy that our team experienced has been illustrated in several descriptions of the team's activities in the field: housekeeping, balancing leisure and work, data gathering, data interpreting, and reinforcing team member ideas. A final illustration is the definition of a preferred research modality. (For an account of the obstacles and discomfort caused by project codirectors with disparate models of research, see Riesman and Watson, 1964).

Each issue tested the team's ability to withstand internal differences of perspective, as shown by this excerpt from a transcript of a team discussion:

Tamar: *I want to ask Sara if it doesn't seem profitable to conduct our discussion in terms of giving people the opportunity to enhance what they are already doing. For instance, first we talked about the clubhouse, then medical services in terms of how to improve the people's ability to use their services. You don't see this as correct?*

Sara: *I see this as a second stage.*

Tamar: *Why?*

Sara: *First we have to get the facts, and then we can make suggestions.*

Tamar: *I think the opposite and I'll tell you why. We did not come here to do research in the scientific manner, so we do not have to defend the conclusions as if we had arrived at them scientifically. What we are really talking about is perspectives; looking at the same things that other people look at. We are not talking about more than that. And I think that not only is it permissible that we do what we are doing, but I think it is desirable to do it this way. We are not going to consult with the "committee on neighborhoods" or with the nurses in the form of a scientific symposium in which it is first necessary to say why we approached the problem the way we did, what our assumptions are, how we collected the data, etc. All that is irrelevant, in my opinion.*

Sara: *(still protesting) It will be relevant for the report, though.*

Tamar: *I don't even know.*

SR: *We don't have to decide that now.*

Tamar: *Right. Now we are preparing for our consultation with the committee and the nurses.*

SR: *(feeling very uncomfortable about Sara being railroaded, and changing the subject) Let's talk about some more health problems we discovered.*

Tamar: *OK, but Sara still has reservations about this approach.*

SR: *(trying to resolve the difference by putting the solu-tion differently) We don't have to be 100 percent sure, but we have to be able to generate ideas. Maybe a large portion of what we have needs further clarifi-cation, but it is giving us the opportunity to think.*

Tamar: *Exactly.*

SR: *To see what are the assumptions on which activities are based in this town.*

Tamar: *That's all. . . . My only hope is that the people with whom we consult will leave with the feeling that it is possible to see things in a slightly different way and that it is worthwhile to do so. I think this is extremely important in this town, because it never happens.*

SR: *To disturb the status quo a bit.*

Tamar: *Yes.*

Sara: *Yes, I guess that's what I mean. That's why I think what we did was important, but it seems to me that alternatives . . . well, I guess that it's important. . . .*

Tamar: *Good, then you agree to what we are going?*

Sara: *But we'll never have enough time to get in all these points, but, well . . . . .*

Tamar: *(turning to Dvora) And what do you think?*

Dvora: *I think the way we began was worthwhile, to give a lot of solutions will be very activating. Besides we are finishing up and it isn't good to leave everything un-resolved.*

Tamar: *So you want to continue the way we are?*

Dvora: *Yes.*

Tamar: *You agree, good. . . .*

One way of characterizing this disagreement is to see it as an argument between verification (Sara) and generation (Tamar), in the terms of Glaser and Strauss (1967). The pressure for consensus was great because we were preparing a public presentation of findings, which we believed required a united front. The project coordinator had slipped from her facilitating role to an organizing role in preparation for the consultations, and she therefore asserted more direction than usual. This switch caused confusion as to whether the coordinator would be a "diplomat" or "dictator" (Vidich and Bensman, 1971, p.

323), two effective project director roles. The emergence of the research model issue prior to our public presentation raised once again the unresolved issue of our private agendas for the project. Yancey and Rainwater (1970) consider these conflicts typical: they include "personal idiosyncracies, theoretical and ideological differences in approaches to data, and the nature of the observations being made" (p. 269). The different definitions and demands we brought to the situation allowed our behavior to diverge and threatened the integration of the team.

I worked hard on the project and wanted others to do the same, yet I was also interested in the team's developing high morale. If morale sagged, I felt guilty and responsible to remedy the situation even if I did not know the cause, a reaction that was enervating. When unspoken temporary alliances formed, the group process was crippled. In general, the group process issues became a variation on the phenomenon of internal noise that I had experienced in the mental hospital. The shifting coalitions of our foursome was a constant concern. Many of our conflicts might have been prevented in prefield meetings, but feelings cannot be contracted in advance. Rather, the team worked together for the first time in the field, and we assumed that we shared each other's research perspective. Only when our lack of consensus became clear under the pressure of a public presentation did we confront and attempt to resolve our initial disagreements. Our project was characterized by emerging consensus rather than preplanned agreements. This arrangement could have benefited from early discussion of two basic issues: What is the basic model we will employ to obtain knowledge? And how will the team deal with a lack of consensus?

Some Images of Team Research. This project alerted me to the significance of the research group for the research process. After leaving the field, I tried to discuss our group process with the team members at a meeting in Jerusalem. When I returned to the United States, I sought literature on team fieldwork and interviewed some researchers engaged in teamwork. These sources reiterated the interpersonal complexity of team research. Among anthropologists, teams are frequently composed of husband and wife, and their particular problems have been analyzed (Mead, 1970). "I have thought that the ideal situation in the field would be that of the married couple, since with a team, practical matters could be more easily subsumed to management by dividing them up, and social and intellectual isolation would be automatically avoided. Friends have convinced me, however, that teams have had many of the same problems as the single woman, as well as a problem peculiar to a marriage—that the frustrations and anxieties of the total field situation have all too handy a target and can threaten the marriage itself" (Codere, 1970, p. 144). "Group field parties" have been advocated to provide "an additional measure of control in fieldwork . . . or a system of checks and balances of points of view" (Lewis, 1953, p. 458) or to train students (Whyte, 1951). Group exposure is thus valued as an inducement for accountability and responsibility, particularly in interdisciplinary teams. Nevertheless, people can check each other and still be wrong. "Some of the pitfalls are . . . the low common denominator of common knowledge, the representatives of each discipline being forced into the role of expert, the increased conservatism of participants as their positions are challenged, and the differential status positions of the participants" (Lewis, 1953, p. 460; see also Caudill and Roberts, 1951). If teamwork results in joint publications, moreover, less prestige is awarded to each author than is given to "individual, independent achievement" (Eaton, 1951, p. 708).

The teamwork that is mentioned is usually referred to as an "undifferentiated we," analogous to the "depersonalized researcher" of the solo project. Monolithic teams are sometimes obliterated altogether in the reports, making it unclear if a project was a group or solo effort. Overlooking the group in the report does not mean that the group was unnoticed during the research process. When the work of partners and teammates is mentioned without a comment on their dynamics, there is room for suspicion that the report is an idealized front for public consumption. Do additional parts of the report suffer from retrospective falsification? Equally mysterious are research reports that express concern about establishing a well-functioning team, announce success, and do not explain how this was achieved.

One example of concern for teamwork that produced only a glossed-over description is from an interdisciplinary research project:

> All phases of the research were carried out by the authors (a sociologist and a physician), assisted by nurses, sociologists, and physicians, none of whom had worked together before. Experience indicated that from five to seven years' time would have to be invested. . . . Therefore, the authors agreed that before they committed themselves to a major piece of research one of the first issues they would have to settle was whether or not the physician and the sociologist could work together . . . [so] we decided to make an exploratory study. . . .
>
> [On the basis of a pilot period,] we attempted to create a staff which would work toward commonly recognized goals. Staff meetings were held weekly to discuss any questions that arose. The meetings were valuable in bringing into the open questions that appeared to be bothering a given individual. The different members of the team talked freely of their difficulties and successes of the week; often sharp disagreements occurred between discussants . . . . The staff meetings became an effective form of group therapy. They were also a seminar in which we learned from one another [Duff and Hollingshead, 1968, p. 20].

This is an idyllic picture of seven placid years in which the strains of teamwork were mitigated in "effective group therapy" conducted by the directors. By contrast, Seeley (1971, p. 170) provides an almost frightening description of a troubled research team:

> We walked the brink of a crisis or a succession of crises of identity, individually and collectively, and we led and were led in so doing. The crisis focused on the operation and its aims, the nature of the "team" (or whether indeed it was a team), the division of labor, the intended product, the nature of our sciences "pure" and "applied," and actually, for some, who we were and what we were doing here. Interpersonal conflict, overt and

covert, increased, and so did intrapersonal stress, for some of us, to the point of threatening or breaching habitual defenses.

Hardly one of the senior personnel involved failed to show a sharp career break, objectively visible as well as subjectively palpable. Two of the senior authors ceased to be practicing social scientists, and one retained the definition but played a then largely anomalous or unconventional role.

Eaton (1951, p. 708) conveys a similar image:

Suppressed behind the polite back-slapping in the preface of many a book are some less cordial relationships. Juicy tidbits of gossip concerned with them, much as they would enliven the usual drabness of chapters on "methodology," are carefully censored. Only "insiders" know that the team of A and B so famous for their recent great contribution to the field would rather be dead than talk to each other. They'll never collaborate again. The world may think much of them, but what they think of each other is not fit to be printed.

The project described by Riesman and Watson (1964, p. 236) contained tensions similar to those of our team, although our project was much briefer:

In immersing ourselves in the study of sociability, we found that unconscious or irrational elements of the personality were brought to bear on the research, as well as conscious and rational ones. Similarly, the holistic quality of our individual involvements in the Sociability Project gave more than ordinary weight to those factors of personality which generate interpersonal alliances and antagonisms. The wide differences that existed among us initially with respect to training and experience in research, our different and often opposed commitments regarding the processes and preferred outcomes of research, were sometimes aggravated, often assuaged, and always blurred by the urgent need, which we felt, to discover in our associates congenial partners in research.

A team that studied psychiatric institutions included a section on the "Logic, Techniques and Strategies of Team Fieldwork":

> Unfortunately we did not chronicle, much less analyze, the development of our own teamwork. We were certainly aware of much that was going on among us but did not deal with it as part of our explicit research. We were more directly interested in the teamwork of professionals other than ourselves. Like those we were observing and interviewing, however, we often acted in terms of personal and professional loyalties and requirements. At times we formed subteam coalitions around new or recurrent issues. Probably we were not at all unique in our teamwork and dialogue; the informal parading of interesting findings, the hectic interchange of memos, the scheduled and unscheduled meetings with their moments of debate, humor and excitement are familiar enough [Strauss and others, 1964, pp. 30-31].

Which is most typical of teamwork—Seeley's succession of identity crises, Vidich and Bensman's group research as a "form of torture," Riesman and Watson's unmitigated frustration, or groups such as those led by Strauss or Duff and Hollingshead where the team functions well with or without group therapy? More accounts and systematic analyses are needed to describe accurately the generic and idiosyncratic social psychological processes of a research team as a special form of group behavior. With such accounts we could differentiate the conditions under which team members experience tension and those under which they experience social support. The size of the team and the nature of its stratification, the clarity of the research objective, the reception by the research "subjects," the hidden agendas or private motivations underlying the team members' participation, and the willingness of the project director to accept leadership responsibilities without stifling the creativity of subordinates—all are salient factors in existing cases. Literature on interdisciplinary team functioning in nonresearch settings whose work nevertheless resembles research (clinical practice, for example) reveals analogous tensions despite the continuous commitment to organizing complex work in this manner (Bloom and Parad, 1976; Brill, 1972; Lowental and Reinharz, in press; Luszki, 1958; New and Priest, 1968; Newton and Levinson, 1973).

The Project Director. For a team to function productively and compatibly, there should be a clearly defined leader who devotes considerable time and energy to the team rather than acting as an absentee landlord. An example of the deleterious impact of an absentee research director is found in Rosalie Wax's (1971, p. 71) description of her study of Japanese relocation camps during World War II: "Week followed week without any noticeable improvement in my 'rapport' or my reports. Every letter I received from Dr. Thomas made it clear that I was not doing what she expected me to do. There was no one I could talk to in any meaningful fashion . . . and after two months I began to see myself as a total failure. The anxiety I suffered was so agonizing that I still find it hard to describe." (For a description of this project from the point of view of the director, see Thomas and Nishimoto, 1946).

The director's involvement and support of team members enables the team to withstand the jolts that occur despite the best planning and intentions: "For me the coordinator's functions involved many new roles. . . . My most constant and difficult role turned out to be that of morale builder. . . . Who is there for this job but the coordinator? . . . But who is there to bolster the morale builder's morale?" (Thompson, 1970, p. 60).

The coordinator's attitudes and values pervade a team. In our case, Tamar's excellent relations with the public health nurses led to a kind of "halo effect" or borrowed trust for the team members and an openness in the team's relations with the nurses. Her insider's view of the needs of the nurses to whom we could offer feedback consultation gave direction to our interpretations. But her involvement in their intrigues and controversies created problems in sustaining both an open research mentality and an involved inside perspective. Similarly, her dual responsibilities of working with the research team and the nurse group became a logistic feat, and the fieldworkers resented the interference of her commitment to the nurses. The benefits of the insider-outsider role carried hidden liabilities.

The coordinator set the tone of our deliberations and chose to pursue certain directions over others. For example, when she did not comment on obvious nonverbal signals of personal distress or interpersonal tension, the team concluded that the distress or tension was unmanageable or taboo. In our postfield analysis of the group process, Tamar explained the assumptions underpinning her coordination of the research team:

> *In a situation in which there is anxiety and in which there are unresolved, dividing, and potentially destructive feelings running around in the group, and you face a demanding, anxiety-provoking situation, I feel you have to make a choice, especially if there is limited time. You try and organize yourself with whatever you have. Never mind what you don't have to confront the situation. Rather than taking a sort of introspective path. I think this is why I acted the way I did, because I thought that if we had used that limited time span (and at that point we were struggling with limited time) to try and bring to light all our feelings, this might have had a greater disorganizing effect on us than the disorganization caused by not attending to them.*
>
> *This probably set a precedent, however, for when we did have time and opportunity to uncover our feelings, and you said, 'I want to know what you felt,' it was seen as demanding, almost harsh and overbearing.*
> *[Transcript of postfield discussion]*

The research group generates interaction from which group patterns develop and intensify existing feelings. Research teams decide whether and how to relate to this process: through the so-called group therapy of staff meetings, through analysis of the group process as part of the research task, or through suppression. In a graphic description of interdisciplinary team research, Bronfenbrenner and Devereux (1952) list "team self-analysis" as a *pitfall* of such research. Attempts by some group members to introduce a self-analytic perspective evoked "self-consciousness and resistance both at explicit and covert levels which, for some team members at least, disrupted communication, enhanced insecurity, dampened spontaneous expression, and delayed stabilization of roles and responsibilities" (p. 190). The chief source of the disruptive effects of group self-analysis was the fact that criticism was focused on individuals as persons rather than as task performers, and that consent to engage in the group self-analysis was obtained through group pressure.

Whereas each team member on our project was responsible for her efforts alone, the coordinator was responsible for the team's welfare, the project's success, and its acceptance by various segments of the community. To satisfy these segments' interests, she played multiple roles, some of which were in conflict, some of which overlapped. An unspoken task for each team member was to comprehend and accommodate the coordinator's definition of her role in the project.

Although our team was small, its members came from slightly different professions (social work, community and public health, and sociology); therefore, we were an instance not only of teamwork but of interdisciplinary research. We underwent the processes of interdisciplinary research described by Caudill and Roberts (1951): simplification of points of view, the burden of being the disciplinary representative, managing criticism, and establishing prestige. "Interdisciplinary research is, above all, an interpersonal situation and the smoothness or strain with which work gets done must be analyzed in terms of the structure of the situation as well as in terms of individual personalities" (Caudill and Roberts, 1951, p. 13). We experienced the strained collaboration of an interdisciplinary group with each member also concerned with her own professional socialization and identity formation.

Group Dynamics of Team Fieldwork. I expected the other fieldworkers to share my attitudes toward the project. I assumed we would be three equal fieldworkers working in parallel and guided by the project coordinator. I did not anticipate how powerful the interaction among the team members would be. The group took on a life of its own, with its own process and development, and became a "family in the field" with all the stress and comfort of a natural family. Like the families we were studying, our family had to deal with the threat of shelling. The family metaphor also fit several aspects of our team's activities. The apartment was our joint home in the field—where we ate, slept, and cared for our personal needs. The team addressed its members' emotional concerns and became an informal nurturing group. The family is one arena in which one's basic worth is generally acknowledged and one's experiences confirmed. This expectation, however, places a demand on one's energy and time. The family also has a socializing function—teaching, prodding, encouraging, and molding its members.

The family analogy is also intended to evoke the powerful feelings that characterized our group. Thrown together with barely any previous acquaintance, bound together with a common task, stranded in our apartment island, we went forth daily to study families and coping. The threat surrounding us exposed some primitive themes of family life in our group (sibling rivalry, infantile regression, and adolescent rebellion), softened by the absence of an adult male to complete the family fantasy.

The "work of membership" in this fieldwork family was striking. The group was neither a neutral entity nor an unconditional source of nurturance to replenish my energy, but a complex, ever-changing, demanding web of interdependencies. Whereas in the hospital study I became aware of the significance of the researcher's personal reactions to the social structure of the setting, in this study I believed I had unearthed a relevant factor influencing every phase of a project, namely, the team's group process. This personal discovery opened a new realm of data and now prevents my accepting a team project's product as complete if it omits detailed discussion of the team's process. This discovery transformed my triad for conceptualizing the research process (person, problem, and method) to a four-part entity (person, team, problem, and method). The discovery of the team served to further "contextualize" the research process.

Eaton (1951) has remarked that in research teamwork, relations quickly go from professional to personal. These personal relations then feedback into the professional interaction in numerous ways. If face-to-face contact is frequent, these personal and professional relations coalesce so that "teamwork involves an experience in group therapy for each participant" (Eaton, 1951, p. 709). This group therapy affects all aspects of the research project. In our case, the "therapy" affected not only our relations to the study families and residents in a dangerous setting but also the interpersonal relations within the team and our personal and professional identities.

We not only lived together but got to know each other in marathon intimate talks lasting far into the night. The intensity of these spontaneous sessions, followed by long, equally intense periods of participant observation with the families, followed by fiery debriefing sessions, was extraordinary. Since these private conversations were considered "off duty," and since we requested confidentiality from each other, I have no field notes on this component of the group process.

My analysis of the group process is also hampered by the gradual withdrawal of one of our team members into silence about which she refused to comment. Following the project coordinator's lead, we all treated this member gingerly, protecting her right to adopt this stance even if it left the rest of us confused and feeling guilty. When the project members finally left the field, we reassembled in Jerusalem for social and research purposes. I suggested then that we analyze the interpersonal relations that had developed in the field. This effort met with a stone wall. When my probing attempts were labeled "cruel," I ceased. In private talks between Tamar and myself, however, we sought an explanation for the group dynamics. We formulated the hypotheses of the group pressure to conform, the group's ambivalence to autonomy, its analogy to a family, the members' use of the project for private agendas and personal growth, the instability of a four-member group, and the impact of the pressures of time, danger, and climate.

The description of group dynamics is almost impossible; multiple interactions occur simultaneously, each behavior can have multiple meanings, and the most appropriate conceptual frame with which to analyze the group changes with time. Nevertheless, I will attempt to list some features of our group interaction. We experienced an initial solidarity of purpose in response to our shared situation, a solidarity that was furthered by my open need to cling to others in the face of danger. Simultaneously, however, the differences among us became clarified, and we struggled to determine the extent to which our individual preferences would be vanquished by the group. In our daily debriefings, there was some competition concerning the quantity of the day's data, the depth of our relations with the families, the intimacy of the information we obtained, the cleverness with which we analyzed the incoming data, and the degree to which we impressed the coordinator. There were also complex interpersonal relations among the four of us. In these intense relations, we worked on conscious and unconscious personal problems. Unwittingly we pushed each other into different symbolic roles (for example, the religious one, the academic, the good daughter) that had personal relevance. The combination of the work tensions and these interpersonal relations overwhelmed one member to the point of her withdrawing from interaction and performing her duties perfunctorily. The brevity of the project prevented our knowing whether we had experienced a stage of a larger process that required time to be resolved successfully or if we had discovered the ultimate coping capacities of each member. This fragmentary analysis follows on what was a personal discovery—the existence of a complex group process among research team members.

The perceived benefit of teamwork was the possibility of receiving immediate feedback on every aspect of my work—from the quality of my field notes to the formulations of my conclusions. When a team is stimulating and supportive, its members feel that they are working with and for each other, since one member's materials invariably facilitate another team member's work. Members can corroborate or invalidate emerging generalizations and keep each other in check. Reiss (1968) has shown how the fact that team members come from different backgrounds can be used to obtain varying interpretations of the same phenomenon. Thus, a team can use a consensus model and expect generalizations to be compatible with the findings of each team member; or the team can use a conflict or relativistic model that seeks multiple interpretations of a phenomenon or pattern. Yancey and Rainwater (1970) argue that the study of a community requires a team in which the community's composition is reflected. The conflict that arises from the separate observers and their ideological differences "illuminates the limitations of the nature of the generalizations being made by a single researcher in his network of informants" (Yancey and Rainwater, 1970, p. 269). A responsive group elicits the examination and comprehension of one's personal feelings and theoretical perspective. The group is also capable of examining its own process and of supporting and guiding the team members in the face of research difficulties. The interpersonal bonds formed in these teams are intellectually and emotionally powerful.

Obviously a team can gather more data than can one researcher in the same time period, but the possible benefits of this increase in quantity depend on the team's coordination and communication. More data are not necessarily better data. The team, particularly the coordinator, is torn between securing the proper team conditions and going on with what seems to be the real research activity—the gathering and analyzing of data. "The psychosocial problems of field relationships between researchers and subjects are quite sufficient so that further complications in the form of interpersonal difficulties among team members should certainly be avoided" (Valentine, 1968, p. 181). Large teams can become an "intruding establishment interfering with research" (Valentine, 1968, p. 181), although they promise more data. The complaint that the team consumes energies more appropriately directed at the research problem belies a conceptualization of research as being distinct from researchers. Rather, I am arguing that research must be conceptualized holistically as the coalescence of the researcher as a person (in a team), the methods the researchers practice and experience, and the problem studied.

Even though from the start I felt a need to separate myself from the team, I also experienced a strong sense of community with the team members. Despite our differences in personal habits, life-styles, training, and background, we shared a great deal: youth and the sense of an unpredictable future, an interest in addressing human needs, our commitment to Israel, our concern with the quality of life in the town, and a sense of being on a personal search. These characteristics we brought with us. The strongest sense of commonality, however, arose from discovering that our first reactions to the town were the same.

SR: *Today I kept on having the feeling that I was special or different from everyone here, and I felt almost ashamed. First of all, I will leave this situation which is so dangerous. Also materially, I can go away on trips even during my stay. Is this happening to you also?*
Sara: *Being here for only two weeks increases these feelings.*
Dvora: *This feeling arises because usually we live in the city [meaning, "we are bourgeois"]. All along I knew that one day I would get involved in a place like this; it's not just a feeling that I have today.*
SR: *I don't think I am happier than the people here, I just have more possibilities, opportunities.*
Sara: *In the next two weeks you could figure all this out?*
Dvora: *Not in a complete way, but a little. Why was it that our whole class arose and wanted to come [here] after the shelling? Because of this feeling. Now the problem is, how long will the feeling last? I am participating in danger here, but you can't compare it at all with the life of the people here. But I am still doing something. I didn't come on vacation.*
Sara: *Many times I have seriously considered joining Kibbutz Ramat Magshimim [a religious kibbutz on the Golan Heights]. I'm not sure if I'll do it though.*
Dvora: *That's just what I mean. Today I spoke to you about whether or not to live [here]. I said I wanted to move here.*
SR: *Yes, me too.*
[Transcript of team discussion]

Our personal motivations for joining the project partially overlapped and therefore our emotional response to the town as a symbol was similar.

Our team was neither a solo study nor bureaucratic research (in the sense of Vidich and Bensman, 1971) but rather contained characteristics of each and of its own. As a small, brief, inexpensive project, coordinated by a person concerned with maximizing the team members' personal experiences, it represented a middle category that might be called "small-team research." Our particular project did not become "a form of torture" (Vidich and Bensman, 1971, p. 323), but it did generate group tensions that were difficult for one member to bear. The tensions manifested themselves immediately, and the one member became a casualty within a week. She withdrew further and further from spontaneous participation in our debriefing sessions and became apathetic. Eventually she barely spoke with any of us, nor would she accept offers to help her deal with whatever was bothering her. Her experience and reaction illustrate the potentially deleterious impact of an intense small-team research project on a fragile, sensitive member. We will never know if this member could have been reintegrated into the team had the project lasted longer or if she would have resigned or been fired as happens so frequently in bureaucratic or group research.

CHAPTER 7

Dimensions of an Experiential Sociological Method

Temporary Affiliation Behavior

The end of the last chapter concerned relations among team members in the context of a small-team fieldwork project. The present section shifts to relations between the fieldworkers and the people in the field, a relation I call "temporary affiliation."

Consider the use of space in various research methods. In the survey project discussed in Chapter Two, the team stayed closeted in research headquarters hundreds of miles from the study site. Although this distance is not required in survey research, it is common, since only the research instrument and not the researcher must make contact with the subject. In my mental hospital study, I entered the setting without invitation from the people I studied. I "invaded" their territory to satisfy my own need as a student with an external institutional base. Grateful for their cooperation, I tried to be unobtrusive and helpful. My behavior was oriented to sustaining my presence on their territory or to finding ways of making the territory ours. Even though I took a job in the setting, the size of the institution, my relatively low status as a dance therapist, and the part-time nature of my work left me feeling I was on someone else's territory.

The Israeli project required being with people on their own territory. Our initial entry into the families' homes was obtained through the public health nurses. Three nurses working in the designated neighborhood each selected three families from their caseloads during a group discussion among all the neighborhood nurses. One nurse then accompanied each team member to the three homes, introduced the member to the family, and left. Each family member had to make sense of this ambiguous situation. The public health nurse who introduced me chatted for a minute about the children's health, mentioned that I came as a student and friend, and said the families should be "nice" to me. On this limited foundation, the family and I had to build our relationship. At the end of two weeks the team was to report their observations and interpretations to the entire public health nursing staff and supervisors and to the Histadrut's committee on neighborhood affairs. Using a simple applied research design, the project represented a joining of needs that resulted in our temporarily affiliating with some groups in the town, not as invited guests or invaders, but as short-term partners who would provide feedback.

In any site there are several overlapping territories of the various groups. The group that invites the researchers is rarely the group that is actually studied. In our case, the project coordinator invited the research as a setting member herself after obtaining the public health nurses' guarantee of assistance and funding from a local sponsor (Histadrut). The families we studied, however, were not approached beforehand. We gained access to their space as a second stage after gaining entry into the community. The issue of entry recurs with each new private space within a setting that the researcher wishes to enter. To the study families themselves, we were imposed guests, which to our surprise enabled the families to open their private space in ways that gave them honor and pleasure. This warm treatment was surprising, since it disconfirmed statements such as the following: "[In the case of the poor,] their home is the place in which most contacts with the agency take place. They are typically being investigated in situ and hence have much less of a chance to conceal their private affairs from the superordinate observers. Such an invasion of home territory, because it prevents the usual stage management for the visit of outsiders, is *necessarily experienced as humiliating and degrading*" (Coser, 1965, p. 145, emphasis added).

Our uninvited presence was interpreted by the families not as a cause for humiliation but as a welcome opportunity for sharing thoughts and feelings. Because the contrary expectation is common, the project coordinator considered its disconfirmation a significant finding, which we then reported to the nurses and the Histadrut. The face-to-face contact and space we shared with the nurses, families, and townspeople in general increased my commitment to them and desire to provide useful insights for them. This commitment encouraged a professional attitude coupled with a warm personal approach. Our very presence engendered respect among those with whom we worked, since we were exposing ourselves to their dangers. This respect was reinforced by our interest in understanding but not evaluating the perspectives of the townspeople.

A researcher can gain access to someone's space without gaining access to their heart. I expected this problem with the Indian families—they would be passive, suspicious, and disinterested; I would be tolerated and my departure patiently awaited. Instead, in the nine families studied by the team, we were enthusiastically welcomed and accepted. The initial bewilderment expressed by some disappeared by the second visit:

Dvora: "I have visited two families so far. On the first day I had the impression that one family stood aloof, shrunk away. The theme of the first family was apparent in the first conversation. The mother wanted to share with me as much of herself as possible. She also assembled all the children and told her husband. The fact that one tells one's husband is very significant to her.

"I think her family understood what I wanted. At least she did. They said they weren't going to request anything from me except in one case in which she thought I could help her in connection with a child. Not as a professional but as any other person to whom one can talk. Perhaps she felt that I would understand, but I think this was something exceptional. Her child did not understand what I wanted and it was very difficult to explain it to him. With him I had real difficulties.

"Today I was concerned about the second family, because of its reaction yesterday which looked to me like withdrawal. She was not sure what to tell me, but when I came in the morning, I came at an unexpected time. We had decided on 11 and I came at 8 in order to go to the market with her. When I told her I wanted to go with her to the market, she told me that she had already gone at 6 in the morning. So I said I was willing to just be with her in the house, to help her or just to sit.

"I was very surprised by her reception. Apparently her reaction yesterday had been what I felt. But in contrast now she told me that she had told her children and husband all about me, and the children were so enthusiastic they wanted me to stay and go for a walk with them and stay overnight. I should eat with them and live with them. That's what they want.

" 'And how do I look? Tall, small, how old am I?' they asked. That is what was interesting to the children. And apparently this influenced her because she was full of smiles and didn't ask me for a certificate for what I intended to do. As a matter of fact she talked all the time. She seemed comfortable and I think she understood that I was not a guest. She told me in the morning, 'I will not relate to you as a guest. I will continue my work and you will stand next to me.' I don't know if she always works this way because it seemed to me that she interrupted to talk a lot."
[Transcript of team meeting]

Our acceptance by the families was facilitated by our association with the nurses, who were familiar, respected, and appreciated. It is not uncommon to gain access to the lower class by way of its caretakers. Our appropriate sponsor eased the way, but the team members were then on their own to sustain the acceptance and establish rapport. I, for one, was grateful for their warmth and openness and this attitude was conveyed during the interviewing process. In their private space, I felt somewhat humble and circumspect. The families played the role of hosts and fed us continuously while telling us about their lives. When the team discovered how valuable this "unburdening" was for the families, we recognized that our relations with the families had been reciprocal and not one-sided, as we had feared they would be.

I cannot convey adequately the positive regard with which I viewed and felt enveloped by these families. Lewis (1961, p. xi) has warned of two distorting attitudes to the study of the poor—"oversentimentalization and brutalization." Nevertheless, researchers' feelings toward the people we study do arise and must be understood not only as an influence on findings but as a human product of a project, an outcome in its own right. I found the families physically attractive, with unusual customs and habits, emotionally expressive, full of charm and warmth, and eager to protect me and make me comfortable. The optimism, humor, and vigor of each family were infectious. I came to cherish the families, even if our relations were superficial and brief. Wolff (1971) wrote of the similarity between love and the total involvement of some community studies. Agee (Agee and Evans, 1972) "fell in love" with his families and relished every detail of their lives. When fieldworkers do not write openly about their feelings engendered by their affiliation, those feelings can be glimpsed between the lines.

Related to the issue of private space is the issue of private talk. Which issues are private and which public for a given culture, family, or individual? The willingness and equanimity with which the heads of the families discussed with me their finances and aspects of their sex lives amazed me. The researchers were more reserved and concerned with privacy than were the families.

Talking about personal topics, however, does not guarantee revealing how one actually feels. For example, I received many contradictory responses to my questions concerning fear of the shelling, problems with children, and health.

SR: *What I found to be interesting is that I cannot ac-*
               cept the first answer they give me. I have to ask the
               same question after an hour.
Nurses: *Or after two.*
SR: *For example, yesterday I asked the husband if he*
               has any health problems. "No, I am 100 percent
               healthy. Thank God." Yesterday the wife asked me
               if I wanted something to eat that was spicy. I didn't
               know how to answer because I wanted to eat what
               they eat. I thought they do eat spicy food so I an-
               swered yes. So she said, "Too bad, I can't cook
               spicy food because my husband has an ulcer and he
               was in the hospital and he is not allowed to eat in
               anybody else's house and because of this we can't
               visit other families and I have to cook special foods
               for him."
Nurse R: *My hypothesis is that he fears being dismissed from*
               work or from health insurance if it is known that he
               has a serious disease. Perhaps SR was seen as some-
               one who would tell on them and therefore he said
               he was 100 percent healthy.
Nurse F: *But this is not the case here. It is simply that he re-*
               ceived SR as so pleasant and full of life and he felt
               good and didn't even think of his sickness. After-
               wards when you get to know the family well and go
               deeper into things with them, you will discover
               many not so pleasant things about them.
SR: *And I will receive different answers.*
Nurse F: *Completely different. You shouldn't draw conclu-*
               sions about these matters on the first or second day.
               It will take a bit longer.
[*Transcript of staff discussion*]

As the team analyzed the families' answers to our questions, the
nurses pointed out various determinants of those responses.
According to the nurses' social theorizing, the family's responses should not be taken on face value but should be seen as
part of defensive pleasantness.

    This response style can be understood in terms of a class-
or culture-bound pattern of behavior with strangers (Strauss and
Schatzman, 1955; Deutscher, 1968; Benney and Hughes, 1956).

For example, in Southeast Asia a courtesy bias has been identified—courtesy supersedes truth and demands compliance (Jones, 1963, p. 1). Among the Indian families with whom I affiliated, a courtesy bias might have structured our interaction, but the term "bias" implies a comparison with an unbiased and therefore nonexistent ideal. The courtesy and amiability of the families did not preclude their criticizing me for my mistakes. (For example, I said, "You must be proud" to a grandfather of a large family and was rebuked that "one must never be proud." The last time he had expressed pride, his daughter's son became deaf.) The amiability combined with directness structured their communication with a stranger in their private space.

Finally, interviewing and being with people in their space gives them the controlling power—they can manipulate the space or manage the stage. If we are to have adequate social history and social theory we should obtain records of all social classes produced in an unstructured format in their private space. Since the records of any historical period favor those who create public events or create records (Zinn, 1970), social science fieldwork can balance this distorted view by giving a mouthpiece "to the people." By taking living testimony of people with little power, researchers can convert the invasion of their privacy into an invasion of the readers' awareness: "I reject the belief that the worlds of quiet men and women must go unnoticed or be treated strictly as actuarial or statistical concerns. Lives are recorded because there is inherent value in preserving human experiences, especially those experiences which for political and economic reasons are deemed 'less significant' and 'less profitable' " (Cottle, 1977, p. 13). (See Cottle, 1967, and Rainwater, 1970, for other instances of "mouthpiece sociology.")

Sociological fieldwork is thus potentially a form of *social activism*. One of my informants taught me this as he instructed me to tell others his story. He wished to become an informant in a larger sense.

Mr. F: Shalom chaverim *[dear friends], I want to tell you about this town. It is a big city. There are about*

18,000 people here. There is a large factory, Northern Textile, and 300 people work there, and there is another one, Great Textile, that began in 1968, which employs 900 people. The problem is that the salaries are very low. We live in this town and it is almost impossible to give an education to the children. It .is impossible to have a good house. We have no refrigerator and can only buy things by having debts. My debts will be with me until the end of my life.

The city doesn't care that the children suffer from the poor quality of the kindergarten. We don't have a garden or park. We have to pay a lot for water. Our life, I don't think it is worthy of a man at all. We have only two movie houses in which to enjoy ourselves. One of them is at 6:30 and the other one just at 8 or 9 or something like that. If there is not a good movie, then the whole week you sit at home. We don't have any community centers to enjoy ourselves nicely as we used to where we came from [India].

I am already 16 years in Israel and I can't see that my life is improving at all. I hope you are listening to me carefully, and that you will do something for me, for Israel, and especially for this town, that you will do something so that we can live like men. We want to live like you. We came to Israel like a Jewish brother and we want to live like a Jew. I think the rich Jews should help like a brother, so that our children will receive a good education and will live like human beings. Shalom.

SR: Thank you.
Mr. F: They will hear it?
SR: Of course, if it is on the tape.
[Transcript of taped interview]

The interviewing procedures used by the team were informal, unstructured, and not standardized, in keeping with our interest in understanding the families in their own terms, in getting a sense of families' reality even if members' statements were inaccurate, and in giving them the opportunity to control the situation. We accommodated their realities rather than imposing our conceptual or linguistic categories. If a parent was busy, I talked with the children; if no one wanted to converse, I joined in their work or leisure activity. I took care of my own needs as well as attempted to understand theirs, and in one case took a long nap after being fed mercilessly in the enervating heat. When I awoke we continued our unstructured conversation. This data-gathering approach preserved each family's individuality since in each I established a unique relationship. The lack of predetermined structure left them and me the freedom to formulate questions and discuss tangential issues as we went along. Similarly, I observed the different ways each family organized our conversations as an expression of their individuality.

Our team coined the term "temporary affiliation research" to describe the researchers' stance in combination with the setting members' experience of pleasure and psychological benefit, which they explicitly expressed. This term was intended to convey the human mutuality that was missing in the behavioristic phrase "participant observation." According to the individuals we visited, the very acts of being sought out, studied, and affiliated with reinforced their sense of personal worth. We gave them an opportunity to present themselves positively and a chance to be heard.

I spent the afternoon primarily with the children, since the mother was busy doing her housekeeping. . . . the second oldest, a twelve-year-old son, took charge of filling me in on all the important information. My writing down exactly what he said demonstrated to him that I was listening carefully and appreciating what he was saying. . . .

Immediately after our conversation he took me on a tour of all that was important to him in his backyard. This consisted primarily of the pigeons, rabbits, and other animals that he cared for. But even more significant was his behavior the following day when I returned. He was sitting in the kitchen with me and his brothers and sisters, but looking intently at the clock on the wall. I reflected back to him the nonverbal behavior I observed and asked him why he was looking at the clock. He told me that the next bus would pass through the area in so-and-so many minutes. When I asked him why he was interested in the bus schedule he asked me to produce a pencil and paper so I could take down his story:

"Buses are good when it is raining, when it is hot, or when the shells come. Today I cried a lot. I didn't want to go to school. I was afraid to walk so far. I cried and made a fuss until mother gave me money and so we all went to school by bus [he and his older and younger brothers]. When I got to school I went to the secretary, Ora. She knows me. I told her that I won't come to school if I have to walk; mother gives me money every day but it is very hard for her. Only my father works. Ora said OK, she would arrange it. In recess I saw Ora walk in the direction of the town hall. Later Ora came in front of all the classes and said from now on we would have a free school bus in our neighborhood every day."

Regardless of whether the child actually brought free buses to his neighborhood, his creation of this sequence of events placed him in center stage as the effective manipulator of a painful situation. Our discussion of his fears on the long walk to school and my confirmation of his leadership among the children in his family reinforced his self-confidence and positive fantasies. In the unstructured interview he was treated as a competent, informed, valuable person from which he gathered additional strength to cope with his problems. This Hawthorne-like positive effect on the morale of a studied person or group is not universal. Certain groups would undoubtedly become demoralized or display hostility. Instead my personal discovery was the existence of an impact on those who are studied, which is sometimes beneficial. This impact, if deliberate, can form the basis of a "clinical sociology" (Lee, 1955).

Dvora: "I can give an example from one family in which one member was able to organize things better because she had the opportunity to be heard. The other one didn't have that opportunity and was all confused. When I gave her the chance, she said voluntarily that she felt a change. The people that I talked to actually mentioned and discussed their need to talk. One of them made the distinction between that and having friends. She doesn't really want to talk to friends. She really understood what she was talking about. It seemed very impor-

tant for her to say these things. It just came out, and after the
conversation she actually seemed more organized in the way she
talked, more confident."
[Transcript of field team meeting]

The therapeutic effects of affiliation resulted from various social psychological opportunities for the subject: *catharsis—*
the relief that comes from the chance to express freely to a
stranger thoughts that were previously suppressed for fear of
impropriety or retribution; *reinforcement* or *confirmation—*the
enhancement of self-worth on the basis of the researcher's attention and interest; and *organization of thoughts—*the subject's opportunity and necessity to organize his previously
unsystematized thoughts and statements in order to be comprehensible to the listener. The family members who seized the
opportunity to address the world through my tape recorder
organized their statements chronologically around the theme of
their immigration to Israel, focusing on disappointments in
others and rationales for their own actions.

The nurses attributed the beneficial impact of the interview to two factors: The conversations occurred in the respondent's own space, and the interviewer made no demands, so that
the informant was in charge and could make statements without
any challenges. The project coordinator considered the benefits
from the interviews so important that she reported to the project's sponsoring agency the need to create conditions for more
such affiliating activity. Specifically, she proposed that "temporary affiliation" be developed as a new form of volunteer
work with the emphasis on listening to one another rather than
doing "good deeds." This could have been developed by bringing in outsiders or by creating opportunities among town
members.

When we presented the finding of the "significance of
being listened to" to the Histadrut official, he cynically dismissed it with, "I always let them talk!" The difference between "letting someone talk," which implies controlling their
talk and not necessarily paying attention, and caring or being
open to what is said is the difference between change-oriented
communication and useless, stultifying communication.

The effect of the interview on the interviewee is too broad a topic to discuss here fully. Rather, I am recounting my own process of discovering these unanticipated impacts in the course of this project. The beneficial impact of temporary affiliation was a methodological by-product of this research experience. The interview impact was especially vivid because the sociological tradition avoids such effects as bias, distortion, or contamination.

Although interviewers' influence is disparaged, they unwittingly or intentionally pressure their subjects to respond in certain ways (Sherman, 1967). This "situational demand" is considered an improper interviewing technique, but its existence demonstrates the possibility of harnessing the study situation for its beneficial impact.

Influence and reactivity are inevitable in interaction. Since this is true, then the researcher could abandon the search for nonreactive interactional methods and select the desired effect. Attempting to avoid an effect is a form of subject manipulation just as is the attempt to influence in a particular direction. An open interactive style allows the researcher to discover the subjects' qualities in their own terms. Many people in this Israeli town experienced this direct human approach as beneficial. I propose, therefore, the acceptance and welcome of the influence between the persons engaged in research. The quality of this influence is part of the data to be collected and thereby contributes to our knowledge if it is adequately described. In addition, it is of immediate use to the interviewee.

The moment the research process begins, the researcher intervenes, interferes, and meddles with what otherwise might have occurred. As Isaac Newton demonstrated in the physical world, the same is true for the social: Every action produces a reaction. The researcher's task is to identify and marshal the reaction, not deny or minimize; the task is to capture and understand phenomena in their contexts. Researchers are thus responsible for understanding the impact of their behavior in the research act. They cannot retreat behind the oft-heard excuse that such self-understanding and reactivity awareness are difficult.

Studying a person or a group can increase morale and

self-understanding, even while assessing how poorly the person or group is doing (for example, see Brown, Tshiyama, and Scheibe, 1967). This is one rationale for the current interest in evaluation research. By its very presence, a study can reinforce a group's values and objectives. A group of researchers multiplies these effects (Festinger, Riecken, and Schacter, 1956). The Heisenberg (or uncertainty) principle states that the act of measuring alters that which is measured; the Hawthorne effect states that subjects alter their behavior in response to the research situation; the guinea pig phenomenon (Webb and others, 1966) refers to the special behavior manifested by those being studied; and Yancey and Rainwater (1970, p. 255) claim that "respondents perform for researchers." Studies demonstrate that instruments not only disturb but produce the very items they wish to measure. Reactivity is not the dreaded mark of researcher incompetence but the likely consequence of living in the social world. Furthermore, it can be harnessed for useful ends. Only by abandoning the natural science model and developing its own can social science relinquish the notions of a subject external to and unaffected by the investigator (Barnes, 1963) and of an investigator outside of the social system.

My experience in this loosely structured, applied field study demonstrated that researchers need not come armed with countless forced-choice questions. Rather, they can envisage a study as an encounter and an opportunity for the subject to talk and be heard (Cottle, 1977). The topic will emerge; all is relevant and appreciated. From this accepting attitude and feedback, the subject gains self-understanding. From the wealth of material that is produced in a trusting interchange, the social scientist selects themes of interest that become or reflect the thrust of the research. The researcher's task is to select and organize, not to predetermine. As Freud showed the world, the distinctions between education, research, and therapy are ambiguous. A successful project contains some of each (for example, see Schwitzgebel, 1964).

What is the stance of the researcher who activates all of these properties? Wolff (1971, p. 238) uses the term "total involvement": "In surrender, an individual becomes involved, undifferentiatedly and indistinguishably, with himself, with his act or state, and with his object or partner—just as the lover's 'involvement' refers to all three of these: in both cases differentiation between subject, act, and object disappears." The social science literature contains almost no examples of such surrender, which suggests it is rarely if ever attempted, recorded, or published. Yancey and Rainwater (1970, p. 248) suggest that their fieldworkers who were successful in understanding the community under study were those who surrendered to it. They lifted their own anxiety and exposed themselves fully to the situation at hand. Agee's (Agee and Evans, 1972) description of his state of being with families with whom he "temporarily affiliated" is an attempt to capture the wholeness of the experience. He is almost overwhelmed with the responsibility of conveying the presence of the people he studied and who allowed him to discover himself:

> Here at a center is a creature: it would be our business to show how through every instant of every day of every year of his existence alive he is from all sides streamed inward upon, bombarded, pierced, destroyed by that enormous sleeting of all objects forms and ghosts how great how small no matter, which surround and whom his senses take: in as great and perfect and exact particularity as we can name them:
> This would be our business, to show them each thus transfixed as between the stars' trillions of javelins and of each the transfixions: but it is beyond my human power to do. The most I can do—the most I can hope to do—is to make a number of physical entities as plain and vivid as possible, and to make a few guesses, a few conjectures; and to leave to you much of the burden of realizing in each of them what I have wanted to make clear of them as a whole: how each is itself; and how each is a sharpener [p. 101].

The sensation of truly being with the other has a powerful impact on both the subject and the investigator. Both are learning from one another.

The determination of who is researcher and who is subject in behavioral research is somewhat arbitrary since it depends entirely upon one's point of view—both parties have interacted and have learned something about the other in their exchange. Similarly, the designation of just what are research results and what are irrelevant background data is arbitrary. The researcher, however, assigns the roles of who will play researcher and who will play subject, and he also determines what will be considered as research results. These decisions, in part, are predetermined in accordance with his interests and hypotheses. The subject, however, may choose not to accept the roles which the researcher has assigned. He may decide, unknown to the researcher, to play a research role himself, thus placing the researcher in the role of subject.

The researcher-subject relationship and the research results exist and are integrally related the moment either is initiated. In this sense the research process and research results are completely embedded in and confounded with a set of ongoing researcher-subject relationships [Friedlander, 1967, p. 488].

The changes that accrue to the totally involved researcher have been called "socialization through participation," or "oversocialization of the researcher" (Habenstein, 1970, p. 119). "Involving research" is characterized by changes in the interviewer and subject, by an interchangeability of their roles, and by a fusion of the goals of the process. Erikson (1964, p. 36) goes so far as to claim that psychological "discovery is accompanied by some irrational involvement of the observer, and it cannot be communicated to another without a certain irrational involvement of both." By careful self-examination, investigators uncover both rational and irrational components of their involvement and begin to understand how the changes they undergo are elicited by their subjects' environment, which the researchers temporarily share. In a study of police, for example, the researchers adopted police behavior inadvertently, but so passionately that the police themselves were taken aback (Reiss,

1968). Researchers should explore and then bracket their attitudes toward their subjects so they can differentiate what was brought to the encounter from what was brought away.

Advances in knowledge about psychosocial realities require the assistance of subjects who feel ready and willing to be partners in the enterprise. There must be room for subject involvement in the research. The essential elements of satisfactory field relations have been labeled "participation" and "parity" (Wax, 1972): Participation is the researcher's willingness to share with subjects the experiences and hazards of their lives; parity means acknowledgement of a common humanity shared by researcher and subjects. Relationships devoid of these qualities seem inappropriate for the study of significant human concerns. To achieve parity, researchers must possess personal security and maturity to overcome their ego boundaries. By the time I reached the town I was ready to participate, and to my delight I learned the meaning of Wax's parity. These dimensions became an extension of the participant observation model, which only peripherally, rather than centrally, involves the researcher's self.

This discussion of the beneficial effects of research is intended to balance the typical neutral or alienated perspective that I had internalized during my socialization. Usually the subject is perceived in a dualistic system that splits the researcher from the subject. In this framework the subject is someone who must be manipulated or managed rather than a collaborator or fellow human being, a potential sister or brother. The problem with the nondualist attitude arises when the temporary affiliation must end. Like death, taking leave of the total involvement relationship always comes too soon. In fact, my most glaring error in the Israeli project was to not adequately prepare myself and the families for the project's termination. My guilt feelings about leaving coincided with the team's detection of the unanticipated positive response by the families to the team. The unexpected mutual impact of researcher-subject forced me to revise my definition of research and to reevaluate the problems of the residents of the town.

The Process of Consultation

During our stays in the nine families' homes, the team met three times with the group of public health nurses for consultation, which consisted of our receiving guidance from them and sharing our observations. This first formal consultation experience as part of a research project altered my understanding of research methodology. The demands of action research revised the methods we used in the field to gather and organize our data. (Only later did I find the body of literature in community psychology known as action research, which explicated this method.) The nurses collaborated, oriented us to the project setting, shaped our emerging interpretations, and expected a final seminarlike presentation. The project sponsor expected a verbal report to a representative committee in addition to a summary written statement in exchange for its sponsorship.

The nurses' collaboration took the form of familiarizing us with the community, selecting families from their caseloads based on our criteria, and introducing each team member to her three families. These activities gave the nurses a sense of collaboration, which was expressed in an eagerness to hear our findings. In contrast to the Histadrut committee, the nurses as collaborators were open and not threatened, even if our points were challenging. (The nurses' supervisor, who had not been involved in the study but did attend the feedback session, did appear threatened. She interpreted our consultation as evaluation.)

In our seminar with the nurses, the project coordinator summarized the project's history, and the fieldworkers gave the nurses feedback concerning how they were perceived by the family members we observed. We did not evaluate or judge their performance but merely informed them how their clients saw them in order to introduce the notion of multiple perceptions of a situation. The format we selected was the recounting of representative anecdotes. One example of this feedback approach that I used was the following:

When the head nurse of the well-baby clinic in our neighborhood took me to the second home to introduce me to the family, she also used the opportunity to ask the mother how her new infant was doing and to ask exactly how old he was. When she was told that the baby was six months old, the nurse asked in a very polite, casual way whether the baby had been brought to the clinic for his vaccinations. The mother said no, she was too busy and had no time. The nurse said it was important to bring the baby soon, so the mother replied she would go the following Sunday, in three days' time. The nurse introduced me and left.

Nearly three hours later, in the midst of talking about other things, the mother told her husband that the nurse had been there that morning and had "yelled at her for not bringing the baby to the clinic," adding "Boy, was she mad!"

By no stretch of the imagination could I say that the nurse had yelled at this woman, but it is possible that the woman had perceived it as such. Perhaps her guilt led her to distort the situation. When I told the story to the nurses, the nurse burst out in utter surprise and astonishment, as did the other nurses. To them the incident seemed ironic in the light of this nurse being an especially gentle person. I had observed her interacting with many women and never found her harsh. But my point was not to have the nurses engage in a discussion about whether or not this nurse is actually harsh, but rather to show that the client and the professional can have opposed, or at least different, perceptions of the same situation. These contradictory perceptions can lead to miscommunication and frustration. We then asked the nurses if they could think of other examples in which there might have been differences in interpretation of the same situation.

After illustrating and labelling the phenomenon of multiple interpretations, our second point was to present a general pattern that we believed underlay much behavior and to support the pattern with observations in the field. The team had learned in the field that many of the families' personal problems could be understood as behavior induced by larger social structures. Attributing to the individual or family behavior that is a symptom of broader causes or constraints is to "blame the victim" (Ryan, 1971).

A simple example is the case of children who have ragged shoes and injured legs because their neighborhood has no sidewalks. To save their shoes, which are expensive to replace, the children often go barefoot, which is hazardous. The slovenliness of which they are accused reflects the city's failure to build sidewalks in their neighborhood.

We attempted not only to alter the pattern of victim-blaming, but also to demonstrate how problems manifest on the level of the individual can best be dealt with on the level of community.

Our final consultation strategy was to build on the feedback and training and then to reflect these ideas back onto the nurses' role itself. We combined the "multiple perceptions of a situation" and the social system ideas and applied them to the nurses, assuming that insights concerning oneself are particularly effective in reshaping one's thoughts.

I asked the nurses, "Who defines your role?" A very lively group discussion followed this apparently simple question. Someone blurted out that obviously the role was defined by the Ministry of Health in Jerusalem. I agreed but asked if there was anyone else who defined their role. "Well, there's the school where we are taught, and then there's our supervisor, and there's we ourselves. . . ." A long list was produced. Finally we reached some of the less obvious role definers, such as the other agencies in town with whom the nurses were supposed to coordinate their services and even the clients, each one perhaps doing it in a slightly different way. The nurses recognized that they were part of a multifaceted social network, each component of which defined who the nurses were. These different definitions and expectations either overlapped or contradicted one another. From this line of thought, the nurses saw the need to clarify the way certain agencies in town perceived them so as to enable the nurses to collaborate with these other services. This question, "Who defines one's role?", became a catch phrase used by the nurses to analyze future events.

The feedback consultation gave the team a chance to air and test their findings and interpretations, while the consultees claimed to have gotten alternative perspectives on their work. The tests of the findings were both comprehensibility and applicability. Phillips (1971) would argue that the families, too, should have confirmed our work. Our feedback was nonthreatening, since it was offered without constraints and with acknowledgement that the nurses were the inside experts, while the team offered an alternative point of view. As collaborators, the nurses expected to benefit from the feedback and were therefore open to change. Our actual on-site observations were the data from which our explanations were constructed. We found that this grounding established the nurses' trust. As Glaser and Strauss (1967, p. 98) described, "Since the categories are discovered by examination of the data, laymen involved in the area to which the theory applies will usually be able to understand it." The contrast between the irrelevant results of the survey study of teachers and the utilized findings of the team field study was stark.

I learned that the utilization of research products, whether lengthy reports or single ideas, is a socially complex component of the research process. We had planned only to report our conclusions, but we found ourselves involved in an educational process that took us beyond the scope of our original work.

The role of the collaborators or clients in assessing research conclusions is unresolved. The clients in Jaques' (1952) famous industrial study both utilized and evaluated the research process at every stage. Some social scientists object to using the client's reaction as the test of the findings' truth value: De Josselin de Jong (1967) argues that "Participants who review a model put forth by anthropologists may not be able to see their culture in those terms; they have an idealized version. The participant view is not the anthropologist's view" (De Josselin de Jong, 1967). Since the outside researcher and inside member will necessarily define situations differently, why should the validity of the researcher's analysis depend on the insider's opinion? Would this procedure not compromise the project's integrity? Claiming that the procedure of obtaining the townspeople' approval distorted the findings of the Springdale study in which Vidich and Bensman were research team members, they wrote an additional, separate book (1960) reporting on the project's findings without having the community review it be-

fore publication. To them, community scrutiny or censorship of
a manuscript was equivalent to "selling out." The researcher's
choice of validity criteria depends, in their view, on the ethos—
scientific, bureaucratic, or moral—with which the researcher is
functioning. This choice reflects both the researcher as a person
and the purposes of the research.

The first feedback effort was carried out with the public
health nurses, and the second, in line with our proposal, was
made to a group consisting of a Histadrut official and representatives of the committee on neighborhoods, which he headed.
This group had not collaborated or interacted with the project
but was considered a suitable feedback recipient by the sponsoring agency. Their middleman stance did not engender great
interest in our work. The Histadrut representative was greatly
concerned, however, that no material criticizing his own work
be included in a final report. He contested our findings, challenged our interpretations, and dismissed our suggestions. When
we reported that the families were more concerned with the
malfunctioning of social services than with the shelling, that
their lack of refrigerators despite promises from the appropriate
authorities was an annoyance, and so on, he flatly denied that
such things had been said to us in the field. As I read later:
"Even under the best of circumstances, an impartial study of an
institution or social system is going to be perceived by its officials or functionaries as a criticism. When these men are in fact
engaged in activities of dubious legality or morality, they will be
even more hostile to the conduct of independent research. And
this is exaggerated when fear is present, especially the fear
that those who have been victimized are organizing themselves to challenge their authority" (Wax, 1971, p. 358). The
team had believed naively that this group would be interested in
our findings even though we had not laid the foundation necessary for creating trust.

Acceptance of consultation depends on "pre-evaluative
collaborative work . . . to teach the researchers about the complexity of problems that the practitioner deals with" (Rodman
and Kolodny, 1964, p. 173). Practitioners tend to be suspicious
of outsiders who have not demonstrated their understanding of

the practitioner's work constraints. Whereas this condition was met with the nurses, it was lacking with the Histadrut group. This disappointing experience clarified the consultation feedback process. Reporting to defensive noncollaborators who had not been given an opportunity to see the project in their own self-interest clearly demanded a different approach from consulting with collaborators (Kimball, Pearsall, and Bliss, 1954), yet each seemed most willing to entertain concepts that they could apply to devise their own solutions to their own problems. The different responses of the two groups to our feedback further illuminated the social service environment in which the families had to function.

After the project left the field, the project coordinator continued her work as consultant to individual nurses and to the nurses' group as a whole. She observed that certain questions we posed to the nurses (for example, "Who defines the role of the professional?") were continuously reworked. In addition, the nurses were able to be explicit about their preferred consultation style. Specifically, they rejected problem solving during supervision, since the solutions that were offered frequently did not fit the problem as it was experienced. Similarly, a nurse who raised a problem might have preferred exploring it to solving it. The nurses' continuous feedback reinforced the value of offering concepts consultees can use in their own problem-solving procedures. Premature definitions of a problem or closure on a solution frustrates the consultee. There is an appropriate timing for problem solving, which can create a sense of ownership for the solution so that it is utilized. When I returned to the town three years later, some anecdotes the team had used to portray a pattern of relationships among phenomena were still remembered by the nurses.

Consultants should not make decisions that could be made by insiders, nor should they "deteriorate into action" too quickly. Rather, they should keep thought and communication processes open by delaying closure, bridging the various interests, introducing complexity, suggesting alternatives, encouraging the exposure of hidden information, and metacommunicating about the discussion process. The consultant's impact can thus broaden beyond solving a particular problem to developing problem-solving techniques and behavior.

A final characteristic of the consultation phase is its continuity with the rest of the research process. We utilized the debriefing model of stories, patterns, questions, and concepts employed in our staff debriefing meetings as the basic format of the consultation. After presenting the story of some striking experiences, we wove them into patterns that we asked the consultees to consider. Similarly, the team's group dynamics invited comparison with that of the nurses.

This rudimentary discussion of the feedback phase of our project has been directed to illustrating my personal discovery that conveying findings to audiences in usable form is a distinctive component of research projects. In our attempt to have our work utilized, we uncovered a whole new world of challenges that had been ignored in my previous work, which had been satisfied with the mere production of a written report. I thought I had discovered the consultation dilemmas of applied research until I became aware of the emerging discipline of community psychology, which has made a special discipline of these issues. Thus, my research experiences encouraged my exploration of additional disciplines.

The Issue of Brevity: Is Short Beautiful?

The sections of this chapter—pre-field-entry learning opportunities, approaching the field, team fieldwork, temporary affiliation behavior, and the process of consultation—have presented concepts in order to cluster some of the methodological insights and personal experiences of this project.

It seems remarkable that one study could have generated so much personal learning despite the limited duration of the fieldwork. The assumption that fieldwork must be lengthy provokes this brief discussion of the special features of brief research.

One month elapsed between my decision to participate and my arrival in the town on September 15, 1970. We departed on September 25, 1970, and met twice as a group in

Jerusalem within the next month. The project coordinator then prepared a final report on her own, while I prepared a separate paper on the impact of shelling (Reinharz, 1971). I met with her weekly until June 1971 to work through our materials for my own purposes, to advise each other on our work and personal matters, and to develop a professional and personal bond. In these meetings, we became teachers, students, therapists, friends, and colleagues to one another. Our shared experiences in the field became the start of a rich friendship, which included continuous reworking of the project's findings and implications. Despite this carryover from the original definition of the project, the actual fieldwork was unusually brief, only eleven days, during which we underwent all the fieldwork phases: initial disorientation, arranging living communications, establishing a working routine, gathering data, encountering and resolving problems, formulating interpretations and patterns, evaluating findings, terminating relationships, and departing. Some social scientists would claim that fieldwork of such brief duration is insignificant and does not even qualify as fieldwork, since the prerequisite of good work is lengthy involvement.

> [Anthropological] field work is a total experience. The only qualifications to such a statement are that the usual conditions for field work hold: Some significant length of time should be involved, and a period of just a few months is probably not sufficient; something like genuine cultural displacement is probably also necessary, for it is difficult to see how field work could be a total experience if it comprised easy and long-standing familiarity with the language, ecology, culture, history, and a number of given individuals who are old acquaintances and friends. Field work, therefore, is a total human experience, involving on an hour-by-hour basis our private physical and psychic well-being, the minutiae of daily living, everything we know of our own culture and of our science, and all of these in relation to new problems that demand solution or fresh contexts that provoke reaction and thought without letup [Codere, 1970, pp. 143-144].

Others would agree with this criticism because the initial exposure to a field site can produce erroneous impressions:

> Those first few days were paradise. The mountains are beautiful. Orchids bloom in abundance in May, before the rainy season begins. . . . I was very happy and secure in the reception given me and felt much less lonely and oppressed than I had felt before leaving Cambridge. But how wrong I was in my assessment of the situation!
>
> When two weeks had passed, I was summoned to the priest's house where I was accused of being a Protestant missionary. . . .
>
> The rosy beginning of those first two weeks was now marred by further accusations, and my anger mounted. . . .
>
> What I had considered a paradise during my first two weeks became a hell [Nader, 1970, pp. 99, 100, 103].

Therefore brevity is not only insignificant but distorted. Major sociological studies based on fieldwork have required several years in the field, the first few months of which involved settling in, overcoming barriers, and establishing a working procedure. This tradition would tend to disqualify or at least challenge the value of a brief project such as ours.

But there are also factors that make brief fieldwork desirable. One is the difficulty in suspending commitments outside the field for lengthy periods or in integrating a private life with a lengthy stay in the field. Many anthropologists and sociologists have avoided this problem either by marrying someone with similar professional interests or by remaining single.

A second advantage is that some funding sources are more willing to fund short-term projects. Moreover, short-term projects permit research questions to be studied almost as they arise rather than after being set aside until a large time segment is available. Short-term research can be more easily integrated into teaching and other academic responsibilities. And finally, almost every reflective fieldworker mentions that prolonged work is physically exhausting and debilitating.

The brief field trip provides an excellent opportunity for generating, rather than verifying, theory from data, which Glaser and Strauss (1967) define as a proper sociological task. The project's brevity dashes the researcher's false hopes of collecting *all* the data or creating a complete description. Since this is always impossible, the researcher is more likely to examine the single case to formulate a conceptual category that includes the case and then to devise a theory to incorporate this conceptual category. With this working theory, new cases can be examined as they arise. Brief projects do not generate expectations of expertise among field consultees but abet the generation of alternative perspectives on familiar phenomena.

> [The sociologist's] job is not to provide a perfect description of an area, but to develop a theory that accounts for much of the relevant behavior. The sociologist with theoretical generation as his major aim need not know the concrete situation better than the people involved in it (an impossible task anyway). His job and his training are to do what these laymen cannot do—generate general categories and their properties for general and specific situations and problems. They can provide theoretical guides to the laymen's action. The sociologist thereby brings sociological theory, and so a different perspective, into the situation of the layman. This new perspective can be very helpful to the latter [Glaser and Strauss, 1967, p. 130].

The brief field trip heightens the researcher's attentiveness to the setting because time is precious. The appreciation that can be delayed when time is abundant becomes pressing in the short time period. Brevity forces efficient and effective utilization of time, which is perhaps possible only for short periods. Brevity encourages continuous peak performance unless the allotted time is utterly inadequate and therefore frustrating. I experienced a special drive to do the project justice because I had so little time. There was no chance for boredom or routinization to set in.

Fieldworkers note that the first few weeks of a longer

project are particularly enjoyable: "Once in the field, I, at least, have always experienced a burst of euphoria and vitality. It invariably wears off in time as the new becomes familiar and as the tedium of everyday life anywhere in the world sets in, particularly when associated with long and regular hours of work" (DuBois, 1970, p. 232). A short field trip utilizes the euphoria and vitality that is characteristic of only the first phase of a longer study. The distortion produced by this euphoria should be evaluated in terms of the distortion produced by tedium. The population's reception in the first phase reflects their way of greeting newcomers rather than long-staying outsiders. Each response is characteristic of behavior dealing with strangers; neither should be considered as evidence of the way the people really are. My initial euphoria was experienced as heightened awareness and sensitivity, great motivation and inspiration, and a sense of drive and creativity: ideal qualities for fieldwork.

A brief foray into the field requires help. In my case, the time necessary to gain entry, locate informants, establish rapport, arrange for feedback consultations, and perform other procedures was short-circuited by our insider-outsider structure, which utilized the insider's resources. The prearranged immediate consultation component provided us assistance in rapidly analyzing our data and assessing our analysis.

If "analysis is carried on sequentially, [and] important parts of the analysis [can be] made while the researcher is still gathering his data" (Becker, 1958, p. 653), then the various phases of participant observation are compatible with brief research. Fieldwork of even short duration can include analysis from the very beginning. That which might have been stretched over a long period is thus collapsed into a short time span without distorting the basic processes. Might Parkinson's law play a role in research—is the amount of time it takes to discover something of consequence in large part a function of the amount of time one expects it to take (Gordon Fellman, personal communication, 1976)?

The major problems related to our abbreviated time frame were the following: the limited opportunity to resolve complex interpersonal team tensions and intrapsychic difficulties in the field, the inadequate preparation of our families for the termination of our stay, and the limited time available for writing in the field.

Brief projects need not be irresponsible, although impending departure might engender reckless involvements. No matter what the nature of fieldwork, it is best to preserve the conditions necessary to permit a revisit, unless circumstances in the field preclude the researcher's interest in returning. The brief project does not require the interpersonal work of building relationships good enough to live with, but it does require good termination skills. The interpersonal costs and benefits of living together are thus avoided. On brief trips the researcher is less likely to meddle in the setting's politics or affairs, since there is no chance to follow through. The brief trip thereby functions to keep the researcher firmly in the role of temporarily affiliating outsider. Under these circumstances, the outsider's mistakes are more easily tolerated by setting members.

The brief study is a modification of, not a substitute for, the long study. Fewer data are collected, and the topics amenable to short-range study must be assessed (as in short-term versus in-depth psychotherapy). Our project coordinator reminded us continuously of our short project's limitations but converted its lack of scientific "pretensions" into an asset for freer exploration. With no pretensions of certainty, we were better able to recognize our data as bound by time, circumstance, and our own participation.

Short projects frustrate the researcher's desire to follow leads, explore problems that arise, and obtain information that depends on long-lasting trust with insiders. The first two problems might be mitigated by good division of labor among team members. If each member plays a specific role, additional members can be "floaters" who work on unanticipated concerns. I simply stored interesting questions for future study or reported these ideas to team and setting members. The short project does not allow time for learning languages or other special skills in the field. Short projects suffer if fieldworkers are unable to organize their time or to administer their project well.

Since short and long field trips have different assets and

deficiencies, neither should be used exclusively. The short trip is ideal for pilot studies, training purposes, and the consultation-feedback paradigm of action research, in which a primary objective is to deliver information to the members of a setting. Since short field trips are disparaged in the literature, the exact characteristics of a short trip have not been analyzed. For example, it would be useful to know which topics are most amenable to brief studies, how short-term relations are established in the field, and how data such as archives and other assembled records can be accessed quickly. My description of a brief project is intended as an early contribution to this subject area.

Beginnings of an Experiential Method

This brief project was the occasion of an overarching personal and methodological insight that I have come to call *experiential analysis*. As previously stated, the original substantive objectives of this project were to describe and analyze how certain families in the town coped with intermittent rocket shelling and, secondarily, how they coped with other concerns. As I began the study, I discovered to my surprise that before I could examine the families, I had to attend to my own security needs. Early in the process of doing so, I uncovered my previously unknown and unexamined responses to potential disaster. I found myself recording my own feelings to the same problem to which the families' responses were being studied. Unlike my attitude in the mental hospital study, I no longer considered these personal reactions internal noise that disturbed the research process. Rather, I looked to my reactions as an indicator of general patterns for coping with the continuous threat of potential destruction. This unanticipated study of my own coping behavior crystallized the notion of experiential research. Once I had formulated this personal discovery and given it a label, I began to observe my reactions systematically. I then applied this self-analysis to coping with shelling and to other issues discussed earlier, such as the group dynamics of team fieldwork and the impact of interviewing on the subject.

When I joined this project, my knowledge about coping

with disasters was limited to that of an educated layperson. As a daughter of holocaust survivors, I probably lived with many unexpressed hypotheses about how people react to and survive life-threatening attacks. For this study my plan was to observe and converse with people in the field and then coordinate these observations and conversations with the literature I could locate on my return from the field. An additional source of information was discovered in the field: my own coping strategies. This vehicle for understanding became available to me since my researcher role did not make me immune to the hazards threatening the population. Since I was subject to the same environmental influences as the population, I became an appropriate subject for study. I do not claim that it is proper to make large-scale generalizations from personal experience, but I do claim that since experiential data possess a unique irrefutability, they must be explained by any larger analysis. Experiential data can thus generate concepts that are eventually included in a grounded theory. Experiential data and derived concepts can then be complemented by other kinds of data in a study. Although experiential data complement other data, they are unique in that they do not rely on intervening collecting tools, tricks, instruments, tests, or questionnaires; they are completely naturalistic and unobtrusive. Whereas researchers have direct, immediate access to their experiential data, all information concerning other people is only indirectly known by researchers. Research that utilizes both the researcher's experience and statements and observed behavior of others enables sociology to be both an experiential and a behavioral discipline. If the experience of the researcher is omitted, then the discipline is limited to the study of observable behavior and responses to instruments and contrived situations such as questionnaires. Studies built on such a foundation lack both the experience of the researcher and of the subject since the information concerning the subject is not experiential but an artifact of research procedures.

Although experiential analysis represents my synthesis of methodological discoveries throughout my socialization, the literature contains examples of other researchers who utilized experiential analysis without formulating a new method. In every case, a personal experience presented a solution to the researcher's substantive problem and pointed the way for additional data gathering with which to evaluate the understanding gained from the personal experience. My first example is from Whyte's (1971, pp. 36-37) *Street Corner Society*:

> In April 1938, one Saturday night I stumbled upon one of my most exciting research experiences in Cornerville. It was the night when the Nortons were to bowl for the prize money; the biggest bowling night of the whole season. I recall standing on the corner with the boys while they discussed the coming contest. I listened to Doc, Mike and Danny making their predictions as to the order in which the men would finish. At first, this made no particular impression upon me, as my own unexpressed predictions were exactly along the same lines. Then, as the men joked and argued I suddenly began to question and take a new look at the whole situation. Here was the social structure in action right on the bowling alleys. It held the individual members in their places—and I along with them. *I did not stop to reason then* that, as a close friend of Doc, Danny and Mike, I held a position close to the top of the gang and therefore should be expected to excel on their great occasion. *I simply felt* myself buoyed up by the situation. *I felt* my friends were for me, had confidence in me, wanted me to bowl well. As my turn came and I stepped up to bowl, *I felt supremely confident* that I was going to hit the pins that I was aiming at. I have never felt quite that way before—or since. Here at the bowling alley *I was experiencing subjectively the impact of the group structure upon the individual*. It was a strange feeling, as if something larger than myself was controlling the ball as I went through my swing and released it toward the pins [Whyte, 1971, pp. 36-37; emphasis added].

Whyte's overwhelming sensations produced the insight connecting social position and individual performance. This experiential knowing has been noted by Glaser and Strauss (1967, p. 7):

"The fieldworker knows that he knows, not only because he's there in the field and because of his careful verification of hypotheses, but because 'in his bones' he feels the worth of his final analysis." Some of the best insights of fieldworkers are thus their own reactions to being in the field and not only their interpretations of what they have observed in others. This personal knowledge is completely compelling and becomes the means of structuring future observations.

In contrast with Whyte's serendipitous experience, which enabled him to predict behavior on the basis of a social psychological pattern, Fox (1959, p. 231) used her own experience, as I did in the Israeli project, to make sense of the behavior she observed in others.

It is rather interesting that some of the ways in which my participation in the life of Ward F-Second affected my attitudes and behavior brought me my earliest insights. It was because through my vicarious experience as observer *some of the same things happened to me as to the patients themselves* that I was able to forge my first links between the events I recorded.

The manner in which I "discovered" the humor of F-Second, for example, beautifully illustrates this process. At a nonhospital gathering one evening, *I caught myself* in the act of making a macabre joke, and I can remember speculating on the source of my unlikely new talent. The next morning, as I moved about F-Second, for the first time *I noticed* how much of the ward's conversation was phrased in the language of the grim joke, and how often I responded in kind. *Without realizing it, I had learned* to speak to the men of F-Second in the same way that they talked to each other. Long before this insight occurred, my field notes contained many samples of ward humor. But it was *only by virtue of a self-observation* that I became sufficiently aware of its prevalence to regard it as a phenomenon central to my study [emphasis added].

If experiential analysis is given its place as a pillar of sociological research, then fieldwork can be redefined as the activity in which researchers undergo experiences similar to those of the people being studied. The researcher is someone who not only experiences but also reflects, analyzes, and uses experiences to understand the behavioral environment.

A third example comes from an industrial study in which the investigator (Roy) took a job as a blue-collar worker:

> Sometimes discovery grows out of introspection. For example, on one factory job where there was a great deal of conflict between workers and management over the administration of the incentive or piece-rate system, Roy became aware one day of a satisfaction he was getting out of certain piece-work jobs that had not been noted by any students of organizational behavior. On jobs where he could "make out" (make just enough pieces to get the maximum bonus acceptable to his work group without having to hold back so as to avoid going beyond the group norm), Roy found himself playing a game against the clock. He set his goal and then, hour by hour, kept track of the number of pieces he made as time passed. He checked his watch at frequent intervals to see whether he was ahead of the clock or dropping behind. In this way, Roy reports that he got a feeling of accomplishment that was otherwise absent in a dull job. He also reports that when he had a rate on which he could just make out, the time seemed to go much faster than it did when he had jobs on which he felt he had to hold back production, or on jobs where no matter how hard he tried, he knew he could not make out.
>
> As he discovered these reactions in himself, Roy checked with fellow workers and found that they were likewise playing a game against the clock and in that way gaining certain satisfactions beyond simply the earning of money [Whyte, 1969a, p. 42].

In the bowling contest, Whyte felt the group's impact and got an insight into the relationship between social structure and individual performance. When Fox noticed herself engaging in unexpected behavior, she postulated that it derived from features in her research setting. Roy became aware that he coped with his work's tediousness by manipulating his productivity. In each case, the researcher's own undeniable feelings or activities produced an insight that, when analyzed, illuminated the research problem.

A final example of experiential learning is from Wax (1971, p. 214):

> Trying to get to the teacher-orientation meetings on time taught us an invaluable lesson about reservation life. For though we rose at six and washed, brushed and groomed ourselves like mad, we could never get ourselves to look presentable. The prairie dust covered all of our clothing and toilet articles every day, and we had no closets or heavy trunks, no way to iron creases out of a garment, no really clean water, and no hot water for shaving and no decent mirror. The strain of trying to keep up a respectable middle-class appearance exhausted us. . . . *We now had a heartfelt understanding* of why most people who live "out on the reservation" always look a bit grubby. Or, to put it another way, one must have hot running water, electricity, an iron and ironing board, dustproof closets, and some kind of bathing facility other than a creek if one is to present the slickly clean appearance that the schoolteachers thought Indian children should have. *We also began to understand* why many of the teachers—who had never themselves tried to live without such conveniences—thought that Indian mothers were careless and dirty, and *we began to appreciate* the desperation of some Indian mothers whose children demand that their mothers dress them in a manner that will win the approval of the teachers [emphasis added].

I began to use my reaction to the problem of coping with shelling on my first evening in the Israeli town, when I was most afraid. The following excerpt from my field notes indicates the personal reactions that later formed the foundation of my analysis of the coping behavior of the town's residents:

> *The project coordinator arrived at our apartment to take us to the wedding. Once in the car, however, she said she'd take*

*us on a tour of the town, so that we might be better oriented.
This was very useful, both from the point of view of straightforward information plus insight into my "guide's" perspective
on things.*

*What did she show us? First we drove to the area where
our project would take place. Called "A," this section was on
the east side of the highway which cut through the town. The
east section was in a valley whereas the west contained the
slopes leading up to the cliffs. On the west were shopping facilities, movies, and the health center. The buildings on the east
side were smaller, appeared older, mostly one- or two-family
dwellings, whereas on the west side there were tall 8-story apartment buildings and other modern structures. From appearances,
one might guess that section "A" was on the poorer side of the
tracks.*

*We drove through neighborhood "A" and the coordinator
pointed out streets which had been hit frequently, the houses
which people had deserted, the walls which had been replaced
after having been destroyed. She drove us up and down all the
streets of the area, pointing out different neighborhoods, including a building in which a few young Americans lived after
their ski resort on nearby Mount Hermon had crumbled when
the fellow who led the project was extradited to the U.S. on
criminal charges. One of the girls connected with that scheme
was now working as a midwife in the maternity ward of the
health center.*

*The coordinator pointed out a school built of flimsy ma-
terial which had been hit a few times without anyone being
hurt, but after which the parents had refused to send their children to this school. She showed us how "security rooms" were
being built onto private homes, explaining that the order of
building was related to the number of children in the family.
She demonstrated how new buildings in the area were being
built with security in mind, so that a new daycare center
looked very strong in contrast to the older homes next to it. A
new school was built for retarded children and the neighbors
were angry that this fine building should not be used to protect
normal children, and demanded that they be allowed to use it as
a shelter and sleep in it at night. She explained that this was the
place into which the Indian families had unsuccessfully tried to
come, stressing how a physician who had seen her go out that*

*night to help had told her she was crazy and that he would
never go himself. I began to realize that the rockets bring interpersonal conflict in their wake, some of which can be quite
ugly: do healthy children have priority over retarded ones, do
some people act selfishly in times of crisis thereby endangering
others, do others resent people's courage since it contrasts with
their own cowardice?*

*She showed·us the road that led to the area in which the
families I would visit lived. I was very frightened for she said it
was a little distance from town and I was afraid to leave.* Somehow it was "safer" around people. *I was relieved when she said
we'd go there some other time. . . .*

She drove us to the neighborhood school. It was nearing
twilight. I was becoming more and more nervous. *We got out of
the car and walked over to a plaque that had been put up in
memory of the school custodian and his daughter who had died
in the last shelling. The coordinator told us the story of their
deaths . . . (as I was to hear so many times again). Now no one
will go near the little house, no one will move into it even
though there is a housing shortage. There is a kind of taboo on
it as if the house is unsafe, because that particular unlucky man
lived there; it was the scene of death, as if death lingered on it.
Of course the man wasn't killed in the house or because of the
house, but it belonged to him. I think it is important to look at
the taboo on the house not so much as irrational behavior (certainly the house contains no danger) but as an act (or a negative
act) which people engage in to keep themselves safe. . . .*

*From there we drove to other spots which had been
shelled. Each spot had its accompanying story. . . . Then we
drove to the west side of the dividing highway, beginning to
climb the slopes and foothills. When we reached the highest
point we got out of the car once again and had a view of the
general layout of the town. The coordinator pointed out the
factories and the lights of the various kibbutzim beginning to
twinkle in the valley.* All I wanted to know was where the danger was going to come from. *She showed where Mount Hermon
and Fatahland were. This is where the guerillas operated. The
rockets usually came from the north rather than from the west
over the mountain. It was difficult for me to understand exactly
where the danger could be expected.*

We stopped in a grocery store to buy some provisions for

the next day. The saleswoman was physically deformed; the customers were very pregnant. They were talking about how they had spent lots of time waiting to see doctors at the health clinics. A young boy wandered in and one of the women asked him to deliver her watch to someone. It seemed like everyone knew each other or were even related. I gawked at these people as if they had horns, wondering, "How can you stand living here —it's so dangerous!"

We returned to the car and started driving out of town toward the kibbutz where the wedding was to take place. On the way the coordinator told us that a local community organizer had jokingly told her he was not glad to see her back in town, because since she is studying the effects of shelling, there is bound to be shelling when she's around. She's like a bad omen. (Here was my second example of irrationality, and this time on the part of an educated person.) He also called her a name which is a combination of her name and the Hebrew word designating the rocket. (Here was my first instance of grim humor.)

I asked her when the last shelling was and when the next would be expected. *She answered that the last one was about five or six weeks ago and the next one, "No one knows." People felt that they were in a respite period right now.*

We drove down the main road built on the west side of the valley, at the furthest possible distance from the Golan Heights, with a single file of leafy trees shielding it from the now Israeli-held territory. The road runs along the bottom of the mountains, along the top of which runs the Israeli-Lebanese border, once so quiet, and now so dangerously active. We turned into the kibbutz to which we had been invited and walked into a large, grassy yard where a platform had been erected on which three couples were being married. Many kibbutz members, friends, and relatives were standing around the platform, not paying much attention to the ceremony. Children were scrambling everywhere. The coordinator was very excited to be at the kibbutz because she had many friends there whom she hadn't seen in a while. No one came up to us, however, and I felt lost and out of place. Not knowing any of the couples being married, in addition, made me feel awkward to be at their wedding.

When the ceremonies were over we wandered over to an-

other grassy field where tables had been set up. People began taking seats and we stood awkwardly at the side. After a long while the coordinator went off looking for our host. I was very tired and eventually sat down at one of the tables. After a while the three of us (team members) began to eat. I felt increasingly like the leader of the other two, somewhat less inhibited in terms of asking questions or acting to satisfy my needs. I saw myself asserting myself probably in order to carve out an identity of my own, and not merely to be "one of three." This is probably what was behind my not wanting to clean the apartment and my being the first to sit and eat.

Eventually the coordinator returned and said our host had been waiting for us in her house—there was a table reserved for us elsewhere. We climbed over all the sitting, eating people to get to our new places, our hosts joined us, we exchanged a few words, had some more to eat, and then the festivities began. A show was being presented in honor of the marriages: songs by a trio, a movie, pantomime, jokes, dances, songs by a small choir, and a play. The play was long, complicated, but very well done. I had a hard time understanding it. In the middle of the play I heard loud noises that sounded like thunder, and then quick, sharp sounds that sounded like machine-gun fire. No one appeared to notice it except me. I turned to face the coordinator and she gave me a knowing look. I asked her what it was, and she said, "That's it, those are the booms" (the word used to describe the sound of shells). We couldn't really talk about it right then and there because there was a play going on, but I became incredibly frightened, tried to figure out how close, exactly what it was, was I going to die, why didn't anyone get up and do something? *Must the play go on?* I wanted to get up and run back to Jerusalem. *I didn't want to go on with the "stupid" project. What I couldn't understand was that everyone else seemed to be so calm. Did they live like this everyday? Did they bring up children like this, always hearing terrible noises? Had they already sent out patrols to scout for the enemy? Did everyone but me realize that the booms were really far away and was I just oversensitive, easily frightened?*

The sounds stopped. Eventually the play was over too. I sheepishly brought up the subject of the noises. Our kibbutz host said that a new road was being blasted out. That seemed to end the discussion. Of course I was incredulous. Could they

*really be building a road at night? Was this just a clever way of
frightening the enemy or fending off the danger of working in
daylight? Or was this just a "story" the host had made up to
allay my fears?*

We talked about other things, *walked over to the dining
room and joined in the folk dancing there.* I felt so much safer
when the lights were on *(it had been dark under the open sky
during the play),* when there were people around whom I could
see talking, laughing, doing things. *By the time I was dancing I
had "forgotten about" those horrible sounds. . . .*

*In the car on the way home to the apartment I talked to
the coordinator about how frightened I was, saying, "I don't
want to sound like a little child, but since I am new to this situation and since you have been here many times before, can
you give me any advice as to what to do?"* I can't remember
much of the advice but I know I felt better just for the talking.
*She did say that we should get to know our next-door neighbor
in our apartment building and ask her what she does (we never
did this); we should go downstairs to the reinforced blast wall in
case of a shelling; we should check out the big underground
shelter nearby. The other team members were either not scared
at all or at least less scared than I was. They had lived in Israel
all their lives, had been in the army; one had been in Eilat once
when it had been attacked and claimed she slept right through
it.*

*We drove "home" from the kibbutz to the town. When
we arrived at our building, one of the girls and the coordinator
went inside and the other team member and I walked over to
the large, underground shelter that was a hundred yards or so
away. On the ground surface there were several odd projections
and we had a hard time finding the entrance. After walking all
over the area we found it.* I was extremely frightened again and
had on my mind the point that had been raised during the conference, that some residents of the town are afraid to enter the
shelter at times of danger because they believe there are terrorists hiding in it waiting for the Israelis to come in. I was too
ashamed to admit to my companion that I was troubled by this
rumor. *As I walked down the stairs and turned the various cor-
ners, I was preoccupied by this thought. Inside the large space
of the shelter, however, there was nothing but a few stones and*

some dust. I saw the water supply, the power generator, the thick doors, and the ventilation section. I realized that the shelter I was standing in was called the "deluxe" type because it was large, reinforced, had various conveniences, and was considered effective against gas warfare, in contrast with the older, tinier, shallower shelters.

Nevertheless, unless special provisions were made by the families, I cannot imagine people sleeping there night after night. Did they set up cots, beds, sleeping bags on the floor? How many people used a shelter? What happened with husbands and wives? Could anyone actually sleep, what with conditions inside and shelling outside? Who actually used the shelters, who didn't, and why? What does it mean, symbolically, to crawl back into the earth for shelter? Do people have a sense of security from knowing that they are in the most modern kind of shelter, or feel particularly insecure knowing that such a shelter had to be built for them?

Knowing a little more about the general layout made me more comfortable. Because I noticed a tight feeling in my stomach when I entered the apartment, I asked the coordinator if, in her connection with the health department, she had become aware of special physiological problems related to fear, such as ulcers, heart trouble, nervous disorders. Although she didn't know specifically, she assumed that everyone in town takes pills. Can anyone bear to work at night, or does working through the night enable people to get their minds off their fear?

The coordinator left the apartment. Now I wanted to cling to the team members for safety, *but everyone was tired. My bed was situated right beneath an open window and* I asked them to help me move it to an adjoining wall, which was "further away from Fatahland." *I crawled into bed numb with fear. It was approaching midnight. The radio was at my side and I listened to the news.* The familiar voice of the broadcaster was reassuring; *he was like a friend connecting me with the safe center of the country. I dreaded the end of his calm report. Then the national anthem was played, signaling the end of a broadcast day.* My worst moment was the start of the silence, *the blank void at the end of the anthem.* I prayed to God *to somehow get me through the damn project. I lay tense on the bed,* straining my ears for booms or for the start-up of the siren. The demands of this alertness exhausted me *even further and I fell into a deep sleep.*

This condensed version of my field notes describes the thoughts and feelings I experienced. These reactions became clues to behavior that I noticed later in other people or that were reported to me about other persons. It is evident that certain situations were conducive to stress—night as compared with day, being alone as compared with being with others, passivity as compared with being active, not understanding what was going on as compared with being informed, and not expressing fear as compared with being able to discuss feelings and ask for advice. These preoccupations were not dismissed as personal "static"; instead, they were recorded daily and took shape in the generalization that *being afraid or insecure is* experienced as *a relative state.* I was afraid during the day, but less so than at night. My sense of security was always changing, and the direction of the change accounted for my overall sense of security.

In the feedback-consulting phase of the project, our team suggested that mental health efforts be directed at making people feel *safer,* since they could not guarantee making people feel *safe.* Analysis of my field notes indicated that an increased feeling of security accrued from being active rather than passive. One way of warding off fear and distracting attention from fearful thinking was simply to be active. Having responsibilities was an antidote to feeling powerless. Activity and responsibility gave me the sense of being connected with a future that would arrive because I had commitments to fulfill. Experientially, I discovered the "compulsion to act" by observing myself constantly attempting to do something to feel safer: I moved my bed to the wall opposite the window; I crossed the street to be further from danger; I avoided "suspicious" objects by changing my path; I kept moving rather than standing still (Is a moving target harder to hit?); I tried to go indoors whenever possible, even if the building was not secure; I moved away from windows. If I could find a way of acting on my own behalf, I felt better than if I had done nothing, even if I knew the action I had taken would not physically protect me. My subsequent reading revealed that students of disasters have identified this compulsion to act *after* a disaster has struck:

> A phenomenon operative in disaster situations leads toward an oft-reported "compulsion toward activity." The phenomenon is reminiscent of Parsons' observation that in medical practice, uncertainty and incurability of certain medical cases result in a "bias in favor of operating" which he likens to Pareto's need to manifest sentiments by external acts. Thus Harry Williams writes, "We know that in the early stages of disaster, rescuers, helpers, and officials feel a great urgency to act—to do something" (Loomis, 1962, p. 126).

The phrase I coined to combine the ideas of relative safety and compulsion to act is making oneself (or one's ego extensions or social network) safer by *making differences*. Both rational and irrational acts are undertaken to create a sense of change. One feels safer by virtue of acting. I could walk down a street terrified, or, if I let myself believe that one side of the street was safer, I could deliberately go to that side and continue walking in a more secure frame of mind. My experiential understanding of the psychological value of seemingly irrational behavior became an additional framework with which to review my field notes and to categorize many functional irrational behaviors, such as creating taboos around secondary victims and objects, collecting disaster-related objects as souvenirs, defining evil omens, and projecting danger onto others.

When I heard the booms at the kibbutz wedding, I did not run to the shelters because no one else did. My escape impulse was counteracted by the presence of hundreds of calm people, by the group norms of not interrupting the status quo and ignoring the disruption. My startling experience of the individual's subjugation to the group norm alerted me to the effects of groups on individual behavior: A nervous group made me nervous, a calm group calmed me. What would it take to change a group's morale in a given instance or its coping behavior in general (Ginath and Krasilowsky, 1970)?

The people around me were not only important because they provided norms or morale but because I could imagine myself being physically protected by them in case of an emergency. My desire simply to be with others was an attenuated form of clinging for protection. Perhaps one of the reasons the team members discussed life until the early hours of every morning was because if we had gone to bed immediately, we would have symbolically "let go" and been more afraid. Similarly, while interviewing the father of one Indian household, I suddenly heard a boom and spontaneously reacted by throwing myself into his arms for protection. His initial impulse was to run to the nearest window to see what had happened. Gradually, simply seeing others in their daily tasks or looking them in the eye gave me courage and the feeling that together we would be able to cope.

I also experienced the strength and potential demoralizing effect of rumors. The rumor reported at the symposium that terrorists had invaded the shelters made me reluctant to use them. Although I had been reassured that the rumor was unfounded, I was left with a nagging doubt. The image of security and inviolability of the shelters had been sullied. In addition, their dirty, unkempt appearance made them uninviting. They had a negative image even if they were deluxe. We suggested to the public health nurses and the Histadrut committee that frightening rumors, endemic in situations of uncertainty where people seek information and explanations (Danzig, Thayer, and Galanter, 1958), should be acknowledged and addressed rather than ignored. People display a willingness to believe so that their incomprehensible and frightening situation can be cognitively organized. These rumor-defying or fear-reducing explanations must be plausible. In a kibbutz study, child care workers who explained away the children's fears by saying, "A stupid member of the kibbutz put the siren in action," or by asking "Wasn't it nice in the shelter?" after leaving the shelter at night did not allay the children's fears (Pergamenter, 1970, p. 3). In addition, shelters and other protective devices that appear neglected convey a nonverbal message that they are not highly valued, whereas a well-kept shelter enhances a sense of security.

My ability to think clearly was affected by fright and extreme alertness. Frequently I found myself deaf to what people were saying because my fear crowded out their words. For this reason my initial field notes indicated little retention of the advice of the project coordinator concerning behavior in case of attack. Under stress such as fear, the senses can be partially immobilized. In the very beginning of my stay, I was aware of being afraid to look around too much, as if I became more vulnerable when I opened my eyes. I was told that some people believe that by continuing to read a newspaper held in front of their face, the rocket will not "see" them. The inability to hear, see, concentrate, or move (a modified paralysis of fear) represents an overstimulation of one feeling that crowds out other senses. By contrast, in addition to being unable to hear when obsessed by fear, I began to hear "extra" sounds. I continuously heard sirens despite the fact that not a single civil defense siren was actually sounded while I was in the town. I also experienced optical illusions. Similarly I had the illusion that each evening it appeared more people were in cafes and parks than had ventured out the evening before, although this was undoubtedly not the case.

In the mental hospital study, I described the inability to remain alert for extended periods. Gradually, a normalization effect occurs; the emergency state becomes normal; boredom, fatigue, and everyday concerns arise and predominate. The fact that one has survived the danger thus far needs to be explained: "Maybe I'm one of the lucky ones since I made it until now," or "Maybe I exaggerated the danger since nothing has happened to me." Fear cannot remain at a crisis stage; eventually it becomes routine. The play goes on, the research project makes demands, meals must be prepared, and laundry washed, whether or not one is afraid. The balance between focusing on security needs and satisfying other needs shifted, so that by the end of the project my desire to learn about the team, the families, and the consultation process predominated. I shifted my concern from dealing with fear to planning what I would do in case of a shelling, since I was able to think of the shelling as a future event rather than as an immediate threat. I coped because everyone else did. I developed my own coping strategies and adopted some I observed in others. Coping with fear in the town was both a very public and a very private affair, and my method of experiential analysis helped me understand the relation between the two.

The Whyte, Fox, Roy, and Wax excerpts are examples of researchers' personal experiences that lead to insights into the social psychological dynamics of a setting or phenomenon. In my case, as in theirs, I fortuitously recognized that I was coping with fear as were the families I was studying. And since my interest was both in substantive and methodological issues, I utilized the insights both for understanding my research problem and for defining an extension of sociological method. By labeling it "experiential analysis," I converted some random insights into a deliberate search for sociological understanding. With this "discovery of method," I embarked on a continuous explication of my own experiences, which became an additional source of data. Whereas Fox, Whyte, Roy, Wax, and others describe their field research as if the insight was fortuitous, I developed an ongoing, *deliberately* reflexive method. Realizing that the value of my experience as a data source depended on capturing it in as pristine and uncensored a state as possible, I kept my observations straightforward and exact, recording even fleeting feelings. I distinguished between the experience and its interpretation, which would be undertaken at a later time. My method consisted of intensive self-awareness or self-observation and exact recording of experiences. Were the method to end there, we would have introspective autobiography. In sociology the autobiography can be extended by creating a *concept* that includes the experiential data. Rather than describing all other cases, an idea is proposed that includes the data which generated it and that elucidates other cases. Experiential analysis is a process similar to creating a language. Once the vocabulary becomes rich enough to communicate, the new insights are recycled in the feedback consultation process to see if setting members can learn or use them and thus to determine if the language is private or public.

Experientially grounded sociology also differs from autobiography in that it can be done in teams. Several running records embellish a single experience and provide a check on self-deception. Team self-deception is also possible. The courtesy norm can prevent team members from pointing out one another's self-deception. As long as experiential analysis is grounded in interaction (in this case with team members, family members, and consultees) and its fruits are publicly shared, self-deception is less likely. With increased practice, situations, and sharing, hollow or idiosyncratic statements can be avoided. Glaser and Strauss (1967) suggest the method of "constant comparison" of new cases to check the idiosyncratic nature of a given case. I would add the comparison of the same case by different team and setting members.

Months after our research project left the field, the coordinator and I critically examined each concept for self-deception. We still have doubts about the group dynamics material because the perspective of the member who withdrew is lacking. We now accept the incompleteness of our understanding, particularly since it was subject to the special hazards of group research. Experiential analysis cannot solve all methodological problems, but it can resolve the dilemmas I experienced in my own work using two major research methods. Experiential analysis provided me with a working methodology which will reveal its own particular problems as I use it in future studies.

Experiential Analysis

Experiential analysis is my methodological resolution of the inadequacies of survey empiricism and participant observation. That which constitutes data in this alternative approach enabled me to utilize *the experiences I was having* in the team, with the study families, and with the community professional consultees so that I could better understand the experience of living in this Israeli town. Experiential analysis assumes that what one person experiences is related to or reflects psychosocial arrangements and forces, so that to explicate the former is to illuminate the latter. Everyone has access to his own experience, although people are differentially aware of, interested in, or able to describe their experiences. Some psychologists (S. W. Dixon, 1978; T. R. Dixon, 1978) claim that since almost all people are unable to describe their experiences accurately without training, a "subject empirical" method is needed with which trained psychologists can capture primary units of experience for later use in research designs. It would be unfortunate if experience became the exclusive province of specialists, but it is true that awareness of and reflection on experiences can be greatly enhanced with practice.

The instrument in experiential analysis is the experiencing *self* in its observing, interacting, acting, and sensing. The human or social studies should use human tools for a trained human examination. Speaking of psychiatry, Coles (1975, p. 12) said: "I think that our own lives and problems are part of the therapeutic process. Our feelings, our own disorders and early sorrows are for us in some fashion what the surgeon's skilled hands are for his work. . . . The psychiatrist's hands are himself, his life." Experiential analysis does not require the differentiation of researcher from the people being studied. In that sense, it is a humble methodology. The researcher is not elite or aloof but becomes the subject of his own investigations. The experiential method of the sociologist matches the method of the members of any social unit to make sense of the world. The sociologist shares with others the task of making sense of one's social environment. Unlike interviewing, which requires interviewers to remember and report and thus requires disruption of action, experiential analysis attempts to understand social reality as it is occurring so that nothing will be lost over time or distorted by language.

Experiential analysis violates the ground rule of most social sciences—striving for objectivity. But it does so after criticizing the naive view of objectivity that permits the alteration of phenomena in order to operationalize concepts, create experimental conditions, or produce quantifiability. All of these operations do not create objectivity but a series of "as if" conditions. In social science, objectivity refers to knowledge that can be replicated by other investigators using identical methods, thereby demonstrating that the effects of the particular investigator are inconsequential. The reliance on these substitutes for experience and the mainstream notion that personal experience contaminates objective knowledge have led some researchers to express pride that they are experientially unfamiliar with their research subject: "Because of the timing of the program, there was no way to see a Great Books group in action before the questionnaire was completed. [My record is still perfect. I have never actually seen a Great Books discussion, despite several years of almost full-time work on this project.] " (Davis, 1964, p. 224). This is the paradigm of unembodied sociological research whose yield is not knowledge of reality as it is but rather the reflection of reality on instruments, records, and other tests.

Questionnaires yield information about the way respondents respond to questionnaires or to being questioned under certain circumstances; this information does not necessarily correlate with the respondents' actions, with how they might respond to others, or even with answers to questions worded differently. In the journey from the respondents' confrontation with a questionnaire through all the stages to report publication, information is manipulated, lost, or changed, so that the resultant picture bears dubious resemblance to the "reality" being investigated. Experiential analysis is purposefully direct, collapses the distance of time, and eliminates intervening instruments.

Although experiential analysis stems from a critique of objectivity as the purpose of research, it does not fall into the trap of simple-minded subjectivity. It goes "back behind the objectivity of science to the life-world" (Gadamer, 1975, p. 225). It is a form of research, not a form of being. The introspective subjective position is expanded so that the researcher is reflecting on experiences embodied in action and interaction during the course of ongoing, patterned social events. The meaning is created in between action and reflection, and this is the meaning that the researcher strives to capture. The experiential researcher stands at the intersection of subjectivity and objectivity, between the observer and the thing observed. Eliminating all instruments other than the reflective self experiencing naturally occurring "publically observable events" (Fischer, 1976, p.

5), the experiential researcher looks inward and outward. This stance allows "direct and immediate observation of the interacting social and personal worlds" (Reynolds and Farberow, 1976, p. 33). In the framework of experiential research, setting members become a context and thus create opportunities for the researcher's experience to develop. The researcher's involvement with a human context, rather than detachment as in the objective model, produces an analysis contingent on an involved stance.

If the researcher's self is the instrument by which the investigation proceeds, then that instrument must be well understood. For this reason I have urged the social researcher to undergo some form of systematic self-analysis as part of training. If the researcher's "biographical presence" (Fischer, 1976, p. 6) participates in a context to create perceptions or interpretations, then the biography of events, relationships, and ideas that the researcher has experienced demands clarification. Self-understanding must then be coupled with courage—the ability to describe and disclose publicly the researcher's emerging self-knowledge and understanding of the research site. Only if that selfhood is communicated to the reader as befits a truly rational framework can the reader assess the research project, its instrument, and its findings.

Experiential analysis refers to two kinds of experience: the experience of *being a researcher* and the experiential data collected from subjects or from the researcher with regard to a substantive issue. Experiential analysis seeks to restrict itself to experiential data, remaining on the level of the "inner story." Such an analysis can be produced concerning any condition which would permit a researcher to be a temporarily affiliating insider. Experiential research is presented as a constructed logic-in-use rather than as reconstructed logic. By *constructed* I mean that the research project's relevant components for organizing data emerge in the field instead of being predetermined. In the cases presented in the preceding chapters, the components of dilemmas and blocks, competing identities in fieldwork, group dynamics of team fieldwork, and mutual impact of temporary affiliation became relevant and may have some generalizability;

other projects will construct their own conceptual structures. Only if we abandon our desire to control research will we discover what is really there, because what we see will be what is presented to us rather than what we have created through our control.

The analyses of reflective research contribute to our understanding of the real similarities and differences among research enterprises, in contrast with the contrived uniformity of method. Experiential analyses begin with the reflexive researcher, who can examine settings to which there is no problem of access (see the categories of "timely events, familiar social situations, and special expertise" in Riemer, 1977), or the researcher can adopt the identity of another person in order to approximate that experience (Reynolds and Farberow, 1976). Experiential research is always intentional, however, and thus is distinguished from subjective or intuitive being-in-the-world. The reflective self of the researcher accompanies natural action rather than detached introspection or experimental authoritarianism. Through this natural action, the reflective researcher collects data about the social impact of the environment on persons and relationships.

Attention should be directed toward the feelings, behaviors, and thoughts of others and of the researcher. The quality of this attention is of overriding significance; it is "be here now" consciousness, an openness to the world as it is lived rather than a shrinking fear of bias; it is not a perspective backward to remembered concepts or forward to anticipated analysis. "Be here now" consciousness means that the researcher neither suppresses the self nor tries to repress or control others. The researcher engages, collaborates, lets happen, questions, follows, not knowing the outcome in advance. Such an attitude is crucial lest the researcher waste the opportunity for learning from the natural situation by imposing on it external categories to which his or her attention is directed. We could then criticize not for the problem of bias but for the error of waste.

The phenomenologists' method also consists of experiential analysis, but its intention is the isolation of essences that underpin these experiences. "Husserl does not want any induc-

tion or deduction but solely intuition on the basis of a very
exact analysis and description. None of the methods used by
the other sciences can be of value here, because they have to
presuppose something in addition to what is actually given,
while in the field of primordial phenomena presuppositions are
simply inconceivable. . . . Every originally given intuition is a
legitimate source of knowledge" (Kockelmans, 1967, p. 29).

Schachtel's (1959) comments on childhood consciousness
evoke the intuition of those primordial phenomena. Schachtel
describes the child's ability to have exhilarating, fresh, new,
wonder-full experiences, which are unlabeled, unique, concrete,
and full of life. For example, a preverbal child becomes fas-
cinated with a moving, purring, furry, soft cuddly thing. The
child grasps the thing, has an inchoate idea of it, but can recognize it when it comes around again. Maybe he will even make up
or ask for a word for this thing. The child then learns to collapse his images into the sound "cat" when referring to it.
"Cat" as a sound has no relevance to what the child has sensed,
but the child wishes to please and communicate with his parents, so he allows language to modify and finally replace his
private understanding of the thing.

> There is an incompatibility of experience with lan-
> guage and a consequent forgetting of experience or its
> distortion by the cliché of language. . . . Like the search
> for truth, which never reaches its goal yet never can be
> abandoned, the endeavor to articulate, express, and com-
> municate an experience can never succeed complete-
> ly. . . . The schemata provided by the culture and gradu-
> ally acquired by the growing child cannot accommodate
> his experience in its entirety, but will distort and bias it
> according to the patterns of the culture [Schachtel, 1959,
> pp. 295-297].

The closer we are to the child's original image, the closer
we are to the thing itself rather than to the assumptions, labels,
terms, borrowed notions, clichés, and conventions with which
we are prone to structure reality and thereby forget experience.
The predefined concepts of the social scientists are particularly

effective in conventionalizing experience so that we have difficulty remembering the referents of these predefined concepts in
a reality we can recognize. Phenomena are not the same as their
labels or descriptions. The representation is never the thing itself. The territory is not the map. But there are better and
worse maps. As we label, describe, and construct our linguistic
maps, we move away from the phenomena. If we *start* with
labels, we have excluded experience altogether. In experiential
research, the intention is to notice and explicate experience in
its own terms or in terms that leave the experience whole and
accessible.

Husserl developed a method for constructing a complete
philosophy grounded in perceptions distilled by a process of
continuous reduction to ultimate, original, general essences.
Phenomenology as a method prescribes the continuous reduction of experience to locate essences. Experiential analysis is
similar in its interest in grounding a social science in experience
rather than an interest in instruments or contrived situations,
but it is not the same as phenomenology since I do not regard
experiences as problematic or in need of reduction. Instead,
they are in need of attention, pursuit, analysis, and connection
with other phenomena.

Gendlin (1965-1966) offers a clear discussion of the relation between experience and its explication by proposing two
criteria for explication: First, since we have independent access
to experiences (in other words, we "know" something before
naming it), we can apply a name and see if it leads us back to
the phenomenon. "The formulation must first 'lift out' the phenomenon and make us sense it concretely and specifically. . . . The phenomenon permits independent access. We can
reject the formulation—perhaps it has inconsistencies, bothers
us, is wrong for some purposes, or now seems an insufficient
description of the very phenomenon to which it led us. . . . Still
we do not unnotice the directly noticed phenomenal aspect we
were led to" (Gendlin, 1965-1966, p. 22). We check the formulation's fit by reliving the phenomenon, just as we constructed
the formulation by living the phenomenon.

Gendlin's (1965-1966, pp. 4-5) second validity test is the

presence or absence of a felt response when the formulation is applied. "There is no problem here about recognizing which statements genuinely function in this way, as compared to the thousands of possible statements that would bring about no response in the directly felt datum, lift out nothing, and leave everything unchanged." Proust's *A La Recherche du Temps Perdu* is dedicated to an explanation of this felt response.

In his discussion of the subjective nature of scientific knowledge, Polanyi (1958) described the felt response to a completed theory that helps to explicate *our* experiences rather than only those being accounted for. This felt response in others arises if the researcher communicates the felt response he experienced when generating his explications.

Diesing (1971) described how this process functions in the social sciences.

> One consideration that induces the holist to persevere in using his method despite its weaknesses and despite the slanders heaped on it, is his feeling that it gets at something real that other methods miss. This sense of what is real or unreal is what I have called an "implicit ontology." Perhaps ontology is too formidable a word for what is more a matter of vivid, immediate experience. . . . The experience of which I speak may be described as a sense of communion with something vivid and fulfilling, of being at home with something that reacts and responds to one's actions. . . . A holist finds his experience of reality in the human community [p. 286].

There is a debate as to whether this criterion of a felt response of comprehension or recognition is an alternative to logical or mathematical validity, as is commonly used in social science, or if it must accompany other forms of evaluation. The argument is between the "either/or" position and the "and" position. Are the experiential and so-called objective social science methods mutually exclusive or additive? Are they rivals or allies (Spiegelberg, 1972, p. 361)? In the alliance model, the reliability and validity checks of traditional methods can be applied to the experiential findings (Reynolds and Farberow, 1976), but how then are inconsistencies resolved?

All interpretation, as does science generally, strives for clarity and verifiable proof. Such proof of understanding will be *either* of a rational, i.e., logical or mathematical, *or* of an emotionally emphatic, artistically appreciative, character. Rational proof can be supplied in the sphere of behavior by a clear intellectual grasp of everything within its intended context of meaning. Emphatic proof in the sphere of behavior will be supplied by complete sympathetic emotional participation [Weber, 1964, p. 30; emphasis added].

The experientially oriented sociologist must engage the reader in the same attitudes of engagement as he held toward his own experience and to that of the subjects. Although the criterion of adequacy in experiential analysis is that the explication is true to the experience and thus produces a felt response in the researcher and potentially in the reader (the reader's capacity for openness and comprehension are mitigating factors here), I would argue that to be valid the explication should have viable action outcomes. One should be able to act and understand future events in terms of what has been discovered. Subsequent action thus becomes a source of refinement on the insights derived from experiential analysis. Adequacy draws on the researcher's sense of closure, rather than on an external, nonparticipative judge, to determine that significant parts of the whole are not absent. The explication thereby expresses the humanness of both the researcher and the subject matter studied. An unembodied researcher or a mechanistic subject betrays a lack of experiential analysis.

The following controversial item should be added to this list of alternative indexes of adequate knowledge: The explication must "make sense" to members of the setting. Kaplan (1964) has discussed this problem as the "instrumental function" of adequacy. Embedded in this criterion is the paradox that understanding might arise less from the explication itself than from "the effect produced by helping others see an explanation. The act of explaining produces the effect, not the explanation itself" (A. Kaplan, 1964, p. 356). Factors other than the explanation might create the impression of understanding. This perspective falls within the interactionist tradition of sociology, as exemplified in the works of Becker (1963) and Glaser and Strauss (1967). Such an argument does not invalidate the value of applying this criterion but compels examination of what these other factors are and how they work. These need to be experienced and explicated.

The rigor of experiential analysis is expressed in accountability rather than replicability. Experiential researchers are willing to live by their findings and have those findings subjected to the scrutiny of the setting members because they are grounded in lived experiences. The results of the attempt of application are not definitive since they generate new experiences that need explication and analysis. Even so, accountability is almost nonexistent in most sociological studies since researchers are satisfied with statistical significance without the test of application.

Experiential analysis produces not *information about* something, as is the case in objective studies, but rather intimate *knowledge that* something is the case, knowledge of, or *knowledge for* some purpose. It derives its certainty from the irrefutability of the researcher's having lived through whatever is being studied. Experiential analysis is a pursuit of directness and immediacy; it is not only "instrumentless research" but also the adoption of a stance of complete surrender to the experience.

The phenomenological method, if it can be spoken of as a single approach, reduces experiential data to their essences for the sake of constructing an absolute consciousness. A sociological experiential analysis accepts what is phenomenologically given in experience and then orders, interprets, and associates this material with other aspects of the social environment. The relationship between experiences and the situations that engendered them is sought. The interplay of reflexive, experiential data and the social situations that generate them are explicated in this form of *doing* sociology and *being* a sociologist.

Explication follows experience. Sociological methods with no experiential base create a foundation of imposed, misplaced, and possibly erroneous assumptions. The explication of experiential analysis will be in terms of gestalts, wholes, and perceivable entities that interpenetrate rather than in terms of variables in so-called causal relationships. The explication lifts phenomena from their contexts to display them in their own terms: not how much of something there is or how it compares with something else, but what it is and how it fits. Matza (1969, p. 9) offers a vivid definition of this research perspective, which he calls "naturalism": "There is a preference for concrete detail, an appreciation of density and variability, a dislike of the formal, the abstract, the artificial. Naturalism tends to begin with whatever confronts the human observer in his complete daily living and to endeavor to frame a satisfactory account of it in its own terms."

Experiential analysis studies experiences in their entirety, not dissected into dimensions or variables that have no experiential referent. It would study illness rather than temperature. The rules for such a sociological method can be adopted from the phenomenologists (Beckman and Mulderij, 1977) or from other social scientists (Bruyn, 1966; Reynolds and Farberow, 1976). The researcher can investigate his own experience in the reflexive sociology advocated by Gouldner (1970), adopt the identity of others, or extend participant observation to employ an intentionally introspective perspective. Whatever the case, it is critical that the researcher begin with the experiences themselves—the original experiences, his own. I would urge the researcher to describe and analyze with as few assumptions, presuppositions, or definitions beforehand as possible, to separate interpretations of an event from the events themselves. Remove the instrument and get to the thing measured. Try to see things as they are without blinders, labels, or intermediaries. Try to experience the human dimension in its social context. Do the sociology as if your life depended on it.

In order to train for experiential analysis, the researcher should participate in settings that offer a wide range of experiences. Before beginning the study itself, the researcher should notice his own expectations; some will recede upon illumination, others will remain. As the researcher begins the study, the record of experience begins, which will only produce understanding if preconceptions are set aside. This is a supremely difficult task, which is achieved by adopting an attitude of openness to experiences.

The researcher in the study setting acts, responds, and

notices the experiences. The researcher also withdraws for short periods to reflect, describe, and share with others. The recording is done continuously, systematically. During explication, the action and sensations of the record are examined for patterns and themes. The product of this engagement is completely undefined and has no concern with "contamination." Experiential analysis directs sociologists to acquire their knowledge from their involvement in natural settings. The problem of the study is unknown in advance and emerges from the experiential data produced once the study has begun.

All situations are suitable for experiential analysis. Goffman (1963) and others have even taken "trivial" public behavior as a point of departure. Elaborate laboratories or trips to exotic field sites are not necessary. Experiential analysis can even be performed on situations the researcher did not choose to experience, such as patienthood or incarceration.

Experiential analysis is performed with minimal expectations of what will be created, rather than originating in the interest of supporting or proving a theory. Once the analysis has been conducted, however, its relation to other bodies of literature must be investigated so as to situate the analysis in the context of the shared community of scholarship. The limitation on expectations is always a dilemma, however, because residual attitudes are never suspended:

> At this point I must explain a difficulty I have in giving the reader an idea of the evidence on which I base my hypothesis. . . . I am bound to so describe an incident that it bears out my theory. I obviously must produce my hypothesis because I see events in particular ways, and there is no proof that the way I see them is accurate. The description then becomes little more than a repetition of a hypothesis clothed in terms of concrete events [Bion, 1961, p. 120].

Bion is describing a problem of circularity. This problem is diminished when experiential research is performed in relatively *unfamiliar* situations that force the researcher "to ask questions and study interrelationships among variables in order to survive and function in that role" (Reynolds and Farberow, 1976, p.

36). Hypothesis generation for the sake of one's own understanding is thus tested by the action that one takes.

Additional problems with the experiential method include not being able to explicate experiences that are unavailable to the researcher because they fall outside the realm of his identity attributes, such as race, age, sex, ethnicity, or bodily characteristics. Studies exist, however, in which even these attributes have been altered or disguised in order to gain an insider's view. In addition, other individuals with the appropriate attributes could be trained to obtain this relatively inaccessible data. But if I am prevented from experiencing the world through the personhood of those whose qualities I do not share, so too must I question objectivity-oriented researchers who remove themselves from the experience of others. I will never know the experience of others, but I can know my own, and I can approximate theirs by entering their world. This approximation marks the tragic, perpetually inadequate aspect of social research.

> We believe it is impossible for middle class academicians, white or black, to know, in the personal sense of being fully enmeshed in them, the constraints imposed on the lower class. Even though we lived there, felt the heat, the cold, the anxieties, the highs, the lows, the lack of control and so on, *we knew we could leave.* Going native, constraining ourselves to be without money, remaining for long periods of time, walking the streets with unemployed men, begging dimes on the corner for wine, or waiting in clinic lines with worried mothers and wounded children did not close off the single safety valve of being able to leave when the going got too rough. The social scientist who is supposed to understand and subjectively interpret the adaptations, life-style, values, etc. of the poor is in the position of not being able personally to assume the major underlying premise of lower-class life [Yancey and Rainwater, 1970, p. 247].

My reactions to this problem are twofold: Although I cannot experience the experiences of other people, I can experience their behavior and make statements about my experience, as long as I differentiate between the two (Laing, 1972). This stance requires attention both to my self as researcher and to the context of the observations I am making. The combination of self- and other-awareness is experiential research. The second solution is the notion of *teamwork*. A research team might include different members with different histories and different probable futures. Each member can experientially analyze the "same" set of events and coordinate the analysis around the same issues. Although still an approximation of the lived world, such a composite is richer than the single analysis of any one member. The closest approximation is the composite rather than the common denominator. The unique case is part of the picture. We are aiming for the best picture rather than an artificial cause and effect chain of variables. The approximation dilemma should be reflected in the language used to describe the work. Rather than arrogantly controlling the phenomenon, it seems more appropriate to express the tension of tentativeness, which is reduced by including the accounts of team members, setting members, or future researchers.

My experience as an ethnographer also convinces me that an ethnography can never be a faithful reflection of external reality. It should not be regarded as a direct translation of one realm of experience into another. Social psychiatrists' view of the culture of poverty, like any ethnographic formulation or like a formulation of individual personality or of history, will inevitably represent a dialectic resolution of a state of tension that has been generated between the observer and the material he seeks to understand. A completed ethnography is a tentative synthesis of that tension, a temporary resolution of a prolonged state of dialectic opposition. The tension may return as soon as others disagree with the formulation, either because new facts have come to light or because fresh concepts have been coined which render the account unsatisfactory. . . . Truth in social science is only a relatively stable equilibrium that has been established between the scientist and his critics after he has resolved the tension that existed between himself and the subject matter he sought to understand [Honigmann, 1969, p. 18].

My notion of temporary affiliation is intended to convey both the separateness of the researcher's and subject's experiences and also their commonality in terms of vulnerability and mutual impact.

Other pragmatic problems related to experiential analysis stem from its assessment by funders and publishers who assume a different framework of social research. The intellectual climate is not yet supportive, although there are signs that it is changing (David Reynolds, personal communication, 1978).

Another hazard is the emotional and physical involvement in the setting and with its persons, which enables the researcher to have illuminating experiences but renders him vulnerable. Even if the setting is not dangerous, the researcher opens himself up to the *risk* of being hurt by the community of subjects and scholars:

> Since the surrenderer can and wants to know and change as a result of knowing, he is prepared to sustain injury; and in both surrendering and acting on his catch, he may be hurt in various ways. For instance, my writing and talking about surrender have alienated some persons from me, and my professional prestige has suffered in their eyes—undoubtedly of more than I know. Yet injury sustained in surrender itself is seen by the surrenderer in its bearing on insight and involvement, for it does not come or threaten to come from any desire to hurt or be hurt [Wolff, 1971, p. 240].

Survey studies' risk of vulnerability to either community —that under study or that of scholars—is minimal. The lack of risk with subjects follows from the attempt to minimize "contamination." This makes antiseptic sociology. But the experiential sociology of natural environments renders the sociologist vulnerable to all the dangers that flesh is heir to. To be immune from the oppression, stress, or risk caused by one's subjects is to skew one's understanding completely. On the contrary, experiential study *depends on* the change or trauma occurring within the researcher. Such change is the penetration of the researcher by social reality. The explication of that penetration is experiential analysis.

The instruments of social science are trappings to make it resemble natural science and barriers to keep the researcher safe from involvement or risk. Stripping away instruments other than his self-awareness and powers of observation leaves him vulnerable to direct experience and accountability. Risk-taking researchers bring more than their reasoning powers and borrowed concepts to a study. They bring their bodies, their sense of self, their histories, and their future. Experiential analysis has as an ideal the elimination of distinctions between knowing and the means of knowing, between knower and known, between the dancer and the dance. Similarly, experiential analysis has as its ideal a multi-dimensional research product. In contrast to advancing the understanding of a substantive problem (the typical criterion of objective research), experiential analysis aims to deepen understanding and to change three levels simultaneously: the substantive issue, the research process, and the self of the researcher—person, problem, and method. Since experiential analysis compels critical self-awareness in the context of engagement with others to whom the researcher is accountable, experiential analysis is a form of praxis for the self and society.

CHAPTER 8

The Integration
of Person, Problem,
and Method

Several innovations in sociological concepts have emerged in this book: the characterization of socialization into an academic discipline as the dual search for identity and method; the redefinition of research in terms of the integration of person, problem, and method; and the development of a new method for sociological research—experiential analysis. To explore these issues, a processual rather than structural model of socialization has been adopted (Epstein, 1974). The focus has been on the changing perceptions of the self and the profession as the student moves through the undergraduate and graduate experience, the critical element of which is the sequence of research projects: "Research [is] the major mastery-inducing experience" (Bucher and Stelling, 1977, p. 211). Socialization has been viewed holistically through one case study over a substantial

369

period of time, rather than being dissected and reassembled from a large sample of inadequately understood cases under various conditions. The former approach is grounded in the lived experience of being-in-time of the person being socialized (see Schutz, 1962). An experiential method has thus been applied to a subject concerned with becoming.

One product of this study is the isolation of a tripartite set of criteria by which to evaluate social research. All projects should generate knowledge within the three components engaged in a research project: person, problem, and method. In this scheme, self-knowledge (person) is a necessary and publicly relevant product of social research. When I began my socialization, I adopted the textbook notion of research, which integrates problem and method and considers the researcher-as-person as irrelevant or as a potential source of bias. In the participant observation study, I revised the model to include *person*, problem, and method; in the experiential action study, the model further expanded to include person, team, problem, and method. Each subsequent project led me to recognize additional contextual features. The experiential analytic method that extends participant observation and that is my current resting point contains many desirable components of a valid, humanizing method for social research. I hesitate to propose experiential analysis, however, as the final answer to the search for method. Rather it is a personal but generalizable resolution that has its own problems. The context for its discussion here is "the search," which I have characterized as the dynamic force within the socialization process. It is interesting to contrast my distillation of "the search" as the key element of the socialization process based on my reflexive study with the conclusion of the Bucher and Stelling (1977) study that the experience of socialization is "working at constructing... identities" (p. 270). People being socialized search for a way to do the work of their identities, and in the doing they express their understanding and need for continuing the search.

The purpose of this case analysis has not been to impart an incremental bit of knowledge about a limited problem but to change the consciousness of the reader by questioning the assumptions and practices of various research methods. Such an impact would parallel my own change in outlook as I continuously reexamined various research experiences and their cumulative personal impact. My experience of socialization was the attempt to retain a sense of self as I adopted a new identity as a member of a problematic discipline. My feelings of identity wavered as I attempted to loosen the grip of objective science and reclaim my self as a knowing agent. Since my consciousness was changed during socialization, both with regard to liberation from certain conventions and openness to new forms, the account of that socialization must encourage readers to question their received notions and to envisage alternative modes of being a social scientist and doing research. The report of the search for a humanizing sociology has the potential of humanizing the reader by drawing attention to the reader's own experience.

These chapters have demonstrated the reciprocal relation between the researcher-as-person and the process of research. What do students learn about themselves and how do their perspectives on the profession of sociology become clarified as they become involved in research activities? In the role playing of research, the persons being socialized discover themselves and their profession. My descriptions of several project cases reveal how this mutuality changes over time, changes that reflect past experiences and future anticipations. *The formation of an identity represents the felt sense of completion of the search for a way of being.* Identity is thus the coalescence of learned skills and knowledge, the passage of time, and the resolution of conflicts in the social arena. The phrase "to make it" contains the hint that succeeding, arriving, and creating are interwoven in identity formation. For the socialization of sociologists, the development of identity and the adoption of a method within the context of a methodological stance are simultaneous processes.

There is a debate among psychologists, anthropologists, sociologists, and others about whether the personality changes after childhood (Brim and Wheeler, 1966). Since all societies provide for a sequence of expectable status and role changes for each member, and since contemporary society is characterized by "frequent and momentous passage from status to status" (Becker and Strauss, 1956, p. 263), then identity will change repeatedly throughout the life of an individual even if basic personality does not. The question is, How does the change occur? How do people acquire not only knowledge and skills, but attitudes and values as well? Why is it that some aspects change and others do not? How is it that the self is modified so that new attributes are not only situational but long-lasting? How are new "cognitive and normative frames of reference by which the individual defines and interprets life" (Gottlieb, 1960, p. 5) internalized?

Researchers have studied the changes that occur to persons processed in primary schools (Parsons, 1959), colleges (Feldman and Newcomb, 1969), professional training schools (Becker and others, 1961; Merton, Reader, and Kendall, 1957; Kadushin, 1969; Lortie, 1959; Olesen and Whittaker, 1968), corrections officer training programs (Blum, 1976), the army (Stouffer and others, 1949), occupations (Becker and Carper, 1956), and other social institutions. Those interested in the impact of graduate training (in the academic disciplines) on identity formation have isolated various factors that seem to be statistically significant in producing identity change: the role of the faculty (Gottlieb, 1960), the preliminary exam (Hall, 1968), and the teaching assistantship (Pavalko and Holley, 1974). These results reflect the methods that were used—primarily, analysis of survey questionnaire responses. They mention conflicts both during training and later on the job but do not suggest that identity formation is the very coming to terms with those conflicts. An experiential method, on the other hand, uncovers epistemological and ontological components to identity formation and change (see Becker and others, 1961; Olesen and Whittaker, 1968; Bucher and Stelling, 1977).

The Olesen and Whittaker (1968) study, based on participation with and observation of an entire nursing school class from entry to graduation, found that the students created "a constantly shifting phenomenological milieu in which the student came to ask herself continually where she stood in relation to her fellows, how she was doing vis-a-vis a beloved former self and a desirable future self, how and under what circumstances she should become as a nurse" (p. 291). In other words, socialization into a profession, as studied experientially, requires a true change of identity in that one acquires a new, although gradually approached, way of going about the business of knowing and being.

In accord with these latter studies, my own investigation suggests the importance of conceptualizing socialization not as a process of transfer but as one of development and conflict. Examples of the transfer model of socialization definitions are the following: Socialization is the "intergenerational transmission of culture" (Williams, 1975, p. 1), or socialization is "both cognitive learning and at least minimal internalization of appropriate norms" (Moore, 1969, p. 868). These are views from the socializers' perspective. The implication of the conservative transfer model is that there is a fixed body of skills, attitudes, values, and behavior patterns that students, recruits, novices, and others being socialized must adopt as their own. Students must attempt to acquire that which already exists. The process is complete when the student has incorporated the attitudes and values to such an extent that they are experienced as internal, or belonging to the new member. In this model, before socialization occurs the novice refers to "the profession's" values; after socialization occurs, he refers to them as "mine." Socialization is, therefore, the *cognitive* mastery of knowledge and skills plus *affective* internalization of the parent culture's norms and values, manifested in appropriate attitudes. Moore (1969, p. 869) states three tests of the quality of the introjection of norms: "compliance with norms—even if contrary to other immediate self-interests—in the absence of sanctions; manifestations of moral outrage at the misbehavior of others; and manifestations of guilt following personal misbehavior." Such an analysis presupposes a profession or occupation into which one is being socialized where compliance is possible because there is unanimity, uniformity, and consistency in its norms and visibility in its activity. In a consensus model such as Moore's (1969), "misbehavior," which might in fact be creative

rebellion, must succumb to self-imposed constraints in deference to the culture being internalized.

In his study of the socialization of prison staff, Blum
(1976) has shown that formal training is in conflict with the
real conditions of the job, so that those who have "successfully" internalized the formal norms are physically endangered.
Here again, socialization (the acquisition of an identity and a
method of action) requires the personal resolution of the inherent conflicts, not the simple adoption of the given definitions.
Defining socialization in terms of denying the self in order to
reduce conflict reflects and abets a society in which selves and
autonomous thought are endangered.

The process of socialization by which skills, values, and
attitudes are transferred and internalized, and by which the personality is transformed, occurs (to my mind) by way of the
resolution of problems. Sometimes these problems are encountered during formal training and sometimes shortly after taking
the first job (Lortie, 1959). What are these problems? The problem for many professions is the discrepancy between the
idealized lay image and the reality of the practice—the self is
transformed as the initiate comes to terms with the discrepancy
(see also Hughes, 1958). The problem in sociology is aggravated
by the lack of consensus as to what sociology is and should be
doing. As new members resolve the discrepancy during their
socialization, they simultaneously create an innovation for the
profession. Socialization is not merely the transfer from one
group to another in a static social structure, but *the active creation of a new identity through a personal definition of the situation.* As these resolutions are made, the initiate ventures into
more and more public exposure of private views and is confirmed by significant others. The newly forming self emerges by
way of *the private resolution of dissonance, the intimate interaction with significant others, and the public confirmation of
the new self through various ritualized events.* It might be stated
that socialization occurs through *the process of experiencing
and reducing cognitive dissonance with regard to the nature of
the new identity* (see also Festinger, 1957).

An element supporting my argument that socialization be

viewed either as a creative or as a conformist resolution of dissonance within a discipline is that this social psychological model parallels the Kuhn (1962) hypothesis explaining how research paradigms are institutionalized. In the following quotation, the words referring to changes in the status of science could be replaced by words referring to the individual being socialized:

> *Normal science* [graduate school] is a period of accumulation of knowledge in which scientists [students] work on, and expand, the reigning paradigm. Inevitably, however, such work spawns *anomalies,* or things that cannot be explained within the existing paradigm. If these anomalies mount, a *crisis* stage is reached, which ultimately may end in a *revolution* in which the reigning paradigm is overthrown and a new one takes its place. . . . A new *paradigm* is born and the stage is set for the cycle to repeat itself [Ritzer, 1975, p. 156].

Information about how this process is experienced is available only if sociological researchers make public their experiences as students and researchers. This is done occasionally and has been called "the informal sociology of research methods" (Miller, 1965, p. 39). The writing that does exist illustrates the process of dissonance reduction. "Research represents a series of accommodations from what is desirable to achieve to what is possible within a given social context and within a given folklore of research practices" (Form, 1971, p. 34). If we rely only on the study of others, the data we collect will be distorted by the researcher's or trainee's interest in appearing successful or by otherwise screening their self-reports (see Bucher and Stelling, 1977, p. 273). Socialization produces not only the acquisition of the skills but also knowing how to resolve the psychological and practical conflicts. An example of such a practical problem is the particular strain of role conflict encountered by women who are wives, mothers, and social researchers. Epstein (1970, p. 149) suggests that since the specific tasks of the researcher are not clear-cut, other role obligations encroach: "The researcher further suffers from imprecise deadlines and unfocused sanctions, so that his [sic] tasks easily can be deferred to meet the demands of another role when they become pressing."

My analysis of my own encounter with sociology—the problems it raised, and my accommodations and partial resolutions—is intended not only as a contribution to an understanding of the lived experience of socialization, but also to the body of self-critical research protocols that are so frequently called for. This self-critical literature reveals not only resolutions of problems within the method but also problems with the shaping of the self as a sociologist. If the purpose of sociological analysis is to transform the personal uneasiness of individuals into explicit public troubles (Mills, 1959, p. 5), then the personal uneasiness of my own socialization process is a problem to be explicated. The product of turning the sociological imagination back on itself to study the process of becoming a sociologist is an illustration of reflexive sociology (Gouldner, 1970). The use of experiential data integrates personal and public issues.

In order to be a sociologist and perform sociological research (and not just to teach the sociology created by others), practical conditions such as time, money, equipment, and a supportive network are necessary, but in addition, the sociological problem and method must be formulated. For some students, the substantive issues on which they work and the research methods that they use are taken from their teachers or the literature. For others, such as myself, the inadequacies inherent in the methods and the discrepancies between the formal description of these methods and their actual usage become a source of dissonance and disillusionment. The process of carrying out given methods is interrupted and suspended while the issue of identity strain is engaged. Some students struggle unsuccessfully with these dilemmas and retreat in frustration. They are called socialization failures. Others plunge head on into a confrontation with the inadequacies and contradictions, hoping to formulate a successful resolution that will become a way of doing sociology and becoming a sociologist. In another case similar to mine, as the student set out to do his major research project he tried to "reconcile for [himself] the commonly held approach to research in our field with [his] own personal orientation to reality" (Adshead, 1973, p. 3). He too devised an experiential method as a resolution of the dissonance he experienced in his socialization.

The three research projects I have described illustrate the process by which I grappled with the dilemmas in sociological research methods and attempted to construct tentative resolutions and revolutions. This aspect of my socialization process has progressed almost to the point of accepting a research method that will enable me to assume the identity of a social scientist. Accepting a discovered or a transmitted method and internalizing a professional identity are therefore simultaneous processes. Although one outcome of my search for method was an innovation or extension (experiential analysis), my companion discovery was that many "methods problems" are not resolvable but are dilemmas that must be experienced and endured. Being a sociologist will always mean becoming a sociologist and struggling with the continuously unmasked difficulties or inconsistencies in the field.

The basic dilemma of my socialization was the tension between becoming a member of the group and retaining my individuality and critical perspective. Could I become sufficiently, rather than completely, socialized? Socialization seemed to imply conformity. How much resistance is possible without diluting the identification? Is there room for deviance and innovation in the socialization process?

As the newcomers adopt and master appropriate skills and values, the peer group of fellow students and faculty supervise the transformation from recruit to member. It must always be kept in mind, but is frequently overlooked, that the recruit does not begin socialization abruptly or in a vacuum. Rather, students bring with them a set of anticipations, private agendas, and a web of social relations. The transformation of the "raw" student to the "fully cooked" member during training makes it possible for departments to exchange and therefore guarantees the social cohesiveness and continuity of the discipline (Stinchcombe, 1975; Diesing, 1971). The ultimate test of socialization is not merely the quality of the student's research but also the student's incorporation into the discipline's social network. Par-

ticipation and acceptance into the network reflect the evaluation of the student by the "exchange managers" and "keepers
of the myths" necessary for this exchange. The novice risks his
or her incorporation into the network by revealing the socialization experiences of dissonance, uncovered anomalies, and disillusionment. Ultimately, identity transformation involves personal work: learning not to be bothered, not to wonder, and
not to worry.

Becoming a sociologist means joining a team or clan and
demonstrating "loyalty to the collectivity" (Moore, 1969, p.
876) if one hopes to receive the benefits of membership. The
discipline as a "collective other" continuously checks the newcomer's behavioral products to determine appropriateness and
adequacy. The persistent possibility of failure perpetuates continuing occupational commitment. But fear of failure is accompanied by guilt of betraying the investment made by the elder:
"The creation of this obligation solidifies occupational attitudes
and loyalties. . . . The person feels he must remain what he has
become in order not to let down his sponsor" (Becker and
Carper, 1956, p. 298). The specific personalized commitment to
the socializers is generalized to an overall loyalty to the group in
which the socializers are imbedded and through which the rewards are produced. These processes underscore stability rather
than innovation, experimentation, or other forms of productive
deviance, such as eclecticism.

Socialization is complicated for those novices who recognize that there is conflict concerning the definition of sociology, the role model for the sociologist, and the proper role performance with regard to research activities. The struggle of the
initiate is the choice between addressing the myths (Stinchcombe, 1975), anomalies (Ritzer, 1975), and ambiguities
(Hughes, 1958) (thus risking embarrassment) and sustaining the
irrational conventions necessary to assure the functioning of
sociology as a social institution (thus risking alienation). Seeley
(1971, p. 175) expressed this conflict as follows: "For whatever
brave show sociologists might put on for others, and particularly for one another, doubts would not die down (and have not
yet) [for me] as to what sociology 'is'; and given some defini-

tion of what it is, as to whether such an enterprise is possible; and, given its possibility, of positive, zero, or negative utility."

This book traces the stages of my attempt to rid myself of my lay, idealized version of sociology after it had been deflated by my rude awakening as a result of survey research. Alternative models were also inadequate and incomplete. My socialization crisis was resolved only by rejecting the teleological image that posits a fixed identity definition as the culmination of the socialization process. Instead, I attempted to create my own identity definition and then socialize myself into it. My own definition centered on the values of a humanistic sociology that are operationalized in the research method of experiential analysis.

The identity change of professional socialization is propelled by the resolution of tension between *attraction* to certain goals and *rejection* of certain experiences, within an environment that balances control with intellectual freedom. My tension derived from my concern with the dilemmas of sociological method. Socialization into sociology was a process of *overcoming*, not just *becoming*. The overcoming of disillusionment through heightened commitment to the original belief has been documented (Festinger, Riecken, and Schachter, 1956), but disillusionment can also be overcome by a commitment to change. My commitment to change the discipline rather than to change my own belief gave me room for exploration and creativity, while allowing me to become a member of a new collective identity. The very conflicts and discrepancies encouraged my self-reliance. Instead of conceiving of socialization as the mastery of what was given (ritualism), I attempted to fashion my socialization around what was needed (innovation).

This view proposes that socialization be redefined as a system of reciprocal impact between the parent culture and the novice. As Olesen and Whittaker (1968) conclude, "Socialization is a mutual dialogue" (p. 299). The "mutual modification model" considers trainees as changing that which is socializing them. Here is where the revolution in a discipline can take place (Young, 1974) if the profession is modified by those who enter it. Just as parents are trained by their infants (Lewis and Rosenblum, 1974), so too are all social systems affected by newcomers' input. Socialization is an opportunity not only for failure of the initiate but also for renovation of the culture. The parent generation is jeopardized as it socializes the young, since each new generation will not only master but also modify the culture if social controls are not excessive nor the reward system overly confining.

According to the dynamic interactionist model I have sketched, the parent culture is changed by the newcomer, and the individual *forms* rather than *adopts* an identity. The interaction of the incoming novice and the receiving culture can be reconceptualized as a dialectic process that yields a synthesis both for the culture and the individual. In this dialectic, reciprocal, or processual model, socialization is reconceptualized as unending rather than teleological. Socialization is not a leap from one given state to another but a continuous experience of negotiation between the individual and the culture.

To deny the continuity of socialization is to deny the fact that conflicts within a discipline compel the person being socialized to reexamine the position he has adopted. The teleological view of the fixed professional identity coincides with the view of the student's task as limited to *acquiring* skills, values, and attitudes. Instead, the socialization process as experienced seems to involve resolving, rejecting, embracing, synthesizing, and revising. The former view represents an overly socialized conception of the student (Wrong, 1961), oblivious to the ambivalence and dissonance.

The reality shock of professional training has been documented (Hughes, 1958; Lortie, 1959; Davis, 1968; Mauksch, 1963). The major task of socialization is the unlearning or rejection of a lay conception and an acceptance of the "insiders' " understanding of what the profession is. I have tried to show that in sociology this process is particularly difficult, because sociology contains several alternative models in addition to the simplified, distorted, or stereotyped lay conception. Because the parent culture has many competing models, the novice must choose an identity to adopt. The novices rid themselves of the lay conception and move toward the insiders' model by changing their attitude toward themselves and toward the profession. "The shift in choice of models by the student, his definite steps or his drifting into the path that leads to one model rather than others, is a significant part of his . . . education" (Hughes, 1958, p. 123). Commitment emerges from the need to work out the puzzle of competing definitions.

As I have stated, professional identity formation is not only a struggle to become but a struggle to overcome. The problems inherent in the discipline "out there" are experienced as a problem of the self "in here" as internalization proceeds. Joining a discipline means changing one's self-definition. The ambiguities and contradictions imposed by conflicting models of sociology and the insoluble dilemmas that the novice experiences in the formative stages of socialization are either put aside as one becomes a full member or linger, ready to be ignited with each new experience. The problem of seeing sociology as in need of methodological reexamination continues to be both personal and political, since the definition of what a profession is reflects the given balance of power in that profession at any given time. Adult socialization does not end with initiation into a new role, for within that role there is continuous resocialization, change, and development of deeper ramifications and complexities. It is evident that I will always be becoming a sociologist (or social scientist/practitioner of some sort), just as I have always been becoming one. My fascination with the dilemmas of method rather than my acceptance of what is given will take a variety of forms as my socialization into new roles continues. My critical attitude toward the profession's claims, my debunking of the certitude with which methods and their products are presented, and my wish that the social sciences be rehumanized will most likely remain part of my personal perspective. These parts of my self contribute to an emerging professional identity and will remain while I develop temporary resolutions.

The dilemmas of survey research, participant observation, and experiential analysis are not, as I once thought, a defeat for sociology, but rather a challenge. I have learned that I have projected my own conflicts onto the profession while I incorporated the profession's dilemmas into my personal identity. It is quite clear that no work can proceed until suitable, appropriate research methods are delineated and the researcher understands the choices made. Although I recognize now that I need the rest of my life to finish my socialization, I also know that my internalized commitment to the social sciences will stem only from isolating a viable research method that I can use; and from this method will emerge a viable definition of the discipline with which I will fully identify.

References

Abel, T. "A Reply to Professor Wax." *Sociology and Social Research*, 1967, *51*, 334-336.

Adams, R. N., and Preiss, J. J. (Eds.). *Human Organization Research: Field Relations and Techniques.* Homewood, Ill.: Dorsey Press, 1960.

Adshead, F. L. "Patient Life in a Nursing Home: An Experiential Study." Unpublished doctoral dissertation, University of Southern California, 1973.

Agee, J., and Evans, W. *Let Us Now Praise Famous Men.* New York: Ballantine, 1972.

Anderson, C. H. *Toward a New Sociology: A Critical View.* Homewood, Ill.: Dorsey Press, 1971.

Anderson, N. *The Hobo: The Sociology of the Homeless Man.* Chicago: University of Chicago Press, 1923.

Andrew, G. "Some Observations on Management Problems in Applied Social Research." *American Sociologist,* 1967, *2,* 84-89.

Ardon, Y. "How We React to Terrorism: Experts Probe the Public Mind." *Jerusalem Post,* September 11, 1970, pp. 7-8.

Ardon, Y. "The Border Development Town: Poor in Cash, Rich in Children." *Jerusalem Post,* March 9, 1973.

Aron, R. *Main Currents in Sociological Thought.* (R. Howard and H. Weaver II, Trans.) New York: Doubleday, 1970.

Athey, K. R. "Two Experiments Showing the Effect of the Interviewer's Racial Background on Responses to Questionnaires Concerning Racial Issues." *Journal of Applied Psychology,* 1960, *44,* 244-246.

Bain, R. K. "The Researcher's Role: A Case Study." *Human Organization,* 1950, *9,* 23-28.

Baldus, H. "Curt Nimuendajú, 1883-1945." *American Anthropologist,* 1946, *48,* 238-243.

Banks, G., Berenson, B., and Carkhuff, R. "The Effects of Counselor Race and Training upon Counselling Process with Negro Clients in Initial Interviews." *Journal of Clinical Psychology,* 1967, *23,* 70-72.

Barber, B., and Fox, R. C. "The Case of the Floppyeared Rabbits: An Instance of Serendipity Gained and Serendipity Lost." *American Journal of Sociology,* 1958, *64,* 128-136.

Barnes, J. A. "Some Ethical Problems in Modern Field Work." *British Journal of Sociology,* 1963, *14,* 118-134.

Barrett, W. *Irrational Man: A Study in Existential Philosophy.* New York: Doubleday, 1962.

Bateson, G., and others. "Toward a Theory of Schizophrenia." *Behavioral Science,* 1956, *1,* 251-264.

Beals, R. *Politics of Social Research: An Inquiry into the Ethics and Responsibilities of Social Scientists.* Chicago: AVC, 1969.

Becker, H. "Interviewing Medical Students." *American Journal of Sociology,* 1956, *62,* 199-201.

Becker, H. "Problems of Inference and Proof in Participant Observation." *American Sociological Review,* 1958, *23,* 652-660.

Becker, H. *Outsiders: Studies in the Sociology of Deviance.* New York: Free Press, 1963.

Becker, H. "Introduction." In C. Shaw (Ed.), *The Jack Roller: A Delinquent Boy's Own Story.* Chicago: University of Chicago Press, 1966. (Originally published 1929.)

Becker, H. "Whose Side Are We On?" *Social Problems,* 1967, *14,* 239-247.

Becker, H. *Sociological Work: Method and Substance.* Chicago: AVC, 1970.

Becker, H. "Problems in the Publication of Field Studies." In A. Vidich, J. Bensman, and M. Stein (Eds.), *Reflections on Community Studies.* New York: Harper & Row, 1971.

Becker, H., and Carper, J. W. "The Development of Identification with an Occupation." *American Journal of Sociology,* 1956, *61,* 289-298.

Becker, H., and Geer, B. "Participant Observation and Interviewing: A Comparison." *Human Organization,* 1957, *16,* 28-32.

Becker, H., and Horowitz, I. L. "Racial Politics and Sociological Research: Observations on Methodology and Ideology." *American Journal of Sociology,* 1972, *78,* 48-66.

Becker, H., and Strauss, A. "Careers, Personality, and Adult Socialization." *American Journal of Sociology,* 1956, *52,* 253-263.

Becker, H., and others. *Boys in White: Student Culture in Medical School.* Chicago: University of Chicago Press, 1961.

Beckman, T., and Mulderij, K. *Living and Experiencing Phenomenological Work Book for the Social Sciences.* (Loren S. Barritt, Trans.) Amsterdam: Boom Meppal, 1977.

Bell, C. G., and Buchanan, W. "Reliable and Unreliable Respondents: Party Registration and Prestige Pressure." *Western Political Quarterly,* 1966, *29,* 37-43.

"Bene Israel." In *Encyclopedia Judaica.* Vol. 4. Jerusalem: Keter Publishing House, 1972.

Benney, M., and Hughes, E. "Of Sociology and the Interview: Editorial Preface." *American Journal of Sociology,* 1956, *62,* 137-142.

Bennis, W. G. "Future of the Social Sciences." *Antioch Review,* 1968, *28,* 227-255.

Berg, D. N. "Intergroup Relations in an Outpatient Psychiatric Facility." Unpublished doctoral dissertation, University of Michigan, 1978.

Berger, P. *Invitation to Sociology: A Humanistic Perspective.* New York: Doubleday, 1963.

Berger, P. "Sociology and Freedom." *American Sociologist,* 1971, *6,* 1-5.

Berger, P., and Luckmann, T. *The Social Construction of Reality: A Treatise in the Sociology of Knowledge.* New York: Doubleday, 1966.

Berk, R. "Discretionary Methodological Decisions in Applied Research." *Sociological Methods and Research,* 1977, *5,* 317-334.

Bernard, J. "My Four Revolutions: An Autobiographical History of the ASA." *American Journal of Sociology,* 1973, *78,* 773-791.

Bierstedt, R. "Sociology and Humane Learning." *American Sociological Review,* 1960, *25,* 3-9.

Bion, W. R. *Experiences in Groups and Other Papers.* London: Tavistock, 1961.

Bird, C. "Demasculinizing the Professions." In R. Gross and P. Osterman (Eds.), *The New Professionals.* New York: Simon & Schuster, 1972.

Blau, P. M. "The Research Process in the Study of *The Dynamics of Bureaucracy.*" In P. Hammond (Ed.), *Sociologists at Work: Essays on the Craft of Social Research.* New York: Basic Books, 1964.

Bloom, B. L., and Parad, H. J. "Interdisciplinary Training and Interdisciplinary Functioning: A Survey of Attitudes and Practices in Community Mental Health." *American Journal of Orthopsychiatry,* 1976, *46,* 669-677.

Blum, L. "Sources of Influence in the Socialization of Corrections Workers." Unpublished doctoral dissertation, University of Michigan, 1976.

Bogart, L. (Ed.). *Social Research and the Desegregation of the*

U.S. Army: Two Original 1951 Field Reports. Chicago: Markham, 1961.

Bowen, E. S. [pseud.]. *Return to Laughter: An Anthropological Novel.* New York: Harper & Row, 1964.

Briggs, J. L. "Kapluna Daughter." In P. Golde (Ed.), *Women in the Field: Anthropological Experiences.* Chicago: AVC, 1970.

Brill, N. *Teamwork: Working Together in the Human Services.* Philadelphia: Lippincott, 1972.

Brim, S., and Wheeler, S. (Eds.). *Socialization After Childhood.* New York: Wiley, 1966.

Brodbeck, M. (Ed.). *Readings in the Philosophy of the Social Sciences.* London: Macmillan, 1968.

Bronfenbrenner, U., and Devereux, E. C. "Interdisciplinary Planning for Team Research on Constructive Community Behavior." *Human Relations,* 1952, *5,* 187-203.

Brown, B., Tshiyama, T., and Schiebe, R. "The Effects of Psychological Testing on Patient's Perception of Self and Environment." *Journal of Clinical Psychology,* 1967, *23,* 49-53.

Brown, J., and Gilmartin, B. "Sociology Today: Lacunae, Emphases and Surfeits." *American Sociologist,* 1969, *4,* 283-290.

Bruyn, S. T. *The Human Perspective in Sociology: The Methodology of Participant Observation.* Englewood Cliffs, N.J.: Prentice-Hall, 1966.

Bryant, F., and Wortman, P. "Secondary Analysis: The Case for Data Archives." *American Psychologist,* 1978, *33,* 381-387.

Bucher, R., and Stelling, J. *Becoming Professional.* Beverly Hills, Calif.: Sage, 1977.

Burgess, E. "The Influence of Sigmund Freud upon Sociology in the United States." *American Journal of Sociology,* 1939, *45,* 356-374.

Butts, S. "Parsons, Weber, and the Subjective Point of View." *Sociological Analysis and Theory,* 1975, *5,* 185-217.

Cannell, C. F., and Fowler, F. J. "Comparison of a Self-Enumerative Procedure and a Personal Interview: A Validity Study." *Public Opinion Quarterly,* 1963, *27,* 250-264.

Calahan, D. "Correlates of Respondent Accuracy in the Denver Validity Survey." *Public Opinion Quarterly,* 1968, *32,* 607-621.

Casagrande, J. (Ed.). *In the Company of Man: Twenty Portraits by Anthropologists.* New York: Harper & Row, 1960.

Cassell, E. J. "In Sickness and in Health." *Commentary,* 1970, *49,* 59-66.

Caudill, W. *The Psychiatric Hospital as a Small Society.* Cambridge, Mass.: Harvard University Press, 1958.

Caudill, W., and Roberts, B. H. "Pitfalls in the Organization of Interdisciplinary Research." *Human Organization,* 1951, *10,* 12-15.

Caudill, W., and others. "Social Structure and Interaction Processes on a Psychiatric Ward." *American Journal of Orthopsychiatry,* 1952, *22,* 314-344.

Chamberlin, J. *On Our Own: Patient-Controlled Alternatives to the Mental Health System.* New York: Hawthorn, 1978.

Cherniss, C. "Creating New Consultation Programs in Community Mental Health Centers: Analysis of a Case Study." *Community Mental Health Journal,* 1977, *13,* 133-141.

Christie, R., and Lindauer, F. "Personality Structure." *Annual Review of Psychology,* 1963, *14,* 201-230.

Cicourel, A. *Method and Measurement in Society.* New York: Free Press, 1964.

Clausen, A. R. "Response Validity: Vote Report." *Public Opinion Quarterly,* 1968, *32,* 588-606.

Clausen, J. *Sociology and the Field of Mental Health.* New York: Russell Sage Foundation, 1965.

Clinard, M. "The Sociologist's Quest for Respectability." *Sociological Quarterly,* 1966, *1,* 399-412.

Codere, H. "Fieldwork in Rwanda, 1959-60." In P. Golde (Ed.), *Women in the Field: Anthropological Experiences.* Chicago: AVC, 1970.

Coleman, J. "Relational Analysis: The Study of Social Organization with Survey Methods." *Human Organization,* 1958, *17,* 28-36.

Coles, R. *The Mind's Fate: Ways of Seeing Psychiatry and Psychoanalysis.* Boston: Little, Brown, 1975.

Colvard, R. "Interaction and Identification in Reporting Field Research: A Critical Reconsideration of Protective Procedures." In G. Sjoberg (Ed.), *Ethics, Politics, and Social Research.* Cambridge, Mass.: Schenkman, 1967.

Coser, L. A. "The Sociology of Poverty." *Social Problems,* 1965, *13,* 140-148.

Coser, L. A. "Letter to a Young Sociologist." *Sociological Inquiry,* 1969, *39,* 131-137.

Coser, L. A., and others. "Participant Observation and the Military: An Exchange." *American Sociological Review,* 1959, *24,* 397-400.

Cottle, T. J. *Time's Children.* Boston: Little, Brown, 1967.

Cottle, T. J. *Private Lives and Public Accounts.* Amherst, Mass.: University of Massachusetts Press, 1977.

Couch, A., and Kenniston, K. "Yeasayers and Naysayers: Agreeing Response Set as a Personality Variable." *Journal of Abnormal and Social Psychology,* 1960, *60,* 151-174.

Crespi, L. "Survey on Problems of Interviewer Cheating." *International Journal of Opinion and Attitude Research,* 1947, *1,* 93-107.

Cumming, E., and Cumming, J. *Closed Ranks: An Experiment in Mental Health Education.* Cambridge, Mass.: Harvard University Press, 1957.

Daedalus. Issue: "Ethical Aspects of Experimentation with Human Subjects." 1969.

Daniels, A. K. "The Low-Caste Stranger in Social Research." In G. Sjoberg (Ed.), *Ethics, Politics, and Social Research.* Cambridge, Mass.: Schenkman, 1967.

Daniels, A. K. "The Notion of Appropriate Professional Conduct: An Exercise in the Sociology of Knowledge." *American Sociologist,* 1974, *9,* 212-217.

Danzig, E., Thayer, P., and Galanter, L. "The Effects of a Threatening Rumor on a Disaster-Stricken Community." Publication 517. Washington, D.C.: National Academy of Sciences-National Research Council, 1958.

Davis, F. "Comment on 'Initial Interaction of Newcomers in Alcoholics Anonymous.' " *Social Problems,* 1961, *8,* 364-365.

Davis, F. "Professional Socialization as Subject Experience: The

Process of Doctrinal Conversion Among Student Nurses." In H. Becker and others (Eds.), *Institutions and the Person.* Chicago: AVC, 1968.

Davis, J. "Great Books and Small Groups." In P. Hammond (Ed.), *Sociologists at Work: Essays on the Craft of Social Research.* New York: Basic Books, 1964.

Dawe, A. "The Role of Experience in the Construction of Social Theory: An Essay in Reflexive Sociology." *Sociological Review,* 1973, *21,* 25-56.

De Josselin de Jong, P. E. "The Participants' View of Their Culture." In D. G. Jongmans and P. C. W. Gutkind (Eds.), *Anthropologists in the Field.* Assen, Netherlands: Van Gorcum, 1967.

Deane, W. N. "The Reactions of a Non-Patient to a Stay on a Mental Ward." *Psychiatry,* 1961, *24,* 61-68.

den Hollander, A. N. J. "Social Description: The Problem of Reliability and Validity." In D. G. Jongmans and P. C. W. Gutkind (Eds.), *Anthropologists in the Field.* Assen, Netherlands: Van Gorcum, 1967.

Denzin, N. *The Research Act: A Theoretical Introduction to Sociological Methods.* Chicago: AVC, 1970.

Descartes, R. *Discourse on Method and Other Writings.* (A. Wollaston, Trans.) New York: Penguin Books, 1960.

Deutsch, M. "Groups: Group Behavior." In D. L. Sills (Ed.), *International Encyclopedia of the Social Sciences.* Vol. 6. New York: Macmillan, 1968.

Deutscher, I. "The Identification of the Complement of Graduate Nurses in a Metropolitan Area." *Nursing Research,* 1956, *5,* 65-70.

Deutscher, I. "Asking Questions Cross-Culturally: Some Problems of Linguistic Comparability." In H. Becker and others (Eds.), *Institutions and the Person: Papers Presented to Everett Hughes.* Chicago: AVC, 1968.

Devereux, G., and Weiner, F. R. "The Occupational Status of Nurses." *American Sociological Review,* 1950, *15,* 628-634.

Dewey, J. *Experience and Education.* New York: Macmillan, 1954. (Originally published 1938.)

Diamond, S. "Nigerian Discovery: The Politics of Field Work."

In A. Vidich, J. Bensman, and M. Stein (Eds.), *Reflections on Community Studies.* New York: Harper & Row, 1971.

Diesing, P. *Patterns of Discovery in the Social Sciences.* Chicago: AVC, 1971.

Dixon, S. W. "Subject Empirical Approach to Affective Memories." Paper presented at annual meeting of the American Psychological Association, Toronto, Canada, 1978.

Dixon, T. R. "Subject Empirical Approach to the Study of Experience." Paper presented at annual meeting of the American Psychological Association, Toronto, 1978.

Dohrenwend, B. P. "Social Status and Psychological Disorder: An Issue of Substance and an Issue of Method." *American Sociological Review,* 1966, *31,* 14-34.

Dollard, J. *Criteria for the Life History.* New Haven, Conn.: Yale University Press, 1936.

DuBois, C. "Studies in an Indian Town." In P. Golde (Ed.), *Women in the Field: Anthropological Experiences.* Chicago: AVC, 1970.

Duff, R., and Hollingshead, A. *Sickness and Society.* New York: Harper & Row, 1968.

Durkheim, E. *The Rules of Sociological Method.* New York: Free Press, 1964. (Originally published 1927.)

Dynes, R. "Sociology as a Religious Movement: Thoughts on Its Institutionalization in the U.S." *American Sociologist,* 1974, *9,* 169-176.

Eaton, J. W. "Social Processes of Professional Teamwork." *American Sociological Review,* 1951, *16,* 707-713.

Ekstein, R., and Wallerstein, R. *The Teaching and Learning of Psychotherapy.* New York: Basic Books, 1958.

Epstein, C. *Woman's Place: Options and Limits in Professional Careers.* Berkeley: University of California Press, 1970.

Epstein, C. F. "A Different Angle of Vision: The Selective Eye of Sociology." *Social Science Quarterly,* 1974, *55,* 645-656.

Erikson, E. "The Nature of Clinical Evidence." In D. Lerner (Ed.), *Evidence and Inference.* New York: Free Press, 1959.

Erikson, E. *Childhood and Society.* New York: Norton, 1963.

Erikson, E. *Insight and Responsibility: Lectures on the Ethical*

Implications of Psychoanalytic Insight. New York: Norton, 1964.

Erikson, K. "A Comment on Disguised Observation in Sociology." *Social Problems,* 1967, *14,* 366-373.

Evans-Pritchard, E. E. *The Nuer.* Oxford: Clarendon Press, 1940.

Feldman, K. A., and Newcomb, T. M. *The Impact of College on Students.* San Francisco: Jossey-Bass, 1969.

Ferris, A. L. "Educational Interrelations Among Social Sciences." *American Sociologist,* 1965, *1,* 15-23.

Festinger, L. *A Theory of Cognitive Dissonance.* Stanford, Calif.: Stanford University Press, 1957.

Festinger, L., Riecken, H., and Schacter, S. *When Prophecy Fails.* Minneapolis: University of Minnesota Press, 1956.

Fichter, J. H., and Kolb, W. L. "Ethical Limitations on Sociological Reporting." *American Sociological Review,* 1953, *18,* 544-550.

Field, J. *A Life of One's Own.* London: Chatto & Windus, 1936.

Field, M. "Former Soviet Citizens' Attitudes Toward the Soviet, the German, and the American Medical Systems." *American Sociological Review,* 1955, *20,* 674-679.

Filstead, W. J. (Ed.). *Qualitative Methodology: Firsthand Involvement with the Social World.* Chicago: Markham, 1970.

Finney, J. C. (Ed.). *Culture Change, Mental Health, and Poverty.* Lexington: University of Kentucky Press, 1969.

Fischer, A. "Fieldwork in Five Cultures." In P. Golde (Ed.), *Women in the Field: Anthropological Experiences.* Chicago: AVC, 1970.

Fischer, C. T. "Undercutting the Scientist-Professional Dichotomy: The Reflective Psychologist." *Clinical Psychologist,* 1976, *29,* 5-7.

Form, W. "The Sociology of Social Research." In R. O'Toole (Ed.), *Organization Management and Tactics of Social Research.* Cambridge, Mass.: Schenkman, 1971.

Fox, R. *Experiment Perilous: Physicians and Patients Facing the Unknown.* New York: Free Press, 1959.

Freud, S. *The Interpretation of Dreams.* New York: Carlton House, 1931.

Friedlander, F. "Researcher-Subject Alienation in Behavioral Research." In E. Glatt and S. Maynard (Eds.), *The Research Society.* London: Gordon & Breach, 1967.

Friedrichs, R. W. *A Sociology of Sociology.* New York: Free Press, 1970.

Gadamer, H. G. *Truth and Method.* New York: Seabury, 1975.

Galliher, J. "The Protection of Human Subjects: A Re-Examination of the Professional Code of Ethics." *American Sociologist,* 1973, *8,* 93-100.

Galtung, J. *Theory and Methods of Social Research.* New York: Columbia University Press, 1967.

Gamberg, H. "Science and Scientism: The State of Sociology." *American Sociologist,* 1969, *4,* 111-116.

Gans, H. *The Urban Villagers: Group and Class in the Life of Italian Americans.* New York: Free Press, 1962.

Gans, H. "The Participant-Observer as a Human Being: Observations on the Personal Aspects of Field Work." In H. Becker and others (Eds.), *Institutions and the Person: Papers Presented to Everett Hughes.* Chicago: AVC, 1968.

Geer, B. "First Days in the Field." In P. E. Hammond (Ed.), *Sociologists at Work: Essays on the Craft of Social Research.* New York: Basic Books, 1964.

Gendlin, E. T. "Experiential Explication and Truth." *Journal of Existentialism,* 1965-1966, *22,* 1-33.

Ginath, Y., and Krasilowsky, D. "Adaptive Changes of Different Social Structures Facing a Common Hostile Situation." *Israel Annals of Psychiatry & Related Disciplines,* 1970, *8,* 145-162.

Glaser, B., and Strauss, A. L. *The Discovery of Grounded Theory: Strategies for Qualitative Research.* Chicago: AVC, 1967.

Glass, J. "The Humanist Challenge to Sociology." Paper presented at 8th annual meeting of Association for Humanistic Psychology, Miami Beach, Fla., August 1970.

Glazer, M. *The Research Adventure: Problems and Promise of Field Work.* New York: Random House, 1972.

Glotfelty, J. "Group Social Work Intervention in the Ward Group Process." Paper presented to a psychiatric hospital, Belmont, Mass., February 11, 1966.

Goffman, E. *Asylums*. New York: Doubleday, 1961.

Goffman, E. *Behavior in Public Places: Notes on the Social Organization of Gatherings*. New York: Free Press, 1963.

Goffman, E. "Lecture to the Department of Sociology." Brandeis University, 1971.

Goffman, E. *Frame Analysis: An Essay on the Organization of Experience*. New York: Harper & Row, 1974.

Gold, R. "Roles in Sociological Field Observation." *Social Forces*, 1958, *36*, 217-233.

Golde, P. (Ed.). *Women in the Field: Anthropological Experiences*. Chicago: AVC, 1970.

Goldman, A., Bohr, R., and Steinberg, T. "On Posing as Mental Patients: Reminiscences and Recommendations." *Professional Psychology*, 1970, *1*, 427-434.

Gostkowski, Z. "Toward Empirical Humanization of Mass Surveys." *Quality and Quantity*, 1974, *8*, 11-26.

Gottlieb, D. "Processes of Socialization in the American Graduate School." Unpublished doctoral dissertation, University of Chicago, 1960.

Gouldner, A. "The Sociologist as Partisan: Sociology and the Welfare State." *American Sociologist*, 1968, *3*, 103-116.

Gouldner, A. "Personal Reality and the Tragic Dimension in Science." In G. Boalt, *The Sociology of Research*. Carbondale: Southern Illinois University Press, 1969.

Gouldner, A. *The Coming Crisis of Western Sociology*. New York: Basic Books, 1970.

Green, L. W. "East Pakistan: Knowledge and Use of Contraceptives." *Studies in Family Planning*, 1969, *39*, 9-14.

Gruschka, R. "Social Effects of the Security Situation." [Hebrew] Seminar proceedings, Kibbutz Gal-Ed, August 8, 1970.

Habenstein, R. (Ed.). *Pathways to Data: Field Methods for Studying Ongoing Social Organizations*. Chicago: AVC, 1970.

Hall, D. T. "Identity Changes During the Transition from Student to Professor." *School Review*, 1968, *76*, 445-469.

Hammond, P. (Ed.). *Sociologists at Work: Essays on the Craft of Social Research*. New York: Basic Books, 1964.

Hardesty, C. Untitled paper presented to activity therapies staff, a psychiatric hospital, Belmont, Mass., March 12, 1970.

Hart, C. W. "Some Factors Affecting the Organization and Prosecution of a Given Research Project." *American Sociological Review,* 1957, *12,* 514-519.

Hempel, C. G. *Aspects of Scientific Explanation and Other Essays in the Philosophy of Science.* New York: Free Press, 1965.

Henry, J. *On Education.* New York: Random House, 1966.

Henry, J. "My Life with the Families of Psychotic Children." In G. Handel (Ed.), *Psychosocial Interior of the Family.* Chicago: AVC, 1967.

Hill, R. J., and Crittenden, K. S. (Eds.). *Proceedings of the Purdue Symposium on Ethnomethodology.* Institute Monograph Series, No. 1. Institute for the Study of Social Change, Department of Sociology, Purdue University, 1968.

Hodges, H. A. *William Dilthey: An Introduction.* London: Kegan Paul, 1944.

Holleb, G. P., and Abrams, W. H. *Alternatives in Community Mental Health: Why Alternative Counseling Centers Started, How They've Fared, Their Future Role.* Boston: Beacon Press, 1975.

Homans, G. C. *The Human Group.* New York: Harcourt Brace Jovanovich, 1950.

Honigmann, J. J. "Middle Class Values and Cross-Cultural Understanding." In J. Finney (Ed.), *Culture Change, Mental Health, and Poverty.* Lexington: University of Kentucky Press, 1969.

Horowitz, I. L. "The Life and Death of Project Camelot." *Transaction,* 1965a, *3.*

Horowitz, I. L. (Ed.). *The New Sociology.* New York: Oxford University Press, 1965b.

Horowitz, I. L. "The Natural History of Revolution in Brazil: A Biography of a Book." In G. Sjoberg (Ed.), *Ethics, Politics and Social Research.* Cambridge, Mass.: Schenkman, 1967.

Horowitz, I. L. *Professing Sociology: Studies in the Life Cycle of Social Science.* Chicago: AVC, 1968.

Horowitz, I. L. (Ed.). *Sociological Self-Images—A Collective Portrait.* Beverly Hills, Calif.: Sage, 1969.

House of Representatives, Committee on Education and Labor.

"A Task Force Study of the Public School System in the District of Columbia as It Relates to the War on Poverty." June 1966.

Huesler, C. "The Gilded Asylum." In G. Jacobs (Ed.), *The Participant Observer.* New York: George Braziller, 1970.

Hughes, E. C. "The Improper Study of Man." In L. White, Jr. (Ed.), *Frontiers of Knowledge in the Study of Man.* New York: Harper & Row, 1956.

Hughes, E. C. "Professional and Career Problems of Sociology." In *Men and Their Work.* New York: Free Press, 1958.

Hughes, E. C. "Introduction: The Place of Field Work in Social Science." In B. H. Junker (Ed.), *Field Work: An Introduction to the Social Sciences.* Chicago: University of Chicago Press, 1960.

Hughes, E. C. "Teaching as Fieldwork." *American Sociologist,* 1970, *5,* 13-18.

Hyman, H. *Interviewing in Social Research.* Chicago: University of Chicago Press, 1954.

Jacobs, G. (Ed.). *The Participant Observer: Encounters with Social Reality.* New York: George Braziller, 1970.

Jacobs, R. "The Journalistic and Sociological Enterprises as Ideal Types." *American Sociologist,* 1970, *3,* 348-350.

Jaffe, D. T., and Clark, T. *Number Nine: Autobiography of an Alternate Counseling Service.* New York: Harper & Row, 1975.

Janes, R. "A Note on Phases of the Community Role of the Participant Observer." *American Sociological Review,* 1961, *26,* 446-450.

Jaques, E. *The Changing Culture of a Factory.* New York: Dryden, 1952.

Jones, E. *The Life and Work of Sigmund Freud.* New York: Doubleday, 1963.

Jones, M. *The Therapeutic Community.* New York: Basic Books, 1953.

Jongmans, D. G., and Gutkind, P. C. W. (Eds.). *Anthropologists in the Field.* Assen, Netherlands: Van Gorcum, 1967.

Josephson, E. "Resistance to Community Surveys." *Social Problems,* 1970, *18,* 117-129.

Junker, B. *Field Work: An Introduction to the Social Sciences.* Chicago: University of Chicago Press, 1960.

Kadushin, C. "The Professional Self-Concept of Music Students." *American Journal of Sociology*, 1969, *75*, 389-404.

Kaplan, A. *The Conduct of Inquiry: Methodology for Behavioral Science.* San Francisco: Chandler, 1964.

Kaplan, B. (Ed.). *The Inner World of Mental Illness: A Series of First-Person Accounts of What It Was Like.* New York: Harper & Row, 1964.

Kelley, H., and Thibaut, J. "Experimental Studies of Group Problem Solving and Process." In G. Lindzey (Ed.), *Handbook of Social Psychology.* Reading, Mass.: Addison-Wesley, 1954.

Killian, L. *An Introduction to Methodological Problems of Field Studies in Disasters.* Publication 465. Washington, D.C.: National Academy of Sciences-National Research Council, 1956.

Kimball, S. T., Pearsall, M., and Bliss, J. "Consultants and Citizens: A Research Relationship." *Human Organization*, 1954, *13*, 5-8.

King, S. H., and Henry, A. F. "Aggression and Cardiovascular Reactions Related to Parental Control over Behavior." *Journal of Abnormal and Social Psychology*, 1955, *50*, 206-210.

Klein, M. *Street Gangs and Street Workers.* Englewood Cliffs, N.J.: Prentice-Hall, 1971.

Kluckhohn, F. "The Participant Observer Technique in Small Communities." *American Journal of Sociology*, 1940, *46*, 331-343.

Kockelmans, J. (Ed.). *Phenomenology: The Philosophy of Edmund Husserl and Its Interpretation.* New York: Doubleday, 1967.

Kress, P. *Social Science and the Idea of Process: The Ambiguous Legacy of Arthur F. Bentley.* Chicago: University of Illinois Press, 1970.

Kuhn, T. *The Structure of Scientific Revolutions.* Chicago: University of Chicago Press, 1962.

Laing, R. D. *Self and Others.* New York: Penguin Books, 1971.

Laing, R. D. *The Politics of Experience*. New York: Ballantine, 1972.

Landes, R. "A Woman Anthropologist in Brazil." In P. Golde (Ed.), *Women in the Field: Anthropological Experiences*. Chicago: AVC, 1970.

Langness, L. L. *The Life History in Anthropological Science*. New York: Holt, Rinehart and Winston, 1965.

Lantz, H. "Introduction." In G. Boalt (Ed.), *The Sociology of Research*. Carbondale: Southern Illinois University Press, 1969.

Lee, A. M. "The Clinical Study of Society." *American Sociological Review*, 1955, *20*, 648-653.

Lee, A. M. "On Context and Relevance." In G. Jacobs (Ed.), *The Participant Observer: Encounters with Social Reality*. New York: George Braziller, 1970.

Levine, M. "President's Column." Newsletter of the *American Psychological Association, Division of Community Psychology*, 1977, *11*, 1-15.

Levinson, D. "The Mental Hospital as a Research Setting: A Critical Appraisal." In M. Greenblatt, D. Levinson, and R. Williams (Eds.), *The Patient and the Mental Hospital: Contributions of Research in the Science of Social Behavior*. New York: Free Press, 1957.

Lewis, M., and Rosenblum, L. (Eds.). *The Effect of the Infant on Its Caregiver*. New York: Wiley, 1974.

Lewis, O. "Controls and Experiments in Fieldwork." In A. L. Kroeber (Ed.), *Anthropology Today: An Encyclopedic Inventory*. Chicago: University of Chicago Press, 1953.

Lewis, O. *The Children of Sanchez: Autobiography of a Mexican Family*. New York: Random House, 1961.

Liebow, E. "A Field Experience in Retrospect." In E. Liebow, *Tally's Corner*. Boston: Little, Brown, 1967.

Lifton, R. J. *Death in Life: Survivors of Hiroshima*. New York: Random House, 1967.

Lofland, J. "Reply to Davis." *Social Problems*, 1961, *8*, 365-367.

Lofland, J. "Styles of Reporting Qualitative Field Research." *American Sociologist*, 1974, *9*, 101-111.

Lofland, J., and Lejeune, R. "Initial Interaction of Newcomers in Alcoholics Anonymous: A Field Experiment in Class Symbols and Socialization." *Social Problems,* 1960, *8,* 102-111.

Longabaugh, R., Dummer, N., and Forster, C. "An Assessment of Hall Care, Working Report 1: East House." Belmont, Mass.: A psychiatric hospital, April 3, 1968a.

Longabaugh, R., Dummer, N., and Forster, C. "An Assessment of Hall Care, Working Report 2: Upham House." Belmont, Mass.: A psychiatric hospital, October 7, 1968b.

Loomis, C. "Toward Systematic Analysis of Disaster, Disruption, Stress and Recovery—Suggested Areas of Investigation." In G. Baker and L. Cottrell, Jr. (Eds.), *Behavioral Science and Civil Defense.* Publication 997. Washington, D.C.: National Academy of Sciences-National Research Council, 1962.

Lortie, D. "Laymen to Lawmen: Law School, Careers, and Professional Socialization." *Harvard Educational Review,* 1959, *29,* 363-367.

Lortie, D. "Shared Ordeal and Introduction to Work." In H. Becker and others (Eds.), *Institutions and the Person: Papers Presented to Everett Hughes.* Chicago: AVC, 1968.

Lowental, U., and Reinharz, S. "Group Dynamics in Community Mental Health Teams." *Journal of Community Psychology,* in press.

Lowie, R. H. *Robert H. Lowie Ethnologist: A Personal Record.* Berkeley: University of California Press, 1959.

Luszki, M. B. *Interdisciplinary Team Research: Methods and Problems.* Washington, D.C.: National Training Laboratories, National Educational Association, 1958.

McCall, G. "Data Quality Control in Participant Observation." In G. McCall and J. L. Simmons (Eds.), *Issues in Participant Observation.* Reading, Mass.: Addison-Wesley, 1969.

McCall, G., and Simmons, J. L. (Eds.). *Issues in Participant Observation: A Text and Reader.* Reading, Mass.: Addison-Wesley, 1969.

McCartney, J. "On Being Scientific: Changing Styles of Presentation of Sociological Research." *American Sociologist,* 1970, *5,* 30-35.

Mack, R. W. "Intellectual Strategies and Research Tactics." In N. K. Denzin (Ed.), *The Values of Social Science.* Chicago: AVC, 1970.

Madan, T. N. "Political Pressures and Ethical Constraints upon Indian Sociologists." In G. Sjoberg (Ed.), *Ethics, Politics, and Social Research.* Cambridge, Mass.: Schenkman, 1967.

Malinowski, B. "Field Method." In *Argonauts of the Western Pacific.* New York: Dutton, 1961. (Originally published 1922.)

Malinowski, B. *A Diary in the Strict Sense of the Term.* (N. Guterman, Trans.) New York: Harcourt Brace Jovanovich, 1967.

Mandelbaum, D. "Social Stratification Among the Jews of Cochin in India and in Israel." *Jewish Journal of Sociology,* 1975, *17,* 165-210.

Mann, F. "Human Relations Skills in Social Research." *Human Relations,* 1951, *4,* 341-354.

Mann, R. "The Identity of the Group Researcher." In G. S. Gibbard, J. J. Hartman, and R. D. Mann (Eds.), *Analysis of Groups: Contributions to Theory, Research, and Practice.* San Francisco: Jossey-Bass, 1973.

Manocchio, A. J., and Dunn, J. *The Time Game: Two Views of a Prison.* New York: Dell, 1970.

Mao Tse-tung. "On Practice: On the Relation Between Knowledge and Practice, Between Knowledge and Doing." In *Selected Works of Mao Tse-tung.* London: Lawrence & Wishart, 1954.

Maslow, A. *The Psychology of Science: A Reconnaissance.* New York: Harper & Row, 1966.

Matson, F. W. *The Broken Image.* New York: Doubleday, 1966.

Matza, D. *Becoming Deviant.* Englewood Cliffs, N.J.: Prentice-Hall, 1969.

Mauksch, H. O. "Becoming a Nurse: A Selective View." *Annals of the American Academy of Political and Social Sciences,* 1963, *346,* 88-98.

Mead, M. "Field Work in the Pacific Islands, 1925-1967." In P. Golde (Ed.), *Women in the Field: Anthropological Experiences.* Chicago: AVC, 1970.

Means, R. L. *The Ethical Imperative: The Crisis in American Values.* New York: Doubleday, 1969.

Medley, M. L., and Conyers, J. E. (Eds.). *Sociology for the Seventies.* New York: Wiley, 1972.

Merton, R. K. "Selected Problems of Field Work in the Planned Community." *American Sociological Review,* 1947, *12,* 304-312.

Merton, R. K. *Social Theory and Social Structure.* New York: Free Press, 1957.

Merton, R. K. "Social Conflict over Styles of Sociological Work." Transactions of the Fourth World Congress of Sociology. Vol. 3. Louvain, Belgium: International Sociological Association, 1959.

Merton, R. K. "Foreward." In B. Barber, *Science and the Social Order.* New York: Collier Books, 1962.

Merton, R. K. *Sociological Ambivalence and Other Essays.* New York: Free Press, 1976.

Merton, R. K., Reader, G., and Kendall, P. (Eds.). *The Student-Physician: Introductory Studies in the Sociology of Medical Education.* Cambridge, Mass.: Harvard University Press, 1957.

Milgram, S. "Behavioral Study of Obedience." *Journal of Abnormal and Social Psychology,* 1963, *67,* 371-378.

Miller, D. C. "The Impact of Organization and Research Value Structures on Researcher Behavior." In A. W. Gouldner and S. M. Miller (Eds.), *Applied Sociology: Opportunities and Problems.* New York: Free Press, 1965.

Miller, S. M. "The Participant Observer and 'Over-Rapport.' " *American Sociological Review,* 1952, *17,* 97-98.

Millman, M., and Kanter, R. (Eds.). *Another Voice: Feminist Perspectives on Social Life and Social Science.* New York: Doubleday, 1975.

Mills, C. W. *The Sociological Imagination.* New York: Grove Press, 1959.

Mishler, E. "Meaning in Context: Is There Any Other Kind?" Paper presented at annual meeting of American Educational Research Association, Toronto, Canada, March 27-31, 1978.

Mishler, E. G., and Scotch, N. A. "Sociological Factors in the Epidemiology of Schizophrenia." *International Journal of Social Psychiatry,* 1965, *1,* 258-298.

Moore, W. E. "Occupational Socialization." In D. Goslin (Ed.),

Handbook of Socialization Theory and Research. Chicago: Rand McNally, 1969.

Nader, L. "From Anguish to Exultation." In P. Golde (Ed.), *Women in the Field: Anthropological Experiences.* Chicago: AVC, 1970.

New, P., and Priest, R. "Problems of Obtaining a Sample in a Study of Deviancy: A Case of Failure." *Social Science and Medicine,* 1968, *1,* 450-453.

New, P. K. "An Analysis of the Concept of Team-work." *Community Mental Health Journal,* 1972, *8,* 178-188.

Newton, P., and Levinson, D. "The Work Group Within the Organization: A Social Psychological Approach." *Psychiatry,* 1973, *36,* 115-142.

Nicolaus, M. "Remarks at the American Sociological Association Convention." *American Sociologist,* 1968, *4,* 154-156.

Nisbet, R. "Sociology as an Art Form." In M. Stein and A. Vidich (Eds.), *Sociology on Trial.* Englewood Cliffs, N.J.: Prentice-Hall, 1963.

Olesen, V. L., and Whittaker, E. W. *The Silent Dialogue: A Study in the Social Psychology of Professional Socialization.* San Francisco: Jossey-Bass, 1968.

Orlans, H. "Ethical Problems of Research Sponsors and Investigators." In G. Sjoberg (Ed.), *Ethics, Politics and Social Research.* Cambridge, Mass.: Schenkman, 1967.

Oromaner, M. "The Structure of Influence in Contemporary Academic Sociology." *American Sociologist,* 1972, *7,* 11-13.

Parry, H., and Crossley, H. M. "Validity of Responses to Survey Questions." *Public Opinion Quarterly,* 1950, *14,* 66-80.

Parsons, T. "The School Class as a Social System: Some of Its Functions in American Society." *Harvard Educational Review,* 1959, *29,* 297-318.

Paul, B. "Interview Techniques and Field Relationships." In A. L. Kroeber (Ed.), *Anthropology Today.* Chicago: University of Chicago Press, 1953.

Pavalko, R., and Holley, J. W. "Determinants of a Professional Self-Concept Among Graduate Students." *Social Science Quarterly,* 1974, *55,* 462-477.

Pergamenter, R. "Group Work with Metaplot in a Border Kibbutz." Unpublished manuscript, Oranim Child Guidance Center, Kirjat Tivon, Israel, 1970.

Perry, S. *The Human Nature of Science: Researchers at Work in Psychiatry.* New York: Free Press, 1966.

Pettigrew, T. F. *A Profile of the Negro American.* Princeton, N.J.: D. Van Nostrand, 1964.

Phillips, D. *Knowledge from What?* Chicago: Rand McNally, 1971.

Polanyi, M. *Personal Knowledge: Towards a Postcritical Philosophy.* Chicago: University of Chicago Press, 1958.

Polsky, H. *Cottage Six: The Social System of Delinquent Boys in Residential Treatment.* New York: Russell Sage Foundation, 1962.

Powdermaker, H. *Stranger and Friend: The Way of an Anthropologist.* New York: Norton, 1966.

Proshansky, H., and Seidenberg, B. (Eds.). *Basic Studies in Social Psychology.* New York: Holt, Rinehart and Winston, 1966.

Proust, M. *A la Recherche du Temps Perdu.* Paris: Gallimard, 1946-1947.

Radin, P. (Ed.). *Crashing Thunder: The Autobiography of an American Indian.* New York: Appleton-Century-Crofts, 1926.

Rainwater, L. *Behind Ghetto Walls: Black Families in a Federal Slum.* Chicago: AVC, 1970.

Record, J. C. "The Research Institute and the Pressure Group." In G. Sjoberg (Ed.), *Ethics, Politics, and Social Research.* Cambridge, Mass.: Schenkman, 1967.

Redfield, R. "The Art of Social Science." *American Journal of Sociology,* 1948, 55, 181-190.

Reinharz, S. "Some Comments on Friendships Between Patients on the Ward of a Mental Hospital." Unpublished manuscript, 1969. Available from author, Department of Psychology, University of Michigan.

Reinharz, S. "Coping with Disaster." Unpublished manuscript, 1971. Available from author, Department of Psychology, University of Michigan.

Reiss, A. J., Jr. "Stuff and Nonsense About Social Surveys and

Observation." In H. Becker and others (Eds.), *Institutions and the Person.* Chicago: AVC, 1968.

Reynolds, D. K., and Farberow, N. L. *Suicide: Inside and Out.* Berkeley: University of California Press, 1976.

Reynolds, L. T., and Reynolds, J. M. *The Sociology of Sociology: Analysis and Criticism of the Thought, Research and Ethical Folkways of Sociology and Its Practitioners.* New York: McKay, 1970.

Richardson, S. A. "Training in Field Relations Skills." *Journal of Social Issues,* 1952, *8,* 43-50.

Richardson, S. A., Dohrenwend, B., and Klein, D. *Interviewing: Its Forms and Functions.* New York: Basic Books, 1965.

Riecken, H. "The Unidentified Interviewer." *American Journal of Sociology,* 1956, *62,* 210-212.

Riemer, J. "Varieties of Opportunistic Research." *Urban Life,* 1977, *5,* 467-477.

Riesman, D., and Watson, J. "The Sociability Project: A Chronicle of Frustration and Achievement." In P. Hammond (Ed.), *Sociologists at Work: Essays on the Craft of Social Research.* New York: Basic Books, 1964.

Ritzer, G. "Sociology: A Multiple Paradigm Science." *American Sociologist,* 1975, *10,* 156-167.

Rodman, H., and Kolodny, R. "Organizational Strains in the Researcher-Practitioner Relationship." *Human Organization,* 1964, *23,* 171-182.

Rose, A. M. *Libel and Academic Freedom: A Lawsuit Against Political Extremists.* Minneapolis: University of Minnesota Press, 1968.

Rosen, G. *Madness in Society: Chapters in the Historical Sociology of Mental Illness.* New York: Harper & Row, 1968.

Rosenhan, D. L. "On Being Sane in Insane Places." *Science,* 1973, *179,* 250-258.

Rosenthal, R. *Experimental Effects in Behavioral Research.* New York: Appleton-Century-Crofts, 1966.

Roth, J. "Comments on Secret Observation." *Social Problems,* 1962, *9,* 283-284.

Roth, J. "Hired Hand Research." *American Sociologist,* 1966, *1,* 190-196.

Rothschild, S. "Review of Bohanan's *Return from Laughter.*" Unpublished manuscript, 1965a. Available from author, Department of Psychology, University of Michigan.

Rothschild, S. "Some Aspects of the Psychodynamics and the Sociodynamics of Scientific Research." Unpublished manuscript, 1965b. Available from author, Department of Psychology, University of Michigan.

Rowland, H. "Interaction Processes in the State Mental Hospital." *Psychiatry*, 1938, *1*, 323-337.

Rowland, H. "Friendship Patterns in the State Mental Hospital." *Psychiatry*, 1939, *2*, 363-373.

Ryan, A. *The Philosophy of the Social Sciences.* New York: Random House, 1970.

Ryan, W. *Blaming the Victim.* New York: Random House, 1971.

Sanford, N., and Krech, D. "The Activists' Corner." *Journal of Social Issues*, 1969, *25*, 247-255.

Sartre, J. P. *Search for a Method.* (H. E. Barnes, Trans.) New York: Knopf, 1967.

Schactel, E. G. *Metamorphosis: On the Development of Affect, Perception, Attention and Memory.* New York: Basic Books, 1959.

Scheler, M. *The Nature of Sympathy.* (P. Heath, Trans.) London: Routledge & Kegan Paul, 1954.

Schlesinger, A., Jr. "The Humanist Looks at Empirical Social Research." *American Sociological Review*, 1962, *27*, 768-771.

Schutz, A. "On Multiple Realities." In M. Natanson (Ed.), *Collected Papers I: The Problem of Social Reality.* The Hague: Martinus Nihoff, 1962.

Schwartz, M. "The Mental Hospital: The Research Person in the Disturbed Ward." In A. Vidich, J. Bensman, and M. Stein (Eds.), *Reflections on Community Studies.* New York: Harper & Row, 1971.

Schwartz, M., and Schwartz, C. "Problems in Participant Observation." *American Journal of Sociology*, 1955, *60*, 343-353.

Schwitzgebel, R. *Streetcorner Research: An Experimental Ap-*

proach to the Juvenile Delinquent. Cambridge, Mass.: Harvard University Press, 1964.

Seeley, J. "Crestwood Heights: Intellectual and Libidinal Dimensions of Research." In A. Vidich, J. Bensman, and M. Stein (Eds.), *Reflections on Community Studies.* New York: Harper & Row, 1971.

Shaskolsky, L. "The Development of Sociological Theory in America—A Sociology of Knowledge Interpretation." In L. Reynolds and J. Reynolds (Eds.), *The Sociology of Sociology.* New York: McKay, 1970.

Shaw, C. *The Jack Roller: A Delinquent Boy's Own Story.* Chicago: University of Chicago Press, 1966. (Originally published 1929.)

Sherman, S. R. "Demand Characteristics in an Experiment on Attitude Change." *Sociometry,* 1967, *30,* 246-261.

Shils, E. "Sacred and Civil Ties: Some Particular Observations on the Relationships of Sociological Research and Theory." *British Journal of Sociology,* 1957, *8,* 130-145.

Shils, E. "Social Inquiry and the Autonomy of the Individual." In D. Lerner (Ed.), *The Human Meaning of the Social Sciences.* New York: World, 1959.

Sibley, E. *The Education of Sociologists in the United States.* New York: Russell Sage Foundation, 1963.

Simmons, J. L. *Deviants.* Berkeley, Calif.: Glendessary Press, 1969.

Sjoberg, G. (Ed.). *Ethics, Politics, and Social Research.* Cambridge, Mass.: Schenkman, 1967.

Skipper, J. K., Guenther, A. L., and Nuss, G. "The Sacredness of .05: A Note Concerning the Uses of Statistical Levels of Significance in Social Science." *American Sociologist,* 1967, *2,* 16-18.

Smelser, N. J., and Davis, J. A. (Eds.). *Sociology.* Englewood Cliffs, N.J.: Prentice-Hall, 1969.

Spiegel, J. P. "Race Relations and Violence: A Social Psychiatric Perspective." In F. C. Redlich (Ed.), *Social Psychiatry.* Baltimore: Williams & Wilkins, 1969.

Spiegelberg, H. *Phenomenology in Psychology and Psychiatry.* Evanston, Ill.: Northwestern University Press, 1972.

Stanton, A. H., and Schwartz, M. S. *The Mental Hospital.* New York: Basic Books, 1954.

Stein, M. "The Eclipse of Community: Some Glances at the Education of a Sociologist." In A. Vidich, J. Bensman, and M. Stein (Eds.), *Reflections on Community Studies.* New York: Harper & Row, 1971.

Stinchcombe, A. "A Structural Analysis of Sociology." *American Sociologist,* 1975, *10,* 57-64.

Stock, R. W. "Going Stark Native." *New York Times,* February 4, 1973.

Stouffer, S., and others. *The American Soldier: Adjustment During Army Life.* Princeton, N.J.: Princeton University Press, 1949.

Strauss, A., and others. *Psychiatric Ideologies and Institutions.* New York: Free Press, 1964.

Strauss, A., and Schatzman, L. "Cross Cultural Interviewing: An Analysis of Interaction and Communication Styles." *Human Organization,* 1955, *14,* 28-31.

Strizower, S. "Jews as an Indian Caste." *Jewish Journal of Sociology,* 1959, *1* (1), 43-57.

Strizower, S. *Bene Israel of Bombay: A Study of a Jewish Community.* New York: Schocken, 1971.

Sudman, S., and Bradburn, N. *Response Effects in Surveys: A Review and Synthesis.* Chicago: AVC, 1974.

Sullivan, H. S. *The Fusion of Psychiatry and Social Science.* New York: Norton, 1964.

Sullivan, M., Jr., Queen, S., and Patrick, R. "Participant Observation as Employed in the Study of a Military Training Program." *American Sociological Review,* 1958, *23,* 660-667.

Summers, G. F., and Hammonds, A. D. "Effects of Racial Characteristics of Investigator on Self-Enumerated Responses to a Negro Prejudice Scale." *Social Forces,* 1966, *44,* 515-518.

Sussman, M. "The Social Problems of the Sociologist." *Social Problems,* 1964, *11,* 215-225.

Sutherland, E. *The Professional Thief.* Chicago: University of Chicago Press, 1956.

Tarter, D. "Heeding Skinner's Call—Toward the Development of a Social Technology." *American Sociologist,* 1973, *8,* 153-158.

Terkel, S. *Working.* New York: Random House, 1972.

"Test of Coed Living Ends in Michigan." *New York Times,* March 19, 1972, p. 14.

Thomas, D. S., and Nishimoto, R. S. *The Spoilage.* Berkeley: University of California Press, 1946.

Thompson, L. "Exploring American Indian Communities in Depth." In P. Golde (Ed.), *Women in the Field: Anthropological Experiences.* Chicago: AVC, 1970.

Tidball, E. "On Liberation and Competence." *Educational Record,* 1976, *57,* 101-110.

Tiryakian, E. "Existential Phenomenology." *American Sociological Review,* 1965, *30,* 674-688.

Tiryakian, E. (Ed.). *The Phenomenon of Sociology: A Reader in the Sociology of Sociology.* New York: Appleton-Century-Crofts, 1971.

Toby, J. "Undermining the Student's Faith in the Validity of Personal Experience." *American Sociological Review,* 1955, *20,* 717-718.

"Toward a Code of Ethics for Sociologists." *American Sociologist,* 1968, *3,* 316-318.

Trice, H. M. "The 'Outsider's' Role in Field Study." *Sociology and Social Research,* 1956, *41,* 27-32.

Valentine, C. A. *Culture and Poverty.* Chicago: University of Chicago Press, 1968.

Vaughan, T. "Governmental Intervention in Social Research: Political and Ethical Dimensions in the Wichita Jury Recordings." In G. Sjoberg (Ed.), *Ethics, Politics and Social Research.* Cambridge, Mass.: Schenkman, 1967.

Vidich, A. J. "Participant Observation and the Collection and Interpretation of Data." *American Journal of Sociology,* 1955, *60,* 354-360.

Vidich, A. J., and Bensman, J. *Small Town in Mass Society.* New York: Doubleday, 1960.

Vidich, A. J., and Bensman, J. "The Springdale Case: Academic Bureaucrats and Sensitive Townspeople." In A. Vidich, J. Bensman, and M. Stein (Eds.), *Reflections on Community Studies.* New York: Harper & Row, 1971.

Vidich, A. J., Bensman, J., and Stein, M. (Eds.). *Reflections on Community Studies.* New York: Harper & Row, 1971.

Voss, H. L. "Pitfalls in Social Research: A Case Study." *American Sociologist,* 1966, *1,* 136-140.

Wagner, H. "Sociologists of Phenomenological Orientations: Their Place in American Sociology." *American Sociologist,* 1975, *10,* 179-186.

Wahl, J. *A Short History of Existentialism.* (F. Williams and S. Maron, Trans.) New York: Philosophical Library, 1949.

Watson, J. *The Double Helix: A Personal Account of the Discovery of the Structure of DNA.* New York: Atheneum, 1968.

Wax, M. L. "On Misunderstanding Verstehen: A Reply to Abel." *Sociology and Social Research,* 1967, *51,* 323-333.

Wax, M. L. "Tenting with Malinowski." *American Sociological Review,* 1972, *37,* 1-13.

Wax, R. "Twelve Years Later—An Analysis of Field Experience." *American Journal of Sociology,* 1957, *63,* 133-142.

Wax, R. *Doing Fieldwork: Warnings and Advice.* Chicago: University of Chicago Press, 1971.

Webb, E., and others. *Unobtrusive Measures: Nonreactive Research in the Social Sciences.* Chicago: Rand McNally, 1966.

Weber, M. *Basic Concepts in Sociology.* (H. P. Secher, Trans.) New York: Citadel, 1964.

Weidman, H. "On Ambivalence in the Field." In P. Golde (Ed.), *Women in the Field: Anthropological Experiences.* Chicago: AVC, 1970.

West, J. *Plainville, U.S.A.* New York: Columbia University Press, 1945.

Whyte, W. F. "Observational Field Work Methods." In M. Jahoda, M. Deutsch, and S. W. Cook (Eds.), *Research Methods in Social Relations.* New York: Dryden, 1951.

Whyte, W. F. *Street Corner Society: The Social Structure of an Italian Slum.* Chicago: University of Chicago Press, 1961.

Whyte, W. F. *Organizational Behavior: Theory and Application.* Homewood, Ill.: Dorsey Press, 1969a.

Whyte, W. F. "Reflections on My Work." In I. L. Horowitz (Ed.), *Sociological Self-Images: A Collective Portrait.* Beverly Hills, Calif.: Sage, 1969b.

Whyte, W. F. "The Slum: On the Evolution of Street Corner Society." In A. Vidich, J. Bensman, and M. Stein (Eds.), *Reflec-*

tions on Community Studies. New York: Harper & Row, 1971.

Williams, J. A., Jr. "Interviewer-Respondent Interaction: A Study of Bias in the Information Interview." *Sociometry,* 1964, *27,* 338-352.

Williams, T. (Ed.). *Socialization and Communication in Primary Groups.* Paris: Mouton, 1975.

Witmer, H. "Review: Howard Polsky's *Cottage Six: The Social System of Delinquent Boys." Annals of American Academy of Political and Social Sciences,* 1963, *364,* 202.

Wolff, K. "For a Sociology of Evil." *Journal of Social Issues,* 1969, *25,* 111-125.

Wolff, K. "Surrender and Community Study: The Study of Loma." In A. Vidich, J. Bensman, and M. Stein (Eds.), *Reflections on Community Studies.* New York: Harper & Row, 1971.

Wrong, D. "The Oversocialized Conception of Man in Modern Sociology." *American Sociological Review,* 1961, *26,* 183-193.

Yancey, W., and Rainwater, L. "Problems in the Ethnography of Urban Underclasses." In R. Habenstein (Ed.), *Pathways to Data: Field Methods for Studying Ongoing Social Organizations.* Chicago: AVC, 1970.

Young, T. R. "Transforming Sociology: The Graduate Student." *American Sociologist,* 1974, *9,* 135-139.

Zelditch, M., Jr. "Some Methodological Problems of Field Studies." *American Journal of Sociology,* 1962, *67,* 566-576.

Zinn, H. "History as Private Enterprise." In K. Wolff and B. Moore, Jr. (Eds.), *The Critical Spirit: Essays in Honor of Herbert Marcuse.* Boston: Beacon Press, 1967.

Zinn, H. *The Politics of History.* Boston: Beacon Press, 1970.

Znaniecki, F. *The Method of Sociology.* New York: Farrar, Straus & Giroux, 1934.

Name Index

411

Subject Index

417

2961-4
5-16